THE INCONVENIENT LONNIE JOHNSON

EDITOR
Kenneth Womack, Monmouth University

ADVISORY BOARD
Henry L. Carrigan Jr., musician and critic
Walter Everett, University of Michigan
Cheryl L. Keyes, University of California, Los Angeles
Hannah Lewis, University of Texas at Austin
Tim Riley, Emerson College
Larry Starr, University of Washington

Music shapes our world more powerfully than any other cultural product. To fully understand America, we must learn the complex, diverse history of American musical life. The books in this series tell the stories of the artists, forms, and innovations that define the musical legacy of the United States and fashion its ideals and practices.

THE INCONVENIENT LONNIE JOHNSON

Blues,
Race,
Identity

JULIA SIMON

THE PENNSYLVANIA STATE UNIVERSITY PRESS | UNIVERSITY PARK, PENNSYLVANIA

Library of Congress Cataloging-in-Publication Data

Names: Simon, Julia, 1961– author.
Title: The inconvenient Lonnie Johnson : blues, race, identity / Julia Simon.
Other titles: American music history.
Description: University Park, Pennsylvania : The Pennsylvania State University Press, [2022] | Series: American music history | Includes bibliographical references, discography, and index.
Summary: "Explores the work of professional blues musician Lonnie Johnson, demonstrating how his recorded works reveal lyrical and musical themes that call into question critical assumptions about the genre"—Provided by publisher.
Identifiers: LCCN 2021056830 | ISBN 9780271092553 (hardback)
Subjects: LCSH: Johnson, Lonnie, 1894-1970—Criticism and interpretation. | Blues (Music)—History and criticism. | Music and race—United States—History—20th century.
Classification: LCC ML419.J625 S56 2022 | DDC 782.421643092—dc23
LC record available at https://lccn.loc.gov/2021056830

Copyright © 2022 Julia Simon
All rights reserved
Printed in the United States of America
Published by The Pennsylvania State University Press,
University Park, PA 16802-1003

The Pennsylvania State University Press is a member of the Association of University Presses.

It is the policy of The Pennsylvania State University Press to use acid-free paper. Publications on uncoated stock satisfy the minimum requirements of American National Standard for Information Sciences—Permanence of Paper for Printed Library Material, ANSI z39.48–1992.

Contents

vi List of Illustrations

vii Acknowledgments

1 Introduction: Lonnie Johnson, Professional Musician

29 **1** Musical Practice and Place: The Cultural History of New Orleans and St. Louis

49 **2** Self-Construction and Self-Awareness: Lonnie Johnson's Persona

75 **3** Social Relations: Race, Gender, and the Perception of Systemic Complexity

104 **4** The Suffering Self: Isolation and Loneliness

134 Conclusion: Performance and the Socially Embedded Self

151 Notes

180 Discography

199 Bibliography

209 Index

Illustrations

3 1. Lonnie Johnson's Harlem Footwarmers, "Move Over," OKeh 8638

13 2. "Entertainers at Negro Tavern," Chicago, April 1941

22 3. Cover of OKeh Race Records catalog, circa 1926 or 1927

23 4. Ad for Lonnie Johnson's OKeh sides from OKeh catalog, circa 1926 or 1927

24 5. Lonnie Johnson on the cover of *Jazz Journal*, June 1951

57 6. Publicity photograph of Lonnie Johnson from the 1920s

147 7. Lonnie Johnson and Blind John Davis in 1946

Acknowledgments

I wrote this book for serendipitous reasons, "cosmic signs" that signaled that it was the right project for me at the right time. First, my curiosity about Lonnie Johnson was piqued as I worked on other research projects on the blues. I found myself continually amazed, particularly by occasional forceful pronouncements in his lyrics against racism, combined with extremely subtle guitar technique in a wide variety of musical contexts. Second, I lived in St. Louis for seven years and gained some sense of the city and its odd regional character blending North and South, East and West, in unusual ways. Third, my original training in eighteenth-century French cultural studies attracted me to a project that would be rooted in the history of colonies shaped by French conceptions of race. Fourth, and idiosyncratically, Johnson's first name, Alonzo, spoke to me because of my dog named Alonso Quijano (Zo), after Cervantes's Don Quixote. Finally, Johnson's musical background, training, adaptability, and flexibility appealed to me as a musician. Trained as a classical flutist, I made the transition to performing blues as an adult, playing drums first and now bass. As a bass player, I understand what it means to inhabit the zone of the rhythm section, to feel essential and yet underappreciated. I read music but I had to learn to play by ear. For these random reasons, coupled with a lull in my research agenda, I embarked on a project that resulted in this book. Trusting one's instincts is not advice often given to academicians, but something in my gut told me to pursue this work and I am so happy that I listened.

Researching and writing a book under the best of conditions depends on the help and support of others. The work for this book, begun under normal conditions, continued for many months under shelter-in-place and other orders as a consequence of the COVID-19 pandemic. I cannot express enough gratitude to the various people, complete strangers, who went out of their way to help locate materials and answer questions for me. They responded to email queries, often sent into the void—even through online forms! Their generous responses restored my faith in human kindness and decency and assisted me in my work in truly difficult times. I wish to thank Lynn Abbott at the Hogan Jazz Archive at Tulane University and Susan Clermont in the Music Division at the Library of Congress for invaluable assistance with archival materials. At the New York Public Library for the Performing Arts, I express my gratitude to Dave McMullin, Music Librarian, Jessica L. Wood, Assistant Curator,

Music and Recorded Sound, and Danielle Cordovez, Audiovisual Reference and Outreach Librarian. I also thank Auburn Nelson, Librarian at the Jean Blackwell Hutson Research and Reference Division, Schomburg Center for Research in Black Culture, and Nadine George-Graves, Professor and Chair of Dance at The Ohio State University. I also benefited enormously from insights of the two anonymous readers of the manuscript and the astute copyediting of Nicholas Taylor. I cannot thank Ryan Peterson of Penn State University Press enough for his encouragement, engagement, and careful shepherding of this project through to publication.

Finally, the work for this book benefited from endless conversations and listening sessions with Charles Oriel, my partner in life and music. Without his insight and expertise on guitar, this work would not have been possible.

Introduction
Lonnie Johnson, Professional Musician

Alonzo "Lonnie" Johnson is inconvenient for scholars for a variety of reasons, not least of which is the stunning catalog of recorded work that he produced during his lifetime. This study addresses the body of work and not the biography of the person, although traces of the life are to be found in the artistic works. The archive of recorded materials that Lonnie Johnson left invites analysis precisely because of the challenges it presents. To begin with, the sheer number of recordings is staggering. Johnson claimed in an interview with Paul Oliver in 1960 that he recorded 572 songs, adding "I know, I got copies."[1] The discography to the present volume provides a listing of the recordings that I have been able to document, including songs recorded after 1960: 724 songs in all, but that total is likely incomplete.[2] The number alone presents a daunting task of examination and analysis. Complicating the picture, Johnson recorded as a soloist and featured artist, as a backing musician, and as a member of ensembles. In these various roles, he played in a variety of genres and styles: blues, but also jazz, vaudeville, popular song, and ballads. In addition to his work as a vocalist, he also performed on several instruments—violin, piano, harmonium, kazoo, and banjo—before focusing exclusively on guitar. But musical production is only part of the equation. Musicians rely on various intermediaries—owners of venues, producers, recording companies, and others, as well as technology—to bring their work to a public. In the case of Johnson, professional mediation of his work helped shape his artistic output. On the reception end, listening to his music and understanding it through processes of categorization have led to further difficulties. Is he really a blues musician? Is his music "authentic" blues? While his influence is clear in the work of numerous blues singers and blues and jazz guitarists who have come after him, the significance of his own work remains vexing and elusive.[3]

To give one example of Johnson's complicated legacy and the role of mediation in it, on 1 October 1928 in the OKeh studio in New York City, he recorded "Move Over" (fig. 1). Although the label gives composer credit to Duke Ellington and classifies the piece as a foxtrot, the artist is listed as Lonnie Johnson's Harlem Footwarmers. On the same day at OKeh, they also recorded "Hot and Bothered" and "The Mooche" with vocalist Gertrude "Baby" Cox, each of which features a solo by Lonnie Johnson.[4] Both of those tunes were released under the Duke Ellington Orchestra name. Eighteen days later, Ellington was in the Pathé Studio, recording "Move Over" again. This time composer credit was given to Ellington-Mills and the song was released as Cameo 9025 and Romeo 829 with "The Washingtonians" listed on the label as the artist. Johnson was not included in that session. Ellington and his agent-publisher Irving Mills clearly worked the system by having him record on multiple labels, sometimes releasing the same composition under different pseudonyms. Lonnie Johnson, under contract with OKeh, sometimes did the same, recording with Columbia (the parent company of OKeh) or Gennett (a competing label) under various pseudonyms.[5] But it is worth noting that in 1928, Johnson was a big enough draw to have his name, rather than Ellington's, prominently displayed on the first release of "Move Over."[6] The story raises a number of important questions: How can an artist who rivals Ellington in 1928 for billing on a label become relatively unknown? How do recording companies shape archives and, therewith, perceptions, not only of artists but of genres and styles? How did Johnson become associated almost exclusively with the blues? The following study proposes to tackle numerous factors that shape the reception of Lonnie Johnson's corpus and the portrait of the artist that emerges from it with the goal of better understanding the dynamics of blues production, mediation, and reception.

This study is not a biography, but understanding Johnson's music does require taking account of, to the extent possible, his professional experiences in the various places he lived and performed, precisely because of the ways they depart from the usual conception of a blues artist. Before providing an overview of the most significant events in his life relative to his musical career, it is important to address the difficulties the record poses. First, as is the case with most African American musicians born in the late nineteenth and early twentieth centuries, the official record is spotty and unreliable. Birth certificates, marriage certificates, census data, and other documentation produced as a result of contact with state and local authorities is scarce, unreliable, or

FIG. 1 | Lonnie Johnson's Harlem Footwarmers, "Move Over," OKeh 8638. Photo courtesy of New York Public Library for the Performing Arts, Rodgers and Hammerstein Archives of Recorded Sound.

nonexistent.[7] Second, information provided in interviews with both Johnson and others is also unreliable. Because of a variety of factors, ranging from faulty memory to a desire to project a particular image to a specific audience, information provided in interviews may be inconsistent, difficult to corroborate, or even easily falsifiable, especially dates, places, and time intervals.[8] Always aware of the performance entailed in all forms of social interaction, when speaking to white blues and jazz scholars, critics, record collectors, and fans, at different stages in his career, Johnson produced different narrative accounts of his life. But just because information provided in interviews is not 100 percent factually accurate does not mean it does not contain elements of truth. Research in neuroscience suggests that memory is always a kind of reworking of the past, particularly as it involves autobiography. As people remember events, they piece together bits of information from the past and often move them to different spatial and temporal locations, modifying and rewriting rather than preserving exactly.[9] In Johnson's case, racialized power relations tied to reception, as well as financial interest, further complicate an already complex dynamic. Rather than look to interviews for verification of facts, I rather read them as containing a kind of truth about his life and work.[10] If dates and timelines can be proved to be false, that does not mean that Johnson lied, misrepresented, or intentionally misled, although he might have. What he presents in the interviews is an image of himself that, as we will see in chapter 1, is something that he self-consciously constructed and manipulated in relation to what he perceived as his audience throughout his professional career. This self-representation should not be taken at face value, nor should it be entirely discounted as devoid of truth. Instead, the information provided in interviews should be interpreted as part of the archive of performances that Johnson left, akin to the songs themselves. In the end, the recordings present the richest trove of information we have. In addition to the music, recording dates, locations, and personnel rosters provide further documentation that aid in the construction of a chronology. Bearing all these caveats in mind, I provide a plausible narrative account of the timeline of Johnson's professional life. His lengthy career allowed for an unusual variety of musical experiences, in particular, work as both a soloist and ensemble player in a number of styles and genres that shaped his artistic output and profile as a musician.

Johnson's Life: The Early Years

Alonzo "Lonnie" Johnson was born in New Orleans, most likely on 8 February 1894.[11] Scholars indicate dates ranging from 1889 to 1900 for his birth year, citing interviews at various stages in his career with different interlocutors, but 1894 seems most likely.[12] In general, Johnson cited earlier birth dates when he was younger, perhaps telling the truth or perhaps wanting to give the appearance of more maturity and experience, whereas later in life he tended to shave off years, likely according to his perception of his marketability. He was born into a large family with five brothers and six sisters, many of whom played music.[13] When asked about his musical background in an interview with Moses Asch recorded in 1967, Johnson explained, "Well, in the first place, the whole entire family was musicians and I started playing when I was fourteen years old. My father played music, my mother played music, my five brothers played music, and I had two sisters played music. And I just bought an instrument and six months I was holding a good job. I was playing with my father's band."[14] Playing in the family band led to performing in various venues and eventually to jobs gigging in New Orleans.

In addition to his early musical experiences in New Orleans, Johnson also played in rural areas of Louisiana. Ernest "Punch" Miller, jazz trumpet player, recounts performing with Johnson in Raceland, in Lafourche Parish, about forty-five miles southeast of New Orleans: "Me and this boy they call Lonnie Johnson now, we called him Rooster at home, we played on a Saturday evening on big store galleries, see. We'd put our hat down and all the people . . . we didn't have no salary . . . we had enough money to last us all that next week. . . . We might play some guitar, bass and trumpet for white folks on Sunday night."[15] In rural Raceland, Johnson played for both African American and white audiences, as he did in New Orleans. The variety of places, venues, and situations in which Johnson played growing up gave him broad exposure and familiarity with different styles and genres of music in urban and rural settings. He played guitar and violin as a young person, but likely had experience with banjo and piano as well.

Johnson gigged in a number of venues in New Orleans, including in Storyville, the infamous red-light district, from roughly 1908 until 1917. In 1917 he seems to have traveled to England. The year marks the official closure of Storyville, although Johnson did not work exclusively in the district. Its commercial viability had been declining before its closure and musicians had already begun leaving New Orleans by that time.[16] World War I presented opportunities to perform in Europe, and Johnson could have benefited from them, although I cannot discount the possibility that, like Big Bill Broonzy, who likely fabricated military service overseas during the First World War, this story may also be based on information gleaned from the experience of other musicians.[17] Work with Will Marion Cook's Southern Syncopated Orchestra and the comedy team of Glenn and Jenkins in England has been disproved.[18] In all likelihood he was away from New Orleans gaining experience performing in a theatrical setting beginning in 1917. Upon his return to New Orleans in 1919, he learned of the death of most of his family during the 1918 influenza pandemic. Although most sources indicate that all members of his family died, with the exception of his brother James, Dean Alger argues persuasively that his parents may have also survived.[19] The brothers moved to St. Louis in late 1919 or early 1920, a decision presented by Johnson in interviews as motivated by the loss.

It is unclear why they chose St. Louis; perhaps they had employment lined up and/or other connections there. In the early years in St. Louis, Lonnie Johnson was employed by traveling theater troupes and on riverboats performing jazz and popular music, both of which were probably made possible by connections established earlier in New Orleans. It is quite likely that he supplemented touring theater work and playing on the boats with solo and small group gigs in and around St. Louis.[20] The work for traveling shows stands as evidence of prior theatrical experience, possibly in England. Mark Miller notes that "he appears to have started very near the top, albeit in a supporting role, when he travelled on the 'big time' B. F. Keith circuit with the popular African-American song, dance and comedy team Glenn & Jenkins," in the early 1920s.[21] In an interview with Paul Oliver, Johnson said, "Well, I played on the TOBA [Theater Owners Booking Association] and I played on the RKO [Radio-Keith-Orpheum] circuit too. I worked from Coast to Coast on the RKO circuit and I played in everything that was playable. Every theater there was every place they could make into a theater or call a theater. I was with the team of Glenn and Jenkins and I was with them for four years. But the TOBA . . . God, I played the TOBA from end to end."[22] For many years, Johnson worked in vaudeville, here mentioning the blackface comedy and dance team of Glenn and Jenkins he backed, but not in England.[23]

The TOBA was an association of Black vaudeville theaters formed in 1921.[24] A statement published in the *Chicago Defender* shortly after the association's founding lists twenty-five member theaters in Alabama, Arkansas, Florida, Georgia, Kentucky, Louisiana, Michigan, Missouri, North Carolina, Ohio, South Carolina, Tennessee, and Texas, with seven additional theaters indicating interest in joining, adding Indiana and Oklahoma.[25] Johnson describes the work:

> Just every place they had from New York to Texas. . . . TOBA's like any other business, you're on the stage and you do so many shows. At that time on TOBA you work—you do five, six shows a day; you got little money, but everybody was happy. I started on TOBA in Philadelphia—that's where I started from, the old Standard Theater. I first had the band in the theater. Then after they put all the live shows out, then I went on the road, traveling, and I went as far as TOBA can carry you, from Philadelphy to New Orleans. I played the Lyric Theater there—oh God—with Clara Smith and with Mamie Smith—yeah, Clara and Mamie both. I knew Clara real well, she were a lovely piano player and a lovely singer. She played piano and she sure could sing. And worked right back . . . and back again. Played in Atlanty, Georgia at the old 81 Theater.[26]

Interestingly, although Johnson mentions Clara Smith and Mamie Smith to Oliver, perhaps because they were known as blues singers who toured on the TOBA circuit, he does not mention the Whitman Sisters, perhaps the highest paid act on the TOBA, for whom he served as bandleader off and on for nine years.[27]

Around the same time, Johnson performed for the Streckfus Steamers, which had an excursion boat based out of St. Louis with an eight- or nine-piece jazz band and large dance floor as well as smaller boats that operated for four of five months during the summer.[28] George "Pops" Foster, the jazz bass player, reports that work on the boats was year-round, with the boats traveling as far as Pittsburgh, St. Paul, and New Orleans.[29] Johnson would have been familiar with the music on the boats from New Orleans and may have even benefited from connections with musicians who played on them. Fellow guitarist and banjoist Johnny St. Cyr was hired to play on the boats and traveled from New Orleans to St. Louis by train in 1918 and 1919 to perform.[30] Fate Marable was the original bandleader for Streckfus and likely hired Johnson, who claimed to have played with him in an interview with Oliver: "We were playing on the excursion boats out of St. Louis. Well I played a couple of times on it but after that I started playin' violin with Charlie Creath's band on the steamer St. Paul—he taken it over."[31] A cornetist, Creath briefly challenged the Streckfus line with "Blacks-only" cruises during the summer of 1921, but he was eventually hired by Marable.[32] Johnson likely performed on the riverboats from 1919 until 1922, although he may have continued until as late as 1925.[33]

In addition to the ensemble work on riverboats and on theater circuits, Johnson continued to hone his singing and guitar skills as a soloist and in small combos in clubs and other venues during the early 1920s, building out his repertoire in blues. In 1924 he entered and won a blues contest hosted by the Booker T. Washington Theater. The theater originally opened in 1912 in Chestnut Valley, which was still the center of African American musical life in the city in the early 1920s.[34] As part of the TOBA circuit, it "featured appearances by such Black stars as Ethel Waters, Bessie Smith, and Ma Rainey."[35] The theater ran a blues contest as a form of scouting for OKeh records.[36] Jesse Johnson, owner of the De Luxe Music Shoppe, worked as a promoter for Creath's riverboat cruises in addition to his work as a freelance talent scout for record companies.[37] Thus, Lonnie Johnson's artistry, as well as his connections with Jesse Johnson and TOBA, likely helped him win the contest and the prize of a recording contract with OKeh that would last seven years.[38]

Johnson began recording in St. Louis in November 1925 as both a featured artist and a member of Charlie Creath's Jazz-O-Maniacs. From OKeh ledgers, we know that he traveled between St. Louis and New York City, OKeh's headquarters, from November 1925 until November 1927.[39] From December 1927 to May 1928 he covered more territory, recording in Chicago in December 1927 (including for Gennett in Richmond, Indiana, under various pseudonyms), in Memphis in February 1928, and in San Antonio in May 1928.[40] In October 1928, he returned to New York City to finish out his contract with OKeh and remained there until his last session for them, on 12 August 1932.[41]

Johnson's pattern of geographical locations for recording shares something of both blues and jazz artists of the period but is distinctly different from both. Speaking from a jazz perspective, Foster, who was also a member of Charlie Creath's Jazz-O-Maniacs (likely playing with Johnson aboard the *St. Paul* and certainly recording with him), observes, "The big music field was Chicago from 1920 to 1925. From 1925, it was in New York."[42] Indeed, Freddie Keppard, Joe Oliver, Louis Armstrong, Jelly Roll Morton, and other major figures of New Orleans jazz performed and recorded in Chicago beginning in the 1910s, continuing through the first half of the 1920s. Johnson did record jazz with Armstrong and his Hot Five in Chicago, but it was not until December 1927. In 1925, Johnson was debuting in St. Louis, one of OKeh's "field" locations, in jazz and blues. Memphis and San Antonio, where he recorded in 1928, are more typical of locations for sessions with blues artists. Indeed, it is likely that Johnson traveled to Memphis to work as a staff or studio musician, backing blues singers Mooch Richardson and Keghouse, but also taking advantage of the opportunity to record some solo pieces. He did the same in San Antonio with Texas Alexander. It is also possible that tour dates with traveling shows and other bookings made it more convenient for him to record in locations other than St. Louis and New York.[43] The geographical locations and alternation between solo and studio work differentiate Johnson from both solo "folk" blues artists, like Blind Lemon Jefferson and Charley Patton, and also jazz players embedded within ensembles recording in major cities. Johnson's professional experience crosses genre boundaries as well as the line between soloist and sideman, shaping his identity in an unusual way.

After he relocated permanently to New York, the headquarters of OKeh and other companies, he recorded in a variety of genres and styles. In 1928 and 1929, he recorded jazz with Ellington, as noted above, as well as with Armstrong and His Savoy Ballroom Five, and in a duo configuration with white guitarist Eddie Lang.[44] But he also recorded with Victoria Spivey and Spencer Williams, backing them in vaudeville-style songs, while he continued to record his own blues. New York was an ideal location for a "utility player" type of musician: able to perform in jazz ensembles, small combos, as an accompanist and soloist, in a variety of styles and genres.

Copyrights for Johnson's compositions were filed beginning in 1926.[45] "Mr. Johnson's Blues" and "Falling Rain Blues" were registered 8 September 1926, crediting Lonnie Johnson as composer, but granting copyright to

F. Wallace Rega, a music publisher located in Bayside, Long Island, New York. Ironically, "Mr. Johnson's Blues" did not belong to Mr. Johnson. This pattern of copyrighting songs to music companies is typical of the exploitation of blues and other artists by the recording industry. Labels like OKeh were often linked to a music publishing house subsidiary that registered titles with the US Copyright Office in order to collect royalties. "Composers" like Johnson (who was likely able to write out music) as well as artists from the folk tradition or even theatrical stars like Bessie Smith and Ma Rainey (who likely depended on others to write out songs in musical notation for them) often were either pressured to sign away copyrights in exchange for the "privilege" of recording or sold them for a flat fee. Jazz musicians were often pressured in similar ways, as we saw in the example of Ellington above, who granted co-songwriting credit to his manager, thereby forfeiting half of his royalties, although still retaining the right to some. Johnson's songs copyrighted subsequently in 1926 and continuing through January 1927 were registered to Jesse Johnson, the St. Louis promoter and talent scout.[46] In June 1927, copyrights for Johnson's songs began being registered to St. Louis Publishing Co. Telling among the songs of this period, "Tin Can Alley Blues" was composed by Johnson and Porter Grainger, but the copyright was assigned to the professional songwriter Grainger and not Johnson.[47]

Significantly, and atypical of blues artists, during a brief window from 1 September 1928 until 18 November 1929, Johnson filed and was granted copyright on nineteen of his own songs.[48] It is highly likely that Johnson was familiar with the financial benefits of writing out and copyrighting songs from his time in New Orleans and from his collaborations with jazz musicians and professional songwriters. Owners of copyright for compositions received "mechanical royalties" for all recorded performances.[49] As Pops Foster explains, Clarence Williams, the piano player who performed in the mansions of Storyville, aided local musicians, but also helped himself:

> Clarence [Williams] wasn't down there too long when he and Armand Piron opened a little music store and music publishing house. I think that was around 1910 or 1912. We used to rehearse there sometimes. If you had written a number, you'd go to Clarence to write it down. He could write very fast; as fast as you could do the number, he could write it down. After he'd write it down, he'd arrange it and send it to have it copyrighted and published. Clarence always managed to cut himself in on a number. When a number was published, it would have four or five names on it. Clarence would get as much of it as he could. His name

would be in two or three places and the guy who really wrote it was usually way down the line. After he got through, he had more of your number than you did.[50]

So, for a brief time, Johnson benefited from copyright ownership of his own songs, more like a professional songwriter (or A&R man) than a blues artist.

The period of copyright ownership by Johnson was short-lived: with the sole exception of "Deep Minor Rhythm Stomp" written by Johnson and Lang and copyrighted to Johnson, the remaining songs of 1930 were registered to Georgia Music Company of New York. The songs of 1931 and 1932, until the end of his contract with OKeh, were registered either to OKeh or Columbia Phonograph Corp., its parent company.[51] All of the songs copyrighted from 1926 until 1932 remained unpublished, eliminating the possibility of income from sheet music sales.[52]

Throughout the period Johnson was recording, he continued touring as part of professional theater troupes off and on. For example, he was a member of Bessie Smith's Midnight Steppers Tour in fall 1929 and was reported to have been involved in a romantic relationship with her.[53] It is likely that his theater work continued into 1930, at which point the Depression put an end to the profitability of large traveling shows.

As part of a broader context, it is worth remembering that travel for African Americans in this period was not easy, to say the least. Taking a train from St. Louis to New York was probably not too fraught, but Jim Crow restrictions were a significant reality in travel to Memphis, San Antonio, and certainly across the United States, including the South, as a member of show casts and crews. Stops in Atlanta, New Orleans, Birmingham, Little Rock, Memphis, Charleston, Chattanooga, Louisville, Dallas, Houston, and other cities on the TOBA circuit required riding in uncomfortable Jim Crow cars and then finding whatever "colored only" accommodations for eating and spending the night were available. For those traveling by car or bus, "Sundown Towns" dotted not just the South, but the nation: "In 1930, 44 out of the 89 counties that lined Route 66 were all-white communities known as 'Sundown Towns'—places that banned blacks from entering city limits after dark. Some posted signs that read, 'Nigger, Don't Let the Sun Set on You Here.'"[54] Beyond discomfort and humiliation, touring also opened entertainers up to the possibility of violent confrontation.

Johnson had his last recording session with OKeh in New York on 12 August 1932. OKeh, owned by Columbia since 1926, continued putting out occasional race records until 1935 in the 8000 series that had included Johnson, but the Depression crippled record sales and left Johnson seeking new employment.[55]

The Middle Years

Johnson left New York and went first to Cleveland, where he worked with Louis "Putney" Dandridge's Orchestra, en route to Chicago in hopes of continuing in music.[56] Finding no recording possibilities there, he returned to the St. Louis area and worked a series of day jobs. In various interviews, he mentions a steel mill in East St. Louis, hauling railroad ties soaked in creosote in Galesburg, Illinois, working in a steel foundry in Peoria, and an "easy job working at the golf club, taking care of the lawns."[57] It is likely that he continued gigging in this period, as he always had. He specifically mentions a night club he played in Peoria in the interview with Asch.

The recording hiatus ended on 8 November 1937 with Johnson back in the studio with Decca in Chicago. On that day, he cut eight songs, including two solo instrumental pieces. He stayed in Chicago until 1947 (with two brief trips to New York) recording his own material, but also backing blues musicians, such as Ollie Shepard, Alice Moore, and Peetie Wheatstraw, and playing in jazz orchestras, such as those led by Jimmie Noone and Johnny Dodds. During this period, he recorded for Decca, Bluebird (RCA Victor's blues and jazz subdivision), Mercury, Disc, and Aladdin.[58] Sometimes he put in marathon sessions, such as on 31 March 1938 in New York City, when he recorded eight of his own songs, including the masterful "Mr. Johnson's Swing," in addition to ten tunes with Ollie Shepard and His Kentucky Boys. During this period he began recording on electric guitar, likely the first songs backing Wheatstraw on "Truckin' thru Traffic" (Chicago, 18 October 1938) and his own "The Loveless Blues" (Chicago, 2 November 1939).[59] While the two early recordings sound a great deal like acoustic guitar, his recordings for Aladdin in 1947 mark a smooth and seemingly effortless transition to an electric style. Unlike guitarists who had to make stylistic adaptations, such as the Delta guitarists who pioneered the Chicago blues sound, Johnson's controlled single-note style of play and use of sliding half chords are ideally suited for amplification. But this lack of need to evolve likely hampered his legacy for the blues. Without constraints imposed by amplification altering his style and technique, he did not explore the sound capabilities of the electric guitar, making his work in the 1940s and '50s sound antiquated to some.

Changes in recording technology, especially higher-quality microphones and better microphone placement in some of the songs recorded in the mid-1940s, enable subtleties in Johnson's vocal delivery to be captured in more detail than in prior recordings. The 1947 Aladdin sides faithfully reproduce changes in vocal intensity, extended nasals, and even some limited and subtle use of vocal noise[60] not normally associated with Johnson—for example, on "You Know I Do" (Chicago, 2 June 1947). The presence in these recordings of vocal timbre that often serves as a marker of the blues raises the unanswerable question of whether restricted use of growl or other effects produced with vibration in the vocal folds was used by Johnson in earlier recordings, but that poor microphone quality and placement failed to capture it.[61] It is difficult to say how the presence of these qualities and their faithful reproduction might have altered Johnson's image and identity. Clearly, their absence contributed to the questioning of his "authenticity" as a "blues singer."

As was the case in the early years in New York and St. Louis, copyrights for almost all of Johnson's songs from this period were registered to various music companies owned by Lester Melrose, RCA Victor's talent scout for blues and jazz.[62] One anomalous item stands out in the copyright record, an unpublished song titled "Won't You Share My Love Nest," registered 13 April 1938 to Johnson indicating Toronto as his location. I have not been able to locate a recording, nor can I explain the Toronto address.

During the late 1930s and 1940s, musicians worked according to wage scales for both club and recording work established by the Chicago Federation of Musicians, which was divided into segregated locals.[63] Some artists were under contract to record companies who abided by guidelines established by the union; however, union bylaws did not shield artists from financial exploitation.[64] Johnson was likely not under contract in this period, as he recorded for both RCA Victor–Bluebird and Decca in fall 1939. Myra Taylor, a singer who performed with Johnson in Chicago, expressed her dismay at his earnings: "I was kind of disgusted with Lonnie Johnson because his record label was making big bucks off his recordings, but were only paying him $25 a side— and he acted happy to get that. It upset me to no end the way they treated him!"[65] Depending on Johnson's time in the recording studio, the amount is probably accurate.[66] Neither a contract nor the union provided financial protection for musicians.

While in Chicago, Johnson also played in various clubs. He told Oliver, "First club I played in Chicago was the Three Deuces on North State with Baby Dodds on the drums and after that—lots of them. That's right I played a couple of places on East 51st Street. I played at the Boulevard Lounge there

FIG. 2 "Entertainers at Negro Tavern," Chicago, April 1941 (Lonnie Johnson on far left). Photo by Russell Lee for the US Department of Agriculture Farm Security Administration, Library of Congress, Prints and Photographs Division, FSA-OWI Collection, LC-DIG-fsa-8c00653.

on East 51st Street and then at Square's at 931 West 51st Street—I was there about five years, something like that. Then I went into the Flame Club at 3020 South Indiana."[67] The mention of Warren "Baby" Dodds and the names and locations of the venues signal that he was performing jazz. A photo taken by Russell Lee for the Farm Security Administration in 1941 documents a two-guitar and double bass combo (fig. 2). Nighttime work in clubs supplemented meager earnings from daytime recording sessions, as it always had.

The rise of a more aggressive sound for the blues in Chicago decreased Johnson's opportunities for employment in the late 1940s and likely motivated his move to Cincinnati, where he began recording with King Records in December 1947.[68] During this period, he scored a major success with the ballad "Tomorrow Night," which "topped the R&B charts for seven [non-consecutive] weeks in 1948."[69] With King, he recorded a combination of blues—some new and some rerecordings of earlier material—and ballads, in an attempt to duplicate his success with "Tomorrow Night" (Cincinnati, 10 December 1947). He had some minor hits with "Pleasing You (As Long as I Live)" (Cincinnati,

Introduction / 13

13 August 1947), "So Tired" (Cincinnati, 19 November 1948), and "Confused" (Cincinnati, 29 November 1949), but the recordings with King were uneven, including with respect to quality of performance and recording.[70] Stylistic mismatches, as in the driving four-four feel at odds with the swing of Johnson's vocal in "She's So Sweet" (Linden, NJ, 9 May 1949) and the heavy band arrangement with horns that practically drown out his vocal in "You Can't Buy Love" (Cincinnati, 3 June 1952), and silly popular songs like "I Know It's Love" (Cincinnati, 13 August 1947), with an uncharacteristically out-of-tune solo, are interspersed with tunes that showcase Johnson's strengths, like "My My Baby" (Cincinnati, 19 November 1948) and "Little Rockin' Chair" (Cincinnati, 14 September 1950). Most of the copyrights for songs in this period were credited to Johnson but registered to Lois Publishing Co., part of King Records' owner Syd Nathan's music production empire.[71] Although Johnson claimed in an interview with Oliver that "I Found a Dream" was "published in '48," copyright records show that the unpublished song was copyrighted both to his second wife, Kay Armstrong Johnson, and Lois Publishing Co.[72] Johnson toured England in 1952 after his final sessions with King.[73] By 1953, musical taste in America had changed sufficiently that Johnson left Cincinnati and recording, and moved to Philadelphia.

Late Years

In Philadelphia, Johnson returned to day jobs and occasional gigging.[74] He was "rediscovered" in 1959 by Chris Albertson, a jazz and blues scholar, producer, and DJ at WHAT in Philadelphia, who received information from a listener that Johnson was working as a janitor at the Benjamin Franklin Hotel.[75] In the same year, Samuel Charters published *The Country Blues*, encouraging white fans, guided by 78 recordings, to search out blues artists and help them relaunch their careers.[76] Johnson's "rediscovery" led to new recording opportunities in the early sixties as a soloist, in small combos, with Victoria Spivey, on her label Spivey Records, and with Elmer Snowden, released on the Prestige Records subsidiary label Bluesville.[77] His final recording in the United States was with the engineer and executive of Folkways Records, Moses Asch, in 1967. The performance was eventually released as part of the Smithsonian Folkways series in 1993 and included a recorded interview with Johnson.[78] The pattern of copyrights for songs being held by music publishing companies continued through the end of his career.[79]

Johnson was invited to participate in the American Folk Blues Festival Tour of Europe from September through November 1963, alongside other blues artists running the gamut of styles from Victoria Spivey to Muddy Waters.[80] In an interview with *Melody Maker*, he acknowledged the financial benefit to the performers.[81] Invited by two jazz enthusiasts to perform, Johnson decided to move to Toronto in 1965.[82] In November 1965, he recorded five songs on the LP *Stompin' at the Penny* for Columbia with Jim McHarg's Metro Stompers, a group of young traditional jazz musicians based in Toronto.[83] He struggled to find work in Toronto, even briefly opening a club that failed.[84] He was struck by a car on 12 March 1969, which resulted in serious injuries, and then had a series of strokes.[85] He performed two songs at a final show billed as "Blue Monday," accompanied by Buddy Guy on acoustic guitar and Jim McHarg on bass, on 23 February 1970.[86] He died alone in his apartment on 16 June 1970.[87]

Corpus, Genre, and Style

My study treats Johnson's body of recorded work as a corpus. One normally thinks of a corpus as a "body or complete collection of writings" of a particular author, now often analyzed with the assistance of digital technology.[88] I propose rather to analyze Johnson's artistic output according to a more old-fashioned literary understanding of a corpus, in which readings and interpretations are guided by the recognition of repetitions and patterns across a body of work.[89] Analyzing an individual author's or artist's output reveals themes and ideas, patterns of style, expression, and thought, as they are both repeated and change over time.[90] For example, the study of the corpus of a poet, playwright, or novelist may reveal patterns in the choice of verbal expressions or formal attributes across works, enriching our understanding of each work in relation to the whole. Rather than simply interpret a word or phrase according to its usual, historically contextualized usage, the corpus approach enables an interpretation of particular articulations informed by their contextualization among the repetitions and variations across the body of the artist's work. Considering each work as one part of an artistic whole enriches our understanding of phrases and figures as they appear and reappear in new contexts. This enables the recognition of consistency, but also change over time, in modes of expression.

If we take Johnson's corpus to comprise all his recorded works, the approach also allows for the setting aside of genre boundaries, such as those between blues and jazz or blues and popular song, to consider the body of work as a whole.[91] This enables the recognition of musical figures and lyrical expressions as they appear in different stylistic contexts. In Johnson's corpus, similar types of patterns—not only of linguistic usage in lexicon and lyrical phrasing, but also recurring musical ideas and figures—repeat across styles, genres, and instruments. They also repeat in solo performances and duets, accompaniments, and ensemble work. Considered from this perspective, Johnson's recordings demonstrate coherence in his composition and performance styles. James Dalton, having transcribed many of Johnson's recordings, remarks on his consistency: "Throughout his prodigious career Johnson managed to maintain a consistent vocabulary while still fitting into each situation in which he found himself."[92] For example, his use of tremolo in his early violin performances resembles the vibrato in his singing that carries on throughout his life. His impeccable phrasing stands out, whether on guitar or vocal, in blues and in ballads.[93] His sense of rhythm and timing is evident across performances, as a soloist, an accompanist, or as a member of an ensemble. The corpus approach enables a picture to emerge of a musical career shaped not only by Johnson, his artistry, his idiosyncrasies, and his life experiences but also by broader social forces during his lifetime.

Over a very long career, far longer than most blues artists of his generation, Johnson earned a living from his music, performing what he and various intermediaries perceived as what audiences wanted to hear. The variety on display in his corpus represents another inconvenience, posing difficulties in terms of categorizing him as an artist. His early life in New Orleans played a significant role in his attitude toward genre and style. Like many musicians in New Orleans of his generation, for Johnson, distinctions between genres were not clear-cut. Moreover, as jazz scholar Bruce Boyd Raeburn attests, "What I learned on the bandstand was that most New Orleans musicians had extremely eclectic tastes and took pride in their ability to perform beyond (and in spite of) categorical boundaries."[94] Distinguishing styles and genres of music in the early decades in New Orleans is no easy task. As I argue, distinctions between types of music are dependent not only on stylistic features, such as rhythm, tone, timbre, and scale, but also on socioeconomic factors related to performance, such as race, class, and gender. The understanding of stylistic features Johnson developed in New Orleans carried on throughout his career.

Musicians a little older than Johnson and those who were his rough contemporaries often used a different vocabulary to describe distinctions between styles of music than the terms we employ today. The distinctions often apply to the venue, the audience, and the style of music being played, conflating the socioeconomic and the musical.[95] For example, guitarist Danny Barker, who was younger than Johnson, cites his maternal grandfather, the musician Isidore Barbarin, describing Buddy Bolden's music as follows: "I heard Isidore once say of Bolden, 'Sure, I heard him. I knew him. He was famous with the ratty people.' I soon learned what ratty people, ratty joints and dives meant: it meant good-time people, earthy people, who frequent anywhere there's a good time, regardless of the location of the element of social class distinction or position. So, ratty music is bluesy, folksy music that moves you and exhilarates you, makes you dance."[96] Pops Foster makes similar distinctions based on venues, clientele, and types of music: "From about 1900 on, there were three types of bands around New Orleans. You had bands that played ragtime, ones that played sweet music, and the ones that played nothin' but blues. A band like John Robichaux's played nothing but sweet music and played the dicty affairs. On a Saturday night Frankie Dusen's Eagle Band would play the Masonic Hall because he played a whole lot of blues. A band like the Magnolia Band would play ragtime and work the District."[97] In this tripartite division of music in the early period, repertoires are shaped by venue and audience, race and class. Venues ran the gamut of respectability "from the Jeunes Amis, 'the most exclusive, . . . where very few jazzmen ever entered—down to Animal Hall, where even a washboard band was welcome if they could play the blues.'"[98] The blues are associated with the lowest classes, manual laborers and prostitutes in the district. Barker describes "Animule" [Animal] Hall, a working-class venue where only blues was played: "The star attraction at the hall was Long Head Bob's Social Orchestra. The patrons loved Bob's music; in fact, no band would play there but Bob's orchestra. Bob's repertoire consisted of the blues, and only the blues: fast blues, medium blues, slow blues, and the slow, slow drag. . . . The men and women who patronized the hall were very hard-working people: stevedores, woodsmen, fishermen, field hands and steel-driving men, and the women were factory workers, washer-women, etc. All were very strong and physically fit."[99] The mention of the "slow, slow drag" signals not only the music's tempo but its use as a background for slow, sexual dancing. The association between the blues and sex is even more explicit in musicians' descriptions of the music in Storyville and, particularly, the taste of the prostitutes.

Louis Armstrong describes advice he received as a youngster from Cocaine Buddy Martin about earning money: "All you have to do is to put on your long pants and play the blues for the whores that hustle at night. They come in with a big stack of money in their stockings for their pimps. When you play the blues they will call you sweet names and buy you drinks and give you tips."[100] Dude Bottley's remembrance of Buddy Bolden's performances also stresses the association between prostitutes and blues: "I used to love going to Lincoln

Park on Monday nights, all them pretty whores would come to the park all dressed up with their pimps and madames [sic]. That's when you should have heard Bolden blow that cornet. His music was like medicine, made you feel happy and made you feel great. He'd play them low, lowdown-under blues and them whores would perform something terrible 'til they'd get out of hand, shaking down to the floor and dropping their drawers and teddies: that was a beautiful sight to see."[101] In these accounts, blues signals as much where the music is played, and for whom, as it does a style of music. This mode of distinguishing styles of music is not anodyne. As Charles Hersch argues, racial purity and social divisions were maintained in part by segregating sound. As a corollary, styles of music were perceived in terms of respectability.[102]

This conflation of the socioeconomic, racial, and musical does not mean that stylistic differences are a fiction. Perceptible differences of tempo, rhythm, scale, timbre, and musical structure form a sign system that creates different "meanings" for different audiences. For example, although Barker's description of the band in Animal Hall lists "fast," "medium," "slow," and "slow, slow" as possible tempos for blues, tempos could signify degrees of respectability coordinated with class and race. William Howland Kenney argues that Joseph Streckfus constrained musicians aboard his boats to evoke nostalgia for the antebellum South to please the white passengers, by controlling tempos, playing slightly faster than hotel bands and avoiding "slow grinds" and "belly rubs."[103] As Hersch points out, tempos "carr[y] racial and class connotations, impelling listeners to move in particular ways and evoking certain attitudes and experiences."[104] In the case of the "slow, slow drag," extremely slow blues tempos invite sexualized forms of dancing associated with working-class Blacks. Very quick tempos also functioned as markers of "African American music."[105] Lillian Hardin Armstrong recounts a humorous anecdote about a rehearsal session with a singer who makes a revealing error: "We were rehearsing her, and she was singing and she stopped and said, 'I can't sing that song in that temperature.'" Armstrong breaks up laughing and reports that the band at the time did, too. She speculates that the singer meant tempo.[106] "Hot" in the context of music can mean many things. The singer's mistake points to tempo as one distinguishing feature of this "exciting" dance music.

"Hot," with its sexual overtones exploited with titles like "Hotter Than That" that Johnson played on with Armstrong and His *Hot* Five, also refers to rhythms. Andrew S. Berish argues that early critical reception of jazz created a spectrum with racial overtones from "hot" to "sweet" to classify and judge music according to its "authenticity."[107] Syncopated rhythms, in particular, were read as markers of authentic, African American music.[108] Playing ahead of or behind the beat created a feeling of "swing," a rhythm with "a forward-directed motion and bounce to it."[109] Rhythm sections, of which Johnson as a guitarist was an integral part, were the key element in the band for creating grooves to make people move. Rhythm musicians work together, playing with and against one another, to accentuate different beats in the measure. For example, a drummer might maintain a consistent 1 and 3 on the bass drum and accentuate 2 and 4 on the snare (sometimes ahead or behind the beat), with occasional pickups and accents, all accompanied by a shuffle or triplet ride on the cymbals. At the same time, the bass player might "walk" with steady quarter notes with slight accentuations that pull slightly against the snare and bass drum. The guitarist might provide contrastive upticks on the offbeats or alternately join in to complement the bass and drum parts. Together, the beats and rhythms combine to create a swung "groove," especially important in dance music.[110]

These rhythms and grooves are difficult to notate in conventional ways and posed particular challenges at the time, reinforcing conflations of playing "hot" music and playing by ear.[111] Rhythmic but also harmonic and melodic improvisation thus feed into these dichotomies. According to this logic, "authentic" musicians do not read music; they play what they feel, based on what they hear.[112] Trumpeter Thomas "Papa Mutt" Carey's comments about Armstrong are typical in this regard: "Louis makes you feel the number and that's what counts. A man who does something from the heart, and makes you feel it, is great. You see, Louis does that for everything. And one thing, Louis never rehearsed a blues number; he played them just as he felt at the time he was up there on the stand."[113] And, in the context of New Orleans, the distinction between reading and not reading music maps onto racial categories: whites and Creoles are presumed to read music and, therefore, be incapable of playing "hot" music, while Black musicians cannot read and are, therefore, capable of playing "hot" rhythms and dance grooves and improvising.[114]

Finally, the scale and timbral palette of music also carried significance for categorization along the sweet-to-hot spectrum tied to notions of "authenticity" and "race." "Blues" elements—such as "dirty" tone, blue notes, unusual sounds, as well as a pentatonic scale and twelve-bar progression—were associated with working-class African Americans. Elements of timbral and tonal variation, most prominently the use of mutes, can be employed to inject an element of signifying (improvising, altering, and/or varying) even the most staid tune. Indeed, many bands played the head of pieces "straight," followed by choruses of increasing degrees of movement away from a "sweet" sound, often culminating in a very "hot" out chorus.[115]

The Reception of Lonnie Johnson

All these elements of musical performance—tempo, rhythm, groove, improvisation, timbral and tonal palette—are interpreted as part of a sign system related to class and race by audiences, critics, and record companies. In and of themselves, the signs do not have any significance, but within a given context, subtle variations can take on meaning.[116] Venue owners, record producers, critics, scholars, record collectors, and listeners all focus on aspects of musical performance to make identifications such as hot or sweet, jazz or blues, ratty or dicty, authentic or inauthentic, that relate to notions of class, race, and sometimes gender.

While musicians have tastes and tendencies in terms of performance style, they also need to make a living. Musical ability, adaptability, taste, and temperament vary, making some musicians gravitate toward one or the other end of the sweet–hot spectrum or the jazz–blues continuum. Artists' identities and especially their reception often depend on alignment with a particular style or genre situated along a spectrum. For example, in jazz, Guy Lombardo is often cited as the "degree zero" of "sweet," while Joe Oliver, Louis Armstrong, and Benny Goodman are used as points of reference for the "hot" end of the continuum.[117] In the case of blues, rural, male artists like Charley Patton, Blind Lemon Jefferson, and others occupy a similar position in terms of "authenticity" to that of Oliver, Armstrong, and Goodman in jazz.[118] The case of Lonnie Johnson poses particular challenges due to a number of factors that enabled him to perform as a solo artist, accompanist, and ensemble player in a number of styles and genres of music. If one imagines the classificatory schemes in terms of lines in space, his performances could be placed at many different points along the sweet–hot or jazz–blues or rural–urban spectra. In other words, his performances, pinpointed in terms of these criteria, would cover a lot more "territory" than most artists. This enabled him to land more paying gigs as an artist, but it also makes his reception more complicated. If he can perform with Ellington and Armstrong, Texas Alexander and Stovepipe Johnson (a yodeler), Victoria Spivey and Spencer Williams, in addition to his own blues and ballads, how do we understand him as an artist? In the end, versatility as an artist—familiarity with a variety of genres and styles and technical mastery in them—functions as an obstacle to the creation of a legible musical identity, which, in turn, colors critical reception. As a musician, he is skilled and employable. From the perspective of recording companies, this means he is exploitable as both a soloist and a studio musician, precisely because of his adaptability and even malleability in response to changing tastes. But for critics, record collectors, and fans, this means he is a protean, labile, flexible, difficult-to-categorize artist precisely because of the variety represented in the corpus.

All musicians, to some degree or another, can play in different styles. Indeed, jazz and blues depend on citational practices in the creation of new material that complicate genre divisions. Bits and pieces of melody, lyric, rhythm, and groove are lifted from any and every context and varied through signifying to create new songs. But Johnson's case is extreme. To begin with, his mastery of different instruments poses interesting challenges. To cite one example, his performance of blues on violin stands out for its seeming juxtaposition of different musical traditions (figs. 3 and 4). In the context of New Orleans and rural Louisiana, violins were employed in string bands that performed blues, among other styles, but in the context of the idea of the blues created by record companies and scholars working in a folkloric tradition, the violin seems out of place. Likewise, his solo guitar work in jazz ensembles is revolutionary, recorded at a time when guitar and banjo were relegated to the rhythm section. This appearance of a "blues" practice in the midst of jazz orchestras paves the way for revolutionary jazz guitar duet recordings with the white artist Eddie Lang and coverage in jazz publications, although not in jazz scholarship (fig. 5).[119] In the end, his ability to play different instruments in different styles and genres for different performance contexts and audiences hindered the construction of a unitary, fixed identity as an artist. Or, put another way, his expertise in manipulating musical sign systems blocked the construction of his own artistic identity as a stable sign. Keenly aware of the tastes of his various audiences and able to adapt accordingly, the construction of a unitary musical identity was hampered by his deep understanding of the social systems in which music is embedded.

The role of record collectors in the construction of Johnson's identity further complicates the reception of Johnson's varied artistic output.[120] In the early years of jazz and to some degree blues scholarship, record collectors helped shape the lines of inquiry. Rather than pose questions informed by musicology or ethnomusicology, record collectors focused on "facts" involving personnel rosters at recording sessions. Miller summarizes a poignant episode from late in Johnson's life that occurred at the International Association of Jazz Record Collectors (IAJRC) fourth annual convention, held 20–21 July 1967 in Toronto:

> Johnson's presence at the convention allowed [Alexander] Ross [writer for the Toronto *Telegram*] to point up what he saw as the paradox of

IAJRC's preoccupations. "History itself walked in," Ross wrote of the moment, late on the 20th, when Johnson arrived, carrying his guitar in a vinyl bag. "He has a deep, wise face, and he looks like he's spent all of his life in a succession of strange furnished rooms. Somebody grabbed a microphone and introduced him by saying "Lonnie was one of the greatest guitar players who ever . . . Uh, and *still* is." Most of the collectors, though apparently not all, turned their attention Johnson's way as he listened intently to the recording of *Broken Levee Blues* that he had made for OKeh in March 1928. "And just for a moment," Ross noted pointedly, "the International Association of Jazz Record Collectors forgot about their discographies, their transcriptions, their disputed personnel lists, their endlessly accumulating collections, and remembered what jaz[z] was all about."[121]

OKeh Race Records

ELECTRIC RECORDS

LONNIE JOHNSON is weighted with misery... hear him sing the horrors of "St. Louis Cyclone Blues". The wind goes wailing through the song like a gale of madness.

Lonnie Johnson
(Exclusive Okeh Artist)

8512
10 in. .75
- ST. LOUIS CYCLONE BLUES—Vocal with Guitar and Piano
- SWEET WOMAN YOU CAN'T GO WRONG—Vocal with Guitar
  Both sung by Lonnie Johnson

85C5
10 in. .75
- LONESOME GHOST BLUES—Guitar and Singing
- FICKLE MAMMA BLUES—Guitar and Singing
  Both sung and played by Lonnie Johnson

8506
10 in. .75
- BEST FRIEND BLUES—Vocal with Piano and Clarinet
- STINGING BEE BLUES—Vocal with Piano and Clarinet
  Both sung by Margaret Johnson

8514
10 in. .75
- A WOMAN GETS TIRED OF THE SAME MAN ALL THE TIME—Vocal with Stovepipe and Guitar Accomp.
- COURT STREET BLUES—Vocal with Stovepipe and Guitar Accompaniment
  Both played and sung by Stovepipe No. 1 and David Crockett

FIG. 3 (OPPOSITE) Cover of OKeh Race Records catalog, circa 1926 or 1927. Author's collection.

FIG. 4 One-page ad for Lonnie Johnson's OKeh sides from OKeh catalog, circa 1926 or 1927, featuring the only publicity photograph of him with a violin. Author's collection.

Introduction / 23

FIG. 5 Lonnie Johnson on the cover of *Jazz Journal*, June 1951. Reproduced courtesy of *Jazz Journal*, https://jazzjournal.co.uk. Copy in author's collection.

Miller reports that record collectors were more interested in resolving a personnel dispute concerning the Gin Bottle Four recordings of Blind Willie Dunn (Eddie Lang) than anything substantive about his life and work. Stefan Grossman, who has transcribed some of Johnson's pieces, highlights the lost opportunities:

> Lonnie was sadly overlooked in his later years by blues and guitar playing historians. He was never interviewed in depth about either his life or his guitar techniques. . . . What is very unusual is that the tonality and key is the same for so many tunes. He might have his guitar tuned

low, or play it with a capo, or use a twelve string instead of a six string but the chord shapes are always based around the key of D. Document Records... have released a 7-volume CD set Lonnie Johnson—The Complete Recorded Works (each CD containing over 20 titles) and within those 140 plus tracks, you will only find 3 or 4 tunes in a key other than D! Yet, Lonnie's recording output in the 1940s and 1950s has little in common with blues in D, and he in fact rarely played in that key or style during these years. I personally cannot cite another guitarist whose style and technique changed so dramatically, especially after it was so widely acclaimed and imitated. This is a very strange phenomenon that only Lonnie would have helped us to understand.[122]

Grossman's lament about lost opportunities speaks directly to the role played by record collectors who went on to become archivists and authorities on early jazz and blues. Relative amateurs with respect to musical knowledge, they nonetheless shaped the contours of reception for many years. The role played by record collectors in reception adds another wrinkle to the history of the reception of Johnson's work.

As we have seen, Lonnie Johnson's musical identity is not easily reducible to one particular genre or style of music, and yet he has been pigeonholed as a blues artist, largely because of his solo work, and either ignored or labeled as "inauthentic" in recent years because of the stylistic variability that his musical talent enabled.[123] The longevity of his career and the pressures exerted by commercial constraints contributed to the varied content of his corpus. If some artists complained about being limited to the blues, such as Floyd Campbell (drummer and vocalist) who recorded blues with Charlie Creath—"Frankly, I didn't care for the Blues but back in those days that's the only thing they let colored bands record"[124]—generic variety did not help in Johnson's case, for he has still come to be known as a blues guitarist. His work as a studio musician and attempts to adapt to the changing tastes of the listening audience only complicate the picture. Indeed, even more than the work in jazz and vaudeville, the ballads recorded with King have led to charges of inauthenticity. His vocals display prominent vibrato and breath support and a distinct lack of the hoarseness, harshness, or growl associated with "authentic" blues.[125] While the ballads showcase his strengths as a vocalist, later fans expecting a "blues artist" did not appreciate his choice to perform "My Mother's Eyes" and other popular songs in the 1960s.[126] Blues scholar Pete Welding's negative reaction to a performance in Philadelphia in 1960 is representative:

Initially, it must be stated that Johnson is by no stretch of the imagination that authentic blues artist his older *Okeh* and *Bluebird* recordings attest he once was. True enough, he offers a number of blues in his program, such tunes as Bessie Smith's *Backwater Blues*, Handy's perennial *St Louis Blues* and several originals, among which was his hit single, *Mr Jelly Roll Baker*. He does a creditable job on them, but one gets the distinct impression—and this was especially noticeable in the Smith classic—that he doesn't really attach too much significance to them. He doesn't feel them as deeply as he does the sentimental, mawkish ballads which comprise the bulk of his repertoire.[127]

Welding goes on to write that "the blues have lost all meaning for him," and that "he's at his best in the maudlin, saccharine ballads which comprise at least 70% of his program."[128]

If it is not the ballads, it is the "clean" technique, use of major and diminished chords on guitar,[129] "the steady flow of melodic riffs and runs ... [that] were too sophisticated and jazz-oriented,"[130] the vibrato in the vocal as opposed to a rough growl, the clear diction, the long lines of lyrical verse, or some other feature that invites ignoring or dismissing his work.[131] While no one distinguishing marker is definitive in terms of its absence or presence for the blues, jazz, or any other genre of music, the tendency remains to attempt to identify a binary opposition and operate a gesture of exclusion based on it.[132] But in the realm of African American culture, as Stuart Hall reminds us, looking for binary oppositions is a futile endeavor fraught with power dynamics: "By definition, Black popular culture is a contradictory space. It is a site of strategic contestation. But it can never be simplified or explained in terms of the simple binary oppositions that are still habitually used to map it out: high and low, resistance versus incorporation, authentic versus inauthentic, experiential versus formal, opposition versus homogenization. There are always positions to be won in popular culture, but no struggle can capture popular culture itself for our side or theirs."[133] Not only is searching for binaries unproductive, but in the end, it only serves to crush the fragile construct that is performance.[134] In Johnson's corpus, I seek to go beyond the binaries to explore the multiple possibilities for meaning that his performances enable us to hear.

Analyzing and interpreting Johnson's corpus in its entirety is neither feasible nor particularly productive in terms of a greater understanding of the meanings of his work. I have taken my cues from Johnson's performances in selecting avenues of questioning to pursue. Recurring imagery, themes, lexicon, and musical figures trace patterns throughout his corpus. My song selections have been shaped by what I perceive as a degree of overarching coherence that these patterns create. In addition, the corpus cannot simply be read as Johnson's individual acts of expression. His artistic output is embedded within contexts of live performance and recording. The songs reflect the contexts in which they were produced that entailed relations with other people—other musicians, producers, and audiences. My approach to the songs analyzed in the following chapters attends to both Johnson's modes of self-presentation and his reflections on the world around him, a world of production, mediation, and reception.

What emerges from an examination of Johnson's corpus is the articulation of a rare degree of awareness of the self's embeddedness in a social world. As the following chapters will develop, Johnson's early experiences in New Orleans and St. Louis shaped an understanding of how individuals function within larger social configurations that is distinctly different from other blues artists. His experience of urban environments, as well as his professional experiences performing as a soloist and in various group configurations, shaped a notion of self that is less solitary and more embedded within larger networks than what is ordinarily represented in the blues. Working as a soloist but also as a sideman and as a member of larger ensembles enhanced this awareness of an individual identity shaped by broader social forces. Successfully maneuvering as a professional musician depended on adapting and conforming to musical and social expectations. As a musician he relates to other musicians, but also promoters, venue owners, record producers, and audiences. As we will see, this is neither the experience nor the portrait of the typical blues performer. Johnson exhibits none of the single-minded passion and mode of expression of a Charley Patton, Blind Lemon Jefferson, or Son House. Furthermore, the world he inhabits musically and socially is reflected in the world he creates in and through his music. As articulated in his music, Johnson's understanding of himself and of the world in which he is embedded reflects in a way unlike any other blues performer the mediation of the self by social forces. In his lyrics and in his musical performances, individual and community perform a complex dialectical dance of interdependence.

Outline and Technical Details

My study begins with an exploration of the rich sociohistorical contexts of New Orleans and St. Louis—in many respects atypical of the early twentieth-century South—that shape the performance of race, music, and the social world in Lonnie Johnson's archive. Of particular interest are the sites of music performance in their intersection with the understanding and politics of race in those two cities. Chapter 2 explores Johnson's construction of a persona for himself through his recordings. Careful readings of songs reveal a self-conscious manipulation of various kinds of signs to produce an unstable identity that responds to others' perceptions. Johnson's attention to how he is perceived by others determines a musical self-construction that portrays the self as embedded in and dependent on social relations. Chapter 3 turns to the social world that Johnson constructs in his lyrics. The complicated networks of relations that Johnson represents involve a typology of individuals. People occupy positions and perform roles, like his own as a musician, within social structures that shape their behavior. In Johnson's lyrics, deceit and betrayal are often exposed as a function of the roles people play, manipulating and exploiting others. Rather than the oppositional relation between self and other typical of many blues lyrics, Johnson instead understands social interactions as conditioned by prescribed roles and functions, consistent with both his musical and life experiences. Social roles delimit possibilities for modes of interaction for the self and others, allowing Johnson to imagine and represent conflict in more complex ways than most blues artists. His exposure to urban environments afforded him insight into social networks of power relations in which he was himself caught up that he communicates to an audience of listeners.

The manipulation and betrayal in the social world Johnson constructs lead, at times, to loneliness and despair. Being alone is a product of deceit, abandonment, and both voluntary and involuntary isolation. Chapter 4 explores the complicated representation of the isolated self in Johnson's lyrics. Representations of breakups, natural disasters, and homelessness lead to meditations on death. The isolated self is forced to face his or her own mortality and the fact of dying alone. I argue that Johnson's representations of the self alone contain a philosophical dimension. Paradoxically, while we all must die alone, we share this common existential condition. The conclusion explores a key central thread that runs throughout Johnson's corpus: the dialectical relationship between the self and others. With particular attention to his instrumental work, I reframe the question of Johnson's authenticity to ponder what we are listening for in his corpus.

All transcriptions of songs are my own. I have chosen to reproduce pronunciation and words as sung to underscore the poetic quality of Johnson's lines, rather than to "correct" African American Vernacular English.

CHAPTER 1

Musical Practice and Place

The Cultural History of New Orleans and St. Louis

Decades of scholarship on the blues have drawn and intensified a distinction between rural and urban traditions; Lonnie Johnson has been placed on the urban side of the divide.[1] Often the demarcation functions to establish ends of a spectrum with artists and styles falling somewhere between "folk" and "popular."[2] On the "folk" side, most often, are male, self-accompanied artists from rural areas who play in a "spontaneous" style, while the "popular" side often features female artists backed by ensembles of professional musicians performing works composed by musically literate "professionals."[3] In addition to supporting a gendered differentiation, the categories have, to some extent, also reinforced stylistic and racial boundaries, as they play out in styles of music and performance venues. Jukes, picnics, barbeques, sawmills, levee camps, and the like provide a space for an African American audience, often participating in a culture of male performance practice, while tented shows, including minstrel shows, showcase female performers who incorporate elements of vaudeville, ragtime, and popular song for a segregated crowd.[4]

Some more recent work in the blues has sought to interrogate the traces of unexamined assumptions in scholarship on the genre since the 1960s. For example, Paige A. McGinley questions the privileging of the male tradition as "authentic," arguing that rural male performances are as staged as female "professional" ones.[5] Karl Hagstrom Miller has traced the influence of Romanticist notions of folk music held by both record company executives that shaped an archive in accordance with segregated categories of understanding and scholars trained in folklore studies and ethnography.[6] He documents the "segregation of sound" practiced by both record labels and scholars in drawing generic boundaries deploying practices of exclusion, a point to which I return below. What emerges from a critical examination of a large body of blues scholarship is a privileging of a male rural tradition that masks underlying assumptions about segregation of the races and the sexes that go largely unexamined. Given Lonnie Johnson's early career in New Orleans and his professional start in St. Louis, the present chapter aims at two interconnected goals: first, to analyze the historical context for Johnson's musical formation through a presentation of a cultural history of the two cities and, as a corollary, to interrogate what attention to the rural has enabled and disabled in blues scholarship. In other words, attending to the specific contexts of New Orleans and St. Louis in the late nineteenth and early twentieth centuries raises questions related to assumptions about race and gender as they shape understandings of musical production and reception, including across styles of music. Before delving into cultural histories of the two cities that will problematize certain key assumptions, it is important to establish the contours of the rural milieu that has shaped the understanding of blues as a genre.

Focus on the Rural

In what Charles Keil acerbically dubbed the "moldy fig mentality," early scholars of the blues privileged a certain type of performer:

> Samuel Charters, Paul Oliver, Harold Courlander, Harry Oster, Pete Welding, Mack McCormick—even Alan Lomax until recently—share a number of interests or preoccupations, first and foremost of which is a quest for the "real" blues. The criteria for a real blues singer, implicit or explicit, are the following. Old age: the performer should preferably be more than sixty years old, blind, arthritic, and toothless (as Lonnie Johnson put it, when first approached for an interview, "Are you another one of those guys who wants to put crutches under my ass?"). Obscurity: the blues singer should not have performed in public or have made a recording in at least twenty years; among deceased bluesmen, the best seem to be those who appeared in a big city one day in the 1920's, made from four to six recordings, and then disappeared into the countryside forever. Correct tutelage: the singer should have played with or been taught by some legendary figure. Agrarian milieu: a bluesman should

have lived the bulk of his life as a sharecropper, coaxing mules and picking cotton, uncontaminated by city influences.[7]

Keil's mention of Lonnie Johnson's ironic quip to an interviewer stands out for the bluesman's understanding of the kinds of assumptions made by researchers interested in the blues. Sarcastically calling attention to projections made by scholars onto their subjects, Johnson demonstrates his awareness of how audience perceptions shape his identity and reception, underscoring his reluctance to play the game, perhaps because of his perceived lack of fit into their neat categories.[8]

To focus on Keil's final criterion, "agrarian milieu," the pioneering scholarship of Charters, Oliver, Lomax, David Evans, and others had multiple mutually reinforcing reasons for focusing on musical production in rural areas, and specifically in plantation settings.[9] Methodological emphasis on the "origins" of the genre motivated the search for sites of production without many "outside" influences. The world of the large plantations, with one white landowning family and numerous African American sharecropper and tenant families, or of the levee camps and sawmills, represent settings in which the races were largely separated and, hence, music-making occurred in differentiated spheres. The juke, picnic, or barbeque represents an African American space of musical production and consumption largely free from white influence. There, or so the argument goes, African American folk musicians create music that conforms to the needs and desires of an African American public, safe from interference by the white dominant culture. In such settings, the male performer entertains on a portable instrument—guitar and harmonica predominate—and female performers rarely appear due to the hazards associated with travel to and from, as well as at the venues themselves: alcohol, violence, and sexual predation. As a site of origin, the rural juke and other venues present neatly cordoned-off spaces back to which one may trace a vibrant tradition. A narrative structure ties together interrelated biases to produce a coherent story of origin.[10]

In addition to the interest in origins, other motivations also spurred the privileging of rural forms of blues. Folklorist methodology, with its nineteenth-century Romantic heritage, coupled with a social and political agenda about race in the United States, often colored the depiction of the blues in scholarship. Charters, in particular, was candid about his motivations in the 1975 preface to the republication of his seminal 1959 study *The Country Blues*. Written as a form of political action, Charters admits that "*The Country Blues* was two things. It was a romanticization of certain aspects of black life in an effort to force the white society to reconsider some of its racial attitudes, and on the other hand it was a cry for help." In attempting to enlist aid in the enterprise of recording "surviving blues artists," Charters engaged in "romanticism," in that he "was trying to make the journey to find the artists as glamorous as possible, by describing the roadsides, and the farms, and the shacks, and the musicians themselves."[11] While Charters's political ideals may have led him to romanticize depictions of a "lost past," notions of folk culture that privilege the exoticism of the rural—here dubbed "country"—have also contributed to the exclusion of the urban.

Lomax, for different reasons, also roped off the rural tradition for special attention. The work of field recording—preserving precious examples of nearly extinct forms of expression—is predicated on journeys of discovery designed to collect, curate, and protect valuable specimens of a soon-to-be-lost past. This aspect of folklorist methodology, akin to ethnography, functions to privilege artistic expression that is not easily accessible to a broad public.[12] The exoticism of the milieu supports the sense of the rarity of the object being preserved for a largely white public.[13] The publication, many decades later, of manuscripts, transcriptions, and field notes authored by John W. Work III, Lewis Johns, and Samuel C. Adams Jr. has shed some light on the omissions and exclusions operated primarily by Alan Lomax as part of the Fisk University–Library of Congress Study, consistent with the assumptions of folklorist methods.[14]

Ultimately, a notion of purity also informs these methodological practices in a variety of ways. First, there is a belief that the rural setting guarantees that the sample being collected and studied is untouched by forms of music from the "outside." Outside here signals professionalism (ability to read and compose music) associated with other forms, such as popular music, vaudeville, and ragtime.[15] According to this argument, any music touched by professionalism is not blues. The logic requires the exclusion of the blues sung by women singers in tented shows from the canon of authentic works, because "outside" forms "contaminate" their purity. Purity understood as lack of professionalism also aligns with the style's "spontaneous" features: composed in the moment from a stock of licks, riffs, and traditional couplets, in response to the calls from the crowd.[16] But, as Miller has argued, such a conception not only robs the folk practice of its status as art, it also effaces the practice and skill required to perform in this mode.[17]

Related to the "professional" label, the perception of commercialism also serves to distinguish what is and is not "authentic blues." But musicians, if they wish to earn money by performing, must sell what they do, to some extent. Whether it is a private party, a dance, a cabaret, bar, or club, or, as we will explore in detail below, a riverboat excursion or recording studio, musicians make adjustments in their performances to accommodate their listening audience and/or their employers. The exclusion of work perceived to be "commercial" from the body of blues ignores the degree to which the market enters all forms of performance except the most intimate and private—for example, before friends and family—but even there, the influence of exposure to commercial songs and practice for future salability cannot be completely discounted.

Ultimately, the folklorist methodology reveals a set of binary oppositions that undergird the categorization and analysis of blues music: pure/impure, folk/professional, male/female, rural/urban, authentic/inauthentic, et cetera. In each of these pairs, the first term is privileged to define an aesthetic genre according to traits that then serve to exclude other artistic practices. This binary system, to some degree, parallels the disciplinary divide between musicology and ethnomusicology. As "folk" music, the rural, male blues tradition merits study alongside of other folk music practices from around the globe. Complicating the designations here, the understanding of the blues as "popular" in the sense of issuing from the "folk" leaves the women's tradition and other related practices, because of their "professional/commercial" status, outside the field of both folklorist considerations of the blues and of ethnomusicology. Genres with "mixed" pedigrees are rejected because of their perceived "impurity" and, therefore, their unworthiness as objects of study.

The "mixed musical pedigree" of forms of blues, such as the women's "classic" blues (so designated because of their admixture of professionalized styles and commercialism), raises by association the question of race. Underlying the binaries above also lurks a racial division between Black and white. The "real," "pure" blues is performed by African Americans to an African American audience without the interference or contamination of European American forms, paradoxically despite origin stories for the blues that assert "original contact" between European and African musical practices.[18] This assumption underlies the privileging of the rural venues for the racial boundaries they represent spatially, as I argued above, but it also resulted in segregated recording practices. As Miller has argued, and some blues musicians lamented in interviews, record companies designated certain performers and songs as belonging to either the "race," "hillbilly," or "old time" category, despite the crossover in terms of repertoire among Black and white performers. Some blues artists, such as Son House and Charley Patton, recorded a repertoire that included church music.[19] But many blues artists were discouraged from recording music other than blues because it was not perceived as folk music.[20] This division imposed from the outside masked the degree of crossover in terms of both repertoire and audience in actual performance practice. Blues artists in the rural areas were hired to play at white parties and gatherings and to perform popular songs, likely including schottisches, polkas, and ballads. Johnny Shines recounts an anecdote about Robert Johnson that explodes the purist myth about music and performers, claiming that he loved "Tumbling Tumbleweeds" and polkas.[21] The archive of recordings largely papers over this messy conglomeration in terms of repertoire by segregating according to style and race, reinforcing notions of purity. In place of the overlaps and crossovers emerges the portrait of the rural, male musician who performs spontaneous folk music and is largely unaware of other traditions and certainly incapable of performing other types of music.

New Orleans

Lonnie Johnson's birth and early musically formative years in New Orleans implicitly interrogate the privileging of the rural setting, posing multiple problems for a large body of blues scholarship. If Lonnie Johnson is inconvenient for blues research, it is in large measure due to the particular set of difficulties that the sociocultural history of New Orleans (and St. Louis) presents to the neat binarisms outlined above. Alonzo Johnson's most likely birthdate on 8 February 1894, two years before the landmark United States Supreme Court decision in *Plessy v. Ferguson*, places him in the city in which the challenge to legalized segregation arose. The urban space of late nineteenth-century New Orleans called into question aspects of Jim Crow segregation and, especially, its operation according to a logic of binary racial opposition: Black or white. Indeed, Homer Plessy was specifically selected to challenge Louisiana's Separate Car Act because of his racial heritage as seven-eighths white and one-eighth African American.[22] In the context of New Orleans, Plessy's mixed racial heritage symbolized an alternative history of race and racialization to the binarism of the "one-drop rule" that would be imposed systematically throughout the South after the decision upholding racial segregation. Simply put, if before *Plessy v. Ferguson* Homer Plessy was an "octoroon," then after *Plessy* he was "'colored,' 'Negro,' or 'black.'"[23] However, it is important to note that actual practice lagged behind the official ruling: racial lines continued to be blurred.[24]

Unlike the rural settings, and especially the areas of large plantations like the Mississippi Delta with majority African American populations favored by blues scholars, binary racial segregation ran counter to a long history of race and racialization in New Orleans.[25] As part of the French Colonial enterprise in North America, stretching from Canada through the Louisiana Territory, both New Orleans and St. Louis were largely shaped by French conceptions of society, including race, rather than Anglo-American ones. The categorization of people into a three-tiered caste system evolved out of multiple pragmatic exigencies, and recognized "whites, free persons of color, and slaves."[26] But beyond the three-tiered caste system, the society of colonial, antebellum, and even occupied, Reconstruction, and Redeemer New Orleans presents a messy and complicated system of overlapping and interwoven forms of social differentiation and categorization.[27] In addition to the caste stratification into three groups were other complex modes of differentiation including, for race: white, Black, and mixed race (including multiple terms for various combinations, such as mulatto, quadroon, octoroon, etc.);[28] for class: elite, middle class, artisan or working class, and slave in the antebellum period; language: English, French, and Creole;[29] and "creolity": originally designating birth in the Louisiana Territory, but evolving into other designations, including one overlapping with "free people of color" and people of mixed racial heritage.[30] While these systems of socioeconomic, legal, racial, and ethnocultural differentiation underwent permutations and changes over the course of French, Spanish, and American territorial and state rule, by the time of Lonnie Johnson's birth, roughly coinciding with *Plessy v. Ferguson*, New Orleans still presented a challenge in multiple ways to "Americanization." As Arnold R. Hirsch and Joseph Logsdon summarize the historical situation, "The Americanization of New Orleans was more than just a struggle between Americans and creoles. It also involved, for nearly a century, the curious coexistence of a three-tiered Caribbean racial structure alongside its two-tiered American counterpart in an ethnically divided city."[31] New Orleans, in multiple ways, resisted the drawing of the color line through the implementation of segregated spaces.

Cultural historian Grace Elizabeth Hale has argued that the imposition of segregation was necessary for "making whiteness," the constitution of a broad category of racial identification across class and gender lines necessary for the ideology of white supremacy. Pointing out the inherent contradictions of white supremacy and its enactment in practice, Hale argues that segregation enforced a separation of racialized spaces that paradoxically required the penetration of Black spaces by whites and vice versa in order to maintain the power differential. For example, for white supremacists, the creation of specifically African American spaces risked the creation of Black autonomy, requiring the crossing of lines and spaces by whites to reassert authority.[32] This contradiction (one of many) at the heart of segregation as an arm of white supremacy signals the permeability of spaces in a "segregated" rural and urban South. The crossing of racialized spatial boundaries then signals two phenomena: (1) that the spaces are not as segregated as they first appear and, indeed, depend on an underlying permeability (by whites into Black spaces to reassert "control" and by Blacks into white spaces as servants and "inferiors"), and (2) that people move across those spaces as part of the enactment of segregation.

The site of New Orleans and, specifically, the case of musicians there, adds two further wrinkles to the paradoxes Hale exposes in her compelling analysis of the history of whiteness. In Louisiana and other formerly French territories, the two spaces were always already three and perhaps more, because of the heritage of the three-tiered caste system. Moreover, the various "districts," like Storyville in New Orleans (the red-light district "created in an attempt to isolate and thus regulate prostitution" that specialized in "interracial sex, with 'octoroon' prostitutes" for white customers),[33] trafficked in sex across the color line in ways that foregrounded the undermining of racial boundaries. Of course, Storyville and other districts were simply public manifestations of the more private scenarios of interracial rape under slavery and of rape and consensual sex in the rural and urban postbellum worlds that also entailed crossing the color line. The districts, then, create a fourth space of "segregation"—neither white, nor Creole (free people of color), nor Black— but intentionally created to cordon off and limit intimate interracial contact. Ironically, this fourth "segregated" space is one of deliberate and purposeful mingling. And within the districts are musicians who move among the spaces. They not only inhabit the spaces of intermingling, like the districts, but also all the other spaces as well. They serve as reminders of the mobility of persons across and through racialized space. More akin to servants, they provide an acoustic reminder of the kind of racial intermixing and mobility that paradoxically enables and supports racial separation.[34]

For the purposes of my analysis of Lonnie Johnson's musical practice, it is important to highlight that this complex social structure not only resists racial binarism but also, and more importantly, creates spaces (both physical and abstract) within the culture that have more obviously porous boundaries. In other words, if binary dualism in the Jim Crow world of the rural South largely segregated the races in key situations, especially those in which social equality could be inferred through contact,[35] the worlds of New Orleans and St. Louis resist the drawing of clear boundaries in part because of the existence of places and spaces, as well as individuals, that continually challenge the dualism. Bars, honky-tonks, barrelhouses, brothels in the districts (Storyville in New Orleans and Chestnut Valley in St. Louis), streetcars, sporting events, and the Roman Catholic Church, but also Afro-Creoles and octoroon prostitutes for white customers, continually assert the permeability of the boundary between white and Black.[36] As Emily Epstein Landau points out, the geography of the city illustrated this porousness after *Plessy*: "In New Orleans, the legacy of a three-tiered racial structure of whites, free people of color, and slaves endured culturally for years after the color line was sharply drawn. The population had long been distributed along a salt-and-pepper pattern, and lines between and among groups were less than fixed. Class, culture, language, and the physical landscape of the city had as much impact as race in determining patterns of settlement and movement. The struggle to segregate the city was a struggle against centuries of habit in New Orleans."[37] The spaces most "resistant to segregation"—bars, saloons, restaurants, houses of prostitution, et cetera—not only involve "social contact"; they are also places in which music is a key feature.[38] The street itself was also a live music scene in New Orleans, as jazz historian Bruce Boyd Raeburn underscores, broadcasting music to a "public" not necessarily constituted as such.[39] Music not only exists in such spaces but also travels through and across the spaces, along with the people who perform it, permeating and challenging the boundaries, including the stylistic ones. The boundaries still exist, but in ways that require them to be constantly redrawn. As Charles Hersch asserts about the conditions of early jazz musicians, "[They] found ways at times to evade the strictures of segregation, but racism influenced which musicians played together, what kind of music was played for a particular audience, who listened to the music and with whom, and what the music meant to those listeners. *One could not be any race at any time, but musicians exploited and expanded the fuzziness around racial boundaries that did exist.*"[40] Musicians not only move across boundaries and play to different audiences, they also create a cultural product that resists categorization. As we saw during the time of Johnson's life in New Orleans, the distinction between popular music, jazz, and blues, like the others, is messy and complicated.

Lonnie Johnson in New Orleans

Like the date of his birth, the site of Lonnie Johnson's family home is also difficult to pin down. Using both information Johnson provided in interviews and maps of New Orleans from the late 1890s, Dean Alger attempts to locate the precise neighborhood in which Johnson grew up. Much difficulty arises from different street names provided in interviews—"Franklin Street near Rampart" and "Wall Street"[41]—that could indicate a neighborhood in or near Storyville, or northeast of the French Quarter, or even in the southwest corner of the metropolitan area near the river (Alger's best guess). I would argue that establishing the precise location of the house that he grew up in is less important than recognizing that conceptions of space and place are shifting, problematic, and permeable in late nineteenth- and early twentieth-century New Orleans. Although neighborhoods had particular characteristics related to their demographic makeup, as Raeburn asserts, "Tremé, the French Quarter, the Seventh Ward, Central City, the Irish Channel, and Algiers were 'cultural wetlands' characterized by 'crazy quilt' demographic configurations that predated the implementation of segregation in the 1890s, interspersing Creoles, Latinos, Jews, blacks, and whites side by side within blocks."[42] Even after "segregation," these residential patterns continued and, more to Raeburn's point, music moved through the air, available to "everyone within earshot."[43]

Whatever the precise location of his early childhood home, in his early years in New Orleans Lonnie performed on violin, guitar, and possibly banjo in his father's band with other family members, in Johnson's words traversing the city to play "weddings and dances, and, uh, private parties, things like that, dinners."[44] This work requires moving in, through, and across different socioeconomic, racial, and ethnocultural spaces.[45] Filling in what Johnson might have meant by "things like that" requires conjuring the landscape and soundscape of early twentieth-century New Orleans in which a wide variety of social occasions involved music at both indoor and outdoor venues: "festivities that included Carnival, debutante parties, lakefront picnics, train and riverboat excursions, social-aid and pleasure-club parades, church dedications, *soirées dansantes*, jitney and college 'script' dances, theater vaudeville, sporting events (possibly at sporting houses), fish fries and funerals,"[46] but also "bordellos, cabarets, honky-tonks, restaurants, and bars," including in the district.[47] The street itself was the site of multiple musical performances, not only the famous return funeral processions followed by the "second line," but also "dance bands riding around the streets on large furniture wagons engaged in 'cutting contests' to advertise a job or to obtain one,"[48] and, of course, busking musicians. Pops Foster specifically remembers the Johnson family band on street corners: "All around New Orleans area we had street corner players. They used guitar and mandolin and played for coins on the corners.... Those guys would walk down the street and if they'd see a gang of people they'd stop and play them a number. Then they'd pass the hat around. Guys would put a coin in. Lonnie Johnson and his daddy and his brother used to go all over New Orleans playing on street corners. Lonnie played guitar, and his daddy and brother played violin."[49]

The information about playing in his father's band beginning in his teens seems reliable, despite the infamous unreliability of information Johnson gave in interviews. Given the list of venues in which the family band played—weddings, dances, and private parties—it seems plausible they played a broad repertoire, adjusting style and genre according to their audiences' tastes. Johnson told Valerie Wilmer in 1963 that they played "schottisches and waltzes and things, there wasn't no blues in those days."[50] The types of venues and music, plus the fact that Johnson played violin early on, indicate that he was almost certainly able to read music. As Danny Barker, a New Orleans blues player asserts, "Lots of the bands couldn't read too much music. So they used a fiddle to play the lead—a fiddle player could read—and that was to give them some protection."[51] Reading music would enable the band to learn popular tunes from sheet music, if at least one member of the band could read to teach others. Finally, Johnson's remarks about lack of formal schooling, made in an interview with Wilmer in 1963, suggest that his father was educated to some degree, having taught him to read and write. In the same interview he insisted, "It is very important to learn to read music in your early years."[52] Extrapolating from these remarks, and from the kind of music that Johnson would have played in the family band, it is reasonable to assume that he learned to read music from his father.[53]

In addition to this childhood urban experience playing a likely wide variety of popular music, he also had experiences with nonurban music and exposure to a rural musical tradition including blues. Jazz cornetist Ernest "Punch" Miller reported that Johnson spent two or three years in Raceland, Louisiana, in Lafourche Parish playing music in a more rural setting. When asked what kind of music they played, Miller reported popular tunes and "blues, whole lot of blues."[54] While the specifics on dates and time intervals may not be exact, Lonnie Johnson's early experiences in Bayou Lafourche performing with Punch Miller exposed him to rural African American forms of music. The tastes and desires of the rural Louisiana audiences would have dictated the repertoire, Black and white.[55]

While exposure to rural practices is significant, it is also important to recognize that the urban/rural dichotomy in terms of musical style and repertoire is not absolute in practice.[56] Plenty of people living in New Orleans came from rural areas and longed to hear music associated with memories of "home." Roustabouts, longshoremen, and other workers also made contributions to the folk music in the city's soundscape.[57] As we saw in the previous chapter, some saloons, honky-tonks, and dance halls in New Orleans catered to working-class, African American audiences who wanted to hear "ratty" music, including blues.[58] Although Johnson no doubt played more "folk blues" style music in Bayou Lafourche than he did at New Orleans private parties, the boundaries are permeable: some audiences in New Orleans likely requested blues or blues-inflected jazz. Bunk Johnson's remarks about playing with Buddy Bolden attest to the repertoire in Storyville and elsewhere: "Bolden was playing blues of all kinds, so when I got with Bolden, we helped to make more blues."[59] So, despite Johnson's claims that "there wasn't no blues in those days" and that he played "city blues," he was quite capable of playing in multiple styles in different contexts, as his accompaniment of the rural musician Alger "Texas" Alexander and others would later demonstrate.[60]

Johnson's ability to play multiple instruments further serves as an important sign of the kind of dexterity and fluidity that would characterize his entire career. While the violin is often associated with the ability to read music and perform popular songs and dances, the guitar is more associated with unwritten rural forms like blues. Johnson's ability to play both written "popular" and unwritten "folk" music, not only on violin and guitar but also piano, banjo, and harmonium, illustrates his adaptability as a musician. One of his first recordings, "Falling Rain Blues" (St. Louis, 4 November 1925), provides a clear example of this adaptability and boundary-crossing. He was rightfully proud of his uncommon ability to sing and accompany himself on violin, saying "It's hard to play violin and sing at the same time."[61] The recording exhibits a dual training that combines styles and skills in fascinating ways to create something different and hybrid. The unusual bowing technique, including skipping and sliding in the solo, creates an impression of falling raindrops. Although far from smooth, the extended solo performance on violin at the end of the verses provides emotion and depth in a remarkable manner.[62] The particular circumstances of a childhood musical training in New Orleans with time spent in Bayou Lafourche enable such a curious and unique aesthetic manifestation.

As he matured from his father's band to perform with other groups, a young adult Johnson continued to play in New Orleans, in a variety of venues.

In an interview from 1945, he claimed to have begun playing on his own in 1912, but it may have been earlier than that.[63] He told blues researcher Paul Oliver that he "worked at the Iroquois Theater" (a Black variety and vaudeville theater on South Rampart) and "at Frank Pineri's place on Iberville and Burgundy."[64] The street location would place this second venue in the Tango Belt in the Upper French Quarter, an area with numerous jazz clubs.[65] He also mentioned performing in Milneburg where Lake Pontchartrain is located, a site of restaurants, parties, picnics, and other events with music. He also listed Storyville, where he had a steady gig in Punch Miller's jazz band.[66] During these early adult years, Johnson likely played in ensembles requiring an ability to perform a wide repertoire, from blues to jazz to vaudeville to popular dance music, according to the racial, class, and ethnic dictates of taste among listeners.

As a guitar player in a small ensemble before the appearance of guitar as lead instrument—something he had a significant hand in pioneering[67]—it is important to remember that he occupies a central role in the rhythm section. Although his main function in the band is to supply part of the rhythmic backing for the lead instruments, as a violinist capable of reading music, he serves as bridge between the written and improvisational worlds. Like a bass player in later configurations, his role on rhythm guitar is to contribute to the groove while reinforcing the tonal architecture of the song. This requires a knowledge of chordal changes and an ability to respond in the moment to the movements of the improvising soloists. Experience playing violin on popular songs would help him to execute this pivotal function between written and nonwritten worlds, providing rhythm for improvisational lead.

Roughly between 1917 and 1919, Johnson likely left New Orleans and traveled to London to perform, although as Mark Miller points out, this cannot be proved.[68] The dates coincide with a turning point of sorts for conditions in New Orleans related to the entrance of the United States in World War I. First, Storyville closed under pressures from the military and its "health and fitness campaign."[69] But World War I also motivated the beginning of the Great Migration with the availability of more industrial jobs in the North. Finally, the historical moment marks the end of struggles against Jim Crow segregation, especially by the community of Creole people of color.[70] Taken together, these social, political, and economic forces caused many musicians and nonmusicians alike to leave the Crescent City. In the case of Johnson, Europe in wartime may have provided a performance venue for a skilled musician capable of working in an ensemble. Having likely performed in Europe during the First World War, Johnson probably returned to New Orleans in 1919 to find that most of his family had died in the influenza pandemic of 1918.[71] He and his surviving brother, James "Steady Roll" Johnson, moved to St. Louis in late 1919 or early 1920. It is not clear why the Johnson brothers chose St. Louis, but job possibilities and the swift and effective quarantine in response to the pandemic that resulted in the lowest death rate in the ten largest cities of the time may have contributed to their decision.[72]

Lonnie Johnson in St. Louis

While St. Louis may not have been the most obvious choice to relocate for musicians, most of whom would have been attracted to Chicago for recording opportunities, nonetheless, St. Louis may have held an attraction for its similarities with New Orleans, beginning with the cities' shared French colonial heritage.[73] As part of the territory included in the Louisiana Purchase in 1803, St. Louis also bore vestiges of a three-tiered caste system and a Creole elite. But in comparison with New Orleans in the early twentieth century, St. Louis was even less racially segregated, although there was greater overt racial tension.[74] In the decade preceding the Johnson brothers' move to St. Louis, it had experienced significant African American population growth: "St. Louis's industrial activities—steel, iron, meat-packing, glass, brick, railroads and tobacco—outstripped those of any of the other cities that opened onto the Mississippi, [so] African Americans migrated to the Mound City in the hope of finding jobs."[75] With this growth came "inconsistent patterns of segregation. Blacks and whites rode streetcars together, and blacks could use the public library or visit the city's grand municipal park, yet municipal playgrounds and swimming pools were segregating, and at the local 'five and dime' black customers were forced to eat at separate lunch counters."[76]

While the practices of segregation may at first have seemed unfamiliar, nonetheless, many aspects of urban life for a musician would have been quite familiar. St. Louis had a "district," like Storyville, in the Chestnut Valley, with brothels and sporting houses for work.[77] Other St. Louis venues would have also seemed similar: bars, honky-tonks, clubs, and restaurants in St. Louis and across the river in East St. Louis, Illinois. Overall, the Johnson brothers no doubt perceived a great deal of continuity between New Orleans and St. Louis in terms of their lives as musicians, not least of which the foundational role St. Louis ragtime played in the creation of "jazz" in New Orleans.[78]

In addition to the familiar venues, St. Louis was home to the Streckfus Steamers, providing tourist excursions on the Mississippi River with jazz musicians as entertainers, many of whom were from New Orleans. The Johnsons would have been acquainted with the music from the boats, having heard it during the steamers' winter port stays in New Orleans.[79] Blues guitarist Danny Barker stresses the riverboats' sonic presence in New Orleans: "One of the most beautiful sounds in the city of New Orleans was Fate Marable playing his steam calliope about seven in the evening every night. Those calliope concerts from the riverboats *J.S.* and *Bald Eagle* started in the first couple of years after the boats started using music—around 1916 and '17, I'd say."[80] Fate Marable's long tenure as the musical director aboard the steamboats, from 1907 to 1940,[81] shaped the early professional experience of many jazz players, including Louis Armstrong, Warren "Baby" Dodds, George "Pops" Foster, and Johnny St. Cyr, among others, with whom Johnson was acquainted from performing.[82]

The riverboat excursion as a professional venue presented a challenging set of circumstances in which Johnson was likely relatively comfortable. Marable's infamous insistence on being able to sight-read music spurred the oft-quoted quip repeated by New Orleans drummer Zutty Singleton: "When some musician would get a job on the riverboats with Fate Marable, they'd say, 'Well you're going to the conservatory.'"[83] The insistence on reading music highlights the kind of music played on the boats: waltzes, rags, and jazz that was notated, with occasional improvisation.[84] The fact that the line was owned by a German American family and catered to a primarily white audience exerted constraints on the music. Cultural historian William Howland Kenney documents the pressure applied by Joseph Streckfus on Marable and his bands to produce "an adaptation of black New Orleans music to the repertoire, tempi, and sensibilities of stock dance band arrangements."[85]

With the usual caveats about the reliability of information Johnson provided in interviews, he may have worked with Marable, but was certainly hired by Charles Creath, the trumpet player and bandleader, for excursions on the *St. Paul*.[86] Given Johnson's experience with both written, "professional" music culture and an unwritten culture of improvisation, he would have had little difficulty navigating the constraints imposed by the riverboat context. Although much is made in jazz scholarship of the divide between reading music and improvising, especially given Louis Armstrong's infamous firing for failing to show up for music lessons with Marable, the dichotomy requires some revision and attenuation.[87]

Marable had multiple reasons for constraining his musicians to perform in a particular way, not least of which were the demands of his employer that were aimed at the commercial interest of pleasing the passengers.[88] An African

American band performing for a white clientele required "professionalism" in multiple forms, including musicianship, to disrupt racial stereotypes, including those associated with blackface minstrelsy.[89] Written music performed according to strict guidelines, especially with respect to tempo, met the needs of this racialized commercial performance context. In this respect, commercialism and professionalism limit the possibilities of "free" improvisation and the use of "hot" and slow tempos. But it is also true that the constraints imposed by a written score only appear to conflict with improvisation when the distinction is perceived as one between freedom to improvise and constraint to perform what is written—a distinction often emphasized by musicians such as Armstrong. The reality of performance practice lies somewhere between the two extremes.

All written scores require interpretation in performance, especially in the context of vernacular music with rhythmic and tonal subtleties beyond the capabilities of elite European notation systems, like jazz and blues.[90] Within the riverboat music culture, musicians more adept at reading taught the others to play the tunes. Indeed, musical literacy, like literacy in general, is a spectrum with a range of capacities rather than a binary opposition: it is possible to read enough to get the basic notes and then supplement by ear.[91] More importantly for jazz musicians, the score is only a starting point. "Signifying" on a melody requires inserting notes and rhythms spontaneously in performance: the notated melodies represent the germ of an idea to be elaborated.[92] As different soloists take the lead and improvise around the melody, those in the ensemble are required to respond in the moment to the movements of the lead. Not only is the distinction between reading music and improvising often overstated in the jazz context, but the distinction between the improvisation of the soloist and the reliance on reading of the rhythm ensemble is also an overstatement. In truth, performance always requires adjustments and adaptations in the moment by the ensemble players in response to the lead. As with literacy, freedom in improvisation is also a matter of degree. As we saw in the previous chapter, dichotomies in jazz scholarship that have parallels in blues scholarship, particularly concerning "authenticity" and "inauthenticity," associate "commercial compromise" with stock arrangements, occluding overlaps, crossovers, and blurred boundaries.[93] As we have seen, Lonnie Johnson's early experiences on violin and guitar enable him to navigate both worlds, as well as the places and spaces in between, making him highly suited to the hybrid environment of riverboat jazz culture.

Although the clientele on the Streckfus boats was largely white, and the musical arrangements catered to this audience, Monday nights were reserved for African American passengers—although as in permeable spaces in New Orleans, whites were sometimes aboard to witness what went on.[94] By 1920, when Lonnie Johnson arrived in St. Louis, Charlie Creath was a bandleader on the Streckfus line, holding his musicians to standards like Marable's,[95] but also catering to the tastes of the African American audience on Monday nights.[96] Creath's footprint in St. Louis included an office on Market Street in Chestnut Valley, the center of African American music in St. Louis, near the Rosebud Café, Jazzland (a dance hall), and the Booker T. Washington Theater.[97] The Monday night cruises were promoted by Jesse Johnson, someone with ties to the African American music scene in St. Louis.[98] Creath teamed with the promoter, Johnson, to expand Black cruise offerings, even directly competing with Streckfus for a time.[99] Eventually, Creath and Jesse Johnson controlled most of the Monday night cruises. While we do not know for a fact that Lonnie Johnson played in Marable's bands, we do know with certainty that he worked and recorded with Creath.[100] Given his musical training and background, he was no doubt comfortable playing on Monday nights, as well as on the other nights of the week, under Creath's direction, making subtle alterations and adaptations of performance style according to the audience.

The St. Louis music community formed a network of ties that connected Lonnie Johnson to Jesse Johnson, Creath, and others.[101] Year-round work was possible on the riverboats. "Tramp" trips traveled north as far as St. Paul and east as far as Pittsburgh in the summer, but it was also possible to winter in New Orleans and summer in St. Louis, playing sometimes daily and always nightly excursions. Playing for the Streckfus line afforded the opportunity to get off the boats and play venues in the St. Louis area.[102] Johnson played venues such as Jazzland, Chauffeur's Club, Revere Club, and Katy Red's in East St. Louis.[103]

Henry Townsend, the blues singer, guitarist, and pianist from St. Louis, heard Johnson when he was young:

> I saw Lonnie Johnson at the Booker Washington—although by that time he had been all over in East St. Louis, but at that time it wasn't too convenient for me to get to those places. So my first time of seeing Lonnie Johnson was there. When I first saw him he's already recorded. I used to sneak in and see him. He also played at a few places where Luella Miller and them got started at—I can't call the street now, but it's a couple

of blocks from Market Street. Lonnie Johnson used to be over there and on Twenty-Second Street there, them speakeasy joints and things. . . . Occasionally I'd see Lonnie Johnson around East St. Louis. Several places over there he used to work, like down around Third Street and all down in there.[104]

Although Townsend did not see Johnson until after he was recording for OKeh, the account is representative of the kinds of venues in which he played before and after the contract. Aside from the Booker T. Washington Theater, these are mostly African American clubs where Johnson performed as a soloist, or possibly in a duo with his brother or small ensemble, including Katy Red's in East St. Louis.[105]

The Booker T. Washington Theater was a large venue that featured soloists and also staged traveling acts. John J. Wright Sr. explains that "the theatre had a seating capacity of 1000 and featured vaudeville and other live entertainment, as well as motion pictures."[106] The connection between the riverboat experience and work in the theater is direct: as a promoter and booker, Jesse Johnson worked for both venues. More significantly, according to Townsend,

> Jesse Johnson was one of the first promoters out of the city of St. Louis for black artists, and he got to be known nationally from the material he sent to those companies. RCA wasn't accepting too much, and I think he broke the ice in getting them to accept black artists. He was also doing things for Okeh, Brunswick, and Paramount Records, because I was on trips with him for some of them. I don't know who the first group of people that come through him and recorded were, but I know it wasn't too long before Roosevelt Sykes was involved. That's also where Victoria Spivey got her trip to Okeh Records from.[107]

Thus, the Booker T. Washington Theater represents an important venue, not only for the exposure to the African American music audience in St. Louis but also for its connections for a professional musical career with acts in the TOBA, as well as recording companies.

As is often the case, the network of professional music is small, with key promoters, bookers, and club owners playing a central role in enabling artists to work. In the case of Lonnie Johnson, the Booker T. Washington Theater also served as a launching point for a recording career. He told Oliver, "They had a blues singing contest at the Booker Washington Theater in St. Louis. It was mostly a talent scout contest. See the scouts for Okeh Records started that off. Whoever win the contest that week got a contract—three weeks in the theater or got a recording contract."[108] While his claims to Oliver were exaggerated about how many weeks he won the contest and the length of his contract with OKeh, the significance of the professional music connections are clear. For Johnson, being connected to a network of African American promoters, scouts, venues, and players enabled him to succeed as a musician in both live and recording contexts. His "professionalism" enabled his commercial success, but not in the sense of selling out.

The Streckfus riverboats and Johnson's contact with jazz musicians, bookers, and promoters opened up opportunities for work in multiple venues, including in TOBA theaters and the B. F. Keith and RKO circuits.[109] The singing contest in the TOBA theater led to a recording contract doing solo, ensemble, and "studio work." The TOBA connection likely enabled his recording work with Victoria Spivey, Clara Smith, Clarence Williams, and others. These experiences also provide an important context for understanding his recordings with Louis Armstrong's and Duke Ellington's bands.[110] Johnson was a seasoned musician capable of playing in a variety of styles, lead and rhythm, with and without written music.

Johnson was uniquely positioned to work for a relatively long period of time without resorting to day jobs, unlike many other musicians, and especially blues artists. His adaptability and flexibility enabled movement across genres and styles, making him skilled in lead roles, as well as part of ensemble play. His discipline and professionalism, evident in his work on the Streckfus boats and on theater circuits, coupled with his improvisational ability shaped a multifaceted career that does not fit into the categories established by some blues and jazz scholarship. Johnson's work demonstrates the fundamental permeability and porousness of boundaries related to genre. His work moves between, among, across, and through styles and the places associated with those styles. Like sound, it crosses boundaries shaped by economic, racial, and social hierarchy, as well as musical categorization that in many ways resonates with the cultural contexts of New Orleans and St. Louis.

Johnson's experiences in New Orleans and St. Louis shaped his understanding of musical performance relative to context. These two cities presented a broader array of possible contexts for African American musical performers than in most of the South, allowing talented musicians like Johnson to play across genres and styles to a variety of audiences. As a member of ensembles and duos, but even as a soloist, Johnson is keenly aware of the ways in which, as a performer, he chooses repertoire and style of execution according to his perception of the audience and its tastes. In other words, Johnson views musical performance as a profoundly social activity, embedded in social, racial, and economic relations. The musician's identity depends as much on self-conscious acts of construction as it does on responses to pressures exerted by promoters, producers, venue owners, and listeners. The urban environments of New Orleans and St. Louis placed Johnson in a position to understand music-making, including his identity as a performer, in a profoundly contextualized way. In the next chapter, I turn to Johnson's musical persona as a performance of identity conditioned by his social understanding of human relations.

CHAPTER 2

Self-Construction and Self-Awareness

Lonnie Johnson's Persona

Beginning with his debut song, "Mr. Johnson's Blues" (St. Louis, 4 November 1925), Lonnie Johnson explicitly announces his intention to construct a lasting identity for himself through his music. The instrumental introduction is shaky, sounding like he may have started on the wrong fret; he most certainly missed fingerings as he played descending triplet double stops slightly out of tune. Understandably nervous his first time in the recording studio, he nonetheless settles down as the performance progresses. The forceful entrance of the vocal commands attention and seems to boost his confidence. The lyrics assert the desire to create an impression that will last beyond the singer's lifetime: "I want all you people to listen to my song [2x] / Remember me after the days I'm gone." The self-referential title, read in conjunction with the only verse of lyrics in the song, communicates a desire to create a unique identity through musical performance for an audience of listeners that will be preserved for posterity.[1] Johnson's vocal performance exhibits elements atypical of blues singers that contribute to the construction of his unique identity. The onset of phonation is relatively smooth, consonants are cleanly articulated, and, most importantly, his vocal timbre is distinct. For the held notes on *all* in the A lines, Johnson deploys heavy laryngeal vibrato with wider tonal variance in the second A′ articulation than the first.[2] The two syllables of *peo-ple* are emphasized with a descending tone rather than a slide more typical in the blues. *Song*, the final word of the A lines, is sung with a tighter vibrato than *all*, displaying Johnson's vocal mastery. The control is reemphasized in the performance of *me* in the B line with an almost diphthong vowel with descending melisma and late onset vibrato. Much of his signature vocal quality is produced by sympathetic resonance in the nasal cavities and possibly an expanded pharynx that provides harmonic resonance and projection.[3] Distinctly absent is the "noise" produced by tense phonation, such as growl, hoarseness, or raspiness, associated with "authenticity," especially in the blues.[4] This signature timbre is most prominent on four significant words that encapsulate his self-presentation: *all, people, song, me*. This *me* on display is aware of and references a public for whom he sings with distinctive qualities that communicate determination.[5]

The vocal quality contrasts with the jaunty rhythm of the guitar and piano accompaniment with its rapid decay and relative lack of sustained tones. Johnson accentuates the intensity of his desire to be heard and known by everyone in the juxtaposition of vocal and instrumental sound. Choosing as his first recording to perform a song with only one verse of lyrics and several choruses of guitar solo, Johnson indirectly asserts a desire to be known more for his instrumental virtuosity than his vocal prowess, although his distinctive vocal style is on display. His nerves seemingly disappear as he settles into an initial thirty-six-bar guitar solo. Despite John Arnold's busy piano backing, Johnson's signature half-tone slides, rapid triplet figures, and movement between plucking and strumming, rhythm and lead are showcased. Overall, despite the uneven introduction, the performance communicates precision and mastery on guitar.

On this 78 rpm release, Johnson constructs a musical identity for himself not only on guitar, but also on violin. "Falling Rain Blues" (on the B-side) introduces his innovative approach to blues in a rare occurrence of a vocalist self-accompanying on violin (fig. 4).[6] As in "Mr. Johnson's Blues," "Falling Rain Blues" also showcases Johnson's instrumental virtuosity with violin responses to the vocal, aided by a more subdued piano part by Arnold than in "Mr. Johnson's Blues," and a four-chorus solo that becomes increasingly inventive as it progresses. Johnson advances from rapid, mostly single notes in a swung rhythm in the first twelve bars, to a melody line of bowed chords that moves by half steps in the second chorus, to a skipping or bouncing bow technique similar to *spiccato* that creates a raindrop-like sound in the next twelve bars, to a final chorus of arpeggios in a two-octave range at the end of the song. This reimagining of the blues on violin showcases the artist's adaptability and flexibility as he creates technique on the violin to approximate the palette of sounds and rhythmic possibilities afforded by the guitar. The options enabled by the violin push the sonic boundaries of the blues to incorporate a larger tonal range, different forms of tonal attack with the bow providing new color, and a recontextualized feeling of movement with the ties and arpeggios performed on violin.

The lyrics of "Falling Rain Blues" introduce themes that will recur in Johnson's corpus, most prominently the use of natural phenomena, like storms, to develop psychological portraits of loneliness, despair, and vulnerability. Like much of his work, the lyrics do not reproduce traditional lines and couplets, but rather develop a coherent thematic pattern that weaves together general observations with personal emotional responses within the confines of the traditional AA′B form, albeit with longer lines. The three simple verses invoke a storm to explore feelings of loss and abandonment. Most significant in the lyrics is the third verse whose simile may have provided inspiration for a line in Robert Johnson's "Hell Hound on My Trail" (Dallas, 20 June 1937): "Blues falling like showers of rain [2x] / Every once and a while, think I hear my baby call my name."[7] The plaintive vocal delivery followed by the violin solo that mimics the sound of the rain together create an overall impression of depression and isolation through artistic mastery.

The choices on display in Johnson's debut 78 highlight his efforts to construct a public persona for himself.[8] While all performers engage in efforts to shape and control their public image, the case of Johnson stands out against a backdrop of other blues musicians, from the women of the 1920s—Bessie Smith, "Empress of the Blues"; Sippie Wallace, the "Texas Nightingale"; and Ma Rainey emerging from a giant Victrola on stage—to the men of the rural tradition—Peetie Wheatstraw, the "High Sheriff from Hell" and "Devil's Son-in-Law," and Robert Johnson's pact with the devil. Lonnie Johnson's persona is crafted in ways that bear the traces of racial and class identities as they were understood and performed in early twentieth-century New Orleans and St. Louis for specific audiences. His self-conscious public persona displays an understanding of permeability across racial and class boundaries, as well as lines ostensibly separating musical styles for different groups of listeners.

Race and Performance

Lonnie Johnson's "Mr. Johnson's Blues" not only declares his intention to make a name for himself as a skilled musician, it also violates norms related to race in the South in the early twentieth century. As Dean Alger points out, referencing an episode recounted in Alan Lomax's *The Land Where the*

Blues Began, using the designation *Mister* for a person of color was considered to be not only a deviation from the norm, but also an affront and insult to whites.[9] As a title of respect, its use was reserved for whites and its application enforced. Using *Mr.* in front of an African American's surname signaled a rejection of the customs associated with white supremacy in its undermining of one of the more public indicators of the line demarcating supposed racial superiority and inferiority. Johnson's use of *Mr.* for self-designation represents a significant demand for respect because of its doubleness: from the perspective of white supremacy, it both bestows a designation reserved for whites on an African American, and it does so in a gesture that appropriates the power and authority, also reserved for whites, to insist on a racially exclusive designation.[10]

But, as we have seen, racial distinctions and designations are more complicated in New Orleans and St. Louis than in many parts of the South. In these cities, the foundational binary of the one-drop rule meets the permutations of French colonial understandings of race. As I argued in the preceding chapter, an awareness of racial permeability is a product of multiple factors, including prominent groups in the population with mixed racial heritage recognized in a three-tiered caste system, residential settlement patterns, and places and spaces of significant interracial contact. The prolonged history of efforts to impose segregation in New Orleans underscores the contradictions of the practice of separation according to a simple binary opposition. As Grace Hale writes, "Positing an absolute boundary and the freedom to cross only in one direction, segregation remained vulnerable at its muddled middle, where mixed-race people moved through mixed spaces, from railroad cars to movies to department stores, neither public nor private, neither black nor white."[11] Musicians, in particular, participate in a crossing of racial "lines" for appearances in numerous venues for different audiences. These patterns of racialized interaction lead to not only a sense of permeability in terms of space and place but also an awareness of the performative aspect of race itself.[12] In other words, as musicians move into and out of, through and across spaces to perform in different venues, they become perhaps more aware than others of the sense in which race is also a performance.

The history of blackface minstrelsy supports the argument of heightened awareness among entertainers of race as a kind of performance. Before African Americans began to perform in blackface troupes, European Americans blackened their faces to perform race in savage parodies of "slave culture." As Karl Hagstrom Miller explains, pre–Civil War minstrelsy "involved the performance of supposedly African American song and dance by white actors under blackface masks of burnt cork. From the common use of dialect or malapropisms to represent black speech to the ubiquitous exaggerations of black physical deviation from white norms (often sliding into comparisons with the animal kingdom), minstrelsy traded on images of African American difference and inferiority."[13] Miller asserts that, in the early period, "minstrelsy did all this within the irreducible context of the blackface mask—a prop that performed racial distance under the auspice of racial passing."[14]

But this type of racial performance, despite its ostensible reliance on separation, nonetheless asserts a kind of permeability. Especially after the Civil War, with the "integration" of Black performers into blackface minstrel troupes, the notions of separation, distinction, and distance became more complex. For an African American performer, even more than for a white performer, "donning the mask" meant re-presenting race through the eyes of the dominant white culture. As Karen Sotiropoulos argues, the performances of African Americans in the first decade of the twentieth century relied on "a hyperconsciousness of how they were seen by whites, and equally, of how much they would play to that gaze in order to win audiences."[15] Yet, at the same time, many critics cite the performances of artists such as Ernest Hogan, Bert A. Williams, and George W. Walker as working simultaneously within and against the dominant culture to interject critical distance into their performances of Blackness, pushing against stereotypes.[16] Public performance in theaters and traveling shows required crafting a performance of race composed of cultural elements, including music, that were coded for different audiences in different ways. Hale has coined the term "miscegenated style" to designate the mode through which performers "like Bert Williams . . . staked out a territory of subtle subversion before the 1920s." She includes in this category a range of musicians, composers, and singers who "drew from European, black folk, and black and white popular traditions."[17] For Hale, "passing and mimicking and masking—the creation with more or less self-consciousness of a 'miscegenated' style—became by the late 1920s the ultimate resistance to the racial polarities whites set at the center of modern American life."[18] As we will see below, "miscegenated" style overlaps significantly with the practices that inform jazz performance in the early days in New Orleans.

Race as performance onstage no doubt dovetails with and promotes a heightened awareness of race as performance offstage. James C. Scott stresses the ways in which subordinate groups engage in a kind of conformity that "requires a division of the self in which one self observes, perhaps cynically and approvingly, the performance of the other self."[19] In this critical view, the stereotypes of the dominant are not only a means of oppression but also tools for subversion through appropriation in performance.[20] Performance, then, includes self-awareness both on- and offstage. Indeed, there is a slippage between performance of race acknowledged as such in minstrelsy and performance of race outside of the confines of theatrics, in which forms of "passing" may be part of a lived reality.

For musicians in particular, performance requires meeting the expectations of the audience in attendance, both in terms of the music and also in terms of the persona adopted on- and offstage. In other words, the notion of miscegenated style as a corollary to minstrelsy only makes more apparent the kinds of borrowings and cross-cultural performances that working musicians in New Orleans and St. Louis enacted all the time. Neighborhoods, venues, audiences, and other factors determine elements of the performance, as we saw, for example, with the Streckfus line in the introduction. The Monday night cruise out of St. Louis reflected the tastes and sensibilities of the African American passengers in the mode of performance and self-presentation by the musicians, in contrast with the performances for white passengers the other nights of the week. Musicians make these kinds of subtle and not-so-subtle adjustments all the time. But the specific character of race in New Orleans and St. Louis enabled more opportunities for creating a wider variety of roles.

By playing various roles—performing different kinds of music, in different costumes, in different settings—musicians become aware of the possibility for self-promotion afforded by creating a role for themselves. As I have mentioned, many employ stage names, costumes, props, lore, and other gimmicks. Role-playing onstage functions as part of a marketing strategy. But this practice invites the creation of a role for oneself offstage, in life: self-consciously to construct a "real life" persona.[21] In the context of New Orleans, performers not only adopt names to promote their prowess on their instruments or their sexual appeal—"King" Oliver, "Kid" Ory, et cetera[22]—but musicians also change their names to insinuate different racial and ethnic identities, thereby blurring the onstage and offstage. The case of Jelly Roll Morton is well known. A Creole with a surname of LaMothe, he adopted a non-Creole surname and referenced Storyville with his nickname, and yet nonetheless asserted a Creole as opposed to African American identity for himself.[23] As Charles Hersch asserts, the flexibility of racial categories in New Orleans enabled musicians to perform a variety of racial and ethnic identities, particularly in the context of mixed-race bands. Citing examples like "'Chink' Martin, of Mexican and Filipino background," and "drummer Abby 'Chinee' Foster . . . a racial chameleon,"[24] both of whom took advantage of ambiguous phenotypic attributes,

Hersch highlights the practice of embracing fictive ethnic and racial identities, including through the self-application of derogatory slurs. Such boundary crossing in identity construction eases the crossing of physical boundaries (for example, public transportation or dining) in order to perform music that reflects the tastes of multiple audiences and styles.[25]

While "passing" usually denotes moving from Black to white, in the context of New Orleans the movement is neither unidirectional nor strictly between two categories.[26] Particularly with respect to musical styles, crossing boundaries may entail incorporating elements from a variety of different sources that, like the racial and ethnic categories, do not fall into a neat vertical hierarchy of status and privilege. In discussing King Oliver's Creole Jazz Band's "High Society Rag," Hersch describes the practice of jazz signifying: "Oliver integrates himself into, comments upon, and alters mainstream culture, amplifying ragtime's syncopation and polyphony and transforming it by means of the blues and improvisation. But the musicians also signify through their juxtaposition of sometimes disparate elements into a musical patchwork or collage. Many standard New Orleans jazz tunes were similarly patched together from a variety of sources and genres."[27] Oliver's title underscores the implied juxtaposition of social position enacted in the musical pastiche. Versatility and adaptability as a performer, as well as familiarity with a variety of styles and genres, enabled "straight," "sweet," or "hot" performances. Creativity and virtuosity depend on facility with crossing boundaries and blending stylistic elements.

Against the seeming downward movement signaled by the incorporation of "ratty" elements in "High Society Rag," Oliver's own performance of identity entailed what Hersch dubs "enacting respectability," at times even speaking Creole.[28] Bruce Raeburn interprets Oliver's adoption of "Creole speech and mannerisms" as part of a strategy to "promot[e] an image of refinement and sophistication in his musical endeavors."[29] While Lonnie Johnson did not adopt a Creole name or identity—despite his Spanish-sounding first name (Alonzo)—his strategies of self-presentation align with some of the practices he was acquainted with from New Orleans.[30]

Creating Lonnie Johnson

Little is known about Johnson's persona during his New Orleans years other than that he was a versatile instrumentalist on violin and guitar, likely banjo and piano as well, and that he probably read music. In addition to street performances, by Johnson's account, the family band played weddings and other indoor events, signaling that they had not only the requisite repertoire but also clothing and comportment for such venues.[31] The unverifiable stint in England with a traveling troupe or revue from 1917 to 1919 begins to sketch the contours of a professional persona that becomes sharper during his employment by the Streckfus line in St. Louis. Meeting the stringent requirements of bandleaders like Fate Marable and Charlie Creath meant reading music, attending rehearsals, being punctual, and wearing appropriate attire.[32] Photos of the orchestras on board the boats feature musicians in dark suits with bow ties.[33] Johnson was no doubt familiar with sartorial requirements for musicians from early exposure to the uniforms of brass bands in New Orleans, evening dress for riverboat musicians, and formal clothing for indoor events.

In addition, Johnson's experiences on the Theater Owners Booking Association circuit provided a backstage view of the careful construction of the theatrical personas of Mamie Smith, Clara Smith, Bessie Smith, the Whitman Sisters, and others. These women used dress, hair, jewelry, and other props to craft images of elegant sexuality. As Paige A. McGinley argues, their stage presentations self-consciously contested minstrel imagery: "Rainey and [Bessie] Smith restaged black southern womanhood as a performance of wealth and value, far from the Topsy or mammy figures that preceded them on stage. They did so by embracing the glamour of costume and fashion, aided by fashion's theatrical partner, publicity photography."[34] Johnson learned from this experience.

Photos of Johnson present a refined image of an immaculately dressed musician, particularly the well-known publicity shot from the 1920s (fig. 6). There he appears in a dark jacket, with striped shirt and floral tie, striped trousers and socks, patent and buck leather saddle shoes. His hair is cut short, perhaps in a conk style, combed back.[35] He gently holds a twelve-string guitar in his ring-adorned right hand, while his left hand seems poised to make a chord. His head is cocked to the side and he looks away from the camera, appearing to be absorbed in thought. It is the image of a consummate professional—sophisticated and well-groomed, and yet somehow not explicitly acknowledging the presence of the camera.[36] The image paradoxically proclaims both Johnson's lack of awareness of the camera—his gaze directed away—and his hyper-consciousness of how he presents to an audience in the attention to sartorial detail, use of the prop, and body language. Four decades later, during the 1960s, he was still concerned about projecting the appropriate urbane image. The careful presentation in the photographs and on stage attests to the blurring of the line between Lonnie Johnson "the

FIG. 6 Publicity photograph of Lonnie Johnson from the 1920s. Photo by Michael Ochs Archives / Getty Images.

real person" and his performance persona.[37] Bernie Strassberg, who was instrumental to Johnson's revival and hosted him when he had shows in New York City, attests to his attention to his appearance: "When he would come to town I would pick him up at the bus station. He would be carrying two of the heaviest pieces of luggage imaginable. I got used to the idea that he had twelve suits with him for a one or two week gig. A different suit for every set, but the same stickpin on his tie, a small diamond studded guitar. He believed in an older tradition of the showman looking good for the people."[38]

Johnson carefully cultivated this image, as well as the sound that accompanied it, including his speech patterns. In an interview with Val Wilmer in 1963 he asserted, "I have the correct pronounciation [sic] of my words, not flat and rude and so on."[39] In the same interview he made a point of defining his singing style as distinctly different in this respect:

> I am altogether different from the rest of the people that sing. Some of them sing their words like it's country blues, and some of it is rock'n'roll type singing. I sing city blues. . . . Some of the other blues singers, you can't understand their words 'cause they're not pronounced right, or the words are so bundled up that although they're saying something, it never shows. It is bad because if a person don't understand a thing, how would he like it? The only thing they can enjoy is the music, but the words are smothered and they have to figure out in their mind just what they are saying.[40]

Correct pronunciation and clear diction are not only stylistic traits that distinguish the kind of music that Johnson strives to perform—"city blues"—but also part of a mode of self-presentation that contributes to the construction of his persona as a performer.

Johnson's mode of self-presentation may have been influenced by the ideals associated with the Harlem Renaissance. John Howland underscores how "sight-reading and adherence to orchestrations written by trained arrangers reflects the . . . New Negro ideology, which called upon black professionals, including professional musicians, to aspire to self-control, dignified presentation, education, and an industrious work ethic."[41] Read in this light, Johnson's claim to have performed with Will Marion Cook's Syncopated Orchestra would situate him at the most elite level in the hierarchy of African American entertainment in Harlem in the 1920s and '30s. Whether he actually performed with his orchestra or not, by invoking the celebrated composer and conductor who trained with Antonín Dvořak, Johnson asserts his musical sophistication and professionalism.[42]

Johnson's self-construction out of visual, sonic, social, and musical elements signals some degree of awareness that audiences imagine the origin of sounds in a body marked by race, class, gender, age, and other attributes.[43] By controlling these signifiers of persona through performance, Johnson recognizes the social embeddedness of his identity as a singer within multiple systems of meaning. Exposure to the enactments of race, ethnicity, class, and professionalism performed by musicians in New Orleans, including their linguistic features, no doubt enabled Johnson to adapt these same strategies for his own purposes: constructing the sound to fit the image of an urban, sophisticated blues singer. Specifically, his controlled use of vibrato, careful enunciation of consonants, long lyrical lines with prosodic elements more akin to popular music in their phrasing, and a resonant voice with strong breath support all contribute to the construction of an individual identity for him by the listening audience.[44] That these elements do not match the usual characteristics of the rural blues artist troubles an easy construction of him as a singer of rural and especially impoverished origins. These traits in dress and vocal delivery support the self-designation as *Mr.* Johnson in his debut track, someone worthy of respect, underscoring the fact that his identity depends on others' perceptions of him.

The instrumental performances on both violin and guitar further contribute to the sophisticated persona. Clearly the violin already signals proficiency in reading music and the ability to perform a wide range of styles. Johnson's technique on guitar exhibits traits associated with professionalism rather than rural style, although he was familiar with the latter, as evidenced by his accompaniment of Texas Alexander. His clean precision, particularly in the fretting and picking patterns, and musical sophistication, based on the liberal use of arpeggios and theme and variation structures in the solo on "Mr. Johnson's Blues," already showcase a polished style that matches his mode of self-presentation. His smooth vocal delivery, with clean articulation, deliberate phrasing, and lengthy lines of verse, complete the sonic component of the portrait of a consummate blues professional.

The Johnson Persona in Recordings

After the collapse of race record companies like OKeh during the Depression and a resulting hiatus from recording, Johnson returned to the studio in 1937 to begin a series of sessions with Decca and RCA Victor–Bluebird that mark the resumption of his professional career. In one extraordinary day in Chicago, 8 November 1937, he recorded eight remarkable sides with startling imagery and virtuosic solo performances. Lyrical themes from the earlier work reappear, such as flood waters, disasters, and their psychological effects; cheating women; and false friends. Playing without accompaniment and setting aside the violin, piano, and harmonium, his guitar work is front and center, masterful and precise, aided by advances in recording technology. The two instrumentals recorded that day—"Swing Out Rhythm," with picking and strumming and a teasingly playful variation on a twelve-bar structure, and "Got the Blues for the West End," a variation on a blues with a nod to both the neighborhood in New Orleans near Lake Pontchartrain and the jazz song that made it famous—demonstrate his progress and maturity as a performer. Rather than the range exhibited on various instruments in the previous work and versatility with vaudeville and popular song, in November 1937 the focus is squarely on virtuosic guitar work, powerful vocals, and songwriting that exhibits the patchwork or collage technique characteristic of New Orleans jazz, here applied to urban blues.

On 31 March 1938 he was back in the studio, this time in New York City, working with a small combo including Roosevelt Sykes on piano and a stand-up bass player as well as drummer. His "Mr. Johnson's Swing" provides an opportunity for extended commentary on previous work through the creation of intertexts and a kind of double self-referentiality that elevate the cut's status to that of meta-song: Johnson names himself, citing and reflecting critically on his earlier work while at the same time gesturing to his professional position in relation to jazz greats Duke Ellington and Louis Armstrong.[45] The entire piece serves as a marker of Johnson's achievements through its performance of a gesture of reassertion of professional identity: it both references the past through a kind of recitation that makes earlier recordings echo in this one, but it also asserts the distance between past and present, highlighting Johnson's growth as a performer.

The title, instrumental introduction, and opening verse reference "Mr. Johnson's Blues," but with an added citational move that signals his relation to jazz. The instrumental introduction to the new song reproduces with precision, accuracy, and greater speed and confidence the introduction to "Mr. Johnson's Blues," but now with a faster swing groove. In place of missed fingerings and slightly out-of-tune notes, the experienced professional executes the introduction with more sharply articulated grace notes and a more emphatically syncopated rhythm within the quicker tempo. This may be the same instrumental opening, but the performer benefits from thirteen years in the studio and onstage, not to mention improved recording equipment, to deliver a stunning self-referential statement that asserts both sameness and difference. Here is the new and improved "Mr. Johnson." Following the introduction, the first verse proclaims, "Want all you people to listen while my guitar sing / I want all you people to listen while my guitar sing / If you ain't got that rhythm it don't mean a thing." The line from "Mr. Johnson's Blues" has been altered to emphasize the singing of his guitar, already implicit in the earlier recording's extended guitar solo. Here, the forceful guitar introduction quoting the earlier recording illustrates just how far he has progressed, justifying his reputation as a guitarist. What the newcomer lacked, the experienced professional confidently asserts. The B line of the verse creates an intertext with Ellington's "It Don't Mean a Thing (If It Ain't Got That Swing)" (New York City, 2 February 1932) as a reminder of their collaboration and a possible implied comparison between the two artists. The replacement of the word "swing" with "rhythm" may signal Johnson's desire to render explicit his own participation in the creation of "swing" as a part of the rhythm section in Ellington's orchestra.

As in "Mr. Johnson's Blues," here the first verse is followed directly by a guitar solo, introduced with the spoken "Sing for me guitar." In the solo work in this song and in others, it is difficult to say what constitutes deliberate citation of musical works, whether Johnson's own or others', what amounts to Johnson's own favorite figures and tics of style, and what constitutes part of a collective archive of figures and phrases used ubiquitously in jazz and blues.[46] Given the explicit quotation of the opening of "Mr. Johnson's Blues," it is difficult not to hear some deliberate citation in the remainder of the song. For example, the opening figure of Johnson's solo in "Mr. Johnson's Swing" resembles the signature syncopated three-note gesture of the main melody in Armstrong's version of "West End Blues" (Chicago, 28 June 1928).[47] Despite the fact that many of the recordings that Johnson played on with Ellington and Armstrong had hot tempos with very different rhythms (many of them straight four-fours) than the swung blues that Johnson recorded in 1938, nonetheless there are similarities of rhythm and phrasing that gesture toward the body of recorded jazz work that he contributed to in 1927 and 1928. In particular, some of the triplet figures resemble those Johnson used as counterpoint to Gertrude "Baby" Cox's vocal as part of Ellington's Orchestra in "The Mooche" (New York City, 1 October 1928), although it is also true that the same triplets could be counted among Johnson's signature moves. The strummed double-stop and single-note triplets deployed in the opening of the second guitar solo echo the guitar solo he played on Louis Armstrong and His Hot Five, "I'm Not Rough" (Chicago, 10 December 1927), where a strong attack and sliding half-tones produce an emphatic feel, stronger than the light-hearted movement in "Mr. Johnson's Swing." Nonetheless, the single-note triplet figure, distinctly different from his arpeggio patterns, recalls the earlier recording. While these may not be direct citations, they nonetheless function as allusions in the context of the lyrics that create explicit links between Johnson's blues in the 1930s and his work in jazz in the late 1920s. After the piano solo, Johnson interjects "Thank you so much, so much," with Armstrong's distinctive "growl" timbre on the second *so much*, suggesting more connections between his jazz past and blues present.[48] Taken together, music and lyrics contribute to the creation of Johnson's identity as a self-aware performer who cites his past as part of a continuing effort to construct his public identity.

The verse following the first solo break references Johnson's professional career directly, and, specifically, his hiatus from recording: "Some people think someday, it's because I've been gone so long / Some people think someday, it's because I've been gone so long / I just stopped to see if you would miss me from singing these lonesome songs." In the first line of the couplet he implies that his fans will have noticed his absence. After all, in "Mr. Johnson's Blues" he had asked everyone to "Remember me after the days I'm gone." He then answers the audience's implied wondering about him with an implausible explanation: he was just testing their attachment to him and his music. Referencing his celebrity by mentioning his absence from the recording scene, he teases like a jealous lover to assert indirectly the reason for his return to the spotlight. Johnson suggests that the six-year absence since his last issued sides with Columbia was the result of his deliberate choice and not because of decisions of recording companies responding to financial pressures shaped by a national market.[49] Always the professional, he recasts the hiatus as evidence of his own agency in shaping his career. The casual "I just stopped by to see" effectively effaces the existence of the recording studio and the company behind it, making it seem as though Johnson unexpectedly popped into the living room to sing in person, rather than that his record was played on the phonograph. The casualness of the articulation coupled with the agency implied in the reinterpretation of his absence as voluntary conjure a cool, detached professional, fully in charge of his destiny, rather than a hardworking musician scrambling to make ends meet and dependent on the decisions of recording company executives. In effect, Johnson attempts to efface the traces of the mediation of his persona by outside commercial forces, thereby negating their role in the construction of his identity. He implies that he controls his celebrity and image in the mind of the public.

The solo that follows this verse again demonstrates Johnson's virtuosity on guitar. Rapidly strummed triplets in the opening two bars in a mandolin style give way to swung rhythm figures and half-tone double-stop moves, before Johnson interjects, "Yes, indeed, it's so good, it's so good," complimenting his own playing. After the spoken commentary, Johnson reverts to familiar figures in single- and double-note phrases to round out the first twelve bars. The second chorus of the solo begins with traded figures between guitar and piano, a pattern that seems like it will structure the entire chorus; however, with some playful phrases and movement between rhythm and lead, Johnson's guitar work begins to overshadow Sykes on piano by the seventh and eighth measures. Clearly, this is *Mr. Johnson's* swing and no one else's.

The final verse rewrites again from "Mr. Johnson's Blues," with another nod to jazz: "I want all you people to listen while I swing this song [2x] / If you are born with that rhythm, honest, you can never go wrong." Johnson's will and agency are both on display, as he restates his desire to be heard; but rather than "listen to my song," he wants us "to listen while *I swing my song.*" Not only does he underscore the relation to jazz with a sly alteration of the expected "sing my song," but he also emphasizes his active role in producing the music: "*I* swing." The final line proclaims an innate sense of rhythm ambiguously expressed, which could refer back to Johnson and his bandmates, or more likely extend out to "all you people" who appreciate this kind of music. Whether it intends to affirm or take a swipe at racial stereotypes about rhythm is difficult to say.[50] The ambiguous phrasing leaves it open to interpretation. The swung triplet descending patterns in the fills on piano and guitar and the slightly syncopated cadence provide a lighthearted ending to a song that performs a confident assertion of identity. Johnson puts on masterful display his hyper-awareness of his public persona and his strong sense of self-worth.

Self-Awareness and Self-Deception

While Johnson at times constructs for himself a self-aware identity as a performer, most of his songs do not instantiate a self-referential gesture of this type. Instead, the vast majority construct a narrating persona who is also a protagonist in the story being recounted, but one who is not necessarily identified as Lonnie Johnson the blues musician. In other words, the collapse between protagonist of the story, narrator, and singer is performed by the listener rather than through explicit equations made in the lyrics.[51] Nevertheless, the narrating persona has significant traits in common with the gestures of self-construction on display in "Mr. Johnson's Blues" and "Mr. Johnson's Swing." In particular, the *I* in Johnson's songs often enacts a doubleness born of an internal split between someone who is simultaneously self-aware and self-deceived.

This kind of internal split in the persona is perhaps clearest in his songs that treat the theme of drinking. The act of narrating one's own drunkenness affords a paradoxical division between the drunken self-deceived individual and the one who is self-aware and provides the narration. "Laplegged Drunk Again" (New York City, 31 March 1930) illustrates the paradoxical split between drunken protagonist engaged in self-destructive behavior and self-aware narrator who explains the situation with a degree of detachment. In the first verse he proclaims, "I've been drinking all night long, I've started again today / I've been drinking all night long, started again today / I've been trying my best to drink these weary blues away." The tense of the narration, a past progressive that reaches into the present moment, collapses the protagonist and narrator into the same individual resorting to drink. Although he has been and is still drinking, some part of him is sober enough to recount his situation. This paradox is nicely reflected in the idiosyncratic tripping rhythms in the guitar introduction and the tension provided by the busy piano work of Roosevelt Sykes. The piano, competing at times with both the vocal and the guitar for the spotlight, makes the track feel almost out of control. Dissonant notes and contrasting rhythms hinder musical coherence, echoing the split in the protagonist/narrator persona.

The theme of self-deception is explicitly raised in the second verse as an explanation for drinking: "Some people drink to hide their troubles, but that don't mean a thing / Some people drink to hide their worries and trouble, but that don't mean a thing / When you think your troubles are gone, and you find yourself drunk again." The levels of deception and resulting paradoxes are multiple here. First, the narrator distinguishes himself from those (*some people*) who drink to hide their troubles, despite the admission in the first verse about trying "to drink these weary blues away." He presents himself as someone who knows from experience that drinking cannot hide worries. But the A lines remain ambiguous about who the drinking is supposed to deceive. Are the worries and troubles hidden from the one drinking, or others? The B line suggests in a complex proposition that the deception is self-directed, aimed at the person drinking. The logic seems to go that people drink to hide the blues from themselves, and that drinking should, at some point, lead to no more need of alcohol. Finding oneself unexpectedly "drunk again" reveals that alcohol is no cure; hiding the blues with drunkenness cannot eliminate troubles. But the line also hints at something darker, that drinking only makes the blues worse by promoting self-deception and a false sense of security. At the very least, the belief in drinking as a cure for the blues serves as a rationalization of unhealthy, self-destructive behavior. Ultimately, the narrator positions himself as one who has greater understanding than most about drinking.

The third verse articulates the narrator's difference from others: "Friends, I drink to keep from worrying; I smile to keep from crying / Friends, I drink to keep from worrying; smile just to keep from crying / That's why I cover my troubles, so the public don't know what's on my mind."[52] The address to "Friends" separates the narrator from those who listen and to whom he promises to reveal his insight. While the *friends* seek to hide troubles from themselves and others with alcohol, he seeks to stave off worry and uses other means to control himself and deceive others. In other words, when drinking, he simply tries to forget his troubles temporarily but never believes that they are permanently banished. The second half of the A line goes a step further with a more intimate revelation. He admits that he "smiles to keep from crying." Alcohol cannot accomplish what a deliberate facial expression can. Smiling enables him to hide his sorrow and vulnerability. The complex guitar fills in the A and A' lines call attention to the performer's distinctive identity rooted in control, underscoring the significance of the verse. Together, the intricate guitar work and admission about careful modes of self-presentation underscore the importance of agency and mastery in what one reveals to others.

The B line of the verse makes an even more extraordinary revelation. Taking a step back from the original narrative position—an unidentified, generalized *I* drinking—this verse references the "public," thereby implicitly identifying the narrator with Johnson the performer. In this line, he simultaneously reveals and conceals in a paradoxical gesture that creates intimacy with the audience. He announces that he deceives with a smile to "cover [his] troubles," and that that enables him to hide "what's on [his] mind." In other words, he divulges one secret in order to reveal the existence of others that remain hidden, specifically from the public. With this line, the self-aware performer gestures to the split in his self between the smiling stage performer and the troubled individual behind the mask, simultaneously creating both proximity and distance with his audience.[53] While he and his audience share worries and troubles and a desire to forget them with alcohol, there remains a fundamental divide between them. The musician exercises self-control to deceive the public, while others are simply self-deceived.

Deception and Betrayal

A great many songs in Johnson's corpus deal with the theme of deception as part of generalized romantic and sexual cheating and infidelity. Self-deception is often an important ingredient in situations in which cheating is ongoing: the one being cheated on often ignores clear warning signs of deceitful behavior. The theme of cheating and its discovery is ubiquitous in the blues. What differentiates Johnson's treatment of the theme is his portrait of the society in which it is embedded. The rural blues often stages a moment of realization about cheating, in which the person discovering the betrayal vows to make a change (usually to end the relationship), but the representations most often invoke only the three parties involved: the couple and the outside lover. There are seldom references to cheating as a generalized state of affairs in a broader world. Indeed, romantic and sexual cheating and betrayal stand in for other forms of socioeconomic exploitation in many rural and postwar urban blues. In Johnson's scenarios, cheating is embedded in a broader social world of deception, but the deception does not necessarily reference economically and racially based forms of betrayal. The next chapter explores in detail the theme of social relations, including gendered ones, as they are represented in Johnson's blues. For now, it is important to note that the invocation of a world where cheating and betrayal are generalized affects the construction of the narrative persona that confronts such a world.

"Your Last Time Out" (Chicago, 2 June 1947) illustrates Johnson's treatment of the theme of learning to read the signs of cheating. Implied in the account of the narrator's realization is the idea that he deceived himself by ignoring clear signs: "Baby, you been gone all night and the sun is risin' low / You been gone all night, now the sun is risin' low / Baby, don't tell me that line, 'cause you ain't been to no midnight show / First time you went out, it was a birthday party, why did you stay out all night long? / First it was a birthday party, why did you stay all night long? / Baby, you know I'm not dumb; I know there's something goin' wrong." The B line of the first verse demonstrates his unwillingness to accept implausible excuses from his unfaithful lover. His rejection of her story—"you ain't been to no midnight show"—demonstrates his awareness of the significance of her behavior, as well as his own past gullibility in believing excuses like being at a "birthday party." The lyrics attempt to draw a demarcation between his past gullibility and self-deception and his present clear-sightedness. The upbeat tempo of the song, precise fills on electric guitar, and smooth vocal delivery project his current control of the situation. The following two verses lay down conditions for their continued relationship, including her staying home and letting him know when she will be back, but the final verse asserts his definitive break with the relationship because of her incorrigibility: "I'm through with you forever because it ain't gonna be like that [2x] / Because I want a real woman and I don't want no alley cat." In this instance, trust is irretrievably broken and the narrator asserts agency in moving on, having discovered her deceit.

Recorded the same day, "How Could You" also tackles the theme of cheating, only in this instance the narrator was warned by friends of his lover's unfaithfulness: "I didn't believe them, baby, but now I know [2x] / You in love with my best friend and how could you hurt me so?" Even more painful in this handling of the cheating lover theme, the situation "has been goin' on for eleven long years today" (verse 3). Rather than blame the woman, as in "Your Last Time Out," here in the final line he blames the betrayal on the friend: "It all comes to show you, even your best friend can be a rat." Indeed, whether or not the relationship will continue remains ambiguous because of his pronouncement in the second verse that he still loves her: "Yes, you know I love you, baby, how could you treat me this a-way?" The jaunty tempo established with a steady pulse on piano and restrained acoustic guitar fills belie the pain of the situation. Only the vocal vibrato hints at the emotion of the narrator. The betrayal is finally recognized after years of both deception and self-deception, despite warnings from friends, but the outcome remains unclear.

In both "Your Last Time Out" and "How Could You," the narrator discovers his lover's capacity for deception and his own victimization. "The Last Call" (Chicago, 13 February 1942), one of Johnson's war-themed blues from the 1940s, sketches the scene of a man on the eve of departure for World War II, facing not only the possibility of his own death but also the likelihood of his lover's infidelity during his deployment. In this scenario, it is not the discovery of betrayal but its anticipation that is staged. The opening verse sets up the context of leaving for war, while the second verse offers a generalized pronouncement about loss, seemingly reflecting on war's consequences: "You can't keep the things in life you really love / You can't keep the things you love no matter how you try / Day by day, deep down inside, you can feel your poor self slowly die." The B line, in particular, focuses the risk of loss on the self. But the following verses introduce the theme of fidelity, underscoring his faithfulness to his woman, "But in my poor heart, there'll never be nobody else" (verse 3), in contrast to her infidelity, "In my heart, I know I'm not the only man" (verse 4). By shifting to the theme of fidelity, the lyrics of the fourth verse in particular recast the meaning of the second, making the loss of self a result of her betrayal rather than his imminent departure for war. Although the song ends with him pleading with her to wait for him and promising to bring back "Japs," the fact of infidelity before separation more or less guarantees betrayal during his absence.

A great many of Johnson's songs suggest that infidelity should be expected, even, as in this example, in the context of war. Cheating is ubiquitous and inevitable, and people are deceitful by nature. In many songs, Johnson's narrative persona offers generalized advice to "people," "friends," "all you women," and/or "all you men" about the immoral ways of the world. In these narratives, he positions himself, as in "Laplegged Drunk Again," as someone with insight into deceit and immorality. In contrast to the lyrics representing conversations between lovers in "Your Last Time Out," "How Could You," and "The Last Call," "Men, Get Wise to Yourself" (New York City, 9 February 1932) employs a different narrative strategy. Here, the narrator speaks to a second-person *you* that correlates with the "men" in the title. The narrative positioning hints that he speaks from experience when he addresses the group. The opening verse proclaims, "Workin' and you gotta wake up; you didn't sleep too long [2x] / Nothin' but these pimps and gigolos that's goin' 'round breakin' up your home." The world conjured in this opening verse pits the working man against a universe of vice and corruption that threatens not only to take economic advantage, but also to spread immorality to the private sphere of the home. The *you* in the lyrics seems to refer simultaneously to a generalized audience of men and also to the narrative voice itself, almost functioning like a *we*. This feeling of familiarity with the experience that allows the narrator to make pronouncements becomes more forceful in the second verse: "You go home sometime and there's no supper; your wife is even cross with you / You go home sometime and find no supper; your wife is even cross with you / It's just some no good rat showin' her the place, but she don't need a man like you." It seems the narrator has confronted this scenario and now addresses himself to an audience of men who have also been victimized. Verses 3–7 shift away from the address to *you* and employ *I* and *we* to make pronouncements about generalized immorality: "friends" stabbing other men in the back by stealing their women, "wild," "married women" "chasin' some other woman's man," "homewreckers" deliberately breaking up marriages, and gestures of kindness performed by "we" good men to no avail. The final verse summarizes the futility of actions aimed at motivating fidelity in marriage: "Sometime, we give a social party to make 'em happy as we can [2x] / There will be some no good woman to lead your wife to some no good man." The narrator proclaims the inevitability of infidelity with a clarity of vision born of bitter experience.

The discovery of cheating prompts a variety of responses, from vows to leave, to confrontation, to moral condemnation. In songs such as "I Ain't Gonna Be Your Fool" (New York City, 31 March 1938), the narrator declares from a position of moral superiority that he's had enough of mistreatment and being taken advantage of, and walks away. In others, such as "Nothing but a Rat" (Chicago, 2 November 1939), he confronts the other man, even cursing him: "When your time come to die, I hope you crawl on your belly just like a snail." Still others directly confront and condemn the cheating woman, even going so far as to threaten retribution, such as "She's Making Whoopee in Hell Tonight" (New York City, 7 January 1930) and the variant remake of it, "The Devil's Woman" (Chicago, 13 February 1942). In these lyrics, the narrator menaces violence: "I'm gonna take my razor and cut your late hours; I will be servin' you right," threatening to kill her and send her to hell to be the devil's consort.[54] In the bitterest representations, such as "Good Old Wagon" (St. Louis, 13–14 May 1926), the narrator invokes all the selfless things he has done for his woman, only to be betrayed and abandoned.

The persona constructed in the cheating and betrayal songs is disillusioned and expects bad treatment. He positions himself among the "good men," offering advice to others based on his own experience. Key in these representations is the narrator's trustworthiness as a truthful purveyor of wisdom about the ways of the world. Although there are a handful of songs in which the narrator himself is the guilty party, these only tend to confirm both the honesty of the singer and the ubiquity of unfaithfulness. Typical among them are "When You Fall for Some One That's Not Your Own" (New York City, 16 November 1928) and "Let All Married Women Alone" (New York City, 22 November 1930), in which the narrator as the outside man is nonetheless betrayed by the married woman with whom he is carrying on an affair.[55] Despite his own guilt in these scenarios, the overriding message concerns the folly of trusting anyone. These representations only reinforce the position of the singer/narrator as a victim of the deception perpetrated by others.

Manipulating a Sign System

The large number of songs about cheating and lying in Johnson's corpus focuses attention on the broader phenomenon of people deceiving one another by creating false appearances and misrepresenting actions and circumstances. In effect, they use signs to their advantage to conceal the truth. Discovering the truth involves learning to be suspicious of explanations and looking beyond the surface to interpret signs in a critical manner. Johnson as a singer-songwriter positions himself as one who has greater insight than those in his audience into the human capacity for deceit and betrayal, although he too has been victimized. Because of this experience, he gives advice in his lyrics, speaking as someone wise to the ubiquity of cheating. As we saw in "Laplegged Drunk Again," this special insight not only derives from his past victimization but is also related to his status as a performer. Performing for others on- and offstage requires donning a mask, which makes the performer particularly sensitive to the manipulability of signs. Clothes, hair, speech, comportment, guitar technique, lyrics, and a host of other elements contribute to the construction of a persona for the singer that sets him apart from members of his audience. Most people not engaged with the world of entertainment do not construct a persona for themselves in the deliberate way that Johnson does. In other words, "Mr. Johnson" is a construct, and Lonnie Johnson is keenly aware of his ongoing efforts to create, shape, and maintain it. The narrative persona shares the performer's insights into the possibilities of using signs to control self-presentation.

The efforts at self-construction coincide to a great extent with the efforts of those who would seek to deceive others in the realm of romantic relations. Both manipulate outward signs to benefit the self. Each constructs a persona and narrative to serve a particular end. The main difference lies precisely in the goal. The faithless lover dissembles for immoral ends, encouraging an erroneous interpretation of outward signs that is tantamount to a lie in order to take advantage. By contrast, the performer seeks to promote his career by manipulating signs to create a narrative that constitutes and promotes the self, but that activity is not inherently immoral. Such a distinction underscores the importance of Johnson's narrative construction of himself as dispeller of common social myths and revealer of hidden truths in his lyrics. Unlike cheaters and liars, he uses the power of signs to help others understand the possibilities for deception. He dons the mask in order both to conceal and reveal, demonstrating the fluidity of knowledge and truth. In effect, Johnson constructs a position for himself to occupy before the public so that he may both entertain and provide moral instruction.[56] His awareness of self-construction affords him a privileged position from which to warn others to be wary of deceptive appearances, highlighting the difference between the performer's self-promotion and the cheater's manipulation and lies.

Thus, the activity of self-construction entails awareness of the broader phenomenon of a sign system on which it depends. The performer, in manipulating his own identity, gains privileged insight into how meanings and interpretations are constituted. Despite the implicit assertion about the existence of hidden truths in Johnson's lyrics, the manipulability of signs signals that, ultimately, stable truths do not exist. Instead, there are multiple truths. Meanings and identities are flexible, elastic, and pliable rather than fixed, varying with time and place. As we have seen, performers construct new identities for themselves on- and offstage (Jelly Roll Morton, King Oliver, and Mr. Johnson, etc.), which require constant work to maintain precisely because of their instability. New Orleans as a site of construction of performers' identities provides particularly permeable and unstable conceptions of class, ethnicity, and race that shape a rich field of possibilities. This cultural context is mirrored in the permeability of styles that gives rise to musical compositions, as miscegenated style and signifying are foundational for the construction of jazz and blues.[57] Johnson understands the inherent instability of personal and musical identity, constructing his own through a variety of means.[58] As part of the overall sign system, identity, like "truth," depends on time, place, circumstance, and the tools available to construct it.

If, on the one hand, one can never be certain about identities because of their inherent instability, on the other hand, this instability gives rise to endless possibilities for performance and creativity. Out of amalgamations, collages, juxtapositions, citations, and interweavings come multiple possibilities for identities, genres, and styles. Johnson is acutely aware and extremely adept at deploying the possibilities that this combination and circulation of signs enable. In the space opened up by the circulation of signs and the resulting indeterminacy, Johnson positions himself not only as self-constructed and, therefore, an adept manipulator, but also as a practiced reader of signs.

Awareness of the indeterminacy of meaning is the inevitable result of such an understanding of a shifting system of signification. If Johnson can both manipulate and read signs, he also knows their meaning cannot be fixed. Johnson's most stunning pronouncement about the ultimate undecidability of the meaning of signs occurs in a song recorded, significantly, under the pseudonym Jimmie Jordan (another assumed identity) for Columbia, "Cat You Been Messin' Aroun'" (New York City, 12 January 1932). In his most disturbing invocation of cheating, he also references miscegenation, monstrosity, and violence, in a narrative context that requires interpreting signs. The lyrics begin by depicting the narrator being presented with a child that he asserts is not his. In this song, the child functions as the ultimate sign requiring interpretation to establish paternity.

In the first verse, the narrator addresses the woman directly: "Now, look here, woman; you done lost your mind / This is not my child; you bring me a better line." The reference to "a better line" underscores the existence of a narrative in which signs are embedded for interpretation. Here, the narrator rejects this particular account of the meaning of the child as sign. In subsequent lines we learn that the child's phenotypic features—"his eyes is blue and his hair's brown"—suggest miscegenation. As the story unfolds, the narrator implies that the child's various deformities and possible disabilities ("slew-footing," "long" head, "crossed" eyes, blindness, and being "half nuts") represent genetic traits that are not in his family. And yet the lyrics are also strangely ambiguous, asserting in the first verse as part of a varied refrain: "'Cause there's something wrong, woman, don't start those lies, there's something wrong / I never had such mix-up in my family, since I was born." At first glance, the line seems to mean that he has never witnessed anyone try to introduce children into his family ("mix-up") that were not genetically related. The assertion is consistent with his opening denial of paternity and, therefore, characterizes her narrative as a lie. But various articulations and information provided in subsequent verses shift the meaning of the refrain.

The fourth verse describes the child as having a "nappy head" and alters part of the refrain to "I never had nothin' like that in my family, woman, since I was born," dropping the reference to a "mix-up." This variant begins to suggest an alternate interpretation. The final verse complicates the situation even further, adding multiple new wrinkles: "Now, I said it was my child and you argued me down / Now, my eyes is blue and my hair is brown / Woman, you been messin' around; yes, woman, you been messin' around / So, woman, get out of my face 'fore I take my fist and knock you down." In the first line of this verse, the narrator asserts that he initially claimed to be the child's father and the mother convinced him otherwise, contradicting his rejection of paternity in the opening verse. Here, he says that he claimed paternity and she offered a counternarrative to his interpretation. In other words, he now claims to have presented evidence that he is the father, stating that his "eyes is blue and [his] hair is brown" and she dissuaded him. The shifting narrative incorporates contradictory claims about whether he asserted or denied paternity, muddying the situation and diverting attention away from an even more significant shift.

His assertions of paternity invoke evidence based on his own phenotypic traits, forcing a reinterpretation of the earlier variant of the refrain, "I never had nothin' like that in my family, woman, since I was born." In light of this new information, he could be saying that there have been no signs of mixed-race children born in his family since his own birth. That is to say that he himself exhibits traits of mixed racial heritage. Nonetheless, despite this evidence, he is seemingly convinced by the woman's assertions about paternity. Outward signs, even phenotypic traits, may be interpreted in a number of ways, at least before DNA testing. The song concludes with the narrator telling the woman to leave and making threats of violence provoked by her presumed infidelity. The curious inconsistencies—the woman's assertions and denials about the narrator being the father—resolve in a final determination of the meaning of the child's presence as a sign. The narrator ultimately rejects the mother and child, attempting to fix paternity and establish infidelity, but doubts persist, especially about the narrator's own racial identity. The inherent instability of the meaning of signs cannot be as easily banished as the woman and her child.

In addition to the strange ambiguity of the lyrics and the pseudonym under which it was released, the guitar solos feature, alongside variations on Johnson's signature moves, uncharacteristic figures, including incredibly inventive passages with chromatic movement. His guitar technique also exhibits borrowings from other traditions, most notably an ascending run of right-hand *rasgueos* or frailing performed while he slides up the fretboard chromatically with his left hand. Even the incorporation of right-hand technique from other genres echoes the dilemma of ambiguous origin posed by the child. The downward strumming could come from either flamenco or clawhammer banjo technique dating back to the minstrel era.[59] Johnson no doubt encountered both styles in New Orleans. This incorporation of techniques from other musical styles into his urban blues demonstrates Johnson's uniqueness and artistry as a performer. The originality created through a collage of techniques and styles aligns with the oddity of the deformed child, also presumably a product of intermixing. The implication that the narrator, like the child, is also the product of miscegenation is reinforced by the performer's own blending of styles to form something new, reinforcing the collapse between narrator and performer. Together, the instrumental setting and lyrics unsettle an easy acceptance of the final banishment of the mother and child in an act aimed at determining paternity once and for all. For all its efforts to establish truth and certainty, "Cat You Been Messin' Aroun'" ultimately teaches a powerful lesson about unstable identity, uncertain knowledge, shifting subject position, and situational truths. Racial and ethnic identity, like musical identity, remains elusive, despite threats of violence to put people in their "right" places.[60]

Thus, Lonnie Johnson's persona depends on a performance of identity composed of multiple elements that requires constant attention. He constructs himself in a self-conscious way in order to elicit particular effects. The ongoing activity of self-construction as a performer involving a variety of different signs affords privileged insight into the world of deception and betrayal that structures social relations, and especially romantic and sexual ones. In the following chapter, I turn to the representation of social relations in Johnson's corpus to examine how an awareness of the manipulation of signs informs an understanding of human social interactions.

CHAPTER 3

Social Relations

Race, Gender, and the Perception of Systemic Complexity

As we saw in the previous chapter, Lonnie Johnson's creation of a professional persona depends on his insight into the manipulability of multiple sign systems of dress, appearance, gesture, comportment, diction, musical style, phrasing, and playing technique, to name a few. Signifiers are selected and combined to create performances of a "blues musician" in different contexts for audiences familiar with the codes.[1] Johnson's awareness of how audiences perceive him, evidenced in his attempts to control his reception, finds its corollary in a sensitivity to manipulations practiced by others. His lyrics, often addressed explicitly to a collective audience of "all you people" and "friends," expose deceptive practices deployed to take advantage of unwitting victims.

Romantic and sexual cheating and betrayal represent themes that appear consistently throughout his corpus from 1926 until 1947. Having scored a hit with the ballad "Tomorrow Night" in 1948, his lyrics in the King years (1948–52) are generally less bitter and angry, although the betrayal theme appears occasionally, such as in "Can't Sleep Anymore" (Cincinnati, 3 June 1952). As a "rediscovered blues artist," he returns to the theme in the recordings of the 1960s, possibly as part of a marketing strategy, given its ubiquity in the blues. But unlike other blues artists who focus most often on the pain experienced by the one being cheated on, Johnson instead consistently portrays betrayal as a fate that befalls individuals as part of broader social patterns. Rather than speak solely from a narrative perspective of individual pain and suffering, Johnson positions himself as someone who seeks to reveal the power dynamics inherent in human interactions. Many songs have titles containing an imperative—such as "Don't Be No Fool," "Be Careful," "Treat 'Em Right," "Men, Get Wise to Yourself," "Don't Ever Love," and "Stay Out of Walnut

Street Alley"—that may be interpreted as advice directed both to an individual and a collective audience. In addressing himself to groups of individuals, Johnson asserts patterns of social behavior from his vantage point as a professional performer embedded in complex social relations.

As we have seen, the social world that he paints is most often characterized by deception, lying, and betrayal. In "There's No Use of Lovin'" (New York City, 13 August 1926), recorded with spoken commentary by Victoria Spivey, he provides a general pronouncement consistent with the outlook expressed in many of his songs: "This world is so crooked, you don't know what to do [2x] / When you try to hold up your head, everybody's down on you." Speaking from a position of insight gained through experience, he both commiserates with and warns his audience about the danger of falling victim to the ways of the world. As we have seen, the heightened awareness of deceit that permeates his corpus is articulated through a persona constructed as honest and trustworthy, offering advice to those who have been, are being, or will be victimized.

Performance Venues and the Place of Musicians

Coinciding with the early period of Johnson's career, New Orleans and St. Louis experienced the uneasy imposition of segregation post–*Plessy v. Ferguson* and attempted to demarcate and separate spaces according to the logic of the one-drop rule. Musicians pose particular challenges to separation of this kind, as they move in, across, and through spaces and give performances to multiple audiences. Johnson's heightened awareness of the performative nature of race, ethnicity, class, and musical style stems in part from his permeable experience of racialized space. His performance is not limited to what Erving Goffman terms the "frontstage," the position from which he plays in the performance venue, but also extends to other spaces.[2] While a "backstage" may exist for Johnson, where "relative to a given performance . . . the impression fostered by the performance is knowingly contradicted as a matter of course,"[3] he also negotiates other in-between spaces that require varying degrees of control and self-mastery. In other words, the boundary between "real person" and "persona" becomes blurred as performance extends beyond stages and venues.[4] For example, in the racialized atmosphere on the Streckfus boats, there were no doubt strictly separate backstage areas where musicians could complain about customers, crack jokes, or act in other ways that could potentially undermine the frontstage performance.[5] Although there may have been differences between what musicians could do on a Monday night cruise in the presence of an African American audience and what they could do any other night of the week both on- and offstage, there were nonetheless constraints on behavior in either case that extended the performance to other areas of the boat. In other words, musicians experience multiple "stages" requiring different types of performances. The distance and separation from the audience is never complete, rendering their position closer to what Goffman terms a "discrepant role." In these subordinate, "in-between" positions, musicians interact with the audience from the stage, but also "offstage."[6] Likewise, they interact with employers and other employees within an establishment as part of a "show," never quite being able to trust that they are completely offstage.

Within the racialized atmosphere of early twentieth-century New Orleans and St. Louis, the awareness of never being able to let one's guard down completely—trust that one is truly "backstage"—adds to the tension of quotidian existence. While this sense of performing a racialized role was no doubt part of the daily life of most African Americans in the early twentieth century, particularly in the South,[7] the role of the musician differs in the degree to which performance requires negotiation of supposedly segregated spaces. While the racialized role of maids, cooks, chauffeurs, and others in service positions required performing a subordinate role, including entering through the backdoor of a house or using prescribed modes of address, among other ritualized behaviors, the performance of the role ended when individuals exited the stage, as it were, and returned home. The role of the musician shares many characteristics with these "discrepant" positions, but neither being on the stage area itself, nor exiting it, is as easy and straightforward.

First of all, stages differ depending on the venue, which determines the composition of the audience, its identity and tastes, a point to which I return below. The type of stage, in conjunction with the makeup of the audience, conditions in turn aspects of the performance. And while musicians may eventually go home, there are many spaces to negotiate between the "stage" and the truly backstage, requiring other performances. Complicating the performance further, even the role on the stage for the musician is not as clearly subordinate as other service roles. Musicians have talent linked to the recognition of skill, individuality, and creativity that bring prestige and distinction and work against the ideology of a racial hierarchy. Indeed, performing requires a delicate balancing act between subordination and assertions of superiority. If servants are in a "discrepant role," then musicians occupy a maximally discrepant position, performing on various stages, to varying degrees, for a variety of audiences. This discrepant position offers a "peculiar vantage point,"[8] one enabled both by the need to attend to performance at all times but also by the movement from frontstage to other spaces that form part of the "show." As we have seen in Johnson's lyrical constructions of his persona, a privileged vantage point provides him access to information in a world where separations and demarcations are highly charged. His hyperawareness of performance for specific audiences, and particularly the manipulation of signs on which it is based, affords him insight and knowledge that he imparts to his audience.

Jazz and blues guitarist Danny Barker, in writing about attitudes about drug use, likened the position of "entertainers, musicians, and show people" to that of social scientists, who occupy a privileged position and even represent an avant-garde with respect to society.[9] In a sense, as participant-observers like sociologists and anthropologists, they are simultaneously inside and outside, on the margins and at the center. Being a musician paradoxically creates a kind of invisibility that allows the performer to watch, listen, and interpret. Although being onstage calls attention to the musician, at the same time, the audience's focus is on the performance and not necessarily on other things the performer does. In effect, being onstage creates a kind of shield protecting the person occupying the role, freeing them to eavesdrop and observe. And while playing requires the musician's attention, the repetitious nature of nightly performance enables a split focus: musicians can both perform and observe at the same time. As Jelly Roll Morton recounts in an episode where he catches someone stealing in a club in Los Angeles, "Those days I never looked at the keys, I always watched the entertainers."[10] Depending on lighting and distance from the audience, the performer is in a position to see and hear a great deal.

Different performance venues provide different optics on society for musicians as participant-observers, varying in relation to the limits of the "stage" and the relative distance or proximity to the audience. A spectrum stretches from "stages" that draw a fairly clear line between performer and audience to those where the boundary is blurred. For example, theaters and open-air park venues that employ large bands create spaces to distinguish relatively neatly between audience and performers. Whether it is in terms of height, as in a raised stage or platform, or in terms of surface, such as a hard surface in the middle of grass, a band area creates separation between performers and audience.[11] Attendant with this separation is often a clearer demarcation between on- and offstage. Musicians have a place to prepare (e.g., get dressed and warm up) or rest, away from the public eye. Somewhere in the middle of the spectrum are venues like the Streckfus boats, dance halls, and clubs that have a defined dance floor that separates the band from the audience and either no distinct and separate backstage area or one that is permeable. In these spaces, performers and audience may interact on set breaks and before and after shows. Smaller venues, like bars, restaurants, and private homes offer even less of a physical boundary between on- and offstage, requiring performers to don the mask the minute they walk through the door.[12] All across the spectrum, musicians are participant-observers, mingling and interacting directly with the crowd at times, but never part of the audience.

The relative distance between musician and audience also varies with the identities and tastes of the audience and does not necessarily coordinate with spatial separation. For example, large open-air venues that may employ a raised stage and clear separation usually invite a general public that may include a variety of different racial, ethnic, and class identities or may be relatively uniform. The identity of the performers may overlap or not with some or all of those in the audience. In these cases, physical space is not a reliable indicator of social distance, which can be variable. Likewise, a small venue, like a private party, may require a stricter separation achieved through performance that extends beyond the designated "stage area" in order to clearly demarcate the separation between audience/employer and musician/employee. Despite physical proximity, social distance may be asserted through other means, such as separate eating areas and food, as a way of drawing ethnic, racial, and class distinctions. In all of these situations of greater and lesser degrees of separation and distance between performer and audience—physical and otherwise—musicians both perform and observe social interactions from a peculiar vantage point. The necessity of responding to the nuances of these variables creates a hypersensitivity among performers of the diversity of roles played in different settings.

In some sense, musicians contribute to the settings that foster, and sometimes even shape, social interactions. Music venues are the sites of primarily romantic and sexual interactions, although not exclusively. In early twentieth-century New Orleans and St. Louis, Johnson played in a variety of venues that offered a front-row seat to opposite and same-sex relations as they played out in clubs, bars, and dance halls. As a participant-observer of these interactions, he gained valuable insight that is reflected in his corpus. Beginning with his early days in New Orleans, his gigs in Storyville provided an unobstructed view of human relations in a context of prostitution, gambling, drugs, and violence. Accounts by musicians who played in the district paint a dog-eat-dog world in which people use one another for strategic ends. Desperate women find a means of financial support aided by pimps and madams, some of whom use addiction to keep the women dependent and in prostitution.[13]

Madams and bar owners pay off crooked cops and public officials to keep them from making arrests.[14] Customers are plied with cheap alcohol marked up to turn a profit and are encouraged to spend.[15] Johns are drugged or physically attacked and robbed, and some are even killed.[16] Corruption and the strategic manipulation of people for financial gain run rampant.

Most significantly for the themes in Johnson's corpus, roles are played in order to deceive and profit financially: prostitutes perform mixed racial identities, as in the "exotic" octoroon and other prostitutes in Storyville, and simulate sexual attraction and satisfaction.[17] Men stage competition and combat in the sexual, financial, and other realms. Violence erupts, often when deception in the form of stealing and cheating is revealed, provoking strong emotional reactions.[18] As a musician in the districts of New Orleans and St. Louis, Johnson provided part of the musical accompaniment to this world of zero-sum human relations. Witnessing this behavior on a regular basis likely affected his outlook, voiced in both novelty songs, like the two-part "I Got the Best Jelly Roll in Town" (New York City, 23 January 1930) and "He's a Jelly-Roll Baker" (Chicago, 13 February 1942), and in bleaker songs, like "Stay Out of Walnut Street Alley" (New York City, 12 August 1927). The street location places the action of the latter song in an area of St. Louis with "saloons, brothels, cafes, gambling parlors, and boarding houses [that] sprawled from the Mississippi River levee toward the notorious Chestnut Valley and the Union Railroad Station."[19] In the song, a drunken narrator warns of the dangers of "white mule." The lyrics detail provoking fights with police, disrespecting judges, and making people "get evil and mistreat [their] best friend" under the influence of alcohol.

In less extreme settings than the brothels of Storyville and Chestnut Valley, Johnson and other musicians were witnesses to scenes of flirting, courting, romancing, fighting, and breaking up. Nightly performances in dance halls, bars, honky-tonks, and other establishments provide a view of sexual interactions that run the gamut from the tawdry and financially interested to the sincere. Insight into the theatrical nature of behaviors witnessed between and among the customers derives in part from the musician's own awareness of the role he or she plays, as well as the roles of others in the establishment. While the theatricality witnessed in bars and clubs may not be as extreme and overt as in a brothel, nonetheless, occupying the position of the entertainer in a variety of venues heightens the ability to detect the roles being played not only by the proprietor and waitstaff but also by the customers. The jealousy and mistrust expressed in Johnson's lyrics mirror the lies and deception witnessed, prompting songs of advice in a world of suspicion, deceit, and betrayal.

In "Don't Be No Fool" (Chicago, 22 May 1940), the narrator addresses an unfaithful, hypocritical, jealous, and violent husband who suspects his wife of infidelity. Stalking his wife in an attempt to find evidence of her affair, the narrator, using an ABC lyric pattern, warns that the man will likely drive her to someone else: "The more you watch a woman, the more you'll suffer in life / You're forever beating and doggin', you dogs her both day and night / But still, as always, a man waitin' to treat a good woman right / Don't scorn your woman when she ain't done nothin' wrong / You beat and dogs her when you know you done wrong yourself / Someday she'll find it out and that will drive her to somebody else." While the narrator attempts to offer counsel, the destructive behavior driven by suspicion seems incorrigible.

Dissembling lovers and false friends populate the lyrics of Johnson's songs. In "I'm Just Dumb" (Chicago, 22 May 1940), he sings from the perspective of a lover who has been wronged and "played ... for deaf, dumb, and blind." He accuses the woman directly with evidence from her own mouth—"You talk all night in your sleep, baby, then you wake up lyin'"—and vows to move on. An eerie instrumental accompaniment to Johnson's vocal, with his brother James on violin and De Loise Searcy on piano, provides an anxiety-producing backdrop for "When I Was Lovin' Changed My Mind Blues" (New York City, 19 January 1926). The musical introduction sets the mood with dissonant tremolo on violin. Rather than harmonic support or antiphonal accompaniment, the violin often plays a competing and, at times, distracting countermelody behind the vocal. Screechy bowed chords, out of tune at times, contribute to the unsettled feeling. Here the narrator swears off an ungrateful lover who now turns her back on him: "I helped you when you were down and could not help yourself [2x] / And now I'm down and you want to help somebody else." False friends who steal their friends' wives appear in numerous songs throughout his corpus, like "Men, Get Wise to Yourself," "Sam, You're Just a Rat" (New York City, 9 February 1932), and the much later "You Will Need Me" (Englewood Cliffs, NJ, 8 March 1960, on *Blues by Lonnie Johnson*). In "Baby, Please Tell Me" (New York City, 13 August 1926), hidden truths lurk behind false appearances, poignantly expressed in Johnson's droning self-accompanied vocal performance with his brother on violin. Spoken interjections by James complimenting Lonnie's piano playing highlight a contrast between lively passages in the solo and the otherwise sedate instrumental part. Like other truths, virtuosic talent may lie hidden behind a veneer of maximum control. In the lyrics, the narrator insists on people's inscrutability: "You think some people is happy, but I swear you don't know [2x] / You don't know what's happening after the door is closed." The declaration paradoxically articulates the singer's privileged insight into what most people seek to hide from others. The world of human relations conjured in the lyrics very much resembles the kinds of scenes Johnson no doubt witnessed on a regular basis from his musician's vantage point. The performance of outward behaviors conceals information perceptible to one familiar with the manipulation of signs.

Gender and Love Relations

In the world represented in Johnson's lyrics, everyone is on the take: people are treated as means to an end rather than as ends in themselves.[20] Both women and men use and abuse. As I have argued, the zero-sum attitude toward human sexual relations reflects his bird's-eye view of behavior in the districts, bars, clubs, and other venues he played, not only in New Orleans and St. Louis but no doubt in East St. Louis, New York City, Chicago, Philadelphia, Cincinnati, and other places. In Johnson's representations, human beings assume roles circumscribed by social forces and perform versions of gender, sexuality, race, and class within the possibilities enabled by the context. As a musician, he plays a role along with everyone else.

Use of a first-person male narrative perspective in most songs likely contributes to the tendency among critics to equate the perspective in the songs with Johnson's views of his own personal relations.[21] Dean Alger presumes that the male narrator in some instances voices Johnson's feelings about his relationship with his first wife, the blues singer Mary (née Smith) Johnson, even going so far as to extrapolate "facts" about the marriage and separation based on recording dates and lyric content of particular songs.[22] But the use of a first-person male narrative perspective does not necessarily mean that the views expressed reflect Johnson's reactions to and feelings about episodes in his private life. As I have argued, the milieu of the musician provides ample opportunity to witness the types of scenes depicted in the lyrics without having to suppose that Johnson had direct, personal experience of cheating, lying, betrayal, and violence, although he may have. In other words, the lyrics should not be read as autobiographical, although autobiographical elements no doubt appear. Rather, the world they conjure should be treated as a fictional universe inflected by Johnson's lived experience, but not reducible to it. The voice of the narrator, a role Johnson performs, describes social and sexual relations that reflect his perceptions and interpretations of events around him in which he may have participated personally and actively, but certainly as a participant-observer.

Likewise, the appearance of misogyny in the lyrics does not necessarily mean that Johnson shares this view with the first-person male narrator. Male narrators who condemn immoral behavior by women do not necessarily equate to a misogynistic attitude on the part of the artist: like everything else, misogyny is a discourse that may be performed.[23] Songs such as "You Drove a Good Man Away" (New York City, 13 August 1926), in which a bitter and hurt male lover remembers better times, fuel the desire to conflate the narrator and artist, ascribing misogyny to Johnson: "Once upon a time, I've laid my poor heart in your hand [2x] / Now, just to say, that I'm draggin' through this worried land." Likewise, "Fickle Mamma Blues" (New York City, 11 August 1927) portrays a helpless narrator who can do nothing to escape the power of a woman who "done put that thing on me." Despite catching her cheating with a friend, he cannot bring himself to leave her: "One night I caught her triflin' with a friend of mine called Sam [2x] / I went to her like a lion, and I come away like a doggone lamb." In one of the most fanciful versions of women abusing men, "Man Killing Broad" (Chicago, 8 November 1937) depicts a narrator afraid of being murdered by a cheating partner, urging her to leave: "You've got a hatchet under your pillow, baby, you got ice pick in your hand / You've got a hatchet under your pillow, baby, ice pick in your hand / The best thing you better do is find you another man / You've got a shotgun in the corner, blackjack under your bed [2x] / But you will never catch me asleep; I know you wants to whip my head." In many songs, deceitful women take advantage of and even torment good men.

Stronger still, in other songs the narrator voices righteous indignation at wrongs committed by women, even justifying resorting to violence. In "She's Making Whoopee in Hell Tonight," "Another Woman Booked Out and Bound to Go," and "The Devil's Woman," the narrator threatens murder in response to cheating, at times even depicting it as a reasonable response. While the lyrics express misogynistic views, presuming misogyny on Johnson's part is problematic for a number of reasons. First, like the readings that attempt to extrapolate information about Johnson's marriage from the lyrics, these interpretations presume that there are neither fictional elements nor representations of overheard conversations in the songs. The hyperbolic formulations in "Man Killing Broad" suggest a collage of inventions and perhaps bits of circulating tales of "bad women" and "bad men," especially with formulations like "You put Lysol in my gravy, black potash in my tea [2x] / But I fed it to your man, baby, instead of me." Because the songs are performed in places and spaces in which misogyny is often verbalized and enacted, they are both a product of the milieu and a contributing factor in shaping its discourses and behaviors. Second, this type of autobiographical analysis ignores possible pressure exerted by recording companies based on ideas about marketability that likely influenced the subject matter of songs. The blues are full of misogynistic lyrics, to the degree that misogyny could be considered a trope of the genre as performed by male singers. Audiences expect it; record companies likely encouraged it. But it is dangerous to presume misogyny on the part of the artist. As I have argued, social representations are informed by the artist's peculiar vantage point as participant-observer. Reducing misogynistic lyrics to the artist's point of view ignores possible critical interpretations of the world he or she inhabits. Finally, misogyny may be another part of the performance of a gendered role within the blues, a point to which I return below.

Finally, the readings that focus on misogyny in Johnson's lyrics ignore the songs in which men behave badly, such as "Ball and Chain Blues" (New York City, 13 August 1926), in which the narrator lost his wife and "happy home" to "triflin' women"; or "I Have No Sweet Woman Now" (St. Louis, 14 May 1926), in which the narrator laments, "I was so mean to my baby, I drove my babe away." Most striking is "Treat 'Em Right" (St. Louis, 25 April 1927), which opens with a second-person imperative ambiguously addressed to an individual or group of hypocritical husbands: "You shouldn't scold your wife, when you do wrong yourself [2x] / Because no woman wants to stay home all by herself." The form of address shifts to the first-person plural in the second verse, including the narrator in the collective indictment of male behavior: "We go out and we get drunk and we stay the whole night long / We, men, go out and get drunk and stay the whole night long / But to let us tell, we never do wrong." The emphatic use of *we men* in the A′ line eliminates all ambiguity about the addressee, while the B line calls out self-serving lies in addition to immoral behavior. The subsequent verses explain the inevitable consequences of "ramblin'": men who do not "stay at home sometime" will find their wives "will soon start up with a ramblin' man." "Treat 'Em Right" deploys a male narrator who speaks for all men guilty of immoral behavior, offering analysis and advice expressed in warnings and imperatives. It is men who drive women to cheat in this representation, instead of the other way around. Misogynistic lyrics, then, form part of a representational strategy that indicts both men and women for immoral behavior. The first-person male narrative voice blames women more often than men, but nonetheless recognizes the pervasiveness of means-ends strategic action, particularly in gendered and sexualized human relations.

The use of a first-person, male narrative perspective that passes judgment on the behavior of others invites autobiographical readings that presume an attitude of male superiority. But gender, like race, class, and ethnicity, is also a performance shaped by the constraints of the blues as a genre. As I suggested above, misogyny is a trope in the blues, deployed in a variety of images, figures, and metaphors. It forms part of the arsenal of verbal expressions available for the construction of a gendered persona in blues lyrics. In the same way that Johnson constructs his professional persona using signs from various systems, he also uses misogyny at times to perform gender. This gendered persona articulates what Chris Smith describes as Johnson's "homilies on moral and social etiquette,"[24] creating a male voice that passes judgment and calls out mistreatment. But I would suggest that the mistreatment of men by women (and of women by men) in his lyrics highlights the gendered performance of roles that he witnessed around him, rather than a pronouncement about essential biological difference or even socially constructed, gender-specific roles. In other words, his persona expresses a worldview that represents a critical interrogation of not only immoral actions, but also the gendering of them. The corpus taken as a whole presents contradictory points of view that call into question facile assumptions about the ways men and women behave. Scenes witnessed during nightly performances enable a critical awareness and representation of the social construction of gendered subject positions that use and abuse on both sides of the gender divide.

Social Complexity

Johnson's narrative persona condemns certain forms of gendered personal interaction that victimize through deceit and betrayal, but he also makes more general pronouncements about society pertaining to economics and race. Alongside songs that deal with personal relations are those that discuss other types of victimization. The coexistence of critical representations of abusive personal relations and broader social modes of interaction in Johnson's corpus draws an implicit parallel between them. Ultimately, the scenarios of deceit and infidelity practiced within gendered and sexualized roles resemble those that form part of larger social configurations. The mirroring of the personal and the social opens up the possibility of interpreting much of his artistic output as an intervention in immoral relations in a variety of forms. As we have seen in the depiction of interpersonal relations, deceit and betrayal create situations in which individuals are treated unfairly, dominated, and subjugated through the strategic manipulation of appearances and emotions.

Social forces operate in similar ways, taking advantage of individuals both personally and as representatives of larger groups.

Consistent with representational practices in the blues, Johnson most often deploys indirect means for representing social forms of mistreatment and injustice. There are many reasons for the indirect mode of representation, most significant among them is that access to recording is mediated by companies controlled by whites. In Johnson's case, the pressures and constraints on his recorded corpus were likely greater than those on other artists, predominantly from rural areas, who cut only a handful of sides in isolated sessions. His seven-year contract with OKeh shaped his recorded output as both soloist and studio musician. As we have seen, his professional work prior to the contract with OKeh on the Streckfus Steamers and theater circuits, shaped him into a disciplined performer, able to take direction from others who were driven by commercial and financial interests. While his live performances in a variety of venues likely kept alive more spontaneous forms of artistic production, and perhaps less censored types of verbal and musical utterances, he was clearly capable of following the dictates of directors and producers.

His recording of "Mean Old Bed Bug Blues" (New York City, 11 August 1927) is a good example of the kinds of pressures exerted on recording artists under contract. Johnson did not write the song, but according to Smith, it "was being hawked around race record producers at this time by publisher Joe Davis." Smith asserts that the African American songwriter and pianist Irene Higginbotham penned the song, while attributions on record labels indicate Leo Wood, aka Jack Wood.[25] The problem of identifying the song's composer is indicative of the kinds of financial exploitation at work in the music business. The song was recorded by a number of artists in 1927, including Walter E. "Furry" Lewis and, most famously, Bessie Smith.[26] The lyrics develop a humorous extended metaphor of a bedbug to invoke parasitic personal but also social relations, as the narrator is terrorized by the noxious pests.[27] Though the bedbug could be a metaphor for a destructive lover, its associations with living conditions in poverty suggest its interpretation as a social and economic metaphor as well. While most verses describe being bitten and prevented from sleeping in a somewhat humorous tone, the third verse suggests a more serious threat: "Bedbugs big as a jackass will bite you and stand and grin [2x] / And drink up all the bedbug poison, then come back and bite you again." Although the simile is hyperbolic, the comparison to a jackass and resistance to poison indicate that the bedbugs represent greater threats that cannot be easily eliminated. The relentless, grinning bugs conjure remorseless victimizers who seem to take pleasure in others' suffering. The final verse has the narrator being thrown out of his home and, although the meaning could still be consistent with an interpretation of the bedbug as cruel lover, it could also be read as a reference to eviction, tightening the association between the bedbug and destructive social forces that harm individuals: "I have to set up all night long, my feet can't touch the floor [2x] / 'Cause the mean old bedbug told me that I can't sleep there no more." Johnson's descending strummed triplet fill with an odd interruptive swung rhythm in the final beat of the third measure draws attention to the A line in this verse and underscores the seriousness of the narrator's predicament. Even the instrumental response to the vocal seems affected by the bedbug's torment. The image evokes a compassionless lover and/or landlord, rather than a bedbug, terrorizing a helpless victim.

The depiction of the bedbug is simultaneously humorous and threatening, achieving a kind of indeterminacy appropriate for social critique as policed by record producers, representatives of the white dominant culture. Using humor and metaphor shields both the artist and the record company from any direct attribution of potentially polemical forms of discourse. In addition to the ambiguity achieved through playful language, the penultimate verse further complicates easy interpretation. Positioned directly following the invocation of the huge, grinning, poison-resistant insects, this verse creates a peculiar sympathy for the bedbug: "Something was moanin' in the corner, I tried my best to see / Something was moanin' in the corner, then I walked over to see / It was the mother bedbug prayin' to the good Lord for some more to eat." The somewhat sympathetic portrayal of the bedbug mother troubles any easy condemnation, introducing the notion that the bedbug too is driven by forces outside its control.[28] While the verse likely provokes laughter as a primary response, the implied connection between the bedbug and the person being disturbed and harassed by it upsets the initial interpretation of the bug as deliberately malevolent. The personification of the bedbug, particularly the moaning and praying, asserts commonality between parasite and host. While this may ultimately be rejected in the final verse by a narrator driven away from his home, the momentary appearance of a potential bond of sympathy reveals a deeper connection between abuser and abused. The complexity of social interactions indirectly represented through metaphor enables the articulation of contradictions within our understanding of social and moral relations. Those who abuse may themselves be pressured and driven by external forces. This representation of complicated human dynamics reflects a nuanced understanding of the motivations even in a dog-eat-dog world. Under cover of a humorous metaphor, recording company executives and artists have plausible deniability about the social critique in the song, while the suggestion of momentary sympathy between victim and bedbug creates nuance in an otherwise banal extended metaphor for abusive relations.

Johnson's exposure to the complexity of human interactions in an urban setting affords him a more expansive worldview than artists hemmed in by a rural milieu. As a result, his work depicts social relations with richness and, at times, contradictions uncharacteristic of rural artists and more like the professional songwriter who penned "Mean Old Bed Bug Blues." A life of tenancy or sharecropping, even on a large plantation, provides little occasion to observe and understand the constraints operating throughout the system. Even performers who managed to escape the geographical boundaries of rural life to perform and record in urban areas had limited insight into the monocrop system as a whole and the pressures it exerted on all involved—banks, merchants, landlords, overseers, laborers, and others. For the most part, these artists engage in social critique that calls out injustice from the perspective of the exploited and subjugated croppers, tenants, and day laborers. Most often, anger, frustration, hurt, and betrayal color representations that, like Johnson's, use sexual infidelity to signify other forms of victimization. These representations, shaped by the brutal reality of rural poverty, use the figure of the betrayed lover to portray victims of the exploitative practices of planters and others through an implied analogical relation. Only rarely, if ever, can they conjure a sense of a larger system that structures, shapes, and limits human interactions of all involved.[29] Far less can they imagine sympathy with the oppressor. A limited geographical horizon and the constraints it imposes impede a broader perception and understanding of how the system works to constrain and determine all involved. By contrast, Johnson's corpus, both in the songs of condemnation involving personal and sexual relations and those that engage broader social issues, conjures a world where even the evil are at times represented as pressured by outside forces. Exposure to life in the districts, in dance halls, honky-tonks, theaters, and other venues, and even to the workings of recording companies, makes him keenly aware of the financial and social dynamics that condition and determine behavior.

Although he didn't write "Mean Old Bed Bug Blues," its message is consistent with the representations of social relations in his work. From his peculiar vantage point, it is easier to perceive that everyone is caught in the system of interconnected relations. Personal, social, and financial webs constrain behavior, often leading to exploitation, domination, and victimization. But, as in "Mean Old Bed Bug Blues," the recognition of the existence of outside pressures on everyone does not mean that you cannot signal unfair treatment. Despite momentary empathy for the bedbug, the narrator driven from his home elicits our compassion as listeners. The complexity in the representational strategy simply means that the injustices are embedded in a world of power relations and dynamics that defy simple remedy. Johnson's direct experience of the complicated world that provided the context for both live music performance and the recording industry enabled him to see just how difficult strategic intervention is when multiple vested interests tug, often in opposite directions.[30]

The networks of social and financial relations in the districts, to take one example, while they constrain and determine behavior in negative ways that lead to abuse of various kinds, also create employment. These networks reach into the musicians' world, providing opportunities for work. Moreover, the musical world also has its "social relations" and "power dynamics" that determine aspects of performance practice and style. Musicians who seek to earn a living are not free to perform in any style or manner they choose. Solo artists, in particular, but group acts as well respond to the dictates of the crowd, playing requested numbers for tips and applause. Johnson certainly experienced these pressures busking with his family, playing for private parties and events, and even in smaller venues, like bars, saloons, cafés, and clubs. Playing on the river cruises and other venues as part of a well-rehearsed ensemble required responding to audience requests, but it also entailed discipline and adherence to a written part, as well as rehearsed styles of execution (phrasing, dynamics, tempo, rhythm, etc.) consistent with the perceived tastes of the crowd. Failure to do these things could lead to termination, as in Louis Armstrong's famous firing from the Streckfus boats for not attending rehearsals.[31] Gainful employment as a musician depends on responding, to some extent, to the pressures exerted by the venues, through owners, producers, and audiences, insofar as repertoire and style are concerned.

Furthermore, ensemble play imposes its own constraints on performance, even in genres like jazz and blues that allow for improvisation. "Social relations" may be broadly interpreted to encompass not only the networks of relations that enable booking gigs, playing on tours, or making money on street corners, but also the relations between and among musicians as part of performance. Performing in a particular style or genre, whether "sweet" or "hot," urban or rural, blues or jazz, requires mastering the associated techniques and executing them when called on to do so. As we saw in the introduction, rhythms and tempos are not only extremely variable but also highly charged with respect to distinguishing styles and genres. Pitch areas (for example, blue notes) and scales (major, minor, modal, pentatonic, diatonic, and chromatic) are also invested with tremendous significance when it comes to identifying styles and genres. Like the other sign systems that Johnson deploys, these musical signs mean different things to different audiences in different venues at different times. Mastering the production of these signs and, more significantly, being able to produce them within the constraints imposed by ensemble play, enables participating and earning a living in the world of musical social relations. Failing to do so can result in loss of gainful employment.

Live performance thus requires connections in two interlocking networks of relations: the world of producers and club owners for booking gigs and the world of musicians with whom you perform. Maintaining appearances and contributing to the performance enables earning a living by adhering to codes of conduct, both personal and musical. In addition, Johnson also negotiated the world of recording companies who placed further demands on his performances. His wide repertoire, including solo and small combo blues in rural and urban styles, vaudeville, popular, and novelty songs, and jazz in both duet and larger group configurations, necessitated discipline to maintain his position within a web of musical relations. His long-term relationship with OKeh and with various companies afterward, like RCA Victor, Decca, and King, coupled with his varied experiences of live performance, provided him a particular vantage point on the imbrication of musical performance with social and financial relations. A strategic intervention aimed at addressing injustices in such a complex network of financial interests overlaid with class, racial, ethnic, and musical dynamics, is difficult to imagine.

The complex portrait of systems of social relations in his lyrics finds its corollary in the variety evident in his musical output: in both worlds, Johnson understands the pressures exerted to play a role or prescribed part in order to survive. His ability to perform rural blues with Texas Alexander, with sparse phrases and deep bends, or take a solo chorus with Louis Armstrong and His Hot Five, or play lead guitar in his duets with Eddie Lang speaks to his discipline as a performer who understands the ways in which constraints paradoxically lead to greater opportunities for expression. For example, some of the lean phrases created to accompany Alexander in "Levee Camp Moan Blues" (New York City, 12 August 1927) echo in his electric solo work thirty-three years later in "Four Walls and Me" and "New Years Blues" (Englewood Cliffs, NJ, 28 December 1960, on *Losing Game*). While the collage technique speaks to his familiarity with compositional practices in blues, and especially in jazz, his pragmatic recycling of material created in other contexts for different purposes demonstrates the way in which he makes creative and productive use of artistic constraint. Work in a studio session for a record label in service to another artist benefits his solo repertoire. By extension, a view of the system and one's place in it informs a depiction of a complex social world where change is necessary but difficult to effect. Consistent with Johnson's musical practice, within the context of social complexity, strategic action may be more effective in the form of variation, recontextualization, and repositioning rather than direct challenge.

Types, Class, and Race in Johnson's Corpus

Johnson recognizes that immoral behavior is often conditioned by complex social systems. Individuals react to a variety of incentives and constraints, sometimes in ways that victimize others. His critical representations of the social world include contradictions and ambiguities that signal this understanding. But he also deploys language that categorizes individuals into types, a representational strategy that seems, at first glance, to be at odds with an understanding of contradictory motivations or overdetermined patterns of behavior. But the invocation of types is, ultimately, consistent with his view of a complicated social world. Learning to identify and understand types enables potential victims to predict behaviors and, potentially, avoid abuse at the hands of others. In this respect, Johnson's lyrics function as what Ron Eyerman and Andrew Jamison term a "cognitive praxis": they provide an "interpretive framework" for understanding social roles and systems.[32]

Types fall into two general categories of people in many of Johnson's songs. On one side, Johnson situates the narrator and his "friends," who are taken advantage of by those on the other side, who cheat, lie, and victimize. The songs describe scenarios in which evil individuals victimize the good, establishing broad patterns of behavior. As we saw in "Fickle Mamma Blues," Johnson often uses the name *Sam* to denote individuals who cannot be trusted. Following the verse, cited above, where he catches his friend *triflin'* with his woman, he provides general advice to *friends*. The explicit address to a collective audience reinforces the sense of a world divided into categories of good and bad individuals. In another example using the name Sam, Johnson stages a confrontation between the betrayed narrator and the false friend. In "Sam, You Can't Do That to Me" (New York City, 11 September 1930), the title functions as a refrain that punctuates the detailing of Sam's misdeeds. The refrain's meaning as a warning becomes clear at the end of the song, when the narrator threatens to murder his so-called friend: "Now, I've asked you like a man; I've explained to you, Sam / You just want to take my woman and you just don't give a damn / Sam, you can't do that to me; Sam, you better watch yourself / You'd be better off dead than double-crossing somebody else." While the narrator seems to justify murder by suggesting that Sam is an incorrigible victimizer, he nonetheless warns him to change his ways.

"Nothing but a Rat" (Chicago, 2 November 1939) makes the invocation of types explicit in a song that imagines a conversation between the betrayed narrator and a *rat*, who has been himself double-crossed. The opening verse establishes the unambiguous relation between the two men: "I let you have my money, my clothes, made you welcome into my home / Yes, I trust you with my family while I go out and slave all day long / You were such a lowdown rat that you couldn't let my wife alone." Having betrayed the narrator's trust, the rat finds himself in the same predicament: his wife has been taken by a friend and now, ironically, he seeks the narrator's advice. The lyrics are bitter, even by Johnson's standards, as he excoriates the friend who in the past seemingly has enjoyed homewrecking as a kind of sport. The penultimate verse clearly establishes a category of people who behave in this way: "That's the reason why homes are wrecked today by just such rats as you / Reason why so many good home is wrecked by such a rats as you / You can dish it out, but when you got to swallow it, you don't know what on earth to do." The use of *rats* in the plural underscores the category of persons who engage in this type of behavior. Although the scenario represents a kind of quid pro quo, the song ends with the narrator cursing the victimizer, without any sense of satisfaction or justice: "When your time come to die, I hope you crawl on your belly just like a snail." We are left with a sense of patterns of behavior that will be repeated without hope of correction.

Addressed to an audience of "good" types, the lyrics in these songs seek to prevent future abuse in interpersonal relations. The categories of good and evil denote moral qualities relative to trust and fidelity. But the categories are not limited to interpersonal relations. As I have already suggested, the indictments may be understood more broadly. At times, Johnson makes this explicit. The representation of types of individuals enables him to issue strong critical pronouncements about class- and race-based forms of abuse that resemble those he makes about gendered interpersonal relations. In this respect, Johnson's lyrics differ significantly from those of rural artists. His urban vantage point and representational strategies afford him a degree of protection that rural artists do not enjoy. For artists performing in a rural context, limited horizons and opportunities for escape—from either retaliation or from the system altogether—make contestation almost unimaginable.

Various forms of terrorism practiced in the South squelched any thought of sharply denouncing abuse. Indictments of injustice could be and were interpreted under such conditions as aimed at particular individuals and, hence, muzzled before they ever surfaced.[33] But interracial contact and even strife in New Orleans and St. Louis are distinctly different from the conditions in the rural South or even Memphis.[34] As we have seen, the history of racialization in these cities produced patterns of social life that differed significantly from those in areas settled by Anglo-Americans. Danny Barker, also from New Orleans, expressed the sense of difference in stark terms:

> Mississippi. Just the mention of the word Mississippi amongst a group of New Orleans people would cause complete silence and attention. The word was so very powerful that it carried the impact of catastrophies [sic], destruction, death, hell, earthquakes, cyclones, murder, hangings, lynching, all sorts of slaughter. It was the earnest and general feeling that any Negro who left New Orleans and journeyed across the state border and entered the hell-hole called the state of Mississippi for any reason other than to attend the funeral of a very close relative—mother, father, sister, brother, wife, or husband—was well on the way to losing his mentality, or had already lost it. The states of Alabama, Florida, Texas, and Georgia were equally fearsome concerning their treatment of Negroes when the least bit of friction with white folks occurred.[35]

Although Barker speaks for all African Americans, musicians in rural areas internalized the terror, curtailing overt condemnations of racialized abuse.

This difference explains, in part, the occurrence of references to race and class in Johnson's songs. Urban life, shaped by a French and Spanish colonial past and creolization, provides a view of social relations, and particularly race, ethnicity, and class that enables a different perception and understanding of these categories.[36] Condemnations take the form of general pronouncements that can be more open in some respects, precisely because they are aimed at "types" and not specific individuals. In addition to this strategy of general statements, working within constraints imposed by producers in recording, theater, and other commercial enterprises shields him from intimidation and retaliation, paradoxically affording him more freedom. His broad, urban perspective frames interpersonal and social relations as part of a system that may be critiqued for the kinds of abuse it enables.

Johnson recorded two versions of one song and a variant with a different title that demonstrate his awareness of exploitative social relations and categories of people as well as the evolution of his representations over time. Nearly twenty years, geographical distance, and significant differences in the instrumental settings separate the recordings of "Crowing Rooster Blues" (San Antonio, 13 March 1928), "Crowing Rooster" (Chicago, 7 February 1941), and "Working Man's Blues" (Cincinnati, 11 December 1947). Despite these differences, all three songs begin with the same striking reworking of a standard blues trope to indict class relations: "What makes a rooster crow every morning 'fore day [2x] / To let the pimps [and ramblers][37] know that the working man is on his way." The traditional barnyard symbol that signals the beginning of a workday has been transplanted to an urban setting where the crowing announces a different kind of exploitation. While the rooster in the A lines evokes the oppressive labor of rural agricultural life, the B line transforms the type of labor and exploitation with the expressions "working man" and "pimps." In the 1928 version of the song recorded for OKeh, subsequent verses develop the theme of sexual infidelity with overtones of prostitution to offer an account of a "working man" being taken advantage of. The second verse in the earliest version indirectly evokes the exploitation of johns by prostitutes in describing men who are victims of sexual infidelity: "You can always tell when your woman's man has come to town [2x] / She will put on her best teddies and dress and steal her some sleeping gown." The use of the word "teddy," a word used by musicians to describe the attire of prostitutes in Storyville, feels out of place in the context of the blues, even if the cheating scenario is familiar.[38] Johnson's final verse proffers advice about preventing cheating that also references material goods unthinkable in the rural blues: "If you buy your woman plenty of silk things, don't buy them all in one time [2x] / She will get ramblin' in her brains and some triflin' man on her mind." "Plenty of silk things" lies beyond the grasp of not only the average "working man" referenced in the opening verse but most certainly those ensnared in a life of poverty in the rural South. If the opening verse in this 1928 recording seems to introduce a pointed critique of class and potentially race relations, it moves into a standard narrative of cheating and betrayal with financial implications. Rather than address class difference and exploitation head on, Johnson evokes them implicitly with the mention of material goods that separate the betrayers from the betrayed. He implies that if only the "working man" had enough money, he too could buy fidelity. The broad pronouncements about *ramblin'* and *triflin'* addressed to a group audience in the final verse signal that this type of exploitation is widespread. Despite the divisions invoked, in the end the lyrics construct a kind of solidarity across class and geographical boundaries among the "good types" who fall prey to the bad.

In "Crowing Rooster," recorded for Bluebird in Chicago, and "Working Man's Blues," recorded in Cincinnati for King, Johnson develops a more pointed critique of exploitative relations in an urban context of the 1940s. While exploitation is still coded in terms of gendered roles and practiced by women on men, nonetheless, the later versions of the song make the connection to class and potentially race relations clear. The second verse continues the parallel between agricultural and urban forms of labor but defines the "pimp" as one who takes money from the honest working man. In "Crowing Rooster" Johnson sings, "We're up before sunrise, slavin' sixteen hours a day [2x] / We pay our house rent and grocery bill and the pimps get the rest of our pay."[39] The A line does not specify the type of labor performed, but rather insists on rising "before sunrise" and "slavin' sixteen hours a day," common to both urban and rural forms of exploitative labor. The B line deviates from the resemblance being asserted between country and city life, invoking economic pressures associated more with the urban dweller. More importantly, the line suggests similarities between landlords, shop owners, and pimps, all extorting money from the laborer.

Most striking in the 1941 and 1947 versions of the song is the third verse that interrupts the AA'B lyric structure with a call to action, in "Working Man's Blues": "Men, we got to get together, yes, something's got to be done / We make the money, while the pimp has the fun / You know where there's only grocery and no money, there ain't no fun."[40] The narrator exhorts the "working man" to take action, but without specifying exactly what is to be done to put an end to economic exploitation. Significantly, he employs a call to *men* in a first-person plural imperative (like the one we saw in "Treat 'Em Right") to unite in common cause against *pimps*. In Chicago, where the song was first recorded prior to World War II, rising tension over discrimination fueled increased race consciousness. Racially restrictive housing covenants, coupled with redlining and house contract sales in the context of maximal segregation, sparked awareness and heightened frustration in the Black community over discriminatory economic practices.[41] Population growth throughout the 1930s and 1940s only worsened deplorable living conditions for African Americans on the South and West sides.[42] Labor strife and racially differential unemployment rates and relief checks in the context of the Depression fueled ongoing anger and a resultant willingness to discuss racial inequality more openly in Chicago and other urban areas.[43] Segregation and discrimination in the military during World War II further heightened racial consciousness. The situation in Cincinnati in 1947 is similar to the one in Chicago from the perspective of housing, although not as extreme. In that city, a growing African American population faces segregation, overcrowding, and the formation of a "second ghetto" between 1945 and 1960.[44] Together these social and economic pressures enable a bolder statement about the existence of class and race exploitation.

After the call-to-action verse, Johnson reverts to the theme of infidelity, including backstabbing behavior by best friends: "If your best friend can't get your woman, he'll frame her for somebody else." Despite the retreat to the familiar and safe territory of sexual deceit and betrayal, the song nonetheless makes accusations about economic exploitation and demands action. The lexicon also implicitly evokes a racial coding of economic exploitation, particularly for an African American audience that purchased Bluebird and King records. Implicitly identifying grocers and landlords with pimps equates the vice of red-light districts and its attendant forms of abuse with the discrimination and exploitation faced by everyday working people, especially those of color.

The instrumental performances of the three versions of the song highlight the evolution toward more forceful denunciation of racialized economic exploitation. The 1928 version with solo guitar features a slow tempo that enables very deliberate responses to the vocal in a combination of single-note and chorded fills. The vocal feels almost mournful with heavy vibrato, particularly on elongated syllables featuring vowels. By contrast, the 1941 recording adopts a quicker tempo and accomplishes a jauntier feel with Lil Armstrong on piano and Andrew Harris on double bass, enabling Johnson to execute extremely precise responses in a single-note style with frequent swung rhythms. The vocal feels less mournful in the quicker tempo, especially with the supporting, almost gleeful accompaniment. The 1947 "Working Man's Blues" achieves a kind of compromise between the two earlier versions, with a tempo somewhere between the 1928 and 1941 versions and a smooth, urban sound with the electric guitar, again accompanied by piano and stand-up bass. Ultimately, while the 1928 tone communicates sadness and lack of action, the 1941 and 1947 versions resonate with playful control, communicating empowerment. Although no solution is explicitly proposed, musically the ensemble performances model the possibility for taking coordinated action.

Other songs in Johnson's corpus from different historical moments bluntly call out injustice with a sober realism. In "Broken Levee Blues" (San Antonio, 13 March 1928), he references the deplorable conditions of the 1927 Mississippi

River Flood response. In particular, he describes forced labor by African Americans in perilous conditions. The second verse describes people being rounded up to perform unpaid manual labor: "They want me to work on the levee; I have to leave my home / They want to work on the levee, then I have to leave my home / I was so scared the levee might break and I lay down."[45] The terror experienced because of the floodwaters is evoked, as in other blues from the period, but with an added social dimension.[46] Johnson references police pursuit and forced labor, adding to the sense of trepidation and panic. The evocation of these abuses that the disaster enabled resonates with a Black audience reading exposé accounts in African American newspapers across the country of events in the Lower Mississippi Valley region. For African Americans rounded up and forced to live either on dangerous levees or in concentration camps—without sanitation, proper food, shelter, or medical care—the response to the 1927 Mississippi flood disaster reintroduced slave labor and other abuses under threat of violence.[47] The final verse has the narrator steadfastly refusing to work, despite threats from law enforcement: "The police say, work, fight or go to jail; I said, I ain't totin' no sacks / Police say, work, fight or go to jail; I say, I ain't totin' no sacks / And I ain't fillin' no levee, the plank is on the ground and I ain't drivin' no nails." While enacting this type of refusal may ultimately represent a fantasy, nonetheless its appearance in Johnson's lyrics is empowering for its directness. The song uses the occasion of the flood to call out the injustices perpetrated under the guise of emergency measures that worsened poverty and reintroduced conditions of bondage. These conditions, although extreme, remind an audience of listeners of the everyday reality of race-based economic exploitation.

Johnson's "Racketeers Blues" (New York City, 12 August 1932) provides a distinctly different context to evoke similar uses of terror to subjugate and dominate along race and class lines. The song opens with advice offered in the second person to those pursued for payments by gangs armed with machine guns. While the lyrics depict an urban world of organized crime and large sums of money that no doubt awakened memories of the recent trial and conviction of Al Capone for contemporary listeners, the focus remains on the victims of extortion efforts. Johnson's advice is less moralistic than realistic, as he underscores the futility of attempting to escape those who take money by force: "When they demand your money, you got to give it up with a smile [2x] /And if you refuse, they'll read about you in a short little while." The lyrical evocations are vague enough to suggest other forms of extortion familiar to the average African American listener. Here, the formulation *give it up with a smile* resonates with practices under Jim Crow, in which African

Americans had no choice but to accede to various types of extortion at white hands without showing signs of resistance. Violent forms of "disappearing" occurred in both the urban North and rural South to enforce compliance, consistent with Johnson's B line here. Refusals of any kind often met with violence and even death. The menace of machine guns depicted in the urban setting parallels kidnappings, beatings, drownings, and lynchings—forms of terrorism more commonly practiced in the South. Reinforcing the expansive meaning of *racketeers*, the penultimate verse makes suggestive general statements about economic coercion backed by threat of murder: "You slave hard for your money, just to give it to some other one / You work hard for your money, just to give it to some other one / And if you refuse, the answer will be from a racketeer's gun." A rural agricultural worker may be reminded of and identify with the helplessness and terror being described. The feelings associated with violent intimidation no doubt seemed familiar from episodes at settling time, even if the mobster lexicon seemed exotic. The expression *some other one* invites a capacious understanding of racketeers, resembling other general characterizations in Johnson's corpus. Like the *pimps* in "Crowing Rooster," these *racketeers* may be understood as anyone who engages in fraudulent dealings to extort hard-earned money by force in both urban and rural contexts.

Finally, "Chicago Blues," recorded the same day as "Crowing Rooster" (Chicago, 7 February 1941) with the same personnel, blends themes of economic inequality and race to express bitterness at rejection. The song opens with an explicit mention of racial categories, but seems to deny their significance relative to the importance of money: "Chicago is alright to visit, but please don't hang around / You'll find smooth Blacks and high yellas, boy, and those mellow browns / But when your bankroll is gone, you're just another chump that's dropped in town." Despite the assertion about the greater importance accorded money, the evocation of a racial hierarchy in the B line establishes a context of discrimination and privilege based on gradations of color. The B line implies that such distinctions become irrelevant when money is the primary consideration, hinting that without it, color matters. Although colorism is not mentioned in the remainder of the song, the shift to the theme of a woman only interested in money cannot banish the suspicion of colorism's lingering effects. The narrator recounts his efforts to seduce a woman who already wears "number three shoes" and "number five gloves," and who is blunt about her sole interest: "She said, 'It's money I need, babe, and I don't need love.'" Whether the woman is skeptical, shrewd, and/or harbors racial prejudice is difficult to determine. The narrator does not provide a reason for her rejection of his proposition to take her to New York and buy her "a 1942 Cadillac": "She said, 'I'm sorry, this fine round body will be here when you get back.'" Whether it is lack of trust, self-protection, or some other reason, she is not willing to take a chance. The overall bitter tone of the song and the suggestion of colorism in the opening verse cannot erase the sense of possible racial basis.

Although the number of songs with direct references to racial discrimination and economic exploitation is small relative to Johnson's substantial recorded corpus, these songs nonetheless stand out, for their articulation of an indictment of how the system works to dominate and victimize, especially in comparison with the blues of other artists.[48] His experience with negotiating a position for himself within complex social systems makes him a shrewd observer able to articulate coded warnings about racialized forms of domination. Protections afforded by associations with professional networks, including recording companies, coupled with general statements and an invocation of "types," enable Johnson to utilize his artistic output as a vehicle for social critique that includes forms of racialized inequality.

Paradoxes of Social Critique and Performance

Johnson's privileged position as a performer in urban venues enables him to perceive social complexity and the various kinds of constraints on human behavior. While on the one hand, this insight reveals how some pressures engender exploitative behavior, such as in red-light districts, on the other hand, it enables him to develop strategies for success within a world of "professional" relations. Playing a role within a complex social system creates possibilities for strategic action that can lead to domination and abuse, but it also opens up opportunities to navigate the system effectively for those able to master performances. Johnson's "professionalism" and contacts in interconnected social networks lead to opportunities for success as a working musician. They also provide a peculiar vantage point on how the performance of gendered, racialized, and economically stratified roles within the world he inhabits are a microcosm of society at large.

Johnson's lyrical corpus reflects his perception of the mirroring of social worlds. His lyrics employ general statements, a typology of characters, and the evocation of analogous relations to indict a social system. As we have seen, parallels suggested between the urban and rural worlds enable broad condemnations of abuse based on gender, but especially race and class. His particular focus on deceit and betrayal enables him to use romantic relations to condemn, at times forcefully and directly, social patterns of discrimination and injustice. Moreover, his sensitivity to forms of deception practiced for financial gain reinforces the movement from the personal to the social in his work. Finally, his moralizing tone and tendency to offer advice to groups of individuals also shield him from censorship, despite some sharp denunciations.

Johnson most often offers advice in a world represented as divided between perpetrators and victims, abusers and abused. But the question remains open as to how the songs might inspire, provoke, or enable intervention to change the status quo, which ties into a larger question about whether or not and, if so, how aesthetic works determine or alter historical reality.[49] In the context of Johnson's oeuvre, which stresses advice directed at individuals and groups, it is nonetheless pressing. Complicating the question further, the worldview that informs his representations rests on some key paradoxes: How can he hold out hope for a better world if people act out of self-interest because of complex systems of social relations over which they have, at best, only limited control? If people use and abuse one another because of the roles they are constrained to play, how can Johnson still address a group—*people* and *friends*—that he believes to be honest and good (like himself)? How can you really know who is good and who is bad in a world of performed roles? Such a determination cannot be based on race, gender, or class, since these are also performed roles, so how can we know who is honest and good? In other words, in the end, where could all this advice lead?

Although Johnson addresses groups of listeners in his lyrics, the interpellations do not produce a collective social or political identity, but rather an imagined moral community.[50] The *people* and *friends* he addresses are distinguished by their honesty and hard work, making them potential victims of betrayal and abuse. Such listeners recognize familiar scenarios and feelings in Johnson's lyrics and identify and align themselves with the groups being constituted. And although the representations indirectly and, at times, directly invoke gendered, racialized, and classed identities, the fundamental trait that distinguishes types of people and prompts identification in Johnson's worldview is moral behavior. Even the overt call in "Crowing Rooster" and "Working Man's Blues" to *men* to *get together* to do *something* fails to "create a kind of spontaneous collective identity or facilitate the investment of people's psychological energies"[51] or mobilize a social group.[52] In particular, the passive-voice construction of "something's got to be done" works to diffuse rather than inspire collective formation for action. Throughout Johnson's corpus, communal identity remains elusive. His lyrics provide the possibility for the constitution of imagined groups of likeminded *people* and *friends* based on shared moral feelings but fall short of offering a vision of a better future—much less instructions for how to achieve it. Instead, individual identity remains in tension with group formations, linked to but never entirely accounted for by collective identity.

Moreover, Johnson's recurring theme of deception implies that some truths are hidden, making action more problematic. In the Johnson imaginary, even a song of lost love and regret can be framed in terms of masked emotions, such as "Baby, You Don't Know My Mind" (St. Louis, 14 May 1926). The opening verse proclaims, "Take me back, baby, you don't know my mind [2x] / I may look happy, but I'm almost dyin'." Although the narrator attempts to convey a message of loss and pain to the audience, hope or belief in a different outcome is never articulated. The masking of truth, which echoes across his oeuvre, makes intervention aimed at change difficult to imagine.

Nonetheless, Johnson aims to inculcate behavioral changes. Teaching *people* and *friends* to look beyond deceptive exteriors to discover "truths" represents an important first step. Although Johnson's lessons may resemble the realignment of "interpretive frameworks" that Ron Eyerman and Andrew Jamison recognize as the work of music associated with social movements, his messages most often seek to inspire self-protective individual behavior rather than collective social or political action.[53] The exemplary final verse of "Sweet Woman, See for Yourself" (New York City, 13 August 1926) almost pleads with the listener to trust only what is directly perceived: "Friend, will you please see for yourself [2x] / Then you'll know when your eyes sees, you don't have to believe nobody else." Penetrating false exteriors entails distrusting the word of others and drawing your own conclusions, making the formation of alliances uneasy at best.

Beyond healthy skepticism aimed at avoiding future betrayal, Johnson occasionally offers hope of escape. In "I'm Gonna Dodge the Blues, Just Wait and See" (New York City, 13 August 1926), his final verse repeats the title as a verbal act of defiance: "But I'm going dodge these blues, people, you just watch and see / People, I'm going dodge these blues, you just watch and see / I'm going to stop these blues from worryin' me." But avoidance is not strategic intervention. Beyond avoidance, other songs, such as "Headed for Southland" (New York City, 23 January 1930) and "Southland Is Alright with Me" (New York City, 11 February 1931), propose a fantasy of escape from the cold North. As in the blues of other artists, this trope of escape rings hollow, especially in the early 1930s. An African American audience, aware of the horrors of Jim Crow under the Depression either through direct experience or collective imaginary, finds little solace in vague nostalgia. Johnson's ascending triplet fills and nondescript evocations of a place "where the sun shines every day," and where he loses his "trouble beneath the weeping willow tree," offer no real promise of happiness.

Avoidance and escape hardly answer the clarion call in "Crowing Rooster" and "Working Man's Blues." In other songs, Johnson offers the consolation that "what goes around comes around." Most often, this is expressed in the context of betrayal: the mean mistreater will someday realize what she or he has lost. "How Could You Be So Mean" (New York City, 15 July 1946) frames the comeuppance scenario in multiple ways.[54] The B line of the second verse addressed to the cheating lover declares as a warning, "It's one thing you got to know, what goes up, it must come down," while the final verse announces the realization of this kind of justice: "I tried so hard to make you love me, but you don't seem to understand / Tried so hard to make you love me, but you can't see it my way / And now you're in love with me, baby, and someone else has steal your place." But even scenarios of cosmic karma, especially those framed in vague temporal terms with *someday*, fail to provide much promise of change.

The overwhelming emphasis on deception and betrayal in Johnson's corpus leads consistently to a recommendation of self-protection rather than collective action as the best strategic response. His title that references the Depression, "Hard Times Ain't Gone No Where" (Chicago, 8 November 1937), would seem broadly applicable. Sober realism in the face of fair-weather friends and rigged systems is better than false hope or misplaced trust. The final verse of this song at least offers solace in the idea that the Depression functions as a great equalizer: "People ravin' about hard times, I don't know why they should / People is ravin' about hard times, I don't know why they should / If some people was like me, they didn't have no money when times was good." Even bleaker, his 1960 recording "No Love for Sale" (Englewood Cliffs, NJ, 8 March 1960, on *Blues by Lonnie Johnson*) seems to give up on close personal relations altogether. The narrator declares in the final verse, "What good is lovin' someone, when they in love with someone else? / Yes, what is the good in lovin' someone else, when they in love with someone else? / Better stop while you can, yes, better off by yourself." Putting an end to lying and deceit is not possible; going it alone remains the only safe alternative.

Johnson's lessons about social dynamics reflect his peculiar vantage point as a musician. Witnessing strategic interpersonal relations, such as in the dog-eat-dog world of the districts, taught valuable lessons about role-playing within a world shaped by a variety of forces. His professional experiences involved interactions with fellow musicians, producers, promoters, recording executives, and others that provided an additional framework for understanding how socioeconomic and other pressures shape opportunities and possibilities, and also the performance of identities. Moreover, his own embeddedness in musical relations required playing in a variety of styles, genres, and configurations depending on context, teaching him the value of flexibility and adaptability. Soloist, ensemble player, and also backing studio musician, Johnson's identity is never fully captured by either the profile of a singular individual or as member of a collective.[55] His malleable identity predicated on performance and oriented toward self-protection and survival as an artist enacts a subtle dialectic between individual and community that is mirrored in his message to listeners: it is difficult but not impossible to be embedded in social formations and retain your sense of self. Johnson's consistent address to *friends* signals hope for an imagined community of good people who could interact in honest ways and resist the pressures exerted by social systems, maintaining the delicate balance between individual and collective. Role-playing and deceit will not end anytime soon. Johnson's best advice in the face of widespread deceit and the risk of victimization is to be wise to the show and to try to master your own performance.

CHAPTER 4
The Suffering Self
Isolation and Loneliness

In the world of deceitful human relations depicted in Johnson's lyrical corpus, clear-eyed judgment and a self-protective strategy of cynical distrust would seem to offer the best hope for avoiding victimization. Despite a mode of address to *friends* that imagines a community of like-minded, moral individuals, his overriding message counsels caution and, if necessary, going it alone. The advice in "No Love for Sale" (Englewood Cliffs, NJ, 8 March 1960, on *Blues by Lonnie Johnson*), "Better stop while you can, yes, better off by yourself," represents a contrapuntal theme of solitude to the message of imagined community in Johnson's songs. But being alone guarantees neither safety from harm nor happiness. Johnson's oeuvre contains a rich vein of songs dedicated to loneliness and isolation. The remedy of self-protective estrangement from others may prevent victimization, but it presents another set of dangers to the self. This chapter examines a nexus of songs that treat isolation occasioned by a variety of causes.

The revelation of lying and cheating often leads to the end of a relationship and both voluntary and involuntary forms of separation. The loss and loneliness endured are a result of betrayal. The separation from the other is certainly psychological but may also be physical in these scenarios, as the narrator loses companionship and, sometimes, a "home." Loss of "home" also occurs in Johnson's corpus because of natural disasters, resulting in physical and spatial separation from others. These songs metaphorize psychological isolation in images of destruction and dislocation, giving voice to feelings not only of homelessness but also of abandonment. Finally, Johnson also portrays psychological states, such as the blues or haunting, that isolate the self in an individualized and personal form of suffering that does not necessarily entail spatial distance from others. These songs articulate the fear, anxiety, and suffering associated with solitude.

Breakups and Being Alone

The discovery of a breach of trust often ends relationships. Although sometimes the narrator struggles to cut ties—for example, as we saw in "Fickle Mamma Blues" (New York City, 11 August 1927)—in most cases betrayal leads to separation and loneliness. Because the narrative voice largely focuses on the experience of being alone, the question of blame sometimes remains a secondary consideration. In "Very Lonesome Blues" (New York City, 19 January 1926), a strange musical opening with both Lonnie and James Johnson on violin accompanied by De Loise Searcy on piano, establishes a feeling of tension and anxiety. Syncopated eighth notes followed by ornamental triplets on solo piano in the first two beats of the opening measure give way to a heavier sound of syncopated chords joined by screechy, tremolo violins, which then take over the instrumental introduction in interwoven lines. Adding to the tension, Johnson's vocal suffers from the limitations of the recording equipment, producing an impoverished frequency range in a performance that sounds shouted rather than sung at times. The narrative is ambiguous about the cause of the narrator's present circumstances. The first two verses suggest that his lover cheated: "It's sad and lonesome, when you have to sleep outside yourself [2x] / When the one you love, you lost to somebody else / When you lay down on your pillow, behind you is a empty space / When you lay down on your pillow, behind you lays a empty space / When the one you love has let someone else take your place." Although voiced from a second-person perspective, the B lines of both these verses underscore the narrator's continuing faithfulness by designating the partner as *the one you love*, implying that she is the one that has ended the relationship by cheating. The imagery of being *outside*, and especially of the *empty space behind you*, represent loneliness in spatial terms, as a form of suffering born of physical separation from those you love. Significantly, these invocations underscore the self apart from all others in a large, unpopulated space.

The final verse of the song, after the violin solo, shifts to advice given in a second-person imperative form that implies that the narrator may be the one responsible for his current situation: "When you got a good woman, treat her kind in every way [2x] / Because I want to tell you, ain't a good woman is found every day." The ambiguity surrounding the question of which partner was responsible for the breakup refocuses attention on the "very lonesome blues" experienced by the narrating subject. Ultimately, the lyrics of the verses may be reconciled in an interpretation that both parties are responsible: he for mistreatment and she for turning to another, perhaps in response. The strangely cadenced outro to the song, which features slightly out-of-tune ascending arpeggios on the violins punctuated by staccato chords on the downbeats from the piano, provides no sense of resolution but rather feels tacked on to fill the remaining ten seconds of recording time. Overall, the track communicates anxiety about loneliness, particularly in its advice aimed at preserving relationships.

Four months later, the brothers recorded "A Good, Happy Home" (St. Louis, 14 May 1926), with James on piano accompanying Lonnie on violin. Formally, the first two choruses resemble songs of the "classic" blues women, like Bessie Smith and Victoria Spivey (whom Johnson accompanied), with a sixteen-bar structure in a minor key with an AAA′B lyric pattern. The final chorus of the song and the concluding violin solo shift abruptly to a major key and conform more closely to a more standard twelve-bar blues progression. Although the singing style and traditional lyrical formulations make "A Good, Happy Home" feel like a "blues," other musical features blur genre boundaries by invoking jazz and popular song. In contrast to the ambiguity in the lyrics of "Very Lonesome Blues," the narrative perspective of "A Good, Happy Home" emphasizes regret and guilt over actions that led to the loss of "a good, happy home": "I used to be happy, but I would not let that do / I used to be happy, but I wouldn't let that do / I used to be happy; I would not let that do; I've got no sweet woman to tell my troubles to / I'm all alone, baby, so are you." The final line of the opening verse suggests guilt over the partner's present condition, which introduces the theme of self-castigation. The second verse makes clear that his behavior, "stay[ing out] all night," led his partner to leave with someone else, in slight contradiction with his previous assertion of her being *all alone*, too. Significantly, the second verse ends with an emphatic statement about the narrator's present circumstances: "Now, I'm all alone; I mean I'm all alone." The repetition of *all alone*, which is also a repetition from the previous verse, emphasizes the narrator's solitude and vulnerability in the present moment. The inclusion of *I mean* functions rhetorically to underscore his sincerity by gesturing implicitly to a group of listeners who require further evidence of the truthfulness of his assertion.

After these verses, the song shifts to a more traditional twelve-bar blues progression in a major key with a final verse in an AA′B lyric pattern that counsels preserving the *happy home*. Although not stated explicitly, the lyrics imply that guarding against the narrator's fate requires avoiding his actions. The violin solo following the final verse contains some creative departures from a traditional blues vocabulary, such as interesting, ornamented arpeggios with occasional bowed chords in the opening four measures followed by bowed chords with tremolo in the next four. The final four measures of the complete twelve-bar progression return to a more traditional melody line that sets up for a four-bar, cadenced ending characterized by a simple syncopated melody with rallentando. Classical, jazz, and popular music influences combine with blues in both the instrumental performance and lyrical construction to produce a hybrid creation that nonetheless emphasizes an unambiguous lyrical message: mind your behavior or you will be *all alone*. In contrast to the ambiguity and anxiety expressed in "Very Lonesome Blues," "A Good, Happy Home" stresses regret and self-recrimination over a preventable loss.

The musical settings of "Very Lonesome Blues" and "A Good, Happy Home" complement the messages in different ways. The more traditional blues structure of "Very Lonesome Blues" features unsettling instrumental accompaniment with the two violins reinforcing the overall message of anxiety and uncertainty. The hybrid "A Good, Happy Home" fails to conform to a formal unifying principle with its abrupt shifts, but nonetheless offers less uncertainty in terms of a lyrical message. Unlike "Very Lonesome Blues," it places the blame squarely on the narrator within a context of musical collage. Each song, then, seems to provide a degree of predictability to offset uncertainty or complexity. As representational strategies, they offer different modes for evoking complex emotional states that converge in an attempt to represent multiple facets of the experience of loneliness. The presence of the violin in these early recordings provides a particularly plaintive sound that complements Johnson's vibrato-laden vocal performances with his characteristic nasal resonance, lending a specific color and character to the "voice" of loneliness.

In the final phase of his recording career, Johnson returns to familiar themes in a session in which Elmer Snowden on acoustic guitar and Wendell Marshall on double bass support his fine vocal and electric guitar work. As Lee Hildebrand remarks in the liner notes to the digital remaster, "A deep feeling of loneliness pervades these songs."[1] Particularly outstanding in the collection is "Blue and All Alone," which although listed as composer "unknown" on the release, recycles lyrics and repeats familiar themes from songs in Johnson's catalog, thereby imprinting the piece with his signature. In a spoken dialogue introduction, Johnson says to Snowden, "Yeah, say, listen, let's you and I go way in, down in the alley, it's where it's nice and greasy," using a language of the blues that reverberates with his past in New Orleans and St. Louis. After a brief instrumental introduction that deploys his signature single-note triplet and arpeggio moves in a very deliberate tempo, the song opens with an invocation of the weather to set the scene: "Skies is cloudy, rain is fallin' down [2x] / And tears is streamin' down my face 'cause I'm crazy about the wildest chick in town." His deliberate phrasing elongates *skies* and *rain* dramatically, while the B line draws the metaphorical connection between the raindrops and the physical manifestation of his emotional state in tears. The comparison retrospectively illuminates the foreshadowing of his mood in the artistic choice to stress *skies* and *rain* in the A and A' lines.

Despite its banality, Johnson breathes new life into a prolonged metaphor of rain to represent the emotional state of suffering prompted by his lover's absence and presumed infidelity in four of the six verses. Johnson's use of the metaphor extends beyond the simple mirroring of his psychological state in meteorological phenomena. The second verse suggests that the advent of rain serves as a reminder of powerful feelings and can even provoke them: "Every time it starts a-rainin', my love come tumblin' down / Yes, every time it starts rainin', my love come tumblin' down / Yes, when I'm in need for my baby, that's the time she can't be found." Whereas in the first verse his tears mirror the raindrops and vice versa, here his longing is provoked by the rain. Love is represented as a physical force that *comes tumblin' down* on the narrator. The holding of the final *n* sound in *rainin'* and *down*, a difficult effect to achieve vocally, highlights the intensity of the present moment, causing the listener to focus on the onset of uncontrollable emotional suffering with the commencement of rain. The vocal phrasing and pronunciation, although exhibiting great control, paradoxically magnify the sense of feelings being out of control, physically falling on the narrator.

Verse 4 cites lyrics that occur in "Falling Rain Blues" (St. Louis, 4 November 1925), "The New Fallin' Rain Blues" (New York City, 11 June 1929), and "New Falling Rain Blues" (New York City, 31 March 1938): "Blues fallin' down like drops of rain." In this context, the simile introduces a slight change in the dominating metaphor. While the first verse implies a comparison between the rain and his tears, and the second verse posits a cause-and-effect relation in which the weather elicits particular feelings, the simile of verse 4 privileges the feeling of the blues over the weather, using the rain to describe the experience. These modifications of the extended metaphor over the verses of the song intensify the sense of the difficulty of describing affect, of putting into words and images the experiences of the suffering self. In verse 5, he returns to the strategy of suggested metaphor employed in verse 1, setting the phenomena of weather and emotion again in parallel: "Well, look it's gone and start rainin' again, beating down on my windowpane [2x] / Yes, I love that gal so much, all it give me, worried mind and aches and pains." The introduction of the image of the *windowpane* enables the use of the verb *beating*, which suggests a physical connotation for the *aches and pains* of the B line. These artful, subtle moves establish a continuity of thought and expression through multiple verses. The final rhyme that extends through five of the six lines of these verses with *rain/insane/pane*, culminating with the homonymic, off-rhyme *pains*, pulls all elements of expression tightly together.

Verse 3 momentarily breaks with the dominant metaphor of the song with a focus on the blues and solitude without reference to rain. Here, Johnson colors his tone and employs a melismatic waiver on the extended vowel in *blues* in ways reminiscent of Bessie Smith's style: "Blues, why don't you let me alone [2x] / I try to figure this out by myself, 'cause I'm so blue and all alone."[2] The performance of the lines contributes to the intensification of feeling, as he holds the word *blues* for an entire measure, a fermata echoed in the following verse in "Blues falling down like drops of rain." The personification of the blues as an outside force that pursues him reinforces the metaphoric comparison to rain: the narrator is a victim of his emotional states, unable to control their onset or duration. While ostensibly a break in the continuity of the metaphor, verse 3 functions to focus attention on the uncontrollability of feelings prompted by solitude, drawing together what are really three strands of comparison that run through the lyrics: rain, solitude, and affect.

Thirty-six years of technological advancement in recording and the advent of the electric guitar enable the subtleties of Johnson's performance techniques to shine in "Blue and All Alone." Held words, like *skies*, *rain*, and *blues*, benefit from the "close-up" that microphones provide, particularly of his vibrato and melisma.[3] His phrasing—marked at times by deliberate, even spacing between words, contrasting with fermatas—is faithfully reproduced. For example, in the first half of the A′ line in the second verse, the equal emphasis and spacing of "Yes, every time it starts" contrasts sharply with *rainin'*, underlining the intensity of emotion despite efforts to control it. The held nasal sounds reverberate through the recording with significant sympathetic resonance, adding pathos to the expression. The musical accompaniment of Snowden on acoustic guitar and Marshall on stand-up bass leaves plenty of sonic space for the dynamic range of the vocal to develop, unlike the intrusive accompaniment of the piano and violin in earlier recordings, which compete both in terms of frequency range and in style of play. Finally, the trebly sound of the electric guitar cuts through, like the closely miked vocal, providing sharp response articulations with more expressive range and depth than the earlier violin. In particular, held notes aided by magnetic pickups and long decay do not have to rely on a distracting technique like tremolo in bowing, achieving a closer match with Johnson's vocal timbre. The guitar solo outro provides closure with insistent repeated-note, triplet figures, including with slides and syncopation, before ceding to a single-note swung rhythm melody that ends with some unusual tonal intervals in a descending cadence. Johnson manages to communicate pain, frustration, but also control in this artful solo. His delight in his own performance is evident in the false modesty of his reply to Snowden's compliment in dialogue following the track—Snowden: "Man, that was a killer." Johnson: "You like that?" The portrait of pain and loneliness is powerful, employing an extended metaphor to highlight the difficulty of articulating the intensity of emotional states.

Natural Disasters

The rain metaphor in "Blue and All Alone" echoes representations of natural disasters in other songs throughout Johnson's corpus. He recorded songs about floods at three significant moments in his professional career. The first group of songs was recorded in 1927 and 1928, during the time of his contract with OKeh and coinciding roughly with the Mississippi River Flood of 1927. He returned to the theme after the interruption introduced by the Depression, recording flood songs in 1937 and 1938. Finally, he reprised the flood theme in his sessions with Elmer Snowden in 1960. The recurrence of the theme over the duration of his recording career signals its importance, not only as a means of documenting real-life events but also as a vehicle for creative expression. The recordings no doubt reflect his choice of material in live shows over decades. As we saw in the previous chapter, Johnson's corpus includes songs about floods that not only depict the natural disaster but also the destructive aspects of response efforts, a human contribution to the suffering experienced by flood victims.

References to floods in songs function simultaneously on a number of levels. On a primary level, they refer literally to tragic events experienced on a fairly regular basis by everyone living in various floodplains throughout the South. Intertwined economic and social factors, such as poverty and Jim Crow oppression, resulted in a racially differential impact of floods, worsening their effect on African Americans. A Federal Writers' Project interview conducted in Tennessee in the 1930s with "people in shanty town in city river bottom" offers a glimpse of the reality of dwelling on undesirable land due to poverty.[4] Fan Flanigan describes the regularity of flooding and the response from people outside the immediate community:

> Oh, I tell you I've see that old river come up. And the gov'ment never sent us no notice of what the water was going to do. We jest set and see it come up. See it and know what we's in for. When it begins to git in the houses, we take and move everything up on the bank across the railroad tracks, and we camp there all on top of each other. Well, city folks come trotting up there gitting under our feets. Coming with soup kettle and kivers and half of them wouldn't no more set foot in your house low water times than nothing at all. I ought not to say a word against them and I know it. I 'preciates what they does. But it's mighty hard for them that's had it easy all they lives to know what 'tis to be poor.
>
> They's always one saying to another, "Do you suppose them people's got little enough sense to go back to them shacks when the river goes down?" And that's jest the little sense we've got—to come back to where we got a spot for a garden and a house we've built to live in without putting out rent money when you ain't got money for eats, much less rent. Yes Lord, we'll always go back to Shanty Town till the river rises some day and forgets to go down.[5]

The interconnected cycles of flooding and poverty do not allow displaced people to imagine another place to live. Flanigan's remarks expose the ignorance among those with money of the realities of poverty, such as the necessity of squatting in a shanty in a floodplain to survive. But this was the harsh lived reality of a large number of impoverished Blacks and some whites in the South. As James C. Cobb asserts about the Mississippi Delta, but which was also true of many other areas in which African Americans were concentrated precisely because of the rich alluvial soil produced by flooding, "Often frightening and always massively disruptive, floods were simply a fact of life throughout the nineteenth and early twentieth centuries—the Delta suffered major floods eleven times between 1858 and 1922."[6] Not only squatters near cities, like Flanigan, but also tenants, sharecroppers, and wage laborers lived in rural, flood-prone lowlands of major rivers and tributaries, usually near the most fertile cropland. Even minor floods required families to flee to higher ground. Rising waters meant grabbing a few meager possessions and heading for the nearest safe ground, hoping that when the waters receded there would still be a home to return to and land to work that season.

Regular flooding represents a real economic threat to African Americans across the urban and rural South, entailing loss of goods and sometimes loss of home, as well as invested labor. In cases when floods occurred after a first planting, they increased indebtedness for tenants and sharecroppers who would be charged double in credit advances that would need to be paid off from a single harvest.[7] Landlords foisted expenses associated with two plantings instead of one onto their bound labor force. This is one of the ways that the effects of natural disasters are magnified by racially discriminatory labor practices that shift losses onto those who can least afford them. In addition to the financial losses sustained, as Johnson references in "Broken Levee Blues," floods opened the door to other racialized forms of abuse, including forced labor and horrific living conditions in "concentration camps."[8] Such conditions led to disease and death, not to mention episodes of violent conflict. In the same way that crevasses in manmade levees exponentially increase the destructive power of flood waters, victims of natural disasters become victims of human actions that compound losses and suffering.

In the midst of disasters, personal losses of various kinds also occur: lovers are separated and families are broken up as homes are destroyed. People also die in rising waters, in attempts to repair levees, and as a result of disease and conflicts that lead to violence.[9] Within the context of songs about natural disasters, the multiple levels of meaning are overlaid and bleed into one another: physical, socioeconomic, and personal losses converge in metaphorical representational strategies. The storm and its aftermath signify danger and loss in multiple ways that lead to isolation.

Johnson adopts two different narrative strategies to represent natural disasters. In some songs he alternates between narrative perspectives, one general and the other more personal, while in other songs he sings from the perspective of personal experience throughout. In songs with alternating narrative perspectives, Johnson often begins with lyrics that paint a general picture of flood conditions affecting an entire population. In his cover of Bessie Smith's "Back Water Blues" (St. Louis, 3 May 1927, and Englewood Cliffs, NJ, 5 April 1960, on *Blues and Ballads*, [vol. 1]), her lyrics open with a distanced, third-person narrative recounted in the past tense: "When it rained five days, sky turned dark at night [2x] / And trouble takin' place, in the lowlands that night." There is no indication of the narrator's specific position, as victim, witness, or simple narrator of events that occurred in the past. The scene is set from an impersonal distance.

Much more typical of Johnson's narrative strategies, in "South Bound Water" (St. Louis, 25 April 1927) he sings from a first-person witness perspective set in an ambiguous present/past tense to paint the scene: "I live down in the valley, people come from miles around [2x] / Their little homes was wiped away, they had to sleep on the ground." In this opening verse, the narrator seems to distinguish himself from flood victims who lost their homes. Although their homes were destroyed in the past, he nonetheless asserts continuity through the present tense in the A lines (I *live* down in the valley). In "Flood Water Blues" (Chicago, 8 November 1937), he also opens with a general narrative perspective: "It's been snowin' forty days and nights, lakes and rivers begin to freeze / It's been snowin' forty days and nights, rivers and lakes begin to freeze / Some places through my old hometown, water's up above my knees." In this variant with snow instead of rain, as in "South Bound Water," the third-person witness perspective situates the narrator in the physical place of natural disaster. The continuous present tense of *It's been snowin'* hints broadly that he may be both witness and victim. Another variation, "South Bound Backwater" (New York City, 31 March 1938), deploys the same general narrative technique in the A lines before confirming that the narrator is indeed a victim: "It's been snowin' forty days and the ground is covered with snow / It's been snowin' forty days, ground is covered with snow / I'm snowbound in my cabin and ice up around my door."

The narrative in all of these songs moves from a general perspective on the flood to a firsthand account from the point of view of a victim. In the covers of Smith's "Back Water Blues," the second verse changes from a third- to a first-person voice: "I woke up this morning, couldn't even get out of my door [2x] / There's so much of trouble, make a poor man wonder where he wants to go." "South Bound Backwater" makes the same move: "I woke up this mornin', couldn't even get out my door [2x] / I was snowbound in my cabin and water seepin' up through my floor." The narrative strategy of "Flood Water Blues" is the most complex of the group. Opening with a general narrative perspective, it moves to a first-person plural in the second verse: "Storm begin risin', and the sun begin sinkin' down [2x] / I says, 'Mother and Dad, pack your trunk; we ain't safe here in this town.'" The inclusion of direct discourse addressed to his parents moves the site of narration to a present tense of the experience. Listeners are positioned to overhear the conversation about flight. A later verse returns to the general mode of the opening, to provide the response of "women and children" in direct discourse, from the standpoint of a witness. The shifting narrative stances are set within an overall frame of a deeply personal, first-person perspective. The portrayal of being trapped in the storm is intensely emotional and intimate: "When it lightnin' my mind gets frightened, my nerves begin weakenin' down [2x] / And the shack where we was livin' begin movin' 'round."

Subsequent verses of most of these songs find the narrator, either alone or with family, fleeing home in a boat. "South Bound Water" skips the intermediary step in which the flood victim is trapped inside, and abruptly introduces homelessness in the second verse: "Through the dreadful nights I stood, no place to lay my head [2x] / Water was above my knee and the world had taken my bed." The restlessness, danger, and desperation of homelessness echoes in all the lyrical treatments of the theme. From anticipated homelessness as direct discourse from women and children—"Women and children were screamin', sayin', 'Lord, where must we go?'" ("Flood Water Blues")— to first-person accounts of homelessness, the focus remains on the loss of shelter and home caused by the disaster: "Washed my little valley house away; there's no place I can call my home" ("South Bound Water"); "'Cause my house fell down and I can't live there anymore" ("Back Water Blues"); "Backwater has wrecked my cabin, and I can't live there no more," and "Washed my little valley house away, there's no place I can call my home" ("South Bound Backwater"). The final verse of "Flood Water Blues" even presents a kind of madness, born of fear and desperation: "And begin cloud as dark as midnight, keep raining all the time / I say, 'Oh, I wonder why the sun don't ever shine?' / And the way it keeps rainin', it's drivin' me out my mind." A departure from Johnson's usual smooth verbal mastery, the ungrammatical opening of the A line, as well as the breaking of the AA'B pattern, enhance the feeling of loss of control.

The strategy of alternating general and personal narrative perspectives in these songs enables the articulation of terror and homelessness as both personal and group experiences. Whether in an explicit articulation, such as "There were so many poor people, didn't have no place to go" in the version of "Back Water Blues" recorded in 1960 (on *Blues and Ballads*, [vol. 1]),[10] or through the implication created by the alternating narrative perspective, loss of home is presented as, at once, deeply personal and a collective experience. In effect, the alternation between witness and victim perspectives reflects a grim reality about flooding: many African Americans were often witnesses to the devastation, never knowing when it was going to be "their turn" to lose everything. As a narrative strategy, this alternation is effective at preserving the pain and suffering experienced by the individual. Whereas general narratives from a third-person perspective tend to be distanced and impersonal, this movement allows a collective experience to retain its personal character. Although many have the experience, the trauma itself remains individualized. Group recognition and commiseration form around the feelings of anxiety and desperation, but without the possibility of collective action to attenuate individual suffering. Paradoxically, the complex of feelings around homelessness is depicted as collective in the sense of being replicated among a number of fellow sufferers, but nonetheless isolating in its effects.

While some songs employ an alternating narrative perspective, others present floods from a strictly first-person viewpoint. As we saw in the previous chapter, "Broken Levee Blues" (San Antonio, 13 March 1928) uses a first-person narrative to represent the experience of a flood victim. The track's title references the levee rather than the water, highlighting the manmade aspect of the disaster.[11] The first-person perspective is particularly effective in establishing an opposition between *me* and *them* that draws a distinction between victims and oppressors. While the first verse depicts the narrator trapped by high water, the second verse describes an aggravating human dimension: "I wants to go back to Helena, the high water's got me barred [2x] / I woke up early this mornin', a water hole in my back yard / They want me to work on the levee, I have to leave my home [2x] / I was so scared the levee might break out and I may drown."[12] Flood waters block movement and encroach on the narrator's living space in the first verse, but human beings attempt to press him into forced labor to repair the levee in the second. The use of the indefinite *they*, who want him *to work on the levee*, signals a racial dimension to an audience familiar with the abusive practices of "relief" efforts. The next two verses also deploy this strategy of alternation between the natural and human components of disaster, juxtaposing being forced to flee home due to rising waters and being pursued by the police and jailed: "The water was round my windows and back and all up in my door [2x] / I rather to leave my home 'cause I can't live there no more / The police run me from Cairo, all through Arkansas / The police run me all from Cairo, all through Arkansas / And put me in jail behind those cold iron bars." Like the narrative alternation between a general and personal perspective in the other flood songs, here the alternation between the flood waters and racial oppression compounding the disaster also functions to both personalize and generalize the experience. The me/them opposition invites an understanding of victimization as a collective fate determined by race. By contrast, the personal persecution reinforces the isolation and individualization of the experience, particularly with the narrator *behind those cold iron bars*, foreclosing the possibility of group action beyond empathy.

The racial oppression and domination that magnify the trauma for victims opens the door to a metaphorical understanding of disasters in two ways. First, all disasters may be interpreted as devices for evoking all kinds of trauma. Desperation, anxiety, isolation, and loneliness are emotional responses to a variety of painful experiences. Breakups, as we saw in the opening section, but also poverty and the crises that result from it, can produce these same affective responses. Lack of money or eviction may ultimately produce the same results from the victims' perspective as floods: exposure to danger, food scarcity, and homelessness. Second, the referencing of the social magnification of the trauma around natural disasters also functions as a metaphor for other types of racialized trauma. As we have seen, floods enable a doubling down of forms of oppression and domination that are hidden in plain sight during times of ordinary daily interactions. Having the police round people up to coerce labor on the levees resembles the use of vagrancy and criminal surety laws to bind workers against their will on plantations. In the context of disasters, the use of police force in the service of coerced labor is more obvious and flagrant. In this respect, the representation of floods invites further metaphoric interpretation: not only are disasters symbols of other forms of oppression, but human responses to them are part of widespread racialized oppression and domination.

As we have seen, desperation, isolation, loneliness, and fear characterize the response to trauma produced by both natural and human causes. This potent emotional cocktail issues in a particularly virulent form of "the blues." The remake, "New Falling Rain Blues" (New York City, 31 March 1938), deploys the storm metaphor that we saw in the breakup songs combined with a personification of the blues to evoke the desperation of isolation. Although not a disaster song strictly speaking, the lyrics move from an impending storm to the torment of the blues brought on by loneliness and betrayal in an associative collapse of themes. The first-person narrative conflates a storm with powerful emotional forces: "Storm is risin' and the rain begin to fall / Storm is risin', the rain begin to fall / Trouble is breakin' down my window, blues breakin' down my door."[3] More menacing than "Falling Rain Blues" (St. Louis, 4 November 1925), where the narrator is simply alone ("I am all alone by myself; no one to love me at all"), here the blues are externalized, physical, and threatening. Closer to the lexicon and metaphors employed for flood waters, the blues threaten to invade the narrator's home. The remainder of the verses develop a narrative of betrayal and abandonment in which the narrator confronts the lover about her continuing attachment to her *used to be*. The final verse presents a variation of the simile in "Falling Rain Blues": "Blues fallin' down like showers of rain [2x] / Every once in a while, I can hear my baby call my name."[14] Imagined confrontation cedes to loneliness and abandonment. The emotional association between isolation, betrayal, and stormy weather allows for the metaphorical reflection of psychological phenomena in traumatic experiences and powerful blues. The response to both the psychological trauma of breakup and the intense emotions provoked by natural disaster are put into productive relation, creating resonance throughout Johnson's corpus.

Sonically, the flood songs deploy a number of musical techniques to add tension to the unsettling narratives. John Erby provides glissando and trills on piano to imitate the sound of wind on "Back Water Blues" from 1927.[15] Other songs use off-rhythms, stylistic tension, or techniques on guitar unusual for Johnson that distinguish the songs from his other work. "South Bound Water," with Lonnie and James both on guitar and Erby on piano, includes some competing rhythms and slight dissonance in the guitar parts. In "South Bound Backwater," Roosevelt Sykes's piano accompaniment to Johnson's guitar work creates stylistic tension with a contrapuntal line to the guitar in the fills. Verses 2 and 3, in particular, stand out for dissonant tonal moves and seemingly different senses of where the downbeats fall. The competing rhythms and tones contribute to the sense of a threatening environment, as each musician struggles to establish a sonic footing against the work of the other. The small combos enable greater freedom than solo performances to create tension both between instruments and through the use of weird-sounding fills. "New Falling Rain Blues," also recorded with Sykes, features stylistic tension between the performers, sounding at times like competition. Skyes's busy treble work with trills and triplets never quite supports Johnson's feeling of movement through swung triplet rhythms. In that song, Johnson's otherwise strong performance with rapid triplet arpeggios at times, is marked by a strange note on the first downbeat after the pickup, either a mistake or an intentional foreshadowing of the troubles described in the song. The overall effect of the musical setting enhances the theme of menacing blues by staging a kind of musical agonistics rather than mutual support. Finally, his later work on electric guitar in the small combo with Snowden and Marshall in 1960 features beautiful, idiosyncratic phrasing in the electric guitar responses that mirrors the artistic choices in the vocal phrasing. The sparseness of the guitar lines emphasizes the deliberateness of the vocal delivery, intensifying the song's meditative, elegiac mood.

Even as a soloist, Johnson's performance of one flood song deviates from his usual style. The use of a twelve-string guitar in "Flood Water Blues" provides a fuller sound than a six-string, with even more possibilities for creating differentiation between strummed and single-note patterns. The droning capabilities of the twelve-string complement Johnson's nasal resonance in the vocal, adding to the plaintive sound. Out of character for him, Johnson deploys an extremely repetitive riff in this song with an unusual, complicated rhythm that feels tripping and almost out of control. The other solo performance, "Broken Levee Blues," stands out for its adherence to Johnson's typical performance style. For this song, I can only speculate that perhaps Johnson felt that an unusual instrumental treatment would have detracted from the strong critical message in the lyrics about racial oppression. Whatever the reason behind the choice, Johnson performs his signature alternation between rhythm and lead, strummed chord and single-note fills, with some swung rhythms, without any unusual departures musically.

Overall, the instrumental choices contribute to the emotional effects of the flood songs. Whether achieved through eerie-sounding fills that mimic the sounds of a storm, contrapuntal lines, stylistic mismatches, or unexpected rhythms, tension builds, enhancing the feeling of anxiety on display in the lyrics. Loneliness and isolation are communicated sonically in some songs through a kind of competition of sounds. At times, the vocal seems to struggle to make itself heard against a busy background. At other times, as in the remake of "Back Water Blues" from 1960, the electric guitar's close mirroring of the vocal phrasing cries out in despair and loneliness, intensifying the message.[16] Ultimately, the performances create instrumental metaphors for fear, anxiety, depression, and desperation. Like the floods themselves that function both literally and metaphorically as representations of experiences that provoke panic and terror, the sonic environments enhance listeners' ability to share their feelings through a variety of techniques.

Separation, Distance, and Space

The disaster songs narrate tales of separation and loss along with accompanying fears, anxiety, and depression. Isolation produced by natural disasters leaves the self alone to face both physical and psychological hardships, sometimes compounded by racialized oppression and exploitation. The loss of home creates physical distance, leaving the narrator separated from family and friends. As we have seen, this condition is paradoxically shared, as it is reproduced among members of a group who are unable to come together to offer comfort and support.

The isolation and spatial separation caused by floods finds its corollary in other songs in Johnson's corpus that deploy spatial metaphors to represent the self alone in an empty space. The breakup song "Very Lonesome Blues" discussed above includes one of Johnson's key recurring phrases: "When you lay down on your pillow, behind you is *a empty space.*" The evocation of *empty space* metaphorizes the feeling of isolation from others by rendering it in physical terms. Some songs with this theme employ the road, both literally and as a metaphor for life, while others represent closed spaces of isolation and loneliness to conjure the pain and suffering of the isolated self in spatial terms. These songs represent loneliness as a physical distancing from others that renders particularly acute the feeling of vacant surrounding space.[17]

Like the flood theme, Johnson returns to the lonesome road theme at key moments throughout his career.[18] Modifying the 1927 popular song "The Lonesome Road" (music composed by Nathaniel Shilkret and lyrics by Gene Austin), which Andrew S. Berish aptly dubs an "ersatz spiritual," Johnson reworks the lyrics into several blues songs.[19] In these songs, the metaphor of the road of life is enhanced by a narrator who walks alone, sometimes explicitly toward death. In his recording of "Way Down That Lonesome Road" (San Antonio, 13 March 1928), Johnson evokes the journey of life in both spatial and temporal terms. The unusually repetitive lyrics for him underscore the sense of the tedium of life. The opening verses present the narrator traveling alone toward death: "Look down, look down that long, old lonesome road [2x] / An' look up to the good Lord jus' before you go / That's a long, that's a long, a long old tiresome road / That's a long, it's a long, a long old tiresome road / You'll find troubles and worry that you never found before." The series of repetitions in the lyrics—*look down, long, old tiresome/lonesome road*—and even the consonance with the [l], [o], [n], and [m] sounds, creates both a dark mood and a feeling of stasis, despite the theme of movement. The repetition of the liquid, vowel, and nasal phonemes contributes a sound of lamentation to the desolate theme. The sonic and lyrical repetitions give the impression that the road of life offers few distractions, save variations on "troubles and worry." Imprecations to the Lord offer no solace: "Then your days begin dreary down that long old lonesome road / And your days begin dreary down that long old lonesome road / And you will say, Lord have mercy, how much more further I've got to go?" The narrator is left alone to suffer and wonder. Even reminders of those who will be left behind after the narrator's death, as in the third verse, provide no comfort: "Then look back, look back, and see what you leavin' all alone / Look back, look back, and see what you leavin' all alone / To grieve and worry after the days you gone." Indeed, the impending death of the narrator is presented as contributing to others' loneliness: *what you're leavin' all alone.* The final verse fails to provide any closure: "That's a long old road, a long road that has no end / That's a long old road, a lonesome road that has no end / Then the blues will make you think about all your right-hand friends." At this point in the song, we know that the road does indeed have an end, despite what the narrator says. The final verse underscores the isolation and loneliness that make traveling the road of life feel as though the journey has no end, suggesting that perhaps death would be welcome. In the final line, the expression "right-hand friends" seems to denote those who can be depended on or trusted, but their association with the blues renders their status problematic.[20] The fact that the blues prompts memories of friends suggests that these relationships are in the past, no longer present to provide companionship. Overall, the repetitiousness of the performance, including many strummed triplet fills and fewer single-note responses than usual, reinforces the message of the suffering of tedium and depression produced by isolation.

Johnson reprises many of the elements of "Way Down That Lonesome Road" in "Death Valley Is Just Half Way to My Home" (New York City, 23 January 1930) and "Lonesome Road" (Chicago, 13 February 1942). In these two songs, he embellishes on the theme of walking by adding the detail that no other form of transportation is available. "Death Valley is Just Half Way to My Home" opens with a variant of the opening verse of "Way Down that Lonesome Road" that specifically references the narrator's feet: "Looked down that long, old lonesome road [2x] / My poor feet is getting' tired, but still I've got to go." In the second verse, the narrator declares, "There's no train to my hometown, ain't but the one way to go [2x] / That's mile after mile, trampin' that muddy road."[21] In these songs, the road is both real and metaphorical. The specific mention of tired feet and lack of train reinforces the solitude by eliminating the possibility of taking public transportation. Moreover, the reference to Death Valley in the title functions both literally and metaphorically to create a palimpsest of meaning in the lyrics. Death Valley was the name of part of the African American vice district in St. Louis, just east of Mill Creek Valley.[22] Since Death Valley is "just half way to my home," the narrator seems to live beyond it in an area not served by public transportation. Without a train, the narrator must return home alone, without the possibility of being with others. Moreover, the lack of train may signal a segregated neighborhood to which the narrator returns, indirectly evoking "transit racism."[23] The name also refers to the area, now a national park, within the Mojave Desert of southeastern California. High temperatures (among the hottest in the world), lack of rainfall, areas below sea level, and desolation characterize this Death Valley. Together, lack of transportation, the intimation of segregation, and the confluence of threatening associations with the name Death Valley conjure a treacherous road to be traveled alone. The sense of threat is intensified in the third verse of these songs: "It's just one thing that worries me both night and day / Ain't but one thing that worries me both night and day / There's a place they call Death Valley and it's just half way."[24] The narrator is plagued by a continual sense of dread.

While the final verses of "Lonesome Road" follow fairly closely the themes of "Way Down That Lonesome Road," "Death Valley" introduces new imagery and threats to the narrator. Empty space is evoked in the fourth verse, as the narrator passes through uninhabited areas and travels hyperbolic distances: "You can't see a house, in twenty-five miles around / I can't see nobody goin' towards my ol' hometown / I've still got three hundred miles to go and my poor feet is givin' down." Breaking the AA′B pattern, empty space and great distance combine to create a feeling of anxiety about not being able to continue. The next verse introduces the sounds of wild animals: "I can hear the wild cats and panthers howl when the sun go down / Can you hear the wild cats and panthers howlin' when the sun go down? / And I've got to go through Death Valley to get to my old hometown." Threats, real and imagined, torment the narrator as he makes this physical and spiritual journey through life. Johnson performs ascending triplets in the fill to the A line rather than his usual descending pattern, offering a strange note of hope in the desolate landscape. The delivery of the B line crushes any prospect for deliverance, as his voice cracks poignantly on *town*. The final verse of this song, like the others, provides no closure. We see the narrator continuing on his journey with "three hundred miles to go, trampin' in this mud and clay." The lexicon echoes biblical language, as he has "been trampin' this lonely road forty nights and days." But rather than the desert, the *mud and clay* evoke both the reality of St. Louis and the earthbound language of human existence. Nearly overcome by weariness, the narrator expresses grief and loss about his own life, even while he is still struggling to live it.

Johnson's ballad version of the same theme (with the same title), "Lonesome Road" (Cincinnati, 13 August 1948), which much more closely resembles the Austin popular song recording from 1927, employs a smooth electric guitar sound with a vibrato-laden vocal to recast the lonesome road in the context of romantic parting. With explicit references to religious salvation, such as "Look up, look up, and seek your Maker, before Gabriel blows his horn," the song adopts a narrative strategy of second-person address to a lover, Johnson's addition to the Austin/Shilkret original.[25] Johnson's addition of the lover enables him to depict the moment of leave-taking, in which the narrator advises acceptance and resignation in a mournful tone: "Don't hang, don't hang, your head and cry / The best of friends must part, why not you and I?"

The minor modifications presented by the romantic context and second-person mode of address only revise the lonesome road metaphor slightly. Grief and mourning still permeate the representation of the isolated self. But the new context does provide the occasion to explicitly generalize the solitude of the lonesome road of life leading to death and counsels simple resignation.

Other songs evoke a solitary existence without explicitly referencing the *lonesome road*. In a pair of songs from the 1940s, Johnson contrasts positive and negative views of traveling alone through life. In "Rambler's Blues" (Chicago, 13 February 1942), expert instrumental accompaniment from Blind John Davis on piano and Andrew Harris on double bass in a lively tempo provide the setting for a treatment of solitude as rambling.[26] From the opening line, the lack of home is expressed as freedom from constraint, enabling serial sexual conquests: "I'm a roamin' rambler, my home is in no one place [2x] / And I'll find a sweet, brown-skinned woman that really fills my empty space." Despite the upbeat message, the lyrics nonetheless invoke empty space in the opening verse, suggesting that women are being used to satisfy needs beyond the sexual. The final line of the song further confirms the suspicion that erotic activity merely serves as a distraction for deeper feelings of isolation. Here, the narrator admits that alcohol is his other source of solace: "I can get the best woman that ever was and I don't have to be in my gin."

In other verses of the song, the narrator boasts about his notoriety. "Known in every man's town" by judges, he also affirms his singular identity and happy countenance: "There's no other one can ever take my place" and "Judges all knows me as a man with a smilin' face." But, as in the opening verse, darker themes lurk in the lyrics. Consistent references to strong emotions being expressed by "birds," "kids," and "women" "when the evening sun goes down" hint that rambling may be neither fulfilling nor a choice. The allusion to Handy's "St. Louis Blues" and a list of others who exhibit strong feelings at dusk—*little birds begin weepin', kids all cry and the women scream*—suggest that the narrator may be projecting his own feelings onto them. The time of day intimates that being alone at dusk is particularly painful, as it serves as a prelude to a night alone. Behind the veneer of braggadocio about rambling lies the same solitary traveler down life's lonesome road that appears in the other songs.

"Drifting Along Blues" (New York City, 15 July 1946) functions as a mirror image of "Rambler's Blues." Treating the same theme from the opposite perspective, it unambiguously paints the darker side of life alone on the road: "I'm drifting and drifting, just like a rolling stone [2x] / No one to love me, no place to call my home / Life is lonely, when you have to travel it all alone

[2x] / I long for happiness; that's something I've never known." The most significant difference in the two treatments from the perspective of the lyrics is that "Drifting Along Blues" specifically names a loved one's passing as the reason for restless loneliness: "I had someone to love me, but they was called away [2x] / If they was only 'live now, I wouldn't have to drift this way." Although the final verse asserts that the narrator's solitude will end when he finds someone else, there is little hope expressed, and certainly no sense of closure: "Until I find someone to love me, I'll just keep on drifting along." Without love and companionship to anchor the self to a particular place, the drifting through life strongly resembles the sorrow and loss associated with the flood songs.

Finally, "Deep Sea Blues" (New York City, 26 April 1930) presents an odd stylistic and thematic amalgamation that ends with the invocation of empty space.[27] Elements of the musical style and tempo match Johnson's usual blues patterns of the period: moderate tempo, nasally resonant singing with vibrato, twelve-bar structure, and strummed triplet and single-note swung rhythm fills. The performance also includes Tin Pan Alley elements mixed in, such as chromatic chords, some "double-time" passages in the fills, and a B turnaround featuring a II-V-I chord sequence.[28] The lyrics begin with hokum in an odd, almost parodic catalog of sexual innuendo that in the first three verses moves from deep sea diving to fast cars to baking.[29] The fourth verse shifts away from double entendre descriptions of sexual satisfaction to the threat of betrayal by his lover. The narrator warns of the consequences of his own boasting: "When you get good lovin', don't never spread the news [2x] / 'Cause that's why I'm alone today with these empty space blues." As we have seen before, Johnson gives advice to others, seemingly based on experience. The final verse confirms that his talk about his lover led to her infidelity with a "pal," a scenario familiar from the cheating and betrayal songs discussed in the previous chapter. The first three verses of the song establish a context of playful, almost silly sexual innuendo that shapes listener expectations. The shift in the lyrics disrupts the hokum framework. Suddenly, the listener is confronted with the abstract concept of *empty space blues*.

Although the title and aspects of the musical setting clearly signal blues, the lyrics up to this point provide only lighthearted and meaningless verbal play consistent with musical elements that gesture to popular music. However, the second half of the song turns to the theme of loneliness and drops the double-time passages, adhering to a blues vocabulary, especially in the final verse. Following the mention of *empty space blues*, the penultimate verse of the song echoes formulations from "Very Lonesome Blues": "I don't mind laying down when I'm sleepy, behind me there's an empty space [2x] / But I can't get the one I love to fill that empty place." The conjuring of empty space is consistent with Johnson's associations between loneliness and nighttime. As we saw in "Rambler's Blues," anxiety about loneliness is particularly acute "when the evening sun goes down." Here, lying down alone creates the conditions for the experience of empty space. Being without a partner at night means not only being deprived of sexual satisfaction, but more profoundly, having to confront an experience of being alone. The unsettling imagery conjures not only an empty bed and a feeling of expanded space around the body (*behind me there's an empty space*), but also the suggestion that a space inside the self feels empty: *I can't get the one I love to fill that empty place*.[30] This formulation represents an embellishment on the earlier representations of space around the narrator, as in the flood and lonesome road songs. Here, the sense of emptiness seems to be both outside and inside the narrator. If traveling the road of life alone or confronting homelessness are experiences conditioned by outside factors that leave the solitary self feeling lonely and vulnerable, abandonment produces an awareness of something missing inside the self. The two senses of emptiness, both outside and inside, coincide here to produce a more existential threat.

Finally, the gorgeous late recording "Four Walls and Me" (Englewood Cliffs, NJ, 28 December 1960, on *Losing Game*) develops the theme of enclosed empty space. Rather than the open spaces of homelessness or traveling, here the emptiness is confined within "four walls." The guitar accompaniment is sparse, particularly in the fills, with outstanding phrasing, single-note work, held notes, extensive use of bends, and very little rhythm work. The lead lines resemble his work with Texas Alexander in the late 1920s and perfectly match the tones and timbre of the vocal performance with its heavy nasal resonance and extensive use of vibrato. Rather than homelessness, abandonment here leads to a feeling of confinement. The opening verse intones, "It's five o'clock in the mornin', just these four walls and me / Mmmm, it's five o'clock in the morning, just these four walls and me / I have waited and cried so long, my eyes so swollen I cannot see."[31] His phrasing and holding of the nasals in *mornin'*, the humming, and *me* convey deep sorrow. As in the earlier songs that emphasize evening, the time of day is significant. Rather than dreading the approach of night, here, the narrator has been awake all night and finds himself crying in the early hours of the morning. The night, whether anticipated or endured, represents the apex of solitude in darkness. The theme of empty space with intimations of death permeates the song. Darkness and solitude combine in the context of abandonment to cause the self to turn inward and face a space that conjures the ultimate solitude of death. If death hovers in the open empty spaces of homelessness and travel as an external threat, particularly at nighttime, death threatens in the enclosed space in its resemblance to a coffin.

In this song, Johnson does an outstanding job of developing the psychological effects of loneliness in the context of abandonment by exploiting the feeling of emptiness characteristic of interior spaces. The second verse expertly brings together feelings of confinement, betrayal, and death: "I have watched these four walls so long, the pictures seem to fade away / Mmmm, I've watched these four walls so long, the pictures seem to fade away / It hurts to be hurt by the one you love, to yourself slowly die day by day." Staring at the walls makes their details disappear, intensifying the sense of the emptiness of the space. Moreover, being alone and abandoned prompts an inward feeling of death encroaching. The enigmatic expression *to yourself die day by day* suggests that without a companion, death is slowly self-inflicted.

The final verse and tag line of the song render the emptiness concrete and specific: "When I sit down to eat, there's an empty chair just across from me / When I sit down to eat, there's a empty chair across from me / My poor heart cries out in pain, that's where my baby used to be / Mmmmm, that's where she used to be." The lonely narrator stares at a space once occupied by the absent lover and suffers. The specific empty space of the chair is both real and reverberant with psychological extension. The emptiness is projected out into the room and introjected into the self. The hesitation in the guitar line behind the vocal—the deliberate play with the rhythm—focuses attention intently on the message of the lines. As rhythmic expectations are thwarted, the listener is forced to pause and wait, in a kind of forced imitation of the narrator's loneliness and introspection. The rhythmic effect, along with significant rapid, narrow vibrato and extended nasal hums, invite the listener to join the meditation on emptiness with overtones of death.

Blues and Hauntings

The abandoned narrator experiences empty space both outside and inside himself. The psychological effects of isolation in an enclosed space in "Four Walls and Me" resemble the torment of haunting described in another complex of Johnson's songs. This group of songs, also recorded at key moments throughout his career, uses the theme of a ghost, sometimes explicitly identified as a dead lover, to meditate on isolation, loneliness, and abandonment.

Although at first glance being haunted seems distinctly different from isolation and loneliness, closer examination reveals that the other presence is an emanation of the self that exacerbates the torment of being alone. Parallel to the external empty space that is introjected to create an empty space inside the self, the ghost is a projection outward of the fear and anxiety that occupy the abandoned narrator. These songs implicitly and explicitly equate haunting with the blues, exteriorizing the state of worry, anxiety, depression, and helplessness into an outside force that pursues the isolated self.

In a first pair of songs, the narrator describes sensory experiences of haunting. "Lonesome Ghost Blues" (New York City, 11 August 1927), set in a cemetery, and "Blue Ghost Blues" (New York City, 31 March 1938), set in a haunted house, feature "a black cat and a owl," sensations of "cold arms around me" and "ice lips upon my cheek," and the sound of the voice of the dead lover to represent the feeling of a supernatural presence. Both songs open with humming, despite differences in stylistic treatment—"Lonesome Ghost Blues" is a solo piece with "Spanish" features on guitar, while the "Blue Ghost Blues" includes Roosevelt Sykes on piano, a double-bass player, and sound effects in a quicker tempo. Nonetheless, in both songs, the humming and imagery of the lyrics portray a lonely narrator in contact with the spirit of a deceased lover. In "Lonesome Ghost Blues," the final verse reveals that the trip to the cemetery is voluntary, as the surviving partner seeks to reconnect with his dead lover: "I'm goin' to the graveyard and stay the whole night through [2x] / Hear my dead lover callin' me and these lonesome ghost blues." Although he goes voluntarily, the previous verse voices the trepidation involved: "The graveyard is so lonely, times some I hear her moan / Mmmmmm, mmmmmm, mmmmm / And the ghosts is all so lonesome, please don't leave me here alone." In these formulations, it is clear that the "lonesome ghost" is merely an avatar of his own solitude. Whether physically traveling to the cemetery or not, the narrator experiences the pain of loss as a haunting, projecting lonesome and sympathetic ghosts as representations of his own mourning.

"Blue Ghost Blues" reconfigures haunting as victimization. Here, the narrator is trapped inside a haunted house "for three long years today," pursued by the blue ghost. The opening verse clearly establishes the tone of terror, as opposed to mourning: "Mmmmmm, something cold is creepin' around [2x] / Blue ghost is got me, I feel myself sinkin' down." Rather than communion with other lonely souls, here the narrator experiences the fear of impending death: "My lover's ghost is got me and I know my time won't be long." The faster tempo of the musical setting in the small combo, although it mitigates the sense of fear, enables the inclusion of sound effects of the lover's voice and the "doorknob . . . turnin' 'round an' 'round," rendering the haunting more palpable. The substitution of the characterization of the ghost as *blue* as opposed to *lonesome* hints that, as in "Lonesome Ghost Blues," the spectral presence is a projection of his own emotional state.

The earlier version of "Blue Ghost Blues" (New York City, 9 November 1927) adds threats of violence to the terror of haunting. In this treatment of the theme, Johnson deploys some of the same imagery of rattling windows and turning doorknobs and sensory experiences of "something cold creepin' 'round" in the haunted house, but here the blue ghost is more menacing. Indeed, after describing being trapped in the house (here for six months rather than three years), the fourth verse multiplies the number of ghosts with a plural pronoun: "They got shotguns and pistols standin' all 'round my door [2x] / They haunt me all night long so I can't sleep no more." Here, the terror is rendered concrete and physical in the form of weapons aimed at keeping the narrator trapped inside. Although the final verse returns to language that could describe psychological projections rather than physical threats—"The blue ghost haunts me at night; the nightmare rides me all night long"—it does not diminish the effect of the mention of shotguns and pistols in the preceding verse. The narrator in this iteration of the blue ghost topos seems to face real threats of violence from something or someone other than spectral presences. Recalling the palimpsest of meanings around "Death Valley," this haunting conjures racialized forms of terror that keep solitary individuals awake at night.

The description of the ghost as *blue* in these songs gains further elaboration in "Blues Is Only a Ghost" (New York City, 11 February 1931). The expression *blue ghost* is consistent with the interpretation that the haunting is a projection of feelings of loneliness from his tortured psyche. In this recording, Johnson explicitly equates the blues and haunting, tying together the phenomena of worry at night (something that we saw in the lonesome road and flood songs), insomnia, and torment. As in "Four Walls and Me," the narrator is confined to one room: "Blues leave my room and please don't come here no more [2x] / 'Cause you been nothin' but trouble ever since you darkened my door." Throughout the song, the narrator addresses the blues in the second person, imploring it/them to leave. The expression of the title appears in the penultimate verse as an attempt to lessen the blues' effect: "Blues, you only a ghost, you sleeps all day and worry me all night long [2x] / And then I'm left to suffer in my young life that's comin' on." It is unclear how understanding the condition of the blues as merely a haunting that descends at night will minimize their effect. But the young narrator seems to be concerned that psychological torment will continue throughout his life. The final verse deploys Johnson's elongated and melismatic, wavering pronunciation of *blues* to create a sonic resemblance between the sounds of haunting (boo) and the moaning of someone suffering from worry and depression: "Blues, please, let me alone / Blues, blues, please, let me 'lone / 'Cause you got me so worried, at night I can't sleep at home." At night, in the dark, as we saw in so many songs, feelings of isolation, loneliness, and desperation are particularly acute. In the haunting songs, a projection of the narrator's tormented psychological state increases the anguish of abandonment and solitude.

The Solitary Self and Death

The haunting songs deploy imagery and themes that appear in the breakup, flood, and lonesome road songs to represent a narrator who confronts the terror of separation and isolation from loved ones. Although the thematic reworkings of the theme of isolation highlight different aspects of the experience, the representations converge in their depiction of threats both inside and outside the self conjured in spatial terms as emptiness. The solitary self struggles with homelessness, insecurity, threats to physical safety, grief, and mourning. The terror brought on by the condition of isolation intensifies feelings of loneliness and vulnerability, particularly at night. The narrator, either alone in the dark or facing the prospect of spending the night alone, suffers from insomnia, worry, dread, and fear surrounded by empty space. Taken together, Johnson's representations of the suffering of the isolated self offer a meditation on existence. Distinctly different from the vast majority of blues that represent loneliness as a temporary state caused by a romantic or sexual breakup to be remedied by the next relationship, many of Johnson's portrayals throughout his career dwell on the existential suffering of the subject separated from loved ones.[32] The specter of death looms as the ultimate form of isolation that the self must face. The blues are neither temporary nor can close relationships remedy them. The treacherous journey of life culminates in a singularly isolating experience—death—for which companionship can provide only distraction.

Johnson's two early songs that focus explicitly on death offer two different perspectives. "Death Is on Your Track" (New York City, 19 March 1929), a duet with Spencer Williams in popular song form, warns of death as a result of cheating both sexually and in gambling. Its refrain reminds that "death is on your track." Although a novelty song, the final verse nonetheless warns that death is inescapable: "Death will surely get you, anywhere / Rich or poor, black, old, death don't care / Death is on your track, and you can't turn him back / You'd better pay attention, death is on your track, death is on your track." As a closing reminder, the lyrics depart from the earlier admonishments about immoral behaviors that hasten death to a general reminder about death's inescapability.

Johnson takes up the metaphor of the track again in a more serious way in "Long Black Train" (New York City, 5 August 1930). In this treatment, the narrator describes the engineer on the train of death passing him by as loved ones "board." As in the breakup, flood, and haunting songs, the narrator faces loneliness, abandonment, and solitude, here as a result of the death of others. Because the "engineer" refuses to allow him to ride, the narrator, as in the other songs, faces his mourning in solitude. He mentions losing two best friends, his mother, father, and wife in early verses, before representing his grief in the penultimate verse: "Train started off slowly, tears began streamin' down [2x] / I said, 'Lord why was I left in this God-forsaken town?'" The representation of the suffering of the sole survivor intensifies in the final verse, where he focuses on the loss of his parents: "I watched that headlight shinin' far as my poor, little eyes could see / Watched that headlight shinin' far as my poor, little eyes could see / Often wondered why mother and dad never sent for me."[33] Staring in incomprehension, the portrayal of the abandoned narrator here mirrors the other portrayals. Breakups, betrayals, disasters, and the death of others create solitude and vulnerability that prefigure the ultimate solitude in death. Life on earth, the "God-forsaken town," can provide no answers or solace in the face of the contemplation of one's own death sparked by separation from others.[34]

Johnson's bleakest song considers suicide in response to abandonment and loneliness. "End It All" (Englewood Cliffs, NJ, 13 July 1961, on *Idle Hours*) opens with the image of the rocking chair and the narrator threatening to "rock away from here."[35] In the second verse, the narrator is driven to suicide by the torment of being alone at night: "'Cause I've got rocks in my bed; my mind's going round and round / I've got rocks in my bed and my mind is going round and round / I might as well end it all and jump overboard and drown." The final verse completes the familiar complex of associations around the self alone in Johnson's work with an invocation of homelessness: "Yes, I'm driftin' and driftin', just like a rollin' stone / Yes, I'm driftin' and driftin', no place I can call my own / Yes, and my woman is in love with someone else; no one to call my own." The guitar solo is striking for its incredibly repetitive figures: the first six bars feature the same ascending and descending triplet run on guitar in a straight rhythm, while the following four bars repeat an ascending, gently swung rhythm figure, before a predictable closing in the turnaround. The repetitiveness of the solo seems to reflect the tedious and uninspiring life without the woman he loves. Absence of the other reverberates in the self, sapping any desire to continue living, here expressed explicitly as contemplation of suicide.

The complex of songs in Johnson's corpus that treats loneliness and isolation as either an implicit or explicit meditation on the narrator's mortality extends throughout his recording career. Numerous recordings from the 1920s, 1930s, 1940s, and 1960s that no doubt mirror Johnson's repertoire in live performance address the pain and suffering of separation and isolation. As we have seen, these songs represent a particular kind of blues in which the narrator suffers solitude, loneliness, and despair as a result of conditions beyond his control. Outside, the weather, homelessness, storms, disasters, the open road, and other people create situations in which the narrator feels himself to be alone in empty space. Inside the space of a house, with rain, flood waters rising, or ghosts, the narrator feels trapped and alone in empty space. The external forces that terrorize the isolated self only intensify the feeling of being out of control. Whether unbounded or enclosed, the empty space functions metaphorically as a representation of the narrator's abandonment and isolation. The empty space created by the trauma of separation makes itself felt in both open and closed spaces, a projection of a feeling of emptiness within. The isolation and emptiness prefigure the self's ultimate separation from others in death. In these situations in which empty space is unavoidable, the narrator attempts to come to terms with his own mortality.

Like many of Johnson's other representational strategies, this one is also fundamentally paradoxical. While other people might represent sources of distraction and solace, it is their misdeeds or deaths that create the conditions of abandonment and isolation. We long for comfort from the very people who inflict trauma and suffering. In the face of disasters, separation from loved ones, and the attendant fears and anxieties it produces, intensifies the terror of isolation. Even hauntings that represent the spectral presence of a lost loved one only inflict pain and suffering by reminding the narrator of his abandonment. Deprived of community, the self struggles with the terror of isolation. However, isolation also reveals a fundamental truth: while we may desire companionship and want to trust in the comfort that community of various kinds provides, we all face death alone.

The suffering of isolation forces a reckoning with our existential condition. Yet, characteristic of Johnson's oeuvre, this paramount, individualized experience of the terror of solitude, with which we must all comes to terms, is shared. Paradoxically, we are "together alone."[36] Even in representations that evoke the ultimate form of solitude and isolation, Johnson manages to conjure a bond of community as he creates a dialogue with listeners who will also face death alone. Despite mistrust born of abandonment and victimization, his portrait of the isolated self nonetheless harbors hope for the comfort of a shared experience. Like his invocation of an imagined community of "friends," whom he advises and warns about the dangers of social commerce, his paradoxical representation of the inescapability of solitude nonetheless calls out to a kindred suffering self.

The sonic portraits of the pain of isolation, as we have seen, take many forms. Most often anxiety and fear are represented in the production of tension through a variety of musical techniques. Johnson's timbre, characterized by strong nasal resonance and generous use of vibrato in the vocal delivery, as well as his phrasing, often communicate grief and mourning. The elongated tones carefully set off by deliberate phrasing enable a feeling of emotional expansiveness to develop in the held wavering blue notes. At the same time, musical accompaniments often provide contrast in the form of a competing sense of tonality or rhythm that further accentuates the emotion on display in the vocal delivery. At times, insistent single-note triplets, repeated riffs, and deliberate pauses in lead work underscore the pain and suffering on display in the lyrics. In the later work on electric guitar in the context of a small ensemble, the instrumental and vocal performances coincide to provide a sonic meditation on loneliness.

Particularly exemplary of Johnson's sonic representation of the experience of isolation is the gorgeous, unissued, solo instrumental guitar piece, "Woke Up with the Blues in My Fingers" (St. Louis, 2 May 1927). Johnson alternates between his own rhythm and lead work, varying the sense of pulse in the mid-tempo piece. The song features a riff in an almost duple rhythm with a chord on the downbeat followed by a single-note swung-rhythm figure that most often occurs in the opening four measures of the progression. But interwoven sections without the same regular sense of duple rhythm, featuring single-note runs, strummed and plucked triplets, and more irregular swung rhythms, interrupt the steady pulse of the music.[37] The alternation between rhythm and lead in this performance produces a sense of opposition between individual flights of fancy and a regular pulse. The regular pulse of the rhythm work creates a musical norm that conditions listener expectations. Deviations from the norm in the lead work thwart listener expectations, creating a feeling of individual idiosyncrasy.[38] Like the alternation of narrative perspective in the flood songs, here the contrast in rhythmic sense produces a similar tension between individual idiosyncrasy and communal norm. The regular predictable pulse of the riff is shared by performer and listener, while the creative moves exhibit the freedom of the individual liberated from constraint. In particular, the fourth chorus opens with a palpable sense of the elasticity of the tempo, created with slight holds on the longer notes in the swung rhythms emphasized with bends, which seem to struggle against the regular sense of time imposed by the regular riff when it returns, in this particular chorus on the IV chord. Throughout the piece, Johnson creates complicated swung-rhythm figures (e.g., end of the third chorus), single-note lead passages (e.g., middle of the fifth chorus), strummed triplet figures in a chromatic movement (e.g., middle of the sixth chorus), hesitations, and rubato passages that assert an alternative sense of time against the regular pulse of the riff. Likewise, his choice to employ more diminished chords in passing than usual in the piece creates a more complex sound palette, providing more opportunities for creating a feeling of tension. The mood provided by the diminished chords reinforces the "blues" feeling of the song created through bends and half- and whole-step moves. Moreover, they enhance Johnson's ability to play with tonality in a similar way that he plays with rhythm and tempo to reinforce the sense of idiosyncratic individual expression at key moments.

This struggle over time and tonality function as a musical corollary to the images of the narrator in empty space. Here, in a temporal-sonic equivalent to the narrator's isolation, the "blues in his fingers" seem at odds with the time-space in which they move. In the final chorus, the regular pulse of the downbeat is maintained through the first 5 ½ measures, before giving way to single-note lead that continues through the V chord in measure 9. The final measures begin to execute a variant of the regular riff with a descent to form a cadence, but Johnson then performs a quick ascent, which ends abruptly with a final strum. The controlled moves feel as though, and likely were, cut short by the time constraint of the 78 rpm recording, bringing the piece to an abrupt end.

The solo instrumental performance enacts the struggle of the individual to face the existential condition as both part of and apart from community. The rhythmic and tonal tensions and struggles in "Woke Up with the Blues in My Fingers" come to a sudden end when time runs out, but not before performing a delicate movement between an idiosyncratic and individual sense of rhythm and tempo and a shared, normative, regular pulse. In this productive tension, Johnson's music provides a strategy for representing our condition in life, facing death, "together alone."

Johnson's instrumental and lyrical representations of the self suffering in isolation find multiple ways of expressing a central existential paradox of the human condition. As painful as the loneliness of separation is, it nonetheless prefigures and perhaps prepares us for our ultimate reckoning with death alone. As we have seen, Johnson's various strategies for representing the dialectical relationship between the self and others deploy breakups, natural disasters, the open road, hauntings, and the blues to meditate on the paradox of our shared condition of isolation in death. In addition, his representational strategies, while they most often explore social and psychological themes, at times also incorporate references to racially differential forms of victimization. Mentions of impressed labor, physical threats of violence, and intimations of segregation ground the abstract existential theme in a concrete reality of racialized victimization. Together, Johnson's body of songs on the isolated suffering self sets him apart from other blues artists. His sonic palette and lyrical compositions create a rich, paradox-laden complex of songs that raise deeply disturbing questions about the human condition that offer no easy solutions nor hope for a better future.

Conclusion
Performance and the Socially Embedded Self

Lonnie Johnson is inconvenient for scholars for a number of reasons. As we have seen in the preceding chapters, many dimensions of his career call into question a profile, flexible though it may be, of the "blues artist," constructed by recording company executives, critics, scholars, record collectors, marketing strategists, and blues enthusiasts. While women (especially those who sang the "classic" blues), whites, and others are sometimes excluded from the roster of "authentic blues musicians," or invoked with a metaphorical asterisk after their names to mark their variance from a kind of cultural-aesthetic norm, Lonnie Johnson's case poses different types of challenges. Critics may debate the "authenticity" of Bessie Smith and Victoria Spivey, or the significance of hokum acts like Georgia Tom and Tampa Red or Butterbeans and Susie, or question Eric Clapton's identification as a blues artist, but Lonnie Johnson's corpus raises a different, although related, set of challenges.[1]

Johnson's early childhood experiences in New Orleans at the historical moment of the uneasy and vexed attempts to impose practices in keeping with the "separate but equal" decision in *Plessy v. Ferguson* determined that he was exposed to different performances of race and racialization than artists from other parts of the South, both urban and rural. Segregation was a very different lived experience in New Orleans, especially for musicians navigating neighborhoods and venues in a patchwork quilt of complex identities that posed multiple challenges to a neat binary opposition. As a corollary of the complicated landscape in terms of race, class, and cultural identity, the musical geography of the city also represents a kind of patchwork of its own. Signifying as a musical practice in early jazz and blues depends on the creation of a kind of collage composed from musical elements gleaned from a wide variety of genres and styles. Signifying in this context signals another type of creolization, as stylistic elements are brought together in productive ways by artists who skillfully combine, cite, alter, and invent to create new forms. Thus, musical identity, like social and racial identity, is a more flexible construct in New Orleans (and St. Louis) than in other places across the South. These practices of creative self-construction as part of performance led to a different kind of awareness of the signs that compose musical and also social, ethnic, racial, and class identities. Awareness of the various kinds of signs, and how they may be skillfully manipulated, enables a performance practice that adapts and changes in relation to specific contexts and conditions. These tools of the musical trade that Johnson learned in his early years in New Orleans enable him to change and adapt throughout a lengthy career that spans six decades.

As we saw in chapter 2, Johnson is a master of self-construction. His persona, announced from his first recording, "Mr. Johnson's Blues," takes shape within a lyrical and musical language that Johnson manipulates in a variety of ways. Significantly, his performance practice signals his awareness not only of various types of performances—musical, social, and personal—but also of the underlying sign systems that enable them. In the world of manipulable signs, meaning is never fixed. Although this enables deception and betrayal of various kinds, it also provides infinite possibilities for self-invention through performance. Despite the ever-present danger of falling victim to others' performances, Johnson's corpus nonetheless celebrates the endless capacity of artists like himself to craft a performance composed of many elements to elicit different responses from his multiple audiences. This celebration of the fluidity of meaning exhibited in self-construction differs significantly from the construction of the personas of other blues artists. Rather than the relatively stable invocation of lore, including mythic origins of talent (e.g., Peetie Wheatstraw, Robert Johnson) or claims to royal status among an implied hierarchy of performers (e.g., Empress of the Blues, King of the Blues), Lonnie Johnson's construction of identity exhibits a rare labile quality. His instrumental performances in particular, whether in the role of studio musician providing accompaniment for artists from a wide variety of traditions, or playing within a jazz ensemble, small blues ensemble, or as a solo artist, all display an uncanny flexibility that paradoxically serves as a marker of his identity as a musician. This fluidity challenges notions of performer identity, particularly within the confines of a genre like the blues, where a variety of factors, perhaps most importantly mediation by white-controlled recording companies, but also a scholarly tradition, contribute to relatively stable profiles for performers.[2] Johnson stands out for a self-consciously malleable presentation of identity across a lengthy career.[3]

The manipulability of sign systems and the concomitant lack of fixity and need for interpretation also enables deceit and betrayal. As we saw in chapter 3, Johnson's corpus represents a world of complex human social relations in which people manipulate appearances to exploit others. Johnson's depiction of social relations stands out against a backdrop of other representational strategies in the blues for its invocation of social systems in which human beings are enmeshed. His peculiar vantage point as a professional musician enables him to develop a critical perspective on the ways people become positioned in and pressured to perform particular roles with respect to gender, race, class, and ethnicity within broader systems of exploitation. In effect, the performance of identity has implications for the realm of social relations, as individuals are caught up in complex systems of interaction. The representation of social complexity in his songs enables Johnson to call out racialized forms of injustice more directly than most blues artists. His use of a typology of behaviors provides cover for, at times, pointed critiques, all addressed to an imagined audience of sympathetic "friends." These imagined listeners are taught strategies of self-protection from a narrator made wise from experiences of victimization. As a representational strategy, Johnson's depiction of social relations as webs of interaction conditioned by complicated networks of power deviates significantly from the more widespread use among blues artists of bad romantic and sexual relations to represent other forms of abuse, betrayal, and exploitation, although he also deploys that strategy at times. More importantly, Johnson's recurring address to sympathetic "friends" gestures toward an imagined community of moral individuals, while at the same time it cautions against trusting appearances, paradoxically advising honest people to master their own performances.

Widespread deception, manipulation, and exploitation lead, at times, to the decision to self-isolate and go it alone. As we saw in the preceding chapter, the isolated self struggles with separation from others, despite having fallen victim to others' manipulations. The depiction of the solitary self in Johnson's archive goes beyond the loneliness and depression occasioned by the romantic and sexual breakups of most blues. Although breakups do occur, their aftermath may also result in homelessness and desperation. These representations mirror his songs about natural disasters and life on the open road, in which individuals face not only homelessness but the anxiety and terror occasioned by continuous, sometimes racialized, threats to safety and survival. In the songs about hauntings, extreme blues, and the death of others, the narrator struggles with isolation and abandonment in a prefiguration of the ultimate solitary experience, death. As I argued, Johnson's representations of the solitary self invoke a conception of our existential condition. Paradoxically, we all share the experience of a solitary death; we are "together alone."

At the heart of both Johnson's lyrical constructions and his musical performance practice lies an understanding of the relationship between self and other that differs significantly from representations by other blues artists. Most blues songs stage romantic and sexual relationships as a struggle between self and other. The "other" in these representations, who most often wrongs the narrator-self, metaphorically represents individuals in other roles who also commit wrongs. In this way, a cheating woman can represent a cheating plantation owner or devious landlord who victimizes the narrator. The representations remain focused on the oppositional, even agonistic relationship between self and other. As we have seen, Johnson often positions the betraying party as part of a social network in which he or she performs a role. Rather than the oppositional dualism between two individuals (often enhanced by a third party to create a love triangle) that is represented in a great many blues songs, Johnson instead often situates his narrator within a network of social relations that constrains everyone to perform particular roles—as men, women, friends, rats, pimps, et cetera—narrator and betrayer alike. This broader social view that requires performances of various types proposes a very different understanding of all human relations. Thinking beyond the oppositional self/other pair necessitates imagining people's actions from a variety of angles. Individuals are viewed as embedded in a social world of relations that require performances that vary according to context.

This understanding of the self/other relation as embedded in a broader social world is reflected in Johnson's instrumental practice. His exposure to a wide variety of genres and styles and his early experiences in the family band made him into a very versatile player. Not only was he a multi-instrumentalist very likely able to read music, he had performed in a variety of venues for different kinds of audiences which required him to be adaptable and flexible. These experiences shaped him in a way that enabled him to succeed playing in groups, such as in touring theatrical acts, on the Streckfus riverboats, with Charlie Creath's Jazz-O-Maniacs, Louis Armstrong and His Hot Five, and Duke Ellington and His Orchestra. In these configurations his role is largely subordinate, as part of the rhythm section playing according to charted arrangements. Most often, playing successfully in these configurations requires skills beyond reading music and performing a subordinate role. Playing, particularly in the jazz ensembles, requires adaptability to tempos and grooves, being able to execute rhythmic subtleties that are distinguishable at the microsecond level and timbral variations on a spectrum from clean to dirty. As we saw in the first chapter, these different performances of beat, pulse, tempo, groove, timbre, and tone are highly charged in the world of jazz, where designations like "sweet" and "hot" create a spectrum of reception experiences coded according to race and class. Playing swung rhythms in particular styles or creating a two-beat feel as opposed to a four-beat feel signal meanings beyond the music. Indeed, these stylistic variations are signs in a signifying system which the successful musician must be able to produce with subtlety and nuance in different contexts. As fellow guitarist Johnny St. Cyr explained in an interview, the guitar is central: "Well, uh, the guitar is a rhythm instrument and, uh, it has a tendency to give a dance orchestra some snap. Gives it a regular snap. I mean, it's sort of a foundation to an orchestra."[4] Johnson's early experiences in New Orleans and St. Louis shape him so that he is able to execute these musical signs in ways that are productive within the group formation of the ensemble.

Beyond the ability to contribute productively to stylistically legible performances in a background role as part of an ensemble, Johnson also developed the ability to distinguish himself as an individual player. In a kind of intermediate role between soloist and member of the ensemble, he provides important antiphonal responses as a semi-soloist in Duke Ellington and His Orchestra's recording of "The Mooche" (New York City, 1 October 1928). In this intermediate role, he delivers short, clean syncopated chords in response to Barney Bigard's clarinet solo. Johnson's antiphonal voice on steel-bodied resonator provides important contrast and texture to both the tonal palette created by the long lines and bends in Bigard's low register solo and to Sonny Grear's insistent four-four feel on the drums. In the next chorus, Johnson contributes a single-note plucked line with swung rhythms in counterpoint to Gertrude "Baby" Cox's scat verse. Against the heavy feel of Cox's vocal, which mimics the sound of a muted trumpet with a kind of back-of-the-throat vibrato/growl,[5] Johnson's light, almost tripping, higher-register sound brings out the sustain and depth of the vocal performance. In these two choruses, his role is to provide contrast without stealing the spotlight, to enhance the qualities of the soloist through productive juxtaposition as a distinct individual voice within a group.

Almost a year earlier, Johnson had set a high standard for this type of role in trading twos with Louis Armstrong's scat vocal in "Hotter Than That" (New York City, 13 December 1927). The three-chorus sequence builds from expert transitions between the call and response, in which the "voice" of the guitar finishes the thought of the human voice without ever intruding, to a final chorus backed only by the drums. The first two choruses require impeccable timing to ensure that the voices don't talk over one another. The contrast between Armstrong's register and timbre and the high range and clarity of Johnson's single-note picked solo (that almost sounds like an electric guitar) produces a feeling of playful conversation between partners who know each other well. In these choruses, Armstrong's occasional held notes contrast with Johnson's constantly moving, eighth and swung eighth-note rhythms. The culminating chorus, in which Johnny St. Cyr's banjo and Lil Armstrong's piano drop out, leave the guitar and vocal to speak against only Zutty Singleton's drum part. In place of the complementary contrast of the previous two choruses, here Johnson follows Armstrong's lead. The guitar imitates the vocal lines, effecting a subtle transition from a more jazz-oriented interweaving of lines to a call-and-response pattern that leans more toward the blues.

But beyond perfecting antiphonal supporting roles, Johnson was also able to pioneer a role for solo jazz guitar, as in "I'm Not Rough" (New York City, 10 December 1927), recorded with Armstrong three days prior to "Hotter Than That." This ability to solo as part of a group dynamic no doubt mirrors other early experiences in which he played lead guitar or violin as part of a small group. As Pops Foster noted, "Lonnie Johnson and his daddy and his brother used to go all over New Orleans playing on street corners. Lonnie was the only guy we had around New Orleans who could play jazz guitar."[6] The recording with Armstrong bears this out. Johnson's solo provides contrast in terms of dynamics and timbre to the three preceding choruses that feature Armstrong's trumpet lead, and especially to Armstrong's and Dodds's interwoven lines on trumpet and clarinet in the chorus that directly precedes it. The sudden change in instrumentation produces a dramatic shift that focuses listeners' attention. The solo guitar executes the twelve-bar progression utilizing a number of single-note triplet figures with a very sharp attack produced with a pick. The high register guitar sounds softer in comparison to the volume and timbre of the trumpet, but nonetheless insistent against St. Cyr's four-beat feel on backing guitar-banjo. Chromatic slides in the triplets and swung rhythms contribute a "blues" perspective to the tonal sophistication of the progression as executed by this ensemble.[7] The decreased volume and relative simplicity of the solo paradoxically call attention to the power of the individual voice to command attention through deliberate phrasing and quiet emphasis.[8] As Gene H. Anderson writes, "'I'm Not Rough' is dominated by ensemble work rather than by soloists and contains an unusual amount of timbral, melodic, and rhythmic variety—mostly supplied by Johnson."[9] The contrastive chorus serves as a perfect introduction to Armstrong's only vocal chorus in the song. The voice of the guitar continues and provides a contrapuntal line behind Armstrong's vocal, as well as antiphonal responses. For the majority of the chorus, Johnson remains in the higher register, in sharp contrast to Armstrong's deep voice. But in the pickup to measure 10, Johnson moves suddenly and dramatically to a lower register, away from his contrastive role. The lower-register runs on guitar make a bold statement, competing for the spotlight, which to this point has shone directly on Armstrong. Moving away from subordination to momentarily challenge Armstrong's voice for the listener's attention prepares for the song's playfully rousing finale. The opening bars of the final hot chorus feature forceful lines from Dodds on clarinet punctuated by short bursts from Kid Ory on trombone in stop time, before ceding to a traditional New Orleans polyphonic style in the fifth measure of the progression. Rubato tempo changes led by Armstrong and playful repetitions finish out the remaining seconds of the cut. In this way, Armstrong reasserts his dominance over the band at just the moment the multiple voices return to express their individuality.

Johnson's role in the small jazz ensemble differs from that of the other instrumentalists. While the other voices, particularly the trumpet's, clarinet's, and human's, largely compete for the spotlight because of their timbre and dynamic range, the guitar's voice allows Johnson to move in an intermediate zone between the spotlight and the background, creating contrast and interest without stealing the show. Akin to his ability to seamlessly move between rhythm and lead in solo blues performances (more on that below), his role in the jazz combo also navigates across the traditional musical "division of labor." His solo, while it functions to focus listener attention, deploys the voice of the guitar with its dynamic limitations to introduce different textures and colors to the song at a pivotal moment between the opening instrumental choruses and the vocal performance. His deft use of blues figures, consisting largely of single-note, emphatic triplets, provides a relative simplicity and repetitiveness to contrast with the busyness of the ensemble work. His role, even as a soloist, differs from that of the other members of the ensemble. As a member of the rhythm section stepping into the spotlight, he displays a sense of restraint and understatement to amplify the message of the group by way of contrast. While showy and flashy moves on the trumpet and clarinet play against counter-lines and meters in the ensemble, Johnson's solo recasts the main melodic lines in far simpler terms that attracts attention for its deviation from the style of play until that point. Instead of the usual sense of a soloist pushing his way forward for a moment in the spotlight while players perform noisily as a collectivity behind him, one has the sense of a team player stepping forward while the others quiet themselves in order for this voice to be audible.[10] In a sense, his solo on guitar moves beyond the standard oppositions between soloist and ensemble, lead and rhythm, to create a form of mediation.[11] He may take the musical foreground, but in so doing he lays bare, in a way that other instrumentalists cannot, the cooperative effort necessary to make that happen. In other words, as a "member of the rhythm section" taking a solo, he reveals a more complicated dialectical relationship between individual and collectivity. All instrumentalists, Armstrong included, are part of a network of interlocking relations that enable the jazz ensemble—a particular kind of social group—to function.

Johnson's role as a guitarist within jazz ensembles resembles roles within the social systems that his lyrical constructions also highlight. His instrumental performances call attention to the prescribed roles within musical groups in the same way that his lyrics often categorize individuals according to types whose behavior is determined by social networks of relations. Rather than the usual individual-versus-collective dynamic that we tend to associate with jazz performance,[12] in which the soloist asserts a form of individual identity against the group, here we find on display an individual whose role is clearly produced by, and therefore dependent on, the collective. In other words, it is clear that the group produces a role for the individual to step into and execute. Moreover, this relation between individual and collective is dialectical. The individual also creates the possibility for a group dynamic. In Johnson's case, this is clearest in his subordinate role as part of the rhythm section. Moving between and among roles as soloist, antiphonal responding voice, and part of the rhythm section, his individuality is embedded in the collectivity and vice versa.

The complex self/other dialectic is apparent not only in Johnson's jazz performances and lyrical representations of social relations that we saw in chapter 3 but also in the processes of identity formation that we saw in chapter 2. "Mr. Johnson" is a self-conscious construction that depends on the gaze of others. Johnson's recurring form of address to a group of imagined listeners calls attention to the self's dependence on the gaze of the other. In that very first recording, "Mr. Johnson's Blues" (St. Louis, 4 November 1925), the only lyrics make abundantly clear that identity depends on the recognition of others: "I want all you people to listen to my song [2x] / Remember me after the days I'm gone." The tremendous emphasis in the vocal delivery on *all* counterbalances the significance accorded to the *I* in the lines, serving as an acknowledgment of the self's dialectical dependence on others. Mr. Johnson may assert his identity, but the lines recognize the need for others to listen and remember in order for the self to exist. As we have seen, the construction of Johnson's lyrical persona very often calls out to and, in so doing, recognizes the role of others in creating and maintaining his identity. But if the self is dependent on others for recognition of its own identity, the audience of listeners—real or imagined—is just as dependent on the narrator's call for its identity. Johnson constructs a community by projecting its existence in lyrical addresses to a group. "Men," "women," "friends," and "all you people" come into being as social formations through the singer's words addressed to them. Thus, the relationship between self and other, individual and community, plays out in complex dialectical ways in Johnson's lyrical formulations that echo the relations foregrounded by his instrumental practice within the jazz ensemble.

The recognition of the dialectical relationship between self and other, individual and collectivity, challenges the prototypical conception of the blues artist in a number of ways. First, and stereotypically, the identity of the blues performer is often understood as a distinctly unique and individual one, someone who is not dependent on social relations for his existence. Moving away from the constraints of sharecropping to assert a kind of freedom is often cited as a primary attraction of being a blues artist. Occupying center stage solo, hopping trains, hoboing, moving from place to place in a physical manifestation of his lack of ties, the rambling blues artist, particularly the rural players who are roughly contemporaneous with and one or two generations younger than Johnson, leads an independent existence. This image is constructed lyrically, but also through decades of reception that privileges the portrait of the artist as loner.[13]

As a corollary of this independence, the need for recognition from and, therefore, dependence on, a group of listeners is usually acknowledged only implicitly or obliquely. Many songs of the rural "folk" tradition feature lyrics addressed to cheating lovers in the second person that position the audience as eavesdroppers on a conversation, a technique Johnson also employs. Other songs narrate events that occurred in the past, often in fragmented and/or laconic ways, without an explicitly identified interlocutor. The past tense tacitly acknowledges an audience to whom the lyrics are addressed, although associative leaps make equally likely the possibility that the words represent a kind of monologue addressed to the self.[14] Topics run the gamut from failed love relations, alcohol, hard times, and run-ins with the law to current events and natural disasters. As we have seen, Johnson also deploys a generalized third-person narration at times, although with more cohesion and detail due to the sheer volume of words in comparison to most "folk" artists.

In order to better define the differences between Johnson and the tradition of rural artists, let's take as an example Charley Patton's "High Water Everywhere," parts 1 and 2 (Grafton, WI, ca. October 1929). The song recounts the events of the Mississippi River Flood of 1927 from multiple vantage points. Like Johnson, Patton also opens with a general perspective that seems to address an audience of listeners. But subsequent verses deploy spatial and temporal dislocations and introduce a series of interlocutors that only obliquely acknowledge the presence of an audience. Listeners are presented with both witness and victim accounts in a reportage effect with leaps and gaps from which to piece together a narrative. Patton's narrative technique creates a feeling of fragmentation and disorientation for the listener that mirrors the experience of flood victims. Places, scenes, images, and voices provide materials from which to construct a story.[15] As we saw, Johnson, by contrast, establishes a fixed first-person narrative perspective in the flood songs, even when he alternates it with a general one. The relative clarity of the events presented in the narrative positions an audience and, thereby, implicitly acknowledges its presence. If narrators in the rural tradition acknowledge an audience, it tends to be far more obliquely, usually gesturing toward an immediate context of reception for the song. Moreover, these tacit acknowledgments do not project a group identity or invoke an awareness of a broader social world. As we saw in "Broken Levee Blues," Johnson is even able to indict forced labor on the levees during the 1927 flood, something that Patton's song does not do. Most importantly, the rural tradition of artists like Patton do not usually project a collective identity for listeners in the way that mentions of *friends* and *all you people* do.[16]

Because the acknowledgment of the group identity of the audience is oblique at best in the rural "folk" tradition, there can be few if any formulations that signal the singer's dependence for his individual identity on recognition from others. Instead, the blues artist seems to appear sui generis, independent of the gaze and admiration of an audience for his existence. This privileging of a seemingly sui generis mode of production of identity would explain, in part, some of the critical resistance to the "classic" women blues artists of the 1920s. Women like Bessie Smith, Clara Smith, Mamie Smith, and Victoria Spivey, whom Johnson accompanied, appeared onstage not only with men backing them in an ensemble, but also with props in a theatrical setting. The context of performance renders visible the dependence on others required to produce performance. As a corollary, such a context also foregrounds its need for a group audience through advance publicity and ticket sales. This dependence on staging works not only against the perception of the "independence" of the performer, but also ultimately against the perception of "authenticity" that "independence" generates.

Artists who cultivated a resolutely independent, individual identity, such as Charley Patton, Son House, and Robert Johnson, did at times perform in duo and trio configurations with people like Willie Brown and Johnny Shines, but it is significant that the ensemble play is not viewed as constitutive of their identities as performers. Their collaborations are represented as casual, incidental, and occasional rather than sustained or organized. If they happen to meet up on the road and travel and perform together, they do so as long as it is mutually beneficial. The image projects no need for rehearsal or preparation: these men are viewed as fundamentally solo artists.[17] In this respect, their representations of themselves and the understanding of their performance practice deny the need for cooperation or assuming a subordinate role.[18] The lyrical constructions and reception literature foreground individual talent and downplay the ability to accompany and collaborate.

To what degree this sui generis, loner image is accurate cannot be determined. All musicians have mentors and teachers, even the "self-taught" ones. But the privileging of this portrait of the artist in critical and amateur reception is clear. Johnson's collaborative formation in small groups and ensembles already troubles any perception of him as "authentic" in this respect. His commercial success, a direct result of his early training, further problematizes the critical perception of him. Experience with the TOBA, B. F. Keith, and RKO circuits and the Streckfus Steamers parlayed into a lengthy recording career. Rather than the periodic encounters with record companies that characterize a great many blues artists of Johnson's generation, and the following two as well, Johnson signed a contract with OKeh that lasted seven years. His connection to talent scouts and other music professionals in St. Louis facilitated this coup.[19] The contract is significant not only for the kind of stability it provides but more importantly as an indicator of his kind of talent. His ability to work in ensembles signaled to record producers his capability to function as a staff musician accompanying other performers. This adaptability and flexibility as a musician runs counter to the image of the independent blues artist with his "own unique voice" that presumably cannot be molded to suit the needs of other artists. In Johnson's case, we have someone who can back artists as diverse as Texas Alexander, Keghouse, Clarence Williams, Clara Smith, and Victoria Spivey. The continuity of the contract with OKeh provides an opportunity for these skills to continue to develop, an opportunity most other artists were not afforded.

Johnson's skills as a musician coupled with the duration of his contract with OKeh provide the ingredients for a varied output, even as a featured, "solo" artist. During the first year of his contract with OKeh, in addition to his vocal ability, his dexterity on numerous instruments is on display: guitar, violin, banjo, piano, and harmonium. As Chris Smith remarks in the liner notes to the first volume of the *Complete Recorded Works in Chronological Order, 1925–1932*, Johnson may have been "anxious to show his versatility . . . [and] impress the company with his range."[20] This type of versatility is valuable to a recording company but not part of the portrait of the "authentic" blues artist. Critical and amateur reception has focused on ability to play one or two instruments, usually guitar and harmonica, as the hallmark of the folk musician.[21] Professional training and exposure to contexts with opportunities to develop skills on multiple instruments are not part of the standard profile. In particular, Johnson's skill on violin and piano runs counter to his image as a guitarist that defines his career by the end of 1931. Moreover, in the early OKeh sessions, between November 1925 and May 1927, he often records in a duo or small combo configuration. In the recordings from August 1927 up through 1930, he begins to appear as a soloist, while continuing to perform in duos and trios, foregrounding variability rather than unity of sound.

Changes in the personnel roster during this period produce differing degrees of stylistic complementarity or tension. To take just the pianists during the time with OKeh as an example, he likely played with eleven different musicians and possibly more. Ranging from relatively obscure pianists, like his brother, James "Steady Roll" Johnson, John Arnold, and De Loise Searcy, to slightly better known players like John Erby and Alex Hill, to seasoned professionals like Porter Grainger, Clarence Williams, and James P. Johnson, the collaborations display varying degrees of compatibility. On first consideration it seems surprising that the vaudeville and popular style material recorded with James C. Johnson, Jimmy Foster, James P. Johnson, and Alex Hill really allows Johnson's guitar work to shine. But on further reflection, it is clear that these musicians' professional experiences enabled them to provide opportunities for Johnson's antiphonal responses and solos. Even novelty tunes, like "Wipe It Off" (New York City, 8 January 1930), featuring Clarence Williams singing falsetto and the sound effect of a scraper, display amazing chemistry between Lonnie Johnson and celebrated stride piano player and composer James P. Johnson. The ability to complement, so evident in the jazz ensembles, is clearer here than in some of the recordings with the lesser known "blues" players. For example, "Sun to Sun Blues" (New York City, 19

January 1926) features rhythmic tension between Johnson's guitar part and his brother's piano part. Perhaps his brother's inexperience, desire to be recognized as an independent voice on the recording, relative lack of talent, or some other factor produced a piano line that competes more than complements the guitar part.

There are no consistent patterns for predicting musical chemistry in the Johnson corpus. Johnson's recordings in the early 1940s with Lillian Hardin Armstrong exhibit more tension than his roughly contemporaneous work with Blind John Davis, both professional musicians (fig. 7). It is difficult to know if it is greater familiarity with the blues idiom from recording with Big Bill Broonzy, Sonny Boy Williamson, and others, or just personal chemistry that enabled the boogie-woogie pianist Davis to leave more space for and be more responsive to Johnson's vocal and guitar than Armstrong, known primarily for jazz. Stylistic tension can be enormously productive for skilled players. Johnson's duets with Eddie Lang exemplify this kind of fruitful tension. While contemporary critical reception often pronounced that Lang "didn't swing,"[22] Rich Kienzle describes tracks recorded in November 1928 that "document Lang primarily as an accompanist to Johnson's muscular, articulate 12-string lead guitar. The two masters of their respective styles complement each other beautifully, with Eddie's solid, melodic rhythm work and timing the perfect frame for Lonnie's soloing."[23] It is indeed the sense of rhythmic tension that produces most of the energy, interest, and excitement in these recordings. Degrees of chemistry and tension aside, what is most significant is Johnson's ability to crank out songs with a revolving door of personnel. Even with varying amounts of musical tension or complementarity, he finds a way to work collaboratively to put his musical talent on display.

Johnson's work in duets and ensembles requires the same skill and adaptability that is evident in his seamless movement between rhythm and lead guitar in his solo work. Although seemingly simple to execute, alternating between the two parts is deceptively difficult, especially when accompanying one's own vocal. There is a natural tendency to either speed up or slow down as one moves between rhythm and lead, chords and single-note lines, producing a choppy performance. Johnson's dexterity and ease of movement is truly uncanny, almost unparalleled in the world of blues. Perhaps years of experience within a rhythm section produced a kind of internalized metronome that would not allow him to deviate from tempo or groove as he moved between solo and background behind his own vocal. In some respects, his performances prefigure the division of labor that does not develop in a systematic way in the blues until the post–World War II years. In particular, the Chicago

FIG. 7 Blues guitarist Lonnie Johnson and blues pianist Blind John Davis (John Henry Davis) in 1946. Photo © AGIP / Bridgeman Images.

sound of Muddy Waters' band, with its second guitar, formalizes the significance of rhythm work on guitar. But Lonnie Johnson is unlike Jimmy Rogers or Hubert Sumlin in that he executes both lead and rhythm parts simultaneously in solo work.[24]

Johnson's uncanny movement between rhythm and lead that never loses the sense of tempo or pulse, as I have suggested, indicates a kind of internalized metronome at work even when he responds to his own vocal or assumes the lead voice in solo breaks. The complicated dialectic between self and other manifests itself here as the internalization of the ensemble, creating a kind of common sense of time within the self. Like the non–sui generis portrait of self constructed in his lyrics, his musical practice exhibits a constant awareness of being part of and dependent on a larger whole. In a sense, keeping consistent time is a musical manifestation of the individual's participation in a shared experience. The lack of deviation from the temporal standard signals an individual who relies on the group for his sense of self. In other words, the consistency as Johnson moves from rhythm to lead and back again represents an imagined belonging to a group of musicians who establish temporal guidelines for play. Even in the most inventive performances in which his lead work plays around the pulse, return to rhythm work never deviates from the internalized collective norm.

Johnson's beautiful solo instrumental work also displays this internalized standard, but takes it a step further. Without the vocal lead to back and respond to, Johnson performs a kind of dialogue with himself on guitar, voicing both the "individual" and "collective" parts. In three of four solo instrumental pieces recorded in Memphis on 21 February 1928, he adheres fairly strictly to the tempo, groove, and pulse established by the rhythm part in executing melodic, single-note lines. "Stompin' 'Em Along Slow," "Away Down the Alley Blues," and "Blues in G" contain very little deviation from a metronomic sense of timing. The feeling of dialogism comes from the expert alternation between lead and rhythm in these pieces. However, "Playing with the Strings," recorded the same day, contains slight deviations in the single-note lead from the temporal standard established by the strummed rhythm part, making it feel, at moments, as though the individual voice is expressing itself free of constraint.[25] These temporary departures are followed by strict adherence to the sense of time, making it seem as though one voice is being pulled back toward a common framework. The tension in pulse and groove is complemented by tonal playfulness at times in the lead that also seems to pull away from the norm established in the chording. The dialogism between rhythm and lead makes it feel as though we're listening to two guitarists instead of one. But only one tremendously talented player could ever pull this off. The kind of synchronicity and practice required to stay together through microsecond-level changes would be impossible to achieve with two players. This dynamic of dialogism executed by a solo instrumental player voices the complicated relation between self and other that we have seen all along in Johnson's archive, only here, both "voices" come from a single guitar. His instrumental performance practice and lyrical articulations exemplify the idea that we have all internalized the presence of the other and depend on it for our individual identity, even in order to execute the idiosyncratic performances that are our "selves." Furthermore, this "other" is both an internalization and an outward projection. We are all, ultimately, together alone.

What fuels this philosophical sophistication, this dialogical/dialectical dimension of Johnson's work? In addition to the urban contexts that provided insight into the production of identities of various kinds and the sign systems on which they depend, and the experiences that musical group formations afforded, Johnson also ironically derived insight from the commodification of himself and his work. As we have seen, the social environments and performances as part of musical ensembles enabled an awareness of roles to be played and parts to be executed. Work on the theater circuits, the Streckfus boats, in public establishments, and for private engagements requires conforming to some degree to expectations set by others. The seven-year contract with OKeh, and subsequent work with RCA Victor, Decca, and King, no doubt intensified his awareness of the need to conform to others' expectations. Role-playing of this type, particularly in the service of marketing strategies, shades into a kind of alienation, where performers become aware of the need to execute a particular role for financial success. Given Johnson's first 78 rpm release, "Mr. Johnson's Blues," it seems fair to say that he chose to engage in a kind of self-commodification rather than accept one imposed wholly by others.[26] In this respect, he participates in another dialectic between self and other, but here, crucially, one that explicitly shapes his identity.

Viewed one way, commodification and alienation work against "authenticity," where authenticity is defined as a sincere, honest expression of self. Selling oneself seems to imply manipulating outward appearances away from some kind of essence or true being. In this respect, Johnson has been perceived as less authentic on the spectrum of blues performers, in part for his ability to navigate multiple roles. To some extent, this characterization is true: he certainly was able to perform multiple roles when called upon. But that does not mean that his performances lack authenticity. All performers engage to some degree in controlling appearances in order to stage the presentation of self. The idea of authentic expression of inner being on stage contains an internal contradiction that reveals its status as myth: the moment the internal expression is exteriorized, that movement acknowledges the presence of another, even if only in the form of another manifestation of the self.[27] In Johnson's case, musical talent, urban environments, and professional and commercial experience all combine to produce a performer obviously capable of assuming and executing multiple roles with discipline and artistry.

For Johnson, experiences of commodification and alienation fuel an examination of how the self relates to others that is reflected throughout his corpus. His work exhibits a rare awareness of the degree to which all forms of self-presentation, and particularly those to a "public," are mediated by others. Does this make his blues less authentic? If what you mean by authentic is unself-conscious emanations from an artist unconcerned with recognition from others, then yes. But his work urges us to reframe the question. Ironically, alienation born of commodification produces a sense of the complexity of the relationship between self and other, performer and audience, rendering "authenticity" of this type impossible. The question is no longer about the authenticity of the performer or the performance, but is now focused on the complexity of the process. Performance entails mediation, through staging, producers, and recording companies, who all exert pressures of various kinds to mold both the identity of the performer and the performance itself. Through this process of mediation, performances reach a public, who then engages in an interpretive process that further shapes the performer's identity and the meaning of the performance. What emerges from Johnson's corpus is a sense of this process, this give-and-take between artist and audience, individual and community that can never be stable or fixed. For Johnson, "authenticity" means offering a window into these insights about our social and existential condition. Rather than answers, his work poses difficult questions.

The philosophical investigation of the self/other relationship that motivates Johnson's work over a long and varied career leaves us to ponder our own role as listeners in creating our image of him. Stubbornly addressing a community and yet resolutely alone, the paradox that Johnson and his work present leaves us with inconvenient questions about not only what we recognize and value in "the blues," but also what we leave unexamined, cannot account for, or choose not to hear.

Notes

NOTE ON SOURCES

In the notes, short titles have generally been used. The full entries can be found in the bibliography, except in cases where the short citation is followed by "discog." in parentheses, directing the reader to the recording's details in the discography.

INTRODUCTION

1. Oliver, *Conversation with the Blues*, 122.

2. Due to pseudonyms, unlisted personnel, unreleased titles, and reissues, counting is complicated. The discography documents, whenever possible, matrix numbers, dates, labels, and catalog numbers for original releases. An obituary claims that he "cut more than 1,800 records in his time," which seems like an exaggeration. See "Lonnie Johnson Buried Quietly" (publication source unknown, but N[ew] O[rleans] T[imes] P[icayune] is partially crossed out in the Hogan Archive record).

3. Rich Kienzle writes, "Calling Lonnie Johnson the Louis Armstrong of the blues guitar could not be an overstatement, for Johnson was the single most important figure in establishing blues guitar as a credible instrumental style" (*Great Guitarists*, 12). It is not entirely clear what Kienzle means by "credible," although it may be linked to conceptions of "polish" and "professionalism." He goes on to assert that Johnson "had an impact on every other blues singer and guitarist during his periods of great popularity" (ibid.). B. B. King cites Lonnie Johnson as a significant influence: "Blind Lemon and Lonnie hit me hardest, I believe, because their voices were so distinct, natural, and believable. I heard them talking to me. As guitarists, they weren't fancy. Their guitars were hooked up to their feelings, just like their voices" (King with Ritz, *Blues All Around Me*, 24). Many scholars point out Robert Johnson's debt to Lonnie Johnson: Kienzle, *Great Guitarists*, 13–14; Alger, *Original Guitar Hero*, 98–99; Dalton, "Guitar Style," 49; Obrecht, *Early Blues*, 131; Garon, "Remembering Lonnie Johnson," 20. He was also an influence on pioneering blues guitarist Aaron Thibeaux "T-Bone" Walker. Chris Gill writes that a young Walker was "greatly impressed" by a performance by Johnson in Dallas, which would likely have been in 1928 ("T-Bone Walker," 19). His influence in jazz is equally significant. In the liner notes to Johnson's last jazz recording with Jim McHarg's Metro Stompers, Patrick Scott writes that his solo in "China Boy" "constituted a veritable capsule history of the guitar in jazz from Eddie Lang to Django Reinhardt. Both these giants of jazz-guitar, plus a third, Charlie Christian, are self-acknowledged students of Lonnie Johnson" (*Stompin' at the Penny*, 8; discog.).

4. Kienzle maintains that Johnson "used a steel-bodied resonator guitar to cut through" the band (*Great Guitarists*, 14).

5. The major labels for blues on race records in the early 1920s were OKeh, Paramount, and Columbia. "*Gennett Records*, a division of Starr Piano Company of Richmond, Indiana had one [blues] release" in 1921 and began expanding in 1923 (Tsotsi, "Gennett-Champion Blues," 50). Columbia bought OKeh in 1926; see "About OKeh."

6. A couple of weeks earlier, on 19 January 1928, they recorded "Harlem Twist," a version of "East St. Louis Toodle-oo,"

which had already appeared on Vocalion, Brunswick, and Columbia, this time as Lonnie Johnson's Harlem Footwarmers for OKeh on the A-side of "Move Over." Perhaps the change of title from East St. Louis to Harlem was an ironic acknowledgment of Johnson's hometown.

7. Dean Alger reports that a flood destroyed Johnson family records kept in a Bible (*Original Guitar Hero*, 34). Elijah Wald finds similar difficulties researching Robert Johnson's life and asserts, "I could preface pretty much every sentence . . . with 'it seems' or 'according to some sources'" (*Escaping the Delta*, 105–6).

8. For example, Mark Miller points out an impossible timeline and an incorrect recording date in Johnson's interview with Moses Asch (*Way Down That Lonesome Road*, 22–23).

9. Shute, "Our Brains Rewrite Our Memories." The study described in the article involved the role of the hippocampus in memory; see Bridge and Voss, "Hippocampal Binding of Novel Information."

10. Mark Miller ascribes most of the inaccuracies relative to dates and lengths of time to a desire to impress: "All of these things may well have happened. Indeed many of them most certainly did, though perhaps not quite as dramatically or for as long as Johnson suggested—ever, it seems, trying to impress" (*Way Down That Lonesome Road*, 22–23). In a similar vein, Alyn Shipton recounts a story about Danny Barker's transcriptions of Dude Bottley's memories: "When I asked him outright about whether Dude Bottley was real, or a figment of his imagination, Danny gave me one of his quizzical looks. Of course, he said, when he gave the original draft to Martin Williams, he'd added 'a little monkeyshine,' but the story was in essence true, and he had put it together from many accounts collected over the years" (Barker, *Buddy Bolden*, ix).

11. The name Lorenzo Joel Johnson also appears in copyright records for some songs; see *Catalog of Copyright Entries*.

12. Chris Albertson argues for 1894 ("Lonnie Johnson," 42), as does Alger (*Original Guitar Hero*, 3, 33) and Sallis (*Guitar Players*, 33). Big Bill Broonzy said that Johnson told him he was born in 1894 (*Big Bill Blues*, 118). Johnson told Mark Thomas in an interview in 1945 that he was born in 1889 ("I'm a Roamin' Rambler," 18). Samuel Charters also reports 1889 (*Country Blues*, 74), as does Arnold Shaw (*Honkers and Shouters*, 13) and John T. Schenck ("Hot Club of Chicago's Second Concert," 8). In general, the earlier sources cite 1889 or 1894; see also McCarthy, "Lonnie Johnson," 1. Johnson, asked to "straighten everybody out about my age," insisted he was born in 1900 in an interview with Max Jones in 1963 ("You're in Love," 6); and repeated the assertion to Max Jones in 1969 ("Men Who Make the Blues.") Steve Voce cites both 1889 and 1900, but opts for the latter based on Albertson's authority ("Return of Lonnie Johnson," 12). The birthdate of 1900 would make him too young to be playing in Storyville. The years 1889 and 1894 are both possible and would make him the contemporary of Ernest "Punch" Miller, George "Pops" Foster, Johnny St. Cyr, Warren "Baby" Dodds, and Zutty Singleton, New Orleans musicians with whom he played.

13. Johnson, "The Entire Family Was Musicians," in *Complete Folkways Recordings* (discog.); Alger, *Original Guitar Hero*, 37; Sallis, *Guitar Players*, 33; Cressing, "Profile," 15. Some sources say that there were thirteen children in the family; see, for example, Swenson, "Masters of Louisiana Music," 20; Dicaire, *Blues Singers*, 226; and Albertson, "Lonnie Johnson," 42.

14. Johnson, "The Entire Family Was Musicians," in *Complete Folkways Recordings* (discog.). Cressing's profile in *Jazz Journal* from 1951 specifies, "Papa played the violin, mama played the piano" (15).

15. Miller, "Interview." Jazz scholar Burton W. Peretti mistakenly claims that Johnson was from Raceland, crediting his contribution to early jazz to his "rural" origins (*Creation of Jazz*, 18).

16. Al Rose, *Storyville*, 73. Court Carney reports that musicians had begun to leave in the 1890s ("New Orleans," 310).

17. Bob Riesman demonstrates that Broonzy most likely "did not enter the U.S. Army in 1917, did not travel to France to serve in World War I, and did not personally experience the humiliations of black veterans returning from Europe" (*I Feel So Good*, 33).

18. See Rye, "Southern Syncopated Orchestra," 228. Johnson likely worked with Glenn and Jenkins later, from 1922 to 1924 (Cullen with Hackman and McNeilly, *Vaudeville Old and New*, 1:572).

19. Alger, *Original Guitar Hero*, 52–53.

20. Kienzle mentions work in theaters, on riverboats, and as a solo artist (*Great Guitarists*, 13).

21. Mark Miller, *Way Down That Lonesome Road*, 26.

22. Oliver, *Conversation with the Blues*, 140. Johnson likely conflates theater associations and timelines here.

23. Mark Miller cites a review of the blackface show from 1922 that does not mention Johnson by name (*Way Down That Lonesome Road*, 26).

24. On the history of the Theater Owners Booking Association, see Abbott and Seroff, *Original Blues*, 231–48; and Harrison, *Black Pearls*, 23. Prior to the formation of the TOBA, Black vaudeville theaters and other venues existed, such as Saloon-Theaters and Park Pavilions (Abbott and Seroff, *Original Blues*, 7–66).

25. Abbott and Seroff, *Original Blues*, 246–47.

26. Oliver, *Conversation with the Blues*, 140.

27. George-Graves, *Royalty of Negro Vaudeville*, xi, 127; Cullen with Hackman and McNeilly, *Vaudeville Old and New*, 1:709.

28. Streckfus, "Interview."

29. Foster with Stoddard, *Pops Foster*, 109–11. See also Chevan, "Riverboat Music," 154, 160.

30. St. Cyr performed summer seasons in New Orleans and winter seasons in St. Louis before "tramp" trips began, requiring musicians to stay on the boats as they traveled up and down the river performing ("Interview").

31. Oliver, *Conversation with the Blues*, 107.

32. Kenney, *Jazz on the River*, 102–3. The *St. Paul* was one of the smaller boats operated in the summer. Verne Streckfus specified that "colored bands" were on the "cheap boats" and "white bands" were on "deluxe boats" ("Interview").

33. Thomas claims that Johnson played on the steamers from 1919 until 1922 ("I'm a Roamin' Rambler," 19). Chevan documents that Creath took over in the early 1920s and continued until moving to Chicago in 1936 ("Riverboat Music," 167). Johnson recorded with Charles Creath's Jazz-O-Maniacs in November 1925, indicating that he had an ongoing relationship with him.

34. The Booker T. Washington Theater was located at Twenty-Third and Market Streets, two blocks from Union Station. It was owned by Charles Turpin, brother of Tom Turpin, who owned the Rosebud Café, home of ragtime piano. On the Turpins, see John J. Wright, *African Americans in Downtown St. Louis*, 44–45; Owsley, *City of Gabriels*, 7; and Young, "Your St. Louis and Mine," 345.

35. John J. Wright, *African Americans in Downtown St. Louis*, 45.

36. Oliver, *Conversation with the Blues*, 122.

37. Kenney, *Jazz on the River*, 102–3; Spivey, "Blues Is My Business," 9; Ward and Huber, *A&R Pioneers*, 256.

38. Johnson claimed in interviews to have won the contest eighteen weeks in a row. This cannot be substantiated and, based on contemporaneous newspaper accounts, Mark Miller casts considerable doubt on it (*Way Down That Lonesome Road*, 28).

39. At some point, likely in 1925, he became involved with Mary Smith, a blues singer originally from Mississippi. They may

have officially married, as she adopted the name Mary Johnson, or she may have been his common-law wife. Oliver interviewed her (*Conversation with the Blues*, 121, 178).

40. Obrecht discusses the recording sessions with Gennett in April 1927, the last time the Johnson brothers recorded together (*Early Blues*, 141–42). Alger believes he stayed in Texas beyond May, performing in Dallas (*Original Guitar Hero*, 132).

41. Alger contends that he moved to Philadelphia in fall 1929 before moving to New York (*Original Guitar Hero*, 162). Chris Smith believes they moved to New York as early as 1927 (liner notes, in Johnson, *Complete Recorded Works in Chronological Order, 1925–1932*, vol. 2; discog.).

42. Foster played with Charlie Creath's Jazz-O-Maniacs on the *St. Paul* in 1921 and 1923–25; see Foster, *Pops Foster*, 178.

43. OKeh was headquartered in New York, but "between 1923 and the end of 1926 ... [its] recording crew went repeatedly to Atlanta, to Charlotte and Asheville, to Dallas and San Antonio, to New Orleans, to Kansas City and St. Louis, to Detroit, and to Cincinnati" (Mazor, *Ralph Peer*, 57). Charters reproduces part of a story in a Dallas newspaper that mentions a held-over show by Johnson there (*Country Blues*, 78–79).

44. Eddie Lang was a pseudonym for Salvatore Massaro, a guitarist who also began on violin. For recordings with Johnson he used the name Blind Willie Dunn. For more on Lang, see Obrecht, *Early Blues*, 156–57; Kienzle, *Great Guitarists*, 133–36; Sallis, *Guitar Players*, 53–75; Sallis, "Eddie Lang," 20–32; and Hadlock, *Jazz Masters*, 239–55.

45. See *Catalog of Copyright Entries*. Copyrights are for unpublished songs, words and melody. Any "mechanical reproduction" royalties for covers would have gone to the copyright holder.

46. Victoria Spivey, also scouted by Johnson, accused him of copyrighting her songs under his own name and thereby "stealing" her royalties (Ward and Huber, *A&R Pioneers*, 92).

47. Composition of "Tin Can Alley Blues" was credited to Porter Grainger and Lonnie Johnson, but copyright was registered to Grainger on 15 December 1927.

48. The only exception during this period was "Bullfrog Moan," a piece for which he shared co-composer credit with Eddie Lang, but copyright was registered to Lang. The other co-authored pieces, "Two Tone Stomp" and "A Handful of Riffs," were registered to Johnson.

49. The Copyright Act of 1909 granted "'mechanical royalties' from the record manufacturers to the music copyright holders" for originals and covers (Kenney, *Recorded Music*, 31).

50. Foster, *Pops Foster*, 100. Clarence Williams later moved to New York and "set up a new publishing company at 1547 Broadway, the same building that housed W. C. Handy's publishing firm, Bert Williams's, and Perry Bradford's" (Mazor, *Ralph Peer*, 43).

51. Ralph Peer, A&R man for OKeh, persuaded the record company to "buy and own the full song copyrights for songs they recorded, an added incentive for the company to promote the songs, as well as a revenue stream" (Mazor, *Ralph Peer*, 70).

52. Bill Dahl claims that two of Lonnie Johnson's songs, "Love Story Blues" and "Falling Rain Blues," were published as sheet music, but the copyright records in the Library of Congress indicate that they were unpublished (*Art of the Blues*, 15).

53. Chris Albertson cites comments by Bessie Smith's niece that "it was a constant thing to see Lonnie coming in and out of Bessie's stateroom, and he kept her company the whole tour." For his part, Johnson said in a 1957 interview, "She was sweet on me, but we never got real serious—Bessie had too many things going for her" (*Bessie*, 167).

54. Taylor, "Roots of Route 66." Andrew S. Berish discusses the difficulties encountered by touring bands even in the 1940s (*Lonesome Roads*, 101–3).

55. OKeh was bought out by Columbia in 1926 ("About OKeh"); Columbia used

the Vocalion label until CBS changed the name to OKeh in 1940.

56. Charters, *Country Blues*, 83; Alger, *Original Guitar Hero*, 163–65; Chris Smith, liner notes, in Johnson, *Complete Recorded Works in Chronological Order: 1937–1947*, vol. 1 (discog.). Obrecht believes that he may have worked with Glenn and Jenkins again in the mid-1930s (*Early Blues*, 167).

57. Quotation from Johnson, "The Entire Family Was Musicians," in *Complete Folkways Recordings* (discog.); other information from Alger, *Original Guitar Hero*, 170–72.

58. A recording ban resulting from a dispute about royalties coincided with materials shortages during World War II, halting production. During this period, Johnson was out on the road playing one-nighters (Smith, liner notes, in Johnson, *Complete Recorded Works in Chronological Order: 1937–1947*, vol. 3; discog.).

59. Obrecht, *Early Blues*, 169, 171; Alger, *Original Guitar Hero*, 185, 188. Regarding the parenthetical track information, such citations provide a track's place and date of recording; label, matrix, and release dates are listed in the discography.

60. Victoria Malawey classifies together different effects achieved through pressed or tense phonation producing vibration in the vocal track that are often described as "noise" (*Blaze of Light*, 102–3).

61. On vocal fold vibration, see Heidemann, "System," paragraphs 3.3–3.5.

62. Copyrights are registered to Wabash Music Co. of Chicago, Evergreen Park, Illinois, and Tucson, Arizona, all owned by Melrose, and one to Melrose himself. Melrose was notorious for exploiting musicians, even advancing money to Big Bill Broonzy on credit against his royalties until the musician was in debt (Riesman, *I Feel So Good*, 80–81, 108–9).

63. Clark Halker reports that the union voted a uniform pay scale for club and recording work in 1938 ("History of Local 208," 211–13). The union was not integrated until 1966 ("Chicago Federation of Musicians"). Alger documents Johnson's membership card from 1944 (*Original Guitar Hero*, 33).

64. Charles Keil discusses Phil Chess's exploitative practices in spite of the union (*Urban Blues*, 83–84, 86).

65. Alger, *Original Guitar Hero*, 178.

66. Halker cites a member of the local quoted in *Downbeat* in 1940, saying "Local 208 has the same problems to face as all the locals in the country have. Scale? Hell, here's a recording contract of one of our members from Columbia. He'll receive the regular price—$30 for four sides in three hours, and $7.50 for overtime. Scale is scale in this town, regardless of color" ("History of Local 208," 213). As a point of comparison, St. Cyr reports that artists received $50 a side in the 1920s at OKeh in Chicago ("Interview").

67. Oliver, *Conversation with the Blues*, 153. Chris Smith also mentions club work (liner notes, in Johnson, *Complete Recorded Works in Chronological Order: 1937 to 1947*, vol. 1; discog.). On club work in Chicago, see also Sallis, *Guitar Players*, 44–46.

68. Johnson also made three recordings in 1948 for Paradise in Detroit, a small R&B label, including "Tomorrow Night."

69. "Lonnie Johnson," 227 (*AMG All Music Guide*). Johnson reported to Valerie Wilmer that he received a first check for $41,000 for the song ("Lonnie Johnson," 7).

70. "Pleasing You (As Long as I Live)" reached number 2 in 1948 and "So Tired" reached number 9 in 1949 on the R&B chart, while "Confused" made it to number 11 in 1950. On Johnson's work at King, see Fox, *King of the Queen City*, 138–39. Despite the ballads, the vocal quality in the recordings is uneven with respect to capturing detail and depth, but the ballads prominently feature the vocal in the mix.

71. Nathan claimed co-songwriting credit under the pseudonym Lois Mann for many compositions by his artists, but not Johnson. In addition to King Records, he had

"a recording studio, a pressing plant to manufacture records, a printing plant to print the record covers and promotional materials, a national sales and distribution network . . . , a trucking company . . . and even a line of record players" (Fox, *King of the Queen City*, 50).

72. Oliver, *Conversation with the Blues*, 122; *Catalog of Copyright Entries*, 63. Johnson married for a second time in the early 1940s (Alger, *Original Guitar Hero*, 194).

73. After leaving King, Johnson recorded four songs for Rama Records in New York (Pearlin, liner notes, in Johnson, *Very Best of Lonnie Johnson*; discog.). Johnson appeared at Royal Festival Hall in a visit organized by the National Jazz Federation (see Mike Rowe's liner notes to *The American Folk-Blues Festival DVD*). See also Obrecht, *Early Blues*, 175; Jones, "Men Who Make the Blues"; Wilmer, "Lonnie Johnson," 5; Dicaire, *Blues Singers*, 228; and Albertson, who describes the tour as part of the "'Trad' fever" ("Lonnie Johnson," 47).

74. Alger, *Original Guitar Hero*, 210–12.

75. For Albertson's own account, see "Lonnie Johnson," 38–42. See also Alger, *Original Guitar Hero*, 216–177; Mark Miller, *Way Down That Lonesome Road*, 39; Kienzle, *Great Guitarists*, 15; Obrecht, *Early Blues*, 176; and Sallis, *Guitar Players*, 48–49.

76. Because Charters was guided by 78 rpm record sales figures, he includes a discussion of Lonnie Johnson (*Country Blues*, 73–85).

77. There was also a release of an informal "living room" session held at Bernie Strassberg's house in Forest Hills, Queens, in 1965, released as Johnson, *Unsung Blues Legend* (discog.). Guitarist Elmer Snowden had a substantial jazz background, having played with Ellington, Count Basie, Jimmy Lunceford, and Chick Webb, among others. He, like Johnson, also backed Bessie Smith (Albertson, liner notes, in Johnson, with Snowden, *Blues, Ballads, and Jumpin' Jazz*; discog.).

78. The Smithsonian acquired Folkways Records in 1987 ("Moses Asch"; "Folkways Records").

79. Copyrights were granted to Duchess Music Corp., O-Cal Publishing Co., Prestige Music Co., and MCA Music.

80. For a critical discussion of the problematic framing of blues in the context of revivalist tours, see Cole, "Mastery and Masquerade."

81. Jones, "You're in Love," 6.

82. Mark Miller, *Way Down That Lonesome Road*, 40–41; Obrecht, *Early Blues*, 184.

83. Goddard, "Final Years of Lonnie Johnson," 33; Mark Miller, *Way Down That Lonesome Road*, 64–67.

84. Mark Miller, *Way Down That Lonesome Road*, 74–76.

85. Ibid., 105–6, 112; Obrecht, *Early Blues*, 186; Garon, "Remembering Lonnie Johnson," 20.

86. Bobby "Blue" Bland, Guy, and a local blues band also performed (Goddard, "Final Years of Lonnie Johnson," 36). The obituary in *Coda* describes the final appearance as "a triumph" ("Lonnie Johnson," 31). Johnson was occasionally invited up to perform by local bands when he dropped into clubs after that, including in May 1970 (Mark Miller, *Way Down That Lonesome Road*, 117–20, 124–25).

87. Mark Miller, *Way Down That Lonesome Road*, 127–28.

88. It can also be a "body of written or spoken material upon which a linguistic analysis is based" (*OED Online* [Oxford University Press, June 2021, https://www-oed-com/, s.v. "corpus").

89. Citing jazz pianist Paul Bley, Benjamin Givan argues for going a step further and imagining an artist's "oeuvre as a single piece, and the oeuvre is a lifetime" ("Gunther Schuller," 228).

90. In the mid-nineteenth century, literary scholars began producing concordances for authors with large corpora, such

as Horace, Shakespeare, and Balzac, or canonical poets, such as Shelley and Wordsworth, as well as lexicons and dictionaries as reference works for authors as diverse as Molière and Thackeray. Before digitization, this scholarly production attests to the recognition of the value and significance of the corpus as a whole, as well as its importance to the analysis of individual works.

91. By setting aside, I do not mean negating, as in the position articulated by Christopher Small that "blues, jazz, rock, and so on, are not separate musical categories" (*Music of the Common Tongue*, 5).

92. Dalton, "Guitar Style," 49.

93. Chris Sheridan credits his phrasing on guitar to his early training on violin, citing his use of "arpeggios and various voicings" ("Chapters in Jazz," 16).

94. Raeburn, "Confessions," 310.

95. Compare Toynbee's argument for understanding genre as "social process" (*Making Popular Music*, 103).

96. Barker, *Life in Jazz*, 28.

97. Foster, *Pops Foster*, 41. In African American Vernacular English, "dicty" means high class, snobbish, or pretentious. St. Cyr corroborates Foster's assessment of Robichaux's music ("Interview").

98. Hersch, *Subversive Sounds*, 42, quoting Morton and Lomax, "Library of Congress Narrative."

99. Barker, *Life in Jazz*, 12.

100. Armstrong, *Satchmo*, 58. Bunk Johnson relates something similar about prostitutes singing blues in Armstrong's neighborhood: "That was the Crescent City in them days, full of bars, honky-tonks, and barrel houses. A barrel house was just a piano in a hall. There was always a piano player working. When I was a kid, I'd go into a barrel house and play 'long with them piano players 'til early in the mornin'. We used to play nuthin' but the blues. I knew Mamie Desdoumes real well. Played many a concert with her singing them same blues. She was a pretty good-looking, quite fair, with a *nice* head of hair. She was a hustlin' woman. A blues-singing poor gal. Used to play pretty passable piano around them dance halls on Perdido Street" (Shapiro and Hentoff, *Hear Me Talkin' to Ya*, 7–8.)

101. Barker, *Buddy Bolden*, 20. Dude Bottley is Buddy Bottley's younger brother, owner of a club in New Orleans.

102. Hersch, *Subversive Sounds*, 41–42.

103. Kenney, *Jazz on the River*, 35.

104. Hersch, *Subversive Sounds*, 46; he also discusses working-class African Americans' dislike of schottisches, waltzes, mazurkas, and quadrilles.

105. Kenney reports that "Streckfus timed the beat with a stopwatch and concluded that about seventy beats per minute created the danceable rhythm he wanted" (*Jazz on the River*, 48).

106. Lillian Hardin Armstrong, "Interview."

107. About the "swing era" of the 1930s and '40s, Berish writes, "The term jazz covered a very large cultural terrain and represented a wide range of concerns. Most Americans had a very broad understanding of what fell into the genre, and it included a diverse array of musical practices: sweet milquetoast dance bands that played syrupy arrangements of pop tunes; novelty orchestras that specialized in musical skits and humorous songs; sturdy, workaday dance bands that had at least a toe in the world of hot jazz; and the top-tier hot bands that featured dynamic arrangements and a good deal of solo improvisation. This spectrum of musical styles, from sweet to hot, was often mapped onto race—the hotter the band the "blacker" it was often perceived to be, whether its members were African American or Caucasian" (*Lonesome Roads*, 13; see also 43–44). Raeburn stresses the importance of record collectors in this dynamic (*New Orleans Style*, 2).

108. Hersch reads syncopation as a "deviation" or surprise relative to the norm of the beat (*Subversive Signs*, 46–47).

109. Berish, *Lonesome Roads*, 62. Early critic Richard A. Waterman attributed

the "hot" designation to "West African tribesmen": "A compelling rhythm is termed 'hot'; the more exciting the rhythms, the 'hotter' the music" ("'Hot' Rhythm in Negro Music," 24). Recent empirical studies have attempted to measure the numerical ratio of swung rhythms, for example, Collier and Collier, who conclude that Armstrong is consistently "behind the beat" ("Study of Timing").

110. See Berish's discussion of groove in swing bands (*Lonesome Roads*, 63–64); Charles Keil deploys André Hodeir's notion of "vital drive" to discuss groove ("Motion and Feeling Through Music," 59).

111. St. Cyr maintains that musicians could not write the syncopation they were playing, necessitating learning by ear. Indications such as dotted eighth notes do not quite capture the feeling of swung eighth notes ("Interview").

112. Bunk Johnson distinguishes between musicians who read and those who play "head music," especially blues (Shapiro and Hentoff, *Hear Me Talkin' to Ya*, 36).

113. Shapiro and Hentoff, *Hear Me Talkin' to Ya*, 46–47.

114. Hersch discusses Creole musicians' difficulties with improvisation (*Subversive Sounds*, 104). Early critic Louis Harap uses improvisation as a marker for authenticity in opposition with predictability and profitability ("Case for Hot Jazz," 49). See also Berish, *Lonesome Roads*, 26. This distinction between authentic and marketable overlaps to some degree with the distinction in the critical reception of blues between folk and popular; compare, for example, Evans, *Big Road Blues*, 3.

115. St. Cyr mentions the term "everybody get a window" for the "hot," last chorus during which even the rhythm section can depart from the standard groove. He also refers to "sweet" music and cites Robichaux's band performing uptown at the Imperial as "legit" ("Interview").

116. Brian Harker discusses how Louis Armstrong "used the blues, the most lowly and disreputable idiom of Black popular music in the 1920s, to bring sweet elements into his solo style" (*Louis Armstrong's Hot Five*, 12). See also Nina Sun Eidsheim's provocative study focused on the perception of race in voice (*Race of Sound*).

117. Armstrong's famous admiration for Guy Lombardo's "sweetest" music further complicates the dichotomy; see Wald, "Louis Armstrong Loves Guy Lombardo," 32.

118. See Berish, *Lonesome Roads*, 42–46.

119. Johnson had nothing but kind words about Lang and their collaboration, calling "the sides [he] made with Eddie Lang . . . my greatest experience" (Shapiro and Hentoff, *Hear Me Talkin' to Ya*, 272). Discussions of the two guitarists in jazz scholarship tend to credit Lang for having "created the entire idiom [of jazz guitar] almost singlehandedly," while recognizing Johnson as a "true master of blues guitar" (Kienzle, *Great Guitarists*, 133). This critical perception adheres to a racialized conception of the genre distinction between jazz and blues, particularly when discussing their duets. A more accurate distinction could be drawn between Lang's "novel use of chord voicing" and his variation of "chord position, inversion, or substitution on each beat" in his rhythm play (Sallis, "Eddie Lang," 22; see also Hadlock, *Jazz Masters*, 241) and Johnson's invention of a vocabulary for solo guitar within the jazz ensemble. Broadly speaking, Lang is viewed as a precursor to Charlie Christian, while Johnson is more identified with blues (O'Malley, "Dark Enough," 252–55). Nonetheless, Johnson's popularity among jazz aficionados of various types is attested by his ranking at number 2 on guitar, behind Lawrence Marrero, in the 1945 poll that asked a group of nine critics, editors, arrangers, and musicians to rate the top jazz musicians in a variety of categories (Harris, "1945 Jazz Poll"). Jazz scholarship has largely ignored Johnson with the exception of mention of his contributions to Armstrong's and Ellington's recordings. Gunther Schuller praises his addition of rhythms, chords, and textures

to four Armstrong tunes, but without more discussion (*Early Jazz*, 109–12). Edward Brooks notes his "single-string tremolos" (415), "rhythmic propulsion" (416), blue notes (417), "snatches of counter-melody" (418), and "conversational role" (477) in Armstrong's early recordings (*Young Louis Armstrong*). Gene Anderson provides a detailed analysis of Johnson's contribution to "I'm Not Rough," including a transcription of his solo, and stresses his "tone system" (*Original Hot Five Recordings*, 170–73). Gary Giddins mentions his contributions to recordings by Spencer Williams (50) and highlights his work with Armstrong, writing admiringly of his solo and crediting him with "spur[ring] Armstrong to a greater level of abandon, one that nearly upsets the band's balance" on "Savoy Blues" (*Visions of Jazz*, 96). The relative lack of critical notice of Johnson's contributions to the Ellington recordings may be due in part to the tendency in Ellington scholarship to attribute everything to Ellington himself, despite tremendous heteroglossia and unique individual voices in the orchestra (Berish, *Lonesome Roads*, 123–24).

120. Garon singled out collectors' interest in "pre-war rural artists or post-war urban ones" as responsible for Johnson's lack of recognition ("Remembering Lonnie Johnson," 20).

121. Mark Miller, *Way Down That Lonesome Road*, 92–93, quoting Darby, "Moldy Figs."

122. Grossman, *Early Masters*, 3. See also Obrecht's discussion of Johnson's technique and tunings (*Early Blues*, 130–31).

123. The defensive tone of Alger's *Original Guitar Hero* is testimony to Johnson's relegation to the category of inauthentic or unworthy of scholarly attention.

124. Rusch, "Floyd Campbell," 6, cited in Kenney, *Jazz on the River*, 113. O'Malley makes a similar observation comparing Eddie Lang's opportunities for performing with Johnson's: "Lang's skin afforded him advantages denied to Johnson, who could never escape the 'ghetto' of the blues" ("Dark Enough," 252).

125. Describing kd lang's cover of Leonard Cohen's "Hallelujah," Malawey writes, "Indicative of her experience as a compelling singer of ballads, lang uses vibrato liberally, most likely as a result of her refined technique and evident breath support" (*Blaze of Light*, 39). She notes that listeners often ascribe "authenticity" in a variety of genres of music based on vocal qualities, such as huskiness, creak, strain, growl, and the like (ibid., 99–100, 102–7).

126. Mark Miller, *Way Down That Lonesome Road*, 42–45. A comment in Mike Rowe's liner notes to the *American Folk-Blues Festival* DVD reflects the dislike of ballads: "Even Lonnie Johnson's blues-ballads and sentimental pop songs and Victoria Spivey's dangerous eye-rolling vaudeville efforts were well received by the good-humored crowd" (8). See also Albertson's initial reaction of anger to Johnson's desire to perform ballads ("Lonnie Johnson," 46). One appreciative reception of Johnson's performance on the British tour is documented in a letter from viewers who saw it on television and criticized Muddy Waters and Victoria Spivey, but praised Johnson, "to whom it was left to reveal the true depth and intensity of personal expression which is the essence of the blues" (Barrie and Cillings, "True Blues," 27).

127. Welding, "Lonnie Johnson," 30. Welding goes on to compare Johnson unfavorably to Lightnin' Hopkins, John Lee Hooker, Brownie McGhee, and Jack Dupree. Grossman's assessment of a show in New York is equally harsh: "His singing had a cocktail lounge edge. All in all I was disappointed" (*Early Masters*, 3).

128. Welding acknowledges that the audience was "reverential" and applauded after every song. He admits that he enjoyed the rendition of "Summertime" ("Lonnie Johnson," 30).

129. Kienzle mentions the clean technique (*Great Guitarists*, 13). Dalton writes that "few other blues guitarists have utilized

diminished chords to the same extent that he has" ("Guitar Style," 49). Dan Lambert characterizes the use of diminished chords as "coloration devices" ("From Blues to Jazz Guitar," 38). For a detailed discussion of his use of "sophisticated voicings" in his accompaniment to Texas Alexander and in the duets with Lang, see Lambert, "From Blues to Jazz Guitar," 37–42.

130. Grossman, *Masters of Country Blues Guitar*, 4, quoted in Obrecht, *Early Blues*, 181.

131. Cole concludes his essay on the transatlantic blues revival by suggesting that virtuosity signaled a decisive indicator of "authentic" and "inauthentic" blues for the British audience. Interestingly, this places Spivey and Johnson on opposite sides of another binary opposition: "If Cousin Joe Pleasants, Victoria Spivey and Big Joe Williams masterfully animated the minstrel mask, performers such as Lonnie Johnson, Matt Murphy and Sister Rosetta Tharpe staged a striking deformation of mastery through a virtuosity that refused to be subsumed under the patronizing trope of blackface" ("Mastery and Masquerade," 209). Heidemann asserts that the growl is produced by supraglottic distortion ("System," paragraph 3.10). Johnson employs laryngeal vibrato, creating sound relatively unaffected by movements of the vocal folds (*Complete Vocal Technique Research Site*).

132. My analysis is informed by Jacques Derrida's critiques of the logic of structuralism, beginning with "Structure, Sign, and Play," in *Writing and Difference*.

133. Hall, "What Is This 'Black,'" in *Essential Essays*, 88.

134. Erving Goffman highlights the fragility of performance: "We must be prepared to see that the impression of reality fostered by a performance is a delicate, fragile thing that can be shattered by very minor mishaps" (*Presentation of Self*, 56). Which is not to say that the ballads are a mishap, but rather an aspect of Johnson's performance practice that shatters a crucial feature of the image of him that some would like to preserve.

CHAPTER 1

1. His self-proclaimed allegiance to city blues contributed to this categorization (Wilmer, "Lonnie Johnson," 5).

2. Evans, *Big Road Blues*, 3. Jeff Todd Titon employs a distinction between "downhome" and "vaudeville" also related to compositional practices (*Early Downhome Blues*, xv–xviii). Christopher Small, advocates for the use of the term "vernacular" in opposition to "classic," which includes "popular" and "folk" (*Music of the Common Tongue*, 7).

3. David Evans notes that some blues songs performed by women (often penned by them) featured "traditional verses," but most did not (*Big Road Blues*, 64). Paige A. McGinley persuasively argues that "authenticity" and antitheatricalism in traditional (folkloric) blues criticism produces gender bias (*Staging the Blues*, 7–9).

4. On the history and meanings of jook, see Gussow, *Seems Like Murder Here*, 201–20. For a sense of performance practice within jukes, see Ferris's transcription of a house party in *Blues from the Delta*, 115–56. On blues singers in traveling shows including blackface minstrelsy, see Abbott and Seroff, *Ragged but Right*, 211–14. On the incubation of the blues in Black vaudeville, see Abbott and Seroff, *Original Blues*, 3, 4, 175.

5. McGinley, *Staging the Blues*, 102.

6. Karl Miller, *Segregating Sound*, 9, 240. On the folk versus popular divide and the "inauthenticity" of recorded blues, see also, Hamilton, *In Search of the Blues*, 16–17.

7. Keil, *Urban Blues*, 34–35. The internal quotation is unattributed, but Max Jones quotes Johnson as saying "People expect to see an old man coming out on crutches" ("You're in Love," 6). Albert Murray expresses a similar sentiment (*Stomping the Blues*, 203). Other scholars could be added

to the list, especially Frederick Ramsey and James McKune; see Hamilton's discussion in *In Search of the Blues*, 200, 230. As I noted in the introduction, the same "moldy fig" mentality was present in early jazz scholarship and the attitudes of record collectors.

8. The quip may also explain Johnson's notorious inaccuracy in interviews, perhaps born of a distrust of interviewers; see Alger, *Original Guitar Hero*, 170.

9. To be fair, Paul Oliver wrote a first book on Bessie Smith and admits in the preface to the revised edition of *Blues Fell This Morning* that he focused primarily on recordings on 78 rpm records "made between the mid-1920s and the mid-1950s" in order to demarcate blues that "was solely the music of the black community," deleting music from LPs from the later edition, (xxiii). For a critical discussion of Charters and Oliver in conjunction with conceptions of race, see Cole, "Mastery and Masquerade," 178–80. Alan Lomax had a more expansive notion of folk music than his more conservative father, John, including some commercial recordings; see Hamilton, *In Search of the Blues*, 150.

10. Raeburn outlines a parallel phenomenon in jazz criticism (*New Orleans Style*, 1–4). He also highlights the significance of the desire to create a narrative.

11. Charters, *Country Blues*, xi–xii. Somewhat ironically, Charters included Lonnie Johnson in his discussion of the blues because he relied on sales of 78 records in the African American community to guide his discussion of musicians (ibid., 73–85). Chris Albertson critiques Charters's depiction of Johnson as conforming to the stereotype of the blues singer leading a sad life ("Lonnie Johnson," 38).

12. Karl Miller argues that many of the practices developed in recording international music were used to record "race," "hillbilly," and "old time" records, reinforcing the link between ethnographers, folklorists, and recording companies (*Segregating Sound*, 184).

13. Miller argues that "folklore . . . opened new avenues for the consumption of ideas about primitivism and exoticism that could function as a salve for the alienation of urban, industrial life" (ibid., 9).

14. Work, Jones, and Adams, *Lost Delta Found*.

15. See Peter C. Muir's helpful axes of classification for "folk" and "popular" songs and a spectrum of classification (*Long Lost Blues*, 38–48).

16. See Evans's discussion of the building block elements of songs he calls a "blues core" (*Big Road Blues*, 154–55). W. C. Handy's autobiography also promotes this distinction in his insistence on writing songs from raw materials, setting himself off from nonprofessional musicians (*Father of the Blues*, 142).

17. Karl Miller, *Segregating Sound*, 58–59.

18. Historical origin stories of the blues often emphasize contact between African and European musical traditions in the American context, spurring debates and polemics about African retentions and "Black" music. See, for example, Waterman, "African Influence"; Small, *Music of the Common Tongue*, 201–13; and Floyd, *Power of Black Music*, esp. 35–86. For an excellent debate on the issue of "Black music," see Floyd and Radano, "Interpreting the African-American Musical Past." Paradoxically, while some amount of interracial contact was required to produce the genre, lack of contact is privileged by scholars seeking "authentic" music.

19. Evans points out that among the group of the earliest blues singers in the period between 1926 and 1931, "about half of them also recorded folk ballads, spirituals, minstrel and ragtime tunes, and other older material" ("Development of the Blues," 31).

20. Karl Miller discusses the ways in which record companies exerted pressure on artists' repertoires to "segregate sound" (*Segregating Sound*, 217–27), specifically citing a complaint from Little Brother Montgomery (227). According to Miller, the enforcement of the "color line" in recording coincides with a "folkloric" presentation

of Black southern music, further reinforcing the rural blues as a category (222). For discussion of the repertoire of "folk" blues players, see Evans, *Big Road Blues*, 112–13; Titon, *Early Downhome Blues*, 216; Charters, "Workin' on the Building," 24–25; and on Leadbelly's repertoire, see Hamilton, *In Search of the Blues*, 122, 130. Jazz musicians were also pressured into recording blues, such as the drummer and vocalist Floyd Campbell (Kenney, *Jazz on the River*, 113). Danny Barker discusses the prohibition against male, Black singers performing love songs and ballads on white stages and the segregation of music on jukeboxes as a corollary to the segregation of the market with race records (*Life in Jazz*, 157).

21. Quoted in Wald, *Escaping the Delta*, 118. John W. Work III's research in the Delta as part of the Fisk University–Library of Congress Coahoma County Study reveals an eclectic mix of selections on jukeboxes in Clarksdale, Mississippi, confirming the circulation of styles ("Untitled Manuscript," 85–86).

22. New Orleans and other areas originally settled by the French, mostly in the Caribbean, used the classification "octoroon" to designate people with Plessy's heritage. On *Plessy v. Ferguson* in relation to New Orleans, see Nystrom, *New Orleans*, 214; and Landau, *Spectacular Wickedness*, 46–50.

23. Landau, *Spectacular Wickedness*, 49. Plessy's lawyers objected less to segregation than to his categorization as Black; see Hartman, *Scenes of Subjection*, 191, 205. Landau points out that men, specifically, lost the designations "quadroon" and "octoroon" after *Plessy*, but the terms were retained for women and, especially, prostitutes in Storyville (*Spectacular Wickedness*, 50, 128–29, 147, 171).

24. Charles Hersch argues that Creoles continued to occupy an ambiguous status, including in Louisiana court rulings, and that "the hardening of racial categories created a whole class of cultural impersonators," including among musicians (*Subversive Sounds*, 100–101).

25. When compared to New Orleans and St. Louis, the Mississippi Delta was settled late, in the 1890s, by a largely homogeneous group of men of means seeking to make a fortune with a plantation (Cobb, *Most Southern Place on Earth*, 3–9).

26. Lachance, "Foreign French," 101. On the colonial history of New Orleans related to race and sexual relations, see Baker, "'Cherchez les Femmes'"; Everett, "Free Persons of Color"; Foner, "Free People of Color"; and Spear, "Colonial Intimacies."

27. Jerah Johnson invokes a "reticulated model" to describe colonial New Orleans, in which "individuals belonging to different cultural groups are so enmeshed in an overall stratification system or a shared common culture that the subcultures of the several groups blur or erode in favor of the pervasive shared culture, which assumes its form by drawing elements from the various subcultures" ("Colonial New Orleans," 45). Johnson makes the argument about colonial New Orleans, but I would extend it up until and even after *Plessy v. Ferguson*, as a means of explaining resistance to segregation.

28. On the range of racial designations used in New Orleans, as in the Caribbean, see Dunbar-Nelson, "People of Color in Louisiana," 3–4. Barker mentions these designations in his discussion of caste in relation to venues in New Orleans (*Life in Jazz*, 61).

29. For a discussion of the origin and evolution of Louisiana Creole as a language, see Mosadomi, "Origin of Louisiana Creole."

30. For helpful discussions of the evolution of the meaning of "*creole*," see Klein, "Introduction," xiii–xvii; and Le Menestrel, *Negotiating Difference*, 7–9. Joseph C. Tregle Jr. argues that the expression "*creole of color*" dates from the postbellum period ("Creoles and Americans," 139).

31. Hirsch and Logsdon, *Creole New Orleans*, 189.

32. Hale, *Making Whiteness*, esp. 9, 105, 228–31.

33. Jackson, *New Orleans*, 254; Landau, *Spectacular Wickedness*, 5.

34. Compare Hale's discussion of the construction of "mammy" as a figure who crosses the color line (*Making Whiteness*, 98–105).

35. Bernstein, "Plessy v. Ferguson," 5–6.

36. Nystrom, *New Orleans*, 213. Hirsch and Logsdon argue that "ethnocultural differences" were more deeply rooted than "simply color or legal status" (*Creole New Orleans*, 193). Alecia P. Long stresses the elasticity of the category of "octoroon" for the purposes of sexual commerce in Storyville (*Great Southern Babylon*, 203–14).

37. Landau, *Spectacular Wickedness*, 78. Pressures were also exerted by swampland that blocked geographical expansion. These pressures were alleviated by the installation of pumping systems from 1899 to 1909 (Hirsch and Logsdon, *Creole New Orleans*, 198).

38. Landau notes resistance to segregation in the imposition of the Gay-Shattuck Law in 1908, which "criminalized interracial fraternizing in bars, saloons, and restaurants, and entrepreneurs applying for permits to operate barrooms had to specify which 'race' they would serve. The many instances in which saloon-keepers were arrested for 'selling to whites and negroes' tell us that there was in fact plenty of mixed-race socializing within New Orleans's still mixed-race neighborhoods" (*Spectacular Wickedness*, 169). George "Pops" Foster confirms the presence of lots of whites on the "colored" side of saloons and in Lincoln Park (*Pops Foster*, 64).

39. Raeburn argues that the street defied neat separations and categorizations (*New Orleans Style*, 43–44). See also Hersch's discussion of the street, parades, and processions (*Subversive Sounds*, 79–80).

40. Hersch, *Subversive Sounds*, 12, emphasis added.

41. Alger, *Original Guitar Hero*, 34–36, based on interviews and conversations, including with Johnson's late-in-life booking agent Roberta Barrett, who provides the Wall Street location. Most other sources cite Franklin and Rampart, likely from Thomas, "I'm a Roamin' Rambler," 18.

42. Raeburn, *New Orleans Style*, 8. Hersch argues that these neighborhoods as "pockets of semiautonomy allowed alternative cultures to flourish in the middle of a highly racist society" (*Subversive Sounds*, 25).

43. Raeburn, *New Orleans Style*, 8.

44. Johnson, "The Entire Family Was Musicians," in *Complete Folkways Recordings* (discog.).

45. Movement across racialized space is always fraught, but parades and other kinds of work enable musicians to move more freely than others. George Lipsitz cites Armstrong's view that marching "granted him 'safe passage throughout the city'" (*How Racism Takes Place*, 61).

46. Raeburn, *New Orleans Style*, 7–8. Barker provides a similar list, and adds church-related affairs, such as christenings, communions, and confirmations (*Life in Jazz*, 59).

47. Landau, *Spectacular Wickedness*, 19. Chris Smith writes that Johnson was "working solo in Storyville by 1910" (liner notes, in Johnson, *Complete Recorded Works in Chronological Order, 1925–1932*, vol. 1; discog.).

48. Raeburn, *New Orleans Style*, 65. Johnny St. Cyr describes this work advertising for gigs in detail ("Interview").

49. Foster, *Pops Foster*, 92.

50. Wilmer, "Lonnie Johnson," 6. Vic Hobson characterizes the family group as a "reading band" based on the repertoire and gigs ("New Orleans Jazz," 16).

51. Shapiro and Hentoff, *Hear Me Talkin' to Ya*, 20. See also Barker's distinction between "routine" musicians who played by ear and those who could read (Barker, *Life in Jazz*, 27–28). Barker emphasizes the violinists' ability to sight read, attributing this

opinion to Dude Bottley (*Buddy Bolden*, 11). Foster concurs about fiddlers being able to read music (*Pops Foster*, 75). St. Cyr claims that at least three people in the bands were able to read music ("Interview").

52. Wilmer, "Lonnie Johnson," 6.

53. The copyrights for songs he registered in 1928 and 1929 strongly suggest that he was able to write as well as read.

54. Miller, "Interview."

55. Miller's use of the qualifier "white" to differentiate Sunday night occasions signals that the other performances were for African Americans.

56. Karl Miller documents the emergence of the distinction between urban and rural blues as a ploy by record companies to market music (*Segregating Sound*, 224–27).

57. Hersch discusses the various secular folk musical traditions in New Orleans in the period (*Subversive Sounds*, 90–92).

58. See Hersch's discussion of "ratty" music and its venues (ibid., 29–33).

59. Shapiro and Hentoff, *Hear Me Talkin' to Ya*, 36. Given the historical moment, the boundary between jazz and blues is clearly porous and not well-defined. Hersch also cites interviews with Creole musicians Johnny St. Cyr and Joe Robichaux who felt compelled to learn blues as it gained in popularity (*Subversive Sounds*, 108).

60. Wilmer, "Lonnie Johnson," 5. Typical of the conceits of early blues scholarship, Oliver erroneously makes the opposite point: "A number of singers—Bo Carter, Tampa Red and Lonnie Johnson among them—moved easily between these groups [traditional blues and jazz-blues] but Lonnie Johnson was rare in being a folk blues singer who infiltrated the jazz-blues field" (*Screening the Blues*, 184).

61. Johnson, "The Entire Family Was Musicians," in Complete Folkways Recordings (discog.).

62. Mark A. Humphrey highlights the "crying" sound of the solo, conjecturing that "ideas he first developed on the bowed instrument later reached maturity on the plucked one" ("Bright Lights, Big City," 156). See my discussion of the song in chapter 2.

63. Smith suggests 1910 as the beginning of his solo work (liner notes, in Johnson, *Complete Recorded Works in Chronological Order, 1925–1932*, vol. 1; discog.). No doubt the different birth dates he provided caused other shifts in the chronology of his life that he provided to interviewers.

64. Oliver, *Conversation with the Blues*, 85. Raeburn discusses the significance of theater work for jazz musicians, including at the Iroquois ("Early New Orleans Jazz," 44–45).

65. Slieff et al., "Tango Belt."

66. Thomas, "I'm a Roamin' Rambler," 18; Hahn, "Lonnie Johnson." Rose lists Johnson in his directory of jazz musicians who performed in Storyville (*Storyville,* 204). See Hersch's discussion of Milneburg as a relatively open space with multiple venues for different races and classes, near West End, Bucktown, and Spanish Fort (*Subversive Sounds*, 80–83).

67. Foster claims, "Lonnie was the only guy we had around New Orleans who could play jazz guitar," by which he clearly means lead (*Pops Foster*, 92). Neglect of Johnson's pioneering role for jazz guitar in jazz scholarship is remarkable. Critics often credit Eddie Lang, his duet partner, rather than Johnson; see Kienzle, *Great Guitarists*, 133.

68. Mark Miller, *Way Down That Lonesome Road*, 23.

69. Landau, *Spectacular Wickedness*, 190. Kenney critiques the overstatement of the significance of the closing of Storyville for the migration north of jazz musicians (*Jazz on the River*, 65).

70. Logsdon and Bell, "Americanization of Black New Orleans," 259–60.

71. Alger, *Original Guitar Hero*, 52–53; Humphrey, "Bright Lights, Big City," 156; Mark Miller, *Way Down That Lonesome Road*, 22–23; Shaw, *Honkers and Shouters*, 13.

72. Bernhard, "St. Louis."
73. Nolen, *Hoecakes, Hambone*, 2–3. Barker emphasizes the move from New Orleans to Chicago, stressing the desire to take the Illinois Central Railroad in order to avoid stopping in Mississippi (*Life in Jazz*, 72). He mentions Alabama, Florida, Texas, and Georgia, but not Missouri, as other states to avoid (71). Morton also extols the virtues of Chicago over St. Louis and other cities (Lomax, *Mr. Jelly Roll*, 150, 180).
74. Both Foster and St. Cyr describe guards accompanying musicians on and off the Streckfus boats (Foster, "Interview," recorded 24 August 1958; St. Cyr, "Interview").
75. Kenney, *Jazz on the River*, 93.
76. Dowden-White, *Groping Toward Democracy*, 5. The residential segregation ordinance, approved by voters in 1916 and subsequently struck down by the United States Supreme Court, further signals the struggle over segregation in St. Louis. The practice of using restrictive housing covenants followed the Supreme Court decision (ibid., 7). On the history of restrictive covenants, see Packard, *American Nightmare*, 105–6. Redlining, racial zoning, and violence also contributed to segregation and discrimination in St. Louis (Lipsitz, *How Racism Takes Place*, 75).
77. Blesh and Janis document visits by Lulu White, the madam of Mahogany Hall in Storyville, to madam friends in St. Louis, underscoring the connections between the cities and their sporting districts (*They All Played Ragtime*, 60). See also John A. Wright, *Discovering African American St. Louis*, 22.
78. Foster asserts repeatedly that there is no such thing as "Dixieland." He calls the early music bands in New Orleans played "ragtime," and even cites Joplin's "Maple Leaf Rag" as a tune that bands knew (Foster, "Interview," recorded 21 April 1957; "Interview," recorded 24 August 1958).
79. Shapiro and Hentoff, *Hear Me Talkin' to Ya*, 76; Chevan, "Riverboat Music," 154.
80. Shapiro and Hentoff, *Hear Me Talkin' to Ya*, 75. Verne Streckfus, the youngest of the four sons who were all musicians and captains aboard the boats, states that music began with the excursions in 1895 ("Interview").
81. Chevan, "Riverboat Music," 160.
82. Kenney, *Jazz on the River*, 45.
83. Shapiro and Hentoff, *Hear Me Talkin' to Ya*, 76.
84. Chevan, "Riverboat Music," 163; Kenney, *Jazz on the River*, 38
85. Kenney, *Jazz on the River*, 47.
86. Kienzle writes that Johnson played with Marable without citing sources (*Great Guitarists*, 13).
87. On the firing of Armstrong, see Kenney, who in *Jazz on the River* (75–80) raises questions about the sharp distinction between reading and not reading music. For Armstrong's own account of learning to read under Marable, see *Satchmo*, 181–84 and 191. Verne Streckfus maintains that Armstrong had the band play the songs through once and learned them that way ("Interview").
88. Kenney, *Jazz on the River*, 9, 48.
89. Paradoxically, as Kenney argues, the Streckfus line deployed minstrel stereotypes in its ads to sell excursions (ibid., 29–30). The size of the dance floor, capacity of the boats, and moral sensibilities also contributed to the constraints on musical performance (ibid., 46–48).
90. Blesh and Janis stress Scott Joplin's significant contribution to the writing of vernacular rhythms in ragtime (*They All Played Ragtime*, 42). See also the analysis of "swing" and the difficulties it poses for notation in Butterfield, "When Swing Doesn't Swing."
91. See Foster's admission to standing "by the piano at rehearsals so I could dig the chords from it" (*Pops Foster*, 106), and Kenney's discussion of Louis Armstrong in this regard (*Jazz on the River*, 75–80).
92. Kenney, *Jazz on the River*, 50. The term comes from Samuel A. Floyd Jr.'s extension of Henry Louis Gates's notion of

signifyin(g) as the master trope in African American literature to Black music. Floyd writes, "Musical Signifyin(g) is troping: the transformation of preexisting musical material by trifling with it, teasing it, or censuring it. Musical Signifyin(g) is the rhetorical use of preexisting materials as a means of demonstrating respect for or poking fun at a musical style, process or practice through parody, pastiche, implication, indirection, humor, tone play or word play, the illusion of speech or narration, or other troping mechanisms" (*Power of Black Music*, 8). For a great example of the difference between written and performed jazz incorporating signifying, see the documentary on Punch Miller directed by Philip Spalding, *'Til the Butcher Cuts Him Down*.

93. See the discussion in the previous chapter. Musicians like Louis Armstrong and Bunk Johnson promoted the strict opposition, as did Jack Weber, who called the different kinds of musicians "readers" and "fakers" (Shapiro and Hentoff, *Hear Me Talkin' to Ya*, 36 and 59). David Brackett proposes two slightly different but relevant oppositions in popular music: "artistry vs. commercialism" and "authenticity vs. accessibility" (*Interpreting Popular Music*, 38). The authenticity versus accessibility distinction applies to someone like Charley Patton relative to Lonnie Johnson.

94. Chevan, "Riverboat Music," 156; Kenney, *Jazz on the River*, 76, 102-3. Foster reports seeing white passengers aboard on Monday nights ("Interview," recorded 21 April 1957).

95. Chevan, "Riverboat Music," 167.

96. Louis Armstrong's reappearance on a boat in 1928 illustrates the divergent tastes (Kenney, *Jazz on the River*, 102). Foster suggests that musicians had more fun on Monday nights ("Interview" recorded 21 April 1957).

97. Kenney, *Jazz on the River*, 99. Jazzland was located behind the Booker T. Washington Theater ("Preservation Plan for St. Louis"; John J. Wright, *African Americans in Downtown St. Louis*, 44).

98. Kenney, *Jazz on the River*, 102-3.

99. Chevan, "Riverboat Music," 158; according to Kenney, Creath had competing boats for African American passengers four nights a week (*Jazz on the River*, 102-3).

100. See the discography for the four sides Johnson recorded in St. Louis with Charlie Creath's Jazz-O-Maniacs.

101. Victoria Spivey mentions being introduced to Lonnie by Jesse Johnson ("Blues Is My Business," 9).

102. Foster describes the year-round work (*Pops Foster*, 109-11). On the Streckfus line routes, see Chevan, "Riverboat Music," 154, 160, 170-71, and 174. St. Cyr describes work in St. Louis in summer and New Orleans in winter, but also "tramp" trips that required musicians to sleep on board the boats ("Interview").

103. Alger, *Original Guitar Hero*, 71-73; Spivey mentions seeing Johnson with his brother at Katy Red's ("Blues Is My Business," 9). St. Cyr mentions Chauffeur's Club as another venue he would play when he worked for Marable on the riverboats ("Interview").

104. Townsend, *Blues Life*, 18-19. The locations are in Chestnut Valley and East St. Louis.

105. Spivey, "Blues Is My Business," 9. Obrecht and Miller rely on Spivey's account of seeing him at that venue (Mark Miller, *Way Down That Lonesome Road*, 35-36; Obrecht, *Early Blues*, 139).

106. John J. Wright, *African Americans in Downtown St. Louis*, 45.

107. Townsend, *Blues Life*, 36-37.

108. Like so much of the misinformation provided in interviews, he told Oliver that he won the contest eighteen consecutive weeks and got an eleven-year contract (*Conversation with the Blues*, 122).

109. Oliver, *Conversation with the Blues*, 140; Mark Miller, *Way Down That Lonesome Road*, 26-27. Alger adds that Johnson played the Lyric Theater in New Orleans, perhaps returning after moving to St. Louis (*Original Guitar Hero*, 64).

110. See the recordings in the discography on which Johnson was a guest artist with Louis Armstrong and His Hot Five and with Duke Ellington and His Orchestra.

CHAPTER 2

1. Some blues recordings of male rural artists from the 1920s and '30s have what appear to be ad hoc titles. The song titles were likely created in response to unrelated but reconcilable phenomena: (1) compositional practices among rural artists who rarely performed the exact song twice and, therefore, whose sense of a song likely lacked a title; (2) the record companies' desire to produce "original" material; but also (3) the desire to sell records by creating confusion with similar song titles. On compositional practices among rural blues artists, see Evans, *Big Road Blues*, esp. 265–311; for a discussion of the pressure exerted by recording companies on blues performers to produce "new" material because of copyright concerns, see Suisman, *Selling Sounds*, 132; and Kenney, *Recorded Music*, 132. Some examples of titles with the performer's name include Blind Blake, "Blind Arthur's Breakdown" (Chicago, October 1929), Bo Chatmon, "Bo Carter's Advice" (New Orleans, 15 October 1936), and Blind Lemon Jefferson, "Lemon's Worried Blues" (Chicago, February 1928). I would argue that there is a spectrum of practices of more or less conscious self-naming in song titles that runs from artists with significant contact with traveling shows and other forms of professionalization, such as Jelly Roll Morton, "Mr. Jelly Lord" (Chicago, 10 June 1927) or Ma Rainey, "Ma Rainey's Lost Wandering Blues" (Chicago, March 1924), to the seemingly ad hoc titles among "folk" performers. "Mr. Johnson's Blues" falls on the highly self-conscious end of the spectrum.

2. On vibrato, see Complete Vocal Technique Research Site.

3. Heidemann, "System," paragraph 3.21. Heidemann distinguishes between nasal voices produced by the position of the velum and "voices that produce sympathetic vibrations far forward in the nose or in the nasal passages" (ibid.). An expanded pharynx may account for his projection despite poor-quality recording equipment in 1925.

4. Malawey, *Blaze of Light*, 102–7. Barb Jungr describes these traits as "vocal noise" that she asserts "allow access to deeper feelings of emotion, both for singer and listener alike" ("Vocal Expression," 147).

5. Martha Feldman argues that voice is always perceived within the context of social relations ("Why Voice Now?," 658). This is consistent with Heinemann's analysis of vocal timbre as a product of listening ("System," paragraphs 1.1, 1.2, 1.3, 2.1).

6. Other early blues fiddle players that came after Johnson include Lonnie Chatmon of the Mississippi Sheiks, Eddie Anthony who accompanied Peg Leg Howell, and Andrew Baxter who accompanied his son Jim on guitar, none of whom sing. Most of these artists play in a more rural style of accompaniment in the string band tradition, rarely soloing.

7. Alger points out the likely borrowing (*Original Guitar Hero*, 98); others cite an interview with Johnny Shines in which he claimed that Robert Johnson revered Lonnie so much that he claimed to be related to him (Welding, "Ramblin' Johnny Shines," 29, cited in Wald, *Escaping the Delta*, 174; Sallis, *Guitar Players*, 37–38; Obrecht, *Early Blues*, 131).

8. Paul Gilroy argues for the significance of self-creation through the production of public persona, including in slave narratives, as a "founding motif within the expressive culture of the African diaspora." Artists are particularly valued for this activity (*Black Atlantic*, 69, 79).

9. Alger, *Original Guitar Hero*, 12; Lomax, *Land Where the Blues Began*, 23. Nate (Shaw) Cobb discusses the use of "Mister" in contrast to "Uncle" and "Auntie" (Rosengarten, *All God's Dangers*, 201).

10. The designation amounts to what Erving Goffman characterizes as a "moral

demand" obliging others "to value and treat him in the manner that persons of his kind have a right to expect" (*Presentation of Self*, 13).

11. Hale, *Making Whiteness*, 9.

12. Judith Butler's influential work deconstructing gender binarism stresses performance and the body as "a signifying practice within a cultural field" (*Gender Trouble*, 139). She applies the same conception of performance to race (134–41).

13. Karl Miller, *Segregating Sound*, 4.

14. Ibid., 4–5.

15. Sotiropoulos, *Staging Race*, 40–41.

16. See Abbott and Seroff, *Ragged but Right*, 56; Hale, *Making Whiteness*, 11; Sotiropoulos, *Staging Race*, 9, 46–47; and Baker, *Blues, Ideology*, 194.

17. Hale cites Duke Ellington, Ethel Waters, James P. Johnson, but also Ma Rainey and Bessie Smith. In the blues women she perceives the enactment of a form of African American sexuality that played on white fantasies of availability to express freedom (*Making Whiteness*, 38), consistent with arguments made by Davis (*Blues Legacies and Black Feminism*, 42–65) and Carby ("It Jus Be's Dat Way Sometime").

18. Hale, *Making Whiteness*, 40.

19. Scott, *Domination and the Arts*, 33. This performance is enabled by the double consciousness formulated by Du Bois in *Souls of Black Folk*, 14.

20. Scott, *Domination and the Arts*, 34.

21. Stuart Hall argues that "identity is always in part a narrative, always in part a kind of representation. It is always within representation" (*Essential Essays*, 70). Musicians and other performers are likely more aware of the performance aspect of identity. Auslander asserts that "jazz musicians and symphony conductors present personae just as popular musicians do" (*Performing Glam Rock*, 6).

22. Spalding, *'Til the Butcher Cuts Him Down*.

23. Hersch, *Subversive Sounds*, 167–75; Alan Lomax discusses Morton's race prejudice (viii) and family background (27–38), and asserts that "he always refused to admit he was a Negro" (*Mr. Jelly Roll*, 196). Morton also "passed" as Cuban in order to secure hotel accommodations with white band members in Richmond, Virginia (Reich and Gaines, *Jelly's Blues*, 86).

24. Hersch, *Subversive Sounds*, 106.

25. Ibid. Danny Barker recounts a story in which musicians assert a "Moslem" identity in Springfield, Illinois, in order to stay in a hotel. Rudy (Musheed Karweem) Powell produces a card for a clerk "stamped with a seal, and there were the crescent, the Star of Arabia, some Arabic words and figures and a Washington D.C. address for the bearer to contact if he got into difficulties." Barker suggests that Powell is Muslim but the rest of the band is not (*Buddy Bolden*, 128–30). O'Malley asserts that "'show business' in general thrived as a place of ethnic and racial transgression, expanding the category of people performing race to include performers and executives who were immigrants, like Eddie Lang and the Kapp brothers ("Dark Enough," 236).

26. "Passing" was not uncommon in New Orleans, aided by a number of circumstances discussed in chapter 1. For example, "within the Creole community," the practice of *plaçage*, "an arranged sexual relationship outside the bounds of marriage between white men and typically freeborn mixed-race women," often produced children capable of crossing racial boundaries (Nystrom, *New Orleans*, 57). Of course, "passing" is both aided and thwarted by a caste system attentive to multiple variations of color. Danny Barker draws the connection between skin color, caste, and specific music venues (*Life in Jazz*, 61).

27. Hersch, *Subversive Sounds*, 163. Court Carney traces white, Black, and Creole influences in two generations of early New Orleans musicians ("New Orleans"). Finally, Alger discusses Johnson's exposure to "uptown" and "downtown" styles, and his capacity to blend them (*Original Guitar Hero*, 32).

28. Hersch, *Subversive Sounds*, 97.

29. Raeburn, "Confessions," 306. Raeburn also discusses the case of Edward Ory, who assumed an "Afro-French Creole" identity despite predominantly white heritage. The performance of race by musicians dovetails to some degree with that of prostitutes. Landau argues that "octoroon" was a sexual category more than a racial designation (*Spectacular Wickedness*, 147). Based on census documents, Craig Foster documents the cultural origins of the prostitutes of Storyville, including Jews and Eastern and Southern Europeans, although the data may not be reliable ("Tarnished Angels," 389).

30. I was only able to find four reviews of vaudeville shows that appeared in the *Chicago Defender* in 1924 and 1926 that use the name Alonzo Johnson, specifically as half of a comedy team with Mary Hicks. The musical recordings do not use this name. The only song by Johnson with the word Creole in the lyrics that I am aware of is "New Orleans Blues" recorded on 19 November 1948 (Cincinnati, unissued) and 5 April 1960 (New York City, on *Blues, Ballads, and Jumpin' Jazz*, vol. 2), which specifically references "Creole babies" with "big, bright eyes and coal black, curly hair"—significantly recorded at a moment in his career when Johnson was interested in highlighting his history and background.

31. Foster, *Pops Foster*, 92. Johnson mentions weddings in "Entire Family."

32. Chevan, "Riverboat Music," 162.

33. Chevan includes one photograph of Marable's orchestra taken aboard one of the boats (ibid., 164).

34. McGinley, *Staging the Blues*, 55. See also Carby, "It Jus Be's Dat Way Sometime," 479; and Davis, *Blues Legacies and Black Feminism*, 137. Compare Auslander's discussion of the creation of the persona for glam rockers that deploys many of the same props and techniques (*Performing Glam Rock*).

35. Conk styles refer to the chemical relaxer Congolene, which contained lye, used by many musicians. It was applied to straighten African American hair and was popular from the 1920s until the 1960s ("Jheri Curl, Conk, Dreadlocks, and Afro").

36. In most photos of Johnson, with the exception of the one in the studio with Blind John Davis (fig. 7), he wears a jacket and tie.

37. Auslander, *Performing Glam Rock*, 5–6.

38. Strassberg, liner notes, in Johnson, *Unsung Blues Legend* (discog.).

39. Wilmer, "Lonnie Johnson," 7.

40. Ibid., 5–6.

41. Howland, *Ellington Uptown*, 31.

42. Ibid., 16, 111–13.

43. Inspired by Roland Barthes influential essay "The Grain of the Voice," recent work in musicology examines listeners' constitution of a body of origin for voices with specific characteristics based on timbre and other vocal qualities; see Eidsheim, *Race of Sound;* Heidemann, "System"; Olwage, "Class and Colour of Tone"; and Malawey, *Blaze of Light*.

44. Malawey includes phrasing as part of prosody (*Blaze of Light*, 70).

45. Although "Mr. Johnson's Blues No. 2" recorded in New York City on 11 June 1929 explicitly gestures to the earlier work, repeating the introduction with expert execution and a variant of the sole verse, it then develops a love-sick and depressed theme. It functions more as a rejoinder or reprise rather than a meta-commentary like "Mr. Johnson's Swing."

46. Benjamin Givan helpfully adapts Leonard B. Meyer's terminology developed in the context of European art music composers for distinguishing between dialect, idiom, and intraopus style for jazz improvisation. Johnson as an individual performer works generally in the dialect of blues and incorporates elements of jazz in his individual idiom, which includes figures common to both traditions (Givan, "Gunther Schuller," 211; Meyer, *Style and Music*, 23–25).

47. King Oliver and His Dixie Syncopators, "West End Blues" (Vocalion 1189, 1928) does not have the exact three-note

figure. Johnson covered "West End Blues" with Jim McHarg's Metro Stompers in 1965 for the LP *Stompin' at the Penny.* After a cadenza opening on solo trumpet inspired by Armstrong's but by no means an attempt to copy it, Johnson takes the first two choruses, playing the signature figure in a very deliberate way before embarking on his own improvisations.

48. Heidemann specifically discusses the production of Armstrong's growl ("System," paragraph 3.10).

49. Johnson recorded his last sides for OKeh and Columbia on 12 August 1932: "I'm Nuts About That Gal" and "Racketeers Blues" (OKeh 8946), "Unselfish Love" and "My Love Don't Belong to You" (Columbia 14674-D), in addition to the two unissued songs for Columbia, "Love Is a Song (Your Love Is Cold)" and "Go Back to Your No Good Man."

50. Debates about racial essentialism and "Black music," including the issue of African retentions with respect to rhythm, are ongoing. For an excellent articulation of the positions, see Floyd and Radano, "Interpreting the African-American Musical Past."

51. See my discussion of the roles of protagonist, narrator, and singer in *Time in the Blues* (102–3).

52. Similar lines occur in "I Just Can't Stand These Blues" (OKeh 8886, 1930).

53. Goffman specifically singles out facial expressions in his discussion of theatrical discipline in everyday life, writing "Perhaps the focus of dramaturgical discipline is to be found in the management of one's face and voice. Here is the crucial test of one's ability as a performer. Actual affective response must be concealed and an appropriate affective response must be displayed" (*Presentation of Self*, 217). This is consistent with Goffman's model of information that is revealed only to "teammates" and not members of the audience (206).

54. See Adam Gussow's analysis of the devil in these songs, *Beyond the Crossroads* (171–72). Some critics interpret the lyrics as evidence of trouble in his marriage:

see Alger, *Original Guitar Hero*, 69; Sallis, *Guitar Players*, 38–39; Smith, liner notes, in Johnson, *Complete Recorded Works in Chronological Order, 1925–1932*, vol. 5 (discog.). Mark A. Humphrey characterizes him as "bluntly cynical about love" ("Bright Lights, Big City," 158), while Smith in the liner notes to *Complete Recorded Works in Chronological Order, 1925–1932*, vol. 7, calls him "misogynistic" (discog.).

55. "Roaming Rambler Blues" (New York City, 12 August 1927) provides another example where the narrator has many women.

56. Smith characterizes Johnson's lyrics as containing "homilies on moral and social etiquette" (liner notes, in Johnson, *Complete Recorded Works in Chronological Order, 1937–1947*, vol. 3; discog.).

57. Cultural context and musical style exist in a dialectical relation rather than one of simple causality. Thus, in New Orleans, the sociohistorical, ethnic, and racial context determines musical styles and vice versa.

58. Gilroy writes, "Music and its rituals can be used to create a model whereby identity can be understood neither as a fixed essence nor as a vague and utterly contingent construction to be reinvented by the will and whim of aesthetes, symbolists, and language gamers" (*Black Atlantic*, 102).

59. Odell and Winans mention the possibility that frailing or the clawhammer technique traces back to West African lute playing; see "Banjo."

60. Compare Mats Johansson's discussion of Michael Jackson's lack of stable identity in part due to borrowings across genres ("Michael Jackson," 274–75).

CHAPTER 3

1. See Brackett's discussion of musical codes in relation to the audience's musical competence (*Interpreting Popular Music*, 12).

2. Goffman, *Presentation of Self*, 107.

3. Ibid., 112. Compare Scott's conception of the "hidden transcript," created by subordinate groups as a "critique of power spoken behind the back of the dominant," but which leaves a trace in the dominant culture in the form of the "public transcript" (*Domination and the Arts*, xii).

4. Compare Auslander's discussion of the persona of glam rockers like David Bowie and Suzie Quatro (*Performing Glam Rock*, 5–6).

5. Long-distance cruises provided shipboard sleeping quarters and board, but short cruises did not. Chevan cites an interview by Irene Cortinovis that mentions a bunkroom ("Riverboat Music," 162). Significantly, musicians did not socialize with passengers other than fellow musicians, helping to maintain the separation of performance (ibid., 175).

6. Goffman discusses the position of "non-persons," such as servants and slaves, whose discrepancy is similar to that of the musician in some respects (*Presentation of Self*, 149–50).

7. Episodes that lead to race consciousness often involve learning prescribed behaviors under Jim Crow. For example, Louis Armstrong recounts his first ride on a streetcar, being told that he had to move to the back (*Satchmo*, 14). The collected volume produced out of the *Behind the Veil Project* at Duke University, *Remembering Jim Crow*, provides numerous examples from oral histories of individuals learning to perform racial subordination, including in service positions, often under the threat of violence.

8. Goffman, *Presentation of Self*, 145.

9. Barker specifically mentions folksingers Bob Dylan, Joan Baez, and Woody Guthrie, as well as Louis Armstrong and Cab Calloway, for their permissive attitudes about drug use (*Life in Jazz*, 138).

10. Lomax, *Mr. Jelly Roll*, 160.

11. The park venues near Lake Pontchartrain employed large bands, as did Lincoln Park, an African American outdoor venue. On Milneburg and the Lake Pontchartrain area, see Foster, *Pops Foster*, 15–16; Raeburn, *New Orleans Style*, 65; and Hersch, *Subversive Sounds*, 80–83. On Lincoln Park and its African American audience, see Barker, *Buddy Bolden*, 6–52.

12. New Orleans streets also constitute a venue with almost no separation between performers and crowd. Funerals with a second line, cutting contests, parades, and other events, as well as busking, offer little distance between musicians and audience (Raeburn, *New Orleans Style*, 8, 43–44; Hersch, *Subversive Sounds*, 79).

13. Barker, *Buddy Bolden*, 27. Drug use was common in the district among prostitutes and clients; see Lomax, *Mr. Jell Roll*, 25. Clarence Williams mentions "cocaine, morphine, heroin, and hop" (Shapiro and Hentoff, *Hear Me Talkin' to Ya*, 12). Emma Johnson infamously lured minors into sex slavery, using drugs and alcohol in addition to kidnapping and rape (Al Rose, *Storyville*, 50).

14. Barker, *Buddy Bolden*, 54–55, 71. For a discussion of the various financial interests profiting from Storyville, see Al Rose, *Storyville*, 29–30.

15. Rose estimates a 400 percent markup on alcohol (*Storyville*, 31). See Landau's discussion of liquor ads in the Blue Books and the prosecution of Lulu White for nonpayment of taxes on alcohol (*Spectacular Wickedness*, 114, 149–51). For musicians' accounts of alcohol in the district, see Shapiro and Hentoff, *Hear Me Talkin' to Ya*, 12; and Foster, *Pops Foster*, 30–31.

16. Landau, *Spectacular Wickedness*, 21–23; on violence in brothels, see Long, *Great Southern Babylon*, 152–54.

17. Landau argues that "octoroon" is a sexual rather than racial category, noting that the prostitutes in photographs "in Lulu White's booklet . . . all appear 'white'" (*Spectacular Wickedness*, 147). See also Foster on census data on race from the district ("Tarnished Angels"), although Landau's analysis of shifting racial identities

(*Spectacular Wickedness*, 132–39) casts doubt on declarations in the census.

18. Barker describes a particularly violent fight over gambling in a gay bar (*Buddy Bolden*, 111).

19. Dowden-White, *Groping Toward Democracy*, 30. Townsend specifically mentions Walnut Street as the location of houses of prostitution (*Blues Life*, 15). This area was also well known for music, beginning in the 1890s with the popularity of ragtime, and was home to the Rosebud Café; see Blesh and Janis, *They All Played Ragtime*, 54. Music continued in the area through the 1920s, particularly on Market Street (Kenney, *Jazz on the River*, 99).

20. Treating people as ends in themselves is Immanuel Kant's test of moral behavior (*Critique of Practical Reason*, 136).

21. On the tendency to conflate the narrator persona with the singer-songwriter, see Brackett, *Interpreting Popular Music*, 2; and Auslander, *Performing Glam Rock*, 5–6.

22. Alger reads song lyrics in an attempt to establish a chronology of the marriage. For Alger, songs such as "You Can't Give a Woman Everything She Needs" and "Baby Please Don't Leave Home No More" (New York City, 11 June 1929) present evidence of their separation in 1929 (*Original Guitar Hero*, 68–69). The autobiographical approach makes interpreting "She's My Mary" (Chicago, 2 November 1938) problematic, given the reference to Mary and the upbeat tone and lyrics.

23. Accusations of misogyny in popular music, especially blues and hip-hop, are ubiquitous. For a discussion that reframes the question in terms of corporate interests in rap, see Tricia Rose, *Hip Hop Wars*, 113–31. With reference to Johnson, Smith writes about his recordings from 1931 and 1932 that his "lyrics remained misogynistic," signaling the theme across his corpus (liner notes, in Johnson, *Complete Recorded Works in Chronological Order, 1925–1932*, vol. 7; discog.).

24. Smith, liner notes, in *Complete Recorded Works in Chronological Order, 1937–1947*, vol. 3 (discog.).

25. Smith, liner notes, in *Complete Recorded Works in Chronological Order, 1925–1932*, vol. 2 (discog.). Higginbotham would have been nineteen at the time of composition. Joe Davis was a music publisher and record producer who was her manager and promoter later in her career (Chilla, "Mystery of Irene Higginbothom"). Wood is credited on Johnson's OKeh label, as well as on Furry Lewis's recording on Vocalion and Smith's recording on Columbia. Johnson also recorded "Bedbug Blues Part 2" (New York City, 3 October 1927), written by Porter Grainger who accompanies him on piano, and "Bitin' Fleas Blues" (New York City, 9 November 1927), his own composition.

26. For a listing of versions of the song, see Peterson, "Mean Old Bed Bug Blues."

27. Obrecht recognizes the metaphor in the song to some extent, interpreting it, along with gambling, as representations of "the disillusioned" in Johnson's work (*Early Blues*, 130).

28. Whoever wrote the original lyrics, they contained the mother bedbug verse, because it was performed by Furry Lewis, Lizzie Miles, Bessie Smith, Betty Gray, Kitty Walters, and even Fats Waller with Jack Bland and His Rhythmmakers in 1953. Only the Bobby Leecan and Robert Cooksey recording does not contain it.

29. Songs that reference the penal system, gang labor, or various relief efforts during the Depression evoke social systems, but in ways that highlight how individuals interact with them, not as systems that subjugate and exploit. Even life histories from the Federal Writers' Project rarely express an awareness of broader economic, political, and social forces. One rare exception, from an African American sharecropper in Arkansas interviewed in 1939, links financial exploitation through the extension of credit to political systems (Terrill and Hirsch, *Such as Us*, 56).

30. For example, Rose estimates that twelve thousand people "lived directly off

the income derived from the sin industry of Storyville" (*Storyville*, 96).

31. Joseph Streckfus, famously, was personally involved in selecting repertoire and setting tempos (Kenney, *Jazz on the River*, 35, 50; Chevan, "Riverboat Music," 159–60).

32. Eyerman and Jamison, *Music and Social Movements*, 19. Although Eyerman and Jamison analyze music's function in social movements, the interpretative function is nonetheless relevant for this sociological aspect of Johnson's lyrical corpus.

33. One notable exception is Charley Patton's "High Sheriff Blues" (New York City, 30 January 1934) about his incarceration in Belzoni, Mississippi, that mentions individuals by name. He also sang about being thrown off of Dockery Plantation by the overseer in "34 Blues" (New York City, 31 January 1934).

34. Memphis's geographical position and designation as gateway to the Yazoo-Mississippi Delta create more continuity than discontinuity in terms of race relations with the agricultural area that lies to its south. Although B. B. King and other artists found opportunities in the urban setting unavailable to them in the rural Delta, Richard Wright considered Memphis to be part of the Jim Crow South and moved on to Chicago (*Black Boy*, 300–303).

35. Barker, *Life in Jazz*, 71.

36. Hall argues that "creolization" is a potentially subversive force born of a "syncretic dynamic which critically appropriates elements from the master-codes of the dominant culture and creolizes them" (*Essential Essays*, 213). Johnson's exposure to this process in New Orleans and St. Louis provides critical insight for his lyrical representations.

37. In the 1928 and 1947 versions.

38. Barker attributes to Dude Bottley a description of prostitutes and madams coming out to hear Buddy Bolden play in Lincoln Park on Monday nights that includes *teddies*: "He'd play them low, lowdown-under blues and them whores would perform something terrible 'til they'd get out of hand, shaking down to the floor and dropping their drawers and teddies: and that was a beautiful sight to see" (*Buddy Bolden*, 20).

39. The second verse of "Working Man's Blues" is very similar: "We up before sunrise, workin' 'leven long hours a day [2x] / We pay house rent and grocery bills and the pimp gets the rest of the pay."

40. The 1947 version is slightly clearer than the verse in "Crowing Rooster": "Man, we have got to get together, something's got to be done / We make the money while the pimps really have the fun / And when there's only house rent and grocery bill, no mon' no fun."

41. Drake and Cayton, *Black Metropolis*, 88, 113, 201. The United States Supreme Court eventually ruled in 1940 that racially restrictive housing covenants could be legally challenged (*Hansberry v. Lee*). The case arose when an African American homebuyer brought suit against the Woodlawn Property Owners' League. The restrictive covenant was upheld by the Superior Court of Cook County and the Supreme Court of Illinois before being overturned by the high court on a technicality (*Black Metropolis*, 184). Johnson would have been familiar with struggles over segregation from St. Louis. Voters there approved a segregation ordinance in 1916 by a two-to-one margin that was eventually struck down by the Supreme Court. Restrictive covenants ended in St. Louis in 1948 with the ruling in *Shelley v. Kraemer* (John J. Wright, *African Americans in Downtown St. Louis*, 40, 88).

42. Drake and Cayton, *Black Metropolis*, 202, 204; Seligman, *Block by Block*, 16–17.

43. On racial discrimination in relief efforts during the New Deal, see Mertz, *New Deal Policy*, 56, 89–90, 193–95; Sklaroff, *Black Culture*, 19; Sitkoff, *New Deal for Blacks*, 36–37, 54–55, 69–70.

44. On the formation of the second ghetto in the Avondale neighborhood in Cincinnati, see Casey-Leininger, "Making

the Second Ghetto." Johnson purchased a house in Avondale in 1948 with a conventional loan (Alger, *Original Guitar Hero*, 201).

45. On police pulling African Americans off the street to work on levees and beating or jailing those who refused, see Barry, *Rising Tide*, 195–96.

46. Bessie Smith's "Back Water Blues" (New York City, Columbia 14195D, 1927) and "Muddy Water" (New York City, Columbia 14197D, 1927) were recorded in February and March respectively, before the first major levee crevasses occurred. Advertising produced after the flood connected the songs to it (Evans, "High Water Everywhere," 14). Lonnie Johnson recorded "Back Water Blues" (St. Louis, 3 May 1927) a few days after the flood and, as in the other songs, stresses disaster and emotional responses to it. "Broken Levee Blues" is the only recording that evokes the abuses associated with the flood-response efforts.

47. On concentration camp conditions and life on top of the levees themselves, see Barry, *Rising Tide*, 200–201, 212–17; Parrish, *Flood Year 1927*, 44–45. Exposé accounts in African American newspapers were Johnson's likely sources of information about conditions for refugees, such as Harrington, "Refugees Herded Like Cattle"; Harrington, "Work or Go Hungry"; Harrington, "Flood Refugee Shot to Death"; and Wells-Barnett, "Flood Refugees Are Held."

48. Evans points out that Leadbelly, Big Bill Broonzy, and J. B. Lenoir are exceptions to the general lack of direct mention of racism in blues lyrics, but "only after they had achieved some success with sympathetic northern white audiences" (*NPR Curious Listener's Guide*, 97).

49. There is a massive body of scholarship on the question of the ability of aesthetic works to have a determining effect on historical and, especially, social and political reality. Without rehearsing those arguments here (as they reach back to Plato's *Republic*), it is worth signaling scholarship—such as Pratt, *Rhythm and Resistance*; Eyerman and Jamison, *Music and Social Movements*; Small, *Music of the Common Tongue*; and Floyd, *Power of Black Music*, among others—that argues for a social and/or political function of popular and, specifically, African American music. Supporting Small's contention that all music performs a ritual function (*Music of the Common Tongue*, 77), analysis of the blues tends to highlight audience engagement in performance—for example, Keil, *Urban Blues*, 15, 164; and Murray, *Stomping the Blues*, 38.

50. It is difficult to maintain that Johnson's music summons the "revolutionary force" that Pratt argues appears when the blues give voice to repressed desires, enabling the projection of fulfillment fantasies (*Rhythm and Resistance*, 92–95). Despite Johnson's urban background, his music also does not offer solutions to urban problems in the way that Keil argues for the soul- and gospel-inflected sounds of B. B. King, Albert King, Freddie King, Ray Charles, and Bobby Bland (*Urban Blues*, 76). Instead, the mode of interpellation and content of the messages create a dialectical relation between the individual and an imagined community constituted around moral behavior rather than racial identity or a desire for social and political justice. In this respect, the "imagined community" is distinctly different from the national and political virtual body Benedict Anderson evokes in *Imagined Communities*.

51. Pratt, *Rhythm and Resistance*, 4.

52. Eyerman and Jamison, *Music and Social Movements*, 1–2.

53. Ibid., 19.

54. The eventual justice theme is also articulated in "Trust Your Husband" (Chicago, 2 November 1939) by the narrator who warns a cheating wife that she will eventually get what she deserves, and in "Why I Love You" (New York, 15 July 1946), in which the narrator warns his partner that she will "learn" to love him.

55. In this respect, Johnson's identity seems to be a manifestation of the "musical

individuality within collectivity" that Floyd posits as characteristic of Black music ("Ring Shout," 268).

CHAPTER 4

1. Hildebrand, liner notes, in Johnson, with Snowden, *Blues, Ballads, and Jumpin' Jazz*, vol. 2 (discog.).

2. Bessie Smith's vamp to "Need a Little Sugar in My Bowl" (New York City, 20 November 1931) provides a good example of her extended, vibrato-colored singing of the word "blues."

3. Frith, *Performing Rites*, 187–88.

4. *These Are Our Lives*, vii.

5. Ibid., 375–76. Descriptions and names in the interview, as well as the attempts to reproduce "dialect," suggest that the flood victims are African American.

6. Cobb, *Most Southern Place on Earth*, 128–29.

7. Harrington, "Use Troops in Flood Area."

8. The expression "concentration camp" comes from White, "Walter White Reports." Bluesman David "Honeyboy" Edwards discussed forced labor during floods in an interview: "And sometimes when the water level, when the levee break, high water break, they'd pick the boys up out of the streets and they wouldn't ask you nothing. 'Come on, go on to work,' stacking them there sacks down at the levee, stop the water from comin in the city. They wouldn't say how much they gave you or nothing—just 'Come on, get on the levee, get them sacks and stack them up over there.' 'Yes, sir.' And after you get through they might give you a couple of dollars, but you got to do that. That was a rough time down there, rough time" (Pearson, *Sounds So Good to Me*, 24).

9. Deaths, particularly of African Americans, were notoriously underreported. Motivated by politics, Herbert Hoover lied about the death toll of the 1927 Mississippi River Flood, in which somewhere between 250 and 500 people (and likely more) lost their lives during the immediate emergency and subsequent rescue and relief efforts (Daniel, *Deep'n as It Come*, 10).

10. A variant appears in the version recorded in 1965 as well (Johnson, *Unsung Blues Legend*; discog.).

11. "South Bound Backwater" mentions a levee break without the racialized oppression.

12. This verse resembles and may have inspired Charley Patton's narrative technique in "High Water Everywhere," parts 1 and 2 (Paramount 12909, 1929). See my discussion of the song's narrative structure (*Time in the Blues*, 142–45).

13. The variant "Blues is at my window and trouble is knockin' down my door" occurs in the remake of "Fallin' Rain Blues" (Cincinnati, December 1947) released by King Records in 1951.

14. Hearing the sound of the lover's voice echoes the representational techniques of the haunting songs discussed below.

15. Similar but louder and more pronounced sound effects are also used to imitate the wind on "St. Louis Cyclone Blues" (New York City, 3 October 1927).

16. This is less true of the version recorded in Cincinnati on 13 August 1948 than of the one released on *Blues and Ballads*, [vol. 1].

17. Writing this chapter under a shelter-in-place order from the COVID-19 pandemic makes this all the more palpable, prompting me to wonder about the connections between Johnson's loss of family in the influenza pandemic of 1918 while he was far away from New Orleans and this theme that runs throughout his corpus.

18. Johnson recorded an upbeat, optimistic tune in a swing style with this theme in his sessions with Smithsonian Folkways, "Long Road to Travel," that contrasts significantly with this earlier work (*Complete Folkways Recordings*; discog.).

19. The "Lonesome Road" was recorded for Victor by Gene Austin in September 1927. As Berish explains, "It was a hit, and many cover versions followed," by

various artists from the 1930s to the early 1940s, including for the film adaptation of *Showboat* (*Lonesome Roads*, 29).

20. The song "When You Always by Yourself" also suggests that for Johnson "right-hand" means dependable: "But when you've got love on your side, you've always got a right-hand friend" (*Complete Folkways Recordings*; discog.).

21. "Lonesome Road" contains the slight variant "There's no train to my hometown; there ain't but one way to go [2x] / There's mile after mile, tramping down that long, old muddy road."

22. Belford, *Devil at the Confluence*, 161.

23. Lipsitz, *How Racism Takes Place*, 67–68.

24. "Lonesome Road" (Chicago, 13 February 1942) contains a variant: "Ain't but one thing that worries me night and day / There ain't but one thing, worries me night and day / There's a place they call Death Valley and it's just halfway."

25. Another variant, "That Lonesome Road" (*Complete Folkways Recordings*; discog.), does not contain the second-person form of address.

26. "Roaming Rambler Blues" (New York City, 12 August 1927) is a much earlier treatment of the theme of rambling that expresses more ambivalence, understanding it both as a kind of freedom and a kind of compulsion.

27. Smith dubs "Deep Sea Blues" "a disguised version of "Empty Bed Blues," a Bessie Smith song (liner notes, in Johnson, *Complete Recorded Works in Chronological Order, 1925–1932*, vol. 6; discog.).

28. I am grateful to one of the anonymous reviewers of the manuscript for pointing out these musical elements.

29. In discussing hokum, Evans notes that "a number of the female vaudeville singers and male-female duos also recorded hokum blues in the late 1920s and early 1930s in an attempt to counter slumping record sales that came with the onset of the economic Depression," which would include Johnson ("Development of the Blues," 50). Johnson recorded solo hokum songs—"I Got the Best Jelly Roll In Town," parts 1 and 2 (New York City, 23 January 1930) and "He's a Jelly-Roll Baker" (Chicago, 13 February 1942)—as well as duets with Victoria Spivey: "Toothache Blues–Part 1" (New York City, 17 October 1928), "Furniture Man Blues," parts 1 and 2 (New York City, 18 October 1928), and "Toothache Blues Part 2" (New York City, 18 October 1928).

30. The much later "I Don't Hurt Anymore" (on Johnson, *Blues by Lonnie Johnson*; discog.) in its opening verse also mentions "an empty space inside" produced by a cheating spouse. In this song, the phrase seems to mean that he no longer loves his wife, that the place she once occupied in his heart is now empty. In this song, the upbeat tempo and bold singing style belie the themes of loss and abandonment.

31. The lines are reminiscent of the second verse of Bessie Smith's "In the House Blues" (New York City, 11 June 1931).

32. In the continuation of a theme that dates back to spirituals, some blues songs deal with death as a great equalizer, such as Memphis Slim and the House Rockers' "Mother Earth" (Premium 50-221, 1951). These songs are often consistent with the African American song tradition of invoking a better place, which Berish traces back to the ring shout (*Lonesome Roads*, 5). Johnson's treatment of death is distinctly different.

33. "Nothing but Trouble" (Cincinnati, 20 September 1950) also identifies the loss of his parents as the source of the narrator's distinctly bad luck. Interestingly, based on interviews Johnson gave late in life, Alger speculates that Johnson's parents were spared in the influenza pandemic of 1918, but that he lost all of his siblings except James (*Original Guitar Hero*, 53).

34. The appeal of this theme may explain Johnson's cover of the Ellington song "(In My) Solitude," recorded at Bernie Strassberg's house in Queens in 1965, released on Johnson, *Unsung Blues Legend* (discog.).

35. Similar lyrics associating the rocking chair and suicide appear in Johnson's "Little Rockin' Chair" (Cincinnati, 14 September 1950). The theme may be drawn from Thelma La Vizzo and Richard Jones, "Trouble in Mind Blues" (Chicago, May 1924) and/or Barbecue Bob Hicks, "Motherless Chile Blues" (Atlanta, 5 November 1927), both of which have their roots in spirituals.

36. The expression is inspired by the Crowded House album *Together Alone* and its title track sung in English and Maori, composed by Bub Wehi, Mark G. Hart, and Neil Mullane Finn. The jazz standard "Alone Together," written by Howard Dietz and Arthur Schwartz in 1932 for the Broadway musical *Flying Colors*, expresses the opposite sentiment summarized in its final line, "We can weather the great unknown if we're alone together."

37. Rogers highlights what he calls "Johnson's subconscious awareness of duple and triple meters and his ability to juxtapose them at will in his improvisations," with specific reference to "Blues in My Soul" ("Lonnie Johnson's Instrumental Style," 25).

38. Compare Givan's discussion of deviation from a normative cell in Sonny Rollins's "Blue 7" ("Gunther Schuller," 212) and Brackett's definition of rhythmic signifying as disappointing expectations in a way that "creates a dialogue between what the listener expects and what the artist plays" (*Interpreting Popular Music*, 134).

CONCLUSION

1. Wald suggests thinking of Johnson "as a sort of male blues queen" (*Escaping the Delta*, 29). McGinley argues that a narrative of blues history promoted by critics, scholars, and fans marked as secondary and "inauthentic" a theatrical tradition in the blues practiced largely by women (*Staging the Blues*, 7–9). As an example of this type of scholarship, Evans looks for the use of elements of "folk composition," including traditional verses, to place artists along a spectrum from folk to popular, noting that women's classic blues singers use few traditional verses (*Big Road Blues*, 64). Evans also highlights the impact of commercial interests in standardizing blues and privileging a certain conception of originality (75–86). Commercial interests motivated performances of race in blackface minstrelsy that would be labeled as "inauthentic" in relation to "authentic" folk blues; see Karl Miller, *Segregating Sound*, 142, 150, 276. But as Woods points out, citing cultural historian Lawrence Levine, "Levine also argued in support of the proposition that commerce does not automatically translate into inauthenticity and irrelevancy" (*Development Arrested*, 109). The devaluing of hokum acts may be because of their resemblance to "humorous" representations of race, class, and gender on the vaudeville and minstrel stage. For a discussion of hokum, see Evans, "Development of the Blues," 50. Finally, Clapton's racist, drunken rant onstage in Birmingham in 1976, included in the documentary *Eric Clapton: Life in 12 Bars* (2017), and for which he has apologized many times, only fueled accusations of appropriating and profiting from African American music. For a summary of the controversies surrounding "white blues" and the furor ignited by Lawrence Hoffman's guest editorial in *Guitar Player* in August 1990, see Garon, "White Blues."

2. Charters's *Country Blues*, originally published in 1959, inaugurated the scholarly tradition of providing portraits of artists, including Lonnie Johnson.

3. As in the case of Johnson, cross-genre borrowings also complicate the identity of Michael Jackson. As Mats Johansson points out, he adopted the moniker "King of Pop" to incorporate techniques from multiple musical traditions (including rock associated with white males) into his vocal performances. Ultimately, the pop label enabled more flexibility in constructing an unstable identity for his professional persona that dovetailed with his racial, sexual,

and gender identity ("Michael Jackson," 275).

4. St. Cyr, "Interview."

5. Giddens describes her performance as an "homage-to-Armstrong vocal" (*Visions of Jazz*, 96).

6. Foster, *Pops Foster*, 92.

7. Providing a transcription, Gene Anderson writes, "Johnson's intriguing solo ... is based on the F minor permutation of the A flat pentatonic scale with chromatic passing tones between scale degrees three-four and five-six" (*Original Hot Five Recordings*, 171–72).

8. Harker describes a similar effect of Johnson's "quiet soulfulness that adds greatly to the mood ... and is particularly effective in introducing Armstrong's solo" in "Savoy Blues" (*Louis Armstrong's Hot Five*, 125).

9. Gene Anderson, *Original Hot Five Recordings*, 170.

10. Most New Orleans and Chicago jazz bands, like Armstrong's, employed banjo rather than guitar because of the guitar's volume limitations. As Berish points out, it is not until the mid-1930s that swing bands began employing guitarists (*Lonesome Roads*, 168). I am indebted to Berish's inspired analysis of Charlie Christian's solo with the Benny Goodman sextet in "Flying Home," and particularly for the vocabulary he develops (184–85).

11. Early jazz criticism noted that "the jazz ensemble usually contains three sections, which are not four-part choirs as in the concert orchestra: percussion (double-bass, drums, piano, guitar), brass (cornet, trumpet, trombone), and reeds (saxophones and clarinet)" (Harap, "Case for Hot Jazz," 55). It is normally the reed and brass voices that step forward as individuals and create tension, with the rhythm section providing the backing. Hersch's discussion of jazz improvisation based on a Bakhtinian model of dialogism provides a helpful model for thinking about improvisation in the ensemble beyond the lead player ("Unfinalizable," 273).

12. Berish, *Lonesome Roads*, 95.

13. Evans's description of the first generation of blues artists is typical in this respect: "The ideal of the blues singer was to be free to move about, riding in style when times were good and hoboing when times were tough, hiring himself out to the highest bidder for his manual labor or musical services or else hustling up a living by his own wits and charm, generally living as well as he could and leaving whenever he became dissatisfied or restless. He avoided being tied to the land, either as an owner or through a long-term sharecropping arrangement, as this meant the loss of mobility and acceptance of the social status quo. He preferred to sing and play for tips on street corners and in parks, on passenger trains and riverboats, and at railroad stations, pool halls, bars, cafés, brothels, house parties, dances, traveling shows. It was a dangerous life, but potentially a rewarding one and certainly always interesting" ("Goin' Up the Country," 36–37).

14. See my discussion of tense and narration in *Time in the Blues* (101–7). Johnson's narrative structures tend to be more thematically consistent, with longer lines of lyrics, producing a greater degree of cohesion than songs in the rural tradition.

15. See my analysis of the narrative structure and displacements of "High Water Everywhere," parts 1 and 2, in *Time in the Blues* (142–44).

16. Charley Patton's "High Sheriff Blues" (New York City, 20 January 1934) is exceptional for a number of reasons, including its accusations made against law enforcement officials by name. It contains lines of direct address, such as in the second verse, "Le' me tell you folksies, how he treated me," and the spoken line "Blues I had, boys" after the fourth verse, reinforcing the sense of testifying or bearing witness against police abuse.

17. Wald, summarizing various sources on Johnny Shines traveling and performing with Robert Johnson, writes, "It is not clear when Shines met Johnson, or how often they got together and split up again over the next few years" (*Escaping the Delta*, 115). Alan Lomax recorded Eddie "Son" House, Fiddlin' Joe Martin, Willie Brown, and Leroy Williams performing

"Walking Blues" at Clark Store in Lake Cormorant, Mississippi. The liner notes suggest that "the string band format . . . was common in the Delta Blues but rarely recorded by commercial companies, who wanted less expensive solo recordings" (*Land Where the Blues Began*; discog.). This seems more like a valorization of what Lomax recorded than a statement of fact regarding record companies, since jug bands were recorded.

18. In the case of Robert Johnson, the myth of the lone individual extends to scholarly neglect of Ike Zimmerman's role as his mentor; see Gussow, *Beyond the Crossroads*, esp. 209–12; and Conforth, "Ike Zimmerman."

19. Johnson's connection to Jesse Johnson and others was distinctly different from the role played by H. C. Speir and Ralph Lembo, who scouted talent from the rural areas for recording companies.

20. Smith, liner notes, in Johnson, *Complete Recorded Works in Chronological Order, 1925–1932*, vol. 1 (discog.).

21. Blues piano players pose an interesting challenge to the standard portrait of the blues musician. Lack of portability, which often means urban roots, relatively greater knowledge of music, stylistic affinities to other kinds of music like jazz, ragtime, and popular song, and other issues complicate the perception of them. Leroy Carr, Roosevelt Sykes, Little Brother Montgomery, and others played sawmills, some jukes, but mostly in urban areas with access to pianos, but are not always included among traditional blues players. See, for example, Charters's portrait of Carr, a "city man," in *Country Blues* (137–47).

22. Sallis cites contemporary critics Marty Grosz and Joel Vance ("Eddie Lang," 31–32). Writing with the bias of early blues critics, Charters asserts that "Lang was the finer musician, and had probably more knowledge of the guitar's harmonic possibilities than any musicians of his period, but Lonnie had an emotional sense and emotional intensity that shaded Lang's brilliance" (*Country Blues*, 82).

23. Kienzle, *Great Guitarists*, 135. Lambert characterizes the complementarity by distinguishing between their different approaches to bends: "Lonnie bends notes to make them 'cry,' wringing every last drop of emotion from a note, while Eddie bends notes to give them a slightly 'off,' out-of-tune sound. Lonnie's is the more emotional (bluesy) approach, Eddie's an intellectual (jazzy) approach" ("From Blues to Jazz Guitar," 41).

24. Even though Rogers and Sumlin were able to pursue independent careers fronting bands, it was only by virtue of their significant contributions to the bands of front men like Waters and Howlin' Wolf. The phenomenon of relative lack of recognition for those perceived as secondary players is not limited to guitarists, but extends to pianists, like Otis Spann, and drummers, like Fred Below and Willie "Big Eyes" Smith.

25. Lambert notes that "Lonnie frequently ignores the bar lines, changing chords at will, and any attempt to chart what he's doing rhythmically is at best an approximation" ("From Blues to Jazz Guitar," 38). See his chart of sections of "Playing with the Strings" (ibid., 39–40). Brackett distinguishes "floating above the beat" with techniques of anticipation and delay and "landing squarely on it" (*Interpreting Popular Music*, 92).

26. I do not mean to suggest that he was naïve, but rather saw the advantage in participating in his own commodification. Johnson was certainly aware of the machinations of recording companies and others as evidenced in his remark before performing the song "Looking for My Sweetie" about Rudy Vallée "stealing" and retitling it "Confessin'" because it was not copyrighted (*Complete Folkways Recordings*; discog.).

27. Toynbee stresses that the creative act is "never a pure enactment of subjective intention, it must, as a condition of its possibility, have an awareness of itself as a performed act in a social milieu, at a particular time and place" (*Making Popular Music*, 58).

Discography

JOHNSON, ALONZO "LONNIE": FEATURED ARTIST ORIGINAL RECORDINGS

This list includes documented untitled sides and some reissues on EP or LP released during Johnson's lifetime.

Johnson, Lonnie. "6/88 Glide." OKeh Matrix W81587-B. 31 October 1927. Unissued. Library of Congress LBC-14.
———. "Ain't Gonna Give Nobody None of My Jelly Roll." Bluesville Matrix 2141. 5 April 1960. Unissued.
———. "All My Love Belongs to You." King Matrix K-11892. 27 April 1964. King 5945.
———. *Another Night to Cry*. Prestige Bluesville BVLP 1062. 1962.
———. "Another Woman Booked Out and Bound to Go." OKeh Matrix W403595. 7 January 1930. OKeh 8886.
———. "Away Down in the Alley Blues." OKeh Matrix W400279-A. 21 February 1928. OKeh 8575.
———. "Baby Ain't I Losing You." King Matrix K-5553. 13 August 1947. Unissued.
———. "Baby I Love It." 21 September 1961. Bluesville. Unissued.
———. "Baby Please Don't Leave Home No More." OKeh Matrix W402441-A. 11 June 1929. OKeh 8754.
———. "Baby, Please Tell Me." OKeh Matrix W74271-A. 13 August 1926. OKeh 8376.
———. "Baby, Remember Me." Bluebird Matrix 074071-1. 13 February 1942. Bluebird 34-0714.
———. "Baby, Will You Please Come Home?" OKeh Matrix W80745-B. 25 April 1927. OKeh 8484.
———. "Baby, You Don't Know My Mind." OKeh Matrix 9687-A. 14 May 1926. OKeh 8340.
———. "Back Water [Backwater] Blues." OKeh Matrix W80831-B. 3 May 1927. OKeh 8466.
———. "Ball and Chain Blues." OKeh Matrix W74268-A. 13 August 1926. OKeh 8435.
———. "Be Careful." Bluebird Matrix 053108-1. 22 May 1940. Bluebird B8564.
———. "Beautiful but Dumb." OKeh Matrix W404946-B. 16 June 1931. OKeh 8898.
———. "Bed of Sand." OKeh Matrix W73938-B. 19 January 1926. OKeh 8291.
———. "Bedbug Blues Part 2." OKeh Matrix W81504-B. 3 October 1927. OKeh 8586.
———. "Best Jockey in Town." OKeh Matrix W404969-B. 21 August 1931. OKeh 8916.
———. "Bewildered." King Matrix 5575. 5 January 1947. King 4261. 1948.
———. "Bitin' Fleas Blues." OKeh Matrix W81797-A. 9 November 1927. OKeh 8524.
———. "Blue Ghost Blues." OKeh Matrix W81802-B. 9 November 1927. OKeh 8557.
———. "Blue Ghost Blues." Decca Matrix 63512-A. 31 March 1938. Decca 7537.
———. "Blues and Trouble Has Got Me Down." OKeh Matrix W80744-B. 25 April 1927. Unknown.
———. *Blues by Lonnie Johnson*. Prestige Bluesville BVLP 1007. 1960.
———. "Blues for Everybody." Disc Matrix D 493. 15 July 1946. Disc 6065. 1947.
———. "Blues in G." OKeh Matrix W400280-A. 21 February 1928. OKeh 8575.
———. "Blues in My Soul." Disc Matrix D 495. 15 July 1946. Disc 5065. 1947.

———. "Blues in the Clouds." King Matrix K-5340. 14 December 1947. King 4260.

———. "Blues Is Only a Ghost." OKeh Matrix W404847-A. 11 February 1931. OKeh 8875.

———. "Blues Stay Away from Me." King Matrix K-5806-2. 29 November 1949. King 4336.

———. "Brenda." King Matrix K-11893. 1 June 1964. King 5907, King 45-5907.

———. "Brenda." Arhoolie Matrix 518. 1960s. On *Hear Me Howling! Blues, Ballads, & Beyond: The Arhoolie 50th Anniversary Boxset*. Arhoolie 518A-D. 2011.

———. "A Broken Heart that Never Smiles." OKeh Matrix W80765. 27 April 1927. OKeh 8601.

———. "Broken Levee Blues." OKeh Matrix W400492-A. 13 March 1928. OKeh 8618.

———. "The Bull Frog and the Toad." OKeh Matrix W404041-F. 5 June 1930. OKeh 8802.

———. "Call Me Darling." King Matrix K-5555. 13 August 1948. King 267.

———. "Can't Sleep Anymore." King Matrix K-9147. 3 June 1952. King 45-4553.

———. "Careless Love." OKeh Matrix W401337-B. 16 November 1928. OKeh 8635.

——— ["Jimmy Jordan"]. "Cat You Been Messin' Aroun'." Columbia Matrix W152061. 12 January 1932. Columbia 14647-D.

———. "Chicago Blues." Bluebird Matrix 059210-1. 7 February 1941. Bluebird B8779.

———. "Chicago Blues." King Matrix K-5446. December 1947. King 958.

———. "Clementine Blues." 16 October 1963. On *Portraits in Blues Vol. 6*. Storyville 162. 1964.

———. *The Complete Folkways Recordings*. Folkways Records SFW40067. 1993.

———. "Confused." King Matrix K-5804. 29 November 1949. King 4336.

———. "Crowing Rooster." Bluebird Matrix 59205-1 7 February 1941. Bluebird B8804.

———. "Crowing Rooster Blues." OKeh Matrix W400491-A. 13 March 1928. OKeh 8574.

———. "Darlin'." King Matrix K-9092. 26 October 1951. 4503.

———. "Death Valley Is Half Way to My Home." OKeh Matrix W403668. 23 January 1930. OKeh 8768.

———. "Deep Sea Blues." OKeh Matrix W403987. 23 April 1930. OKeh 8822.

———. "Devil's Got the Blues." Decca Matrix 63518-A. 31 March 1938. Decca 7487.

———. "The Devil's Woman." Bluebird Matrix 074072. 13 February 1942. Bluebird B-9022.

———. "Don't Be No Fool." Bluebird Matrix 053110-1. 22 May 1940. Bluebird B-8530.

———. "Don't Blame Her." Aladdin Matrix 4007. 2 June 1947. Aladdin 3029.

———. "Don't Drive Me from Your Door." OKeh Matrix W4036723-A. 23 January 1930. OKeh 8796.

———. "Don't Make Me Cry Baby." Rama Matrix RR-18. 1953. Rama 9. 1954.

———. "Don't Play Bad with My Love." King Matrix K-5721. 8 April 1949. King 4317.

———. "Drifting Along Blues." Disc Matrix 488. 15 July 1946. Disc 6064. 1947.

———. "Drunk Again." King Matrix K-5353-2. December 1947. Gusto 5039.

———. "Fallin' Rain Blues." King Matrix 5350-1. December 1947. King 4450. 1951.

———. "Falling Rain Blues." OKeh Matrix 9436-A. 4 November 1925. OKeh 8253.

——— ["Jimmy Jordan"]. "The Faults of All Women and Men." Columbia Matrix W1511669. 6 July 1931. Columbia 14622-D.

———. "Feel So Lonesome." King Matrix K-5549. 13 August 1947. King 4245. 1948.

———. "Feeling Low Down." King Matrix K-5352-1. December 1947. King 4388.

———. "Fickle Mamma Blues." OKeh Matrix W81216-B. 11 August 1927. OKeh 8505.

Discography / 181

———. "Five O'Clock Blues." OKeh Matrix 73945-A. 20 January 1926. OKeh 8417.

———. "Flood Water Blues." Decca Matrix 91341-A. 8 November 1937. Decca 7397.

———. "Fly Right, Baby." Bluebird Matrix 074070-1. 13 February 1942. Bluebird 34-0708. 1943.

———. "Four Hands Are Better Than Two." OKeh Matrix W80815-B. 1 May 1927. Columbia CG-33566.

———. "Four-O-Three Blues." Victor Matrix BS-044052-1. 2 November 1939. Bluebird B-8338.

———. "Friendless and Blue." Decca Matrix 63517-A. 31 March 1928. Decca 7487.

———. "Friendless Blues." King Matrix K 5323. 14 December 1947. Federal. 45-12376. 1960.

———. "From 20 to 44." Bluebird Matrix 074066-1. 13 February 1942. Bluebird B-8980.

———. "From a Wash Woman on Up." OKeh Matrix W404947-B. 16 June 1931. OKeh 8898.

———. "From Now on Make Your Whoopee at Home." OKeh Matrix W402439-B. 11 June 1929. OKeh 8722.

———. "Fussing and Fretting." OKeh Matrix 81795-B. 9 November 1927. Unissued.

———. "Get Yourself Together." Bluebird Matrix 053111-1. 22 May 1940. Bluebird B-8530.

———. "Go Back to Your No Good Man." Columbia Matrix W152264. 12 August 1932. Unissued.

———. "A Good, Happy Home." OKeh Matrix 9686-A. 14 May 1926. OKeh 8340.

———. "Good Night Darling." King Matrix K-5548-1. 13 August 1947. King 4450. 1951.

———. "Good Old Wagon." OKeh Matrix 9685-A. 14 May 1926. OKeh 8358.

———. "Got the Blues for Murder Only." OKeh Matrix W404560-A. 22 November 1930. OKeh 8846.

———. "Got the Blues for the West End." Decca Matrix 91344-A. 8 November 1937. Decca 7445.

———. "Happy New Year, Darling." King Matrix 5312. 10 December 1947. King 4251. 1951.

———. "Hard Times Ain't Gone No Where." Decca Matrix 91340-A. 8 November 1937. Decca 7388.

———. "He's a Jelly-Roll Baker." Bluebird Matrix 074074-1. 13 February 1942. Bluebird B-9006.

———. "Headed for Southland." OKeh Matrix W403669-A. 23 January 1930. OKeh 8786.

———. "Heart of Iron." Bluebird Matrix 074073-1. 13 February 1942. Bluebird B-9022.

———. "Hell Is a Name for All Sinners." Columbia Matrix W151666-1. 6 July 1931. Columbia 14667-D.

———. "Home Wreckers Blues." Columbia Matrix W151667. 6 July 1931. Columbia 14667-D.

———. "How Could You." Aladdin Matrix 4005A-1. 15 July 1946. Aladdin 197.

———. "How Could You Be So Mean." Disc Matrix D 489. 15 July 1946. Disc 6061. 1947.

———. "I Ain't Gonna Be Your Fool." Decca Matrix 63519-A. 31 March 1938. 7509.

———. "I Did All I Could." RCA Victor Matrix 059211-1. 7 February 1941. Bluebird B8779.

———. "I Done Told You." OKeh Matrix W80746-B. 25 April 1927. Unissued.

———. "I Found a Dream." King Matrix K-5720. 9 May 1949. King 4297.

———. "I Found a Dream." Rama Matrix RR-42. Rama 20. 1953.

———. "I Got the Best Jelly Roll in Town—Part 1." OKeh Matrix W403670-B. 23 January 1930. OKeh 8786.

———. "I Got the Best Jelly Roll in Town—Part 2." OKeh Matrix W403671-B. 23 January 1930. OKeh 8796.

———. "I Have No Sweet Woman Now." OKeh Matrix 9689-A. 14 May 1926. OKeh 8411.

———. "I Have to Do My Time." OKeh Matrix W404281-B. 8 August 1930. OKeh 8909.

———. "I Just Can't Stand These Blues." OKeh Matrix W403974-B. 26 April 1930. OKeh 8886.
———. "I Know It's Love." King Matrix K-5552. 13 August 1947. King 4261. 1948.
———. "I Love It." Aladdin Matrix 4011. 2 June 1947. Unissued.
———. "I Love You, Mary Lou." OKeh Matrix W81188-B. 5 August 1927. Unissued.
———. "I Want My Baby." King Matrix K-5335. 14 December 1947. King 4225. 1948.
———. "I'm Gonna Dodge the Blues, Just Wait and See." OKeh Matrix 74272-A. 13 August 1926. OKeh 8391.
———. "I'm Guilty." King Matrix K-9144. 3 June 1952. King 45-4553.
———. "I'm in Love with Love." Disc Matrix D 487. 15 July 1946. Disc 5060
———. "I'm Just Dumb." Bluebird Matrix 053109-1 22 May 1940. Bluebird B-8564.
———. "I'm Nuts About That Gal." Columbia Matrix W152259-2. 12 August 1932. OKeh 8946.
———. "I'm Nuts over You (But You Just a Teaser)." Decca Matrix 91346-A. 8 November 1937. Decca 7397.
———. "I'm So Afraid." King Matrix K-5805. 29 November 1949. King 4346. 1950.
———. "I'm So Crazy for Love." King Matrix K-5955. 14 September 1950. King 4411.
———. "I'm So Glad." King Matrix K-5310. 10 December 1947. King 4212. 1948.
———. "I'm So Tired of Living All Alone." OKeh Matrix W400447-A. 9 March 1928. OKeh 8677.
———. "In Love Again." Bluebird Matrix 059212-1. 7 February 1941. Bluebird B-8748.
———. "In Love Again." Disc Matrix D 494. 15 July 1946. Disc 6064. 1947.
———. "In Love Again." King Matrix K-5448. December 1947. King 4225. 1948.
———. "It Ain't What You Usta Be." Decca Matrix 91342-A. 8 November 1937. Decca 7427.
———. "It Was All in Vain." King Matrix K-9025-1. 26 February 1951. King 4473.

———. "It's Been So Long." King Matrix K-5338. 14 December 1947. King 520.
———. "It's Too Late to Cry." King Matrix K-5550-2. 13 August 1947. King unissued. *Me and My Crazy Self.* Charly 266. 1991.
———. "Jelly Killed Old Sam." Columbia Matrix 151668-3. 6 July 1931. Columbia 14662-D.
———. "Jelly Roll Baker." King Matrix K-5374-2. December 1947. King 4388.
———. "Jersey Belle Blues." Victor Matrix BS-044050. 2 November 1939. Bluebird B-8287.
———. "Johnson Trio Stomp." OKeh Matrix 73946-A. 20 January 1926. OKeh 8417.
———. "Just a Roaming Man." OKeh Matrix W404848-A. 11 February 1931. OKeh 8875.
———. "Just Another Day." King Matrix K-9145. 3 June 1952. King 4572.
———. "Kansas City Blues Part 1 and 2" OKeh Matrices W82092-B, W82093-C. 17 December 1927. OKeh 8537.
———. "Keep It to Yourself." OKeh Matrix W403750-A. 7 February 1930. OKeh 8812.
———. "Keep What You Got." Disc Matrix D 485. 15 July 1946. Disc 6062. 1947.
———. "Laplegged Drunk Again." Decca Matrix 63522-A. 31 March 1938. Decca 7537.
———. "The Last Call." Bluebird Matrix 074067-1. 13 February 1942. Bluebird B-8980. 1942.
———. "Layin' on the Strings." OKeh Matrix W81810-B. 10 November 1927. Unissued.
———. "Lazy Woman (Blues)." Bluebird Matrix 059208-1. 7 February 1941. Bluebird B-8748.
———. "Let All Married Women Alone." OKeh Matrix W404561-A. 22 November 1930. OKeh 8846.
———. "Life Saver Blues." OKeh Matrix W81801-B. 9 November 1927. OKeh 8557.

Discography / 183

———. "Little Rockin' Chair." King Matrix K-5957-3. 14 September 1950. King 4423.
———. "Lonesome Day Blues." Paradise 123. 1948.
———. "Lonesome Ghost Blues." OKeh Matrix W81215-B. 11 August 1927. OKeh 8505.
———. "Lonesome Jail Blues." OKeh Matrix 73939-B. 19 January 1926. OKeh 8309A.
———. "Lonesome Road." Bluebird Matrix 074069-1. 13 February 1942. Bluebird 34-0714. 1942.
———. "Lonesome Road." Parlophone GEP 8635. 1957. King Records 395-520. 1958.
———. "Long Black Train." OKeh Matrix W404280-C. 5 August 1930. OKeh 8822.
———. "Lonnie's Got the Blues." OKeh Matrix 9674-A. 13 May 1926. OKeh 8411.
———. *Losing Game*. Prestige Bluesville. 28 December 1960. 1961.
———. "Love Is Just a Song (Your Love Is Cold)." Columbia Matrix W152263. 12 August 1932. Columbia unissued. Library of Congress, LBC-2.
———. "Love Is the Answer." Aladdin Matrix 4006-1. 2 June 1947. Aladdin 197.
———. "Love Me Tonight." King Matrix K-11890. 29 May 1964. King 45-5907.
———. "Love Story Blues." OKeh Matrix 73942-B. 20 January 1926. OKeh 8282.
———. "Love That Gal." King Matrix K-5337. 14 December 1947. On *Lonnie Johnson Sings 24 Twelve Bar Blues*. King 958. 1966.
———. "The Loveless Blues." Victor Matrix BS-044051-1. 2 November 1939. Bluebird B-8338.
———. "Low Down St. Louis Blues." OKeh Matrix W404849. 11 February 1931. Unissued.
———. "Low Land Moan." OKeh Matrix W82043-A. 12 December 1927. OKeh 8677.
———. "Lucky Dreamer." King Matrix K-11891. 29 May 1964. King 45-5945.
———. "Man Killing Broad." Decca Matrix 91339-A. 8 November 1937. Decca 7445.
———. "Matinee Hour in New Orleans." King Matrix K-5576. January 1947. King 4277.
———. "Me and My Crazy Self." King Matrix K-9094. 26 October 1951. King 4510.
———. "Mean Old Bed Bug Blues." OKeh Matrix W81214-B. 11 August 1927. OKeh 8497.
———. "Memories of You." Prestige Bluesville 45-812. 1961.
———. "Men, Get Wise to Yourself." OKeh Matrix W405140-A. 9 February 1932. OKeh 8937.
———. "Mr. Johnson's Blues." OKeh Matrix 9435-A. 4 November 1925. OKeh 9435.
———. "Mr. Johnson's Blues No. 2." OKeh Matrix W402440-C. 11 June 1929. OKeh 8709.
———. "Mr. Johnson's Swing." Decca Matrix 63520-A. 31 March 1938. Decca 7509.
———. "My Baby's Gone." King Matrix K-5334. 14 December 1947. On *Lonnie Johnson Sings 24 Twelve Bar Blues*. King 958. 1966.
———. "My Heart Don't Cry Out for You Anymore." OKeh Matrix W401712. 14 March 1929. Unknown.
———. "My Heart Don't Cry Out for You Any More." OKeh Matrix 401712-A. 14 March 1929. OKeh unissued.
———. "My Last Love." Disc Matrix D 484. 15 July 1946. Disc 6061. 1947.
———. "My Love Don't Belong to You." Columbia Matrix W152262-2. 12 August 1932. Columbia 14674-D.
———. "My Love Is Down." RCA Victor Matrix D4AB-329-1A. 14 December 1944. Bluebird 34-0742. 1946.
———. "My Mother's Eyes." King Matrix K-9093. 26 October 1951. King 4510.
———. "My My Baby." King Matrix K-5581. 19 November 1948. King 4278. 1949.
———. "My Woman Is Gone." Rama Matrix RR-19. 1953. Rama 9. 1954.

———. "The New Fallin' Rain Blues." OKeh Matrix W402442-B. 11 June 1929. OKeh 8709.
———. "New Falling Rain Blues." Decca Matrix 63521-A. 31 March 1938. Decca 7461.
———. "New Orleans Blues." King Matrix K-5588. 19 November 1948. Unissued.
———. "Nile of Genago." OKeh Matrix W73944-A. 20 January 1926. OKeh 8291.
———. "No More Troubles Now." OKeh Matrix W404437. 11 September 1930. OKeh 8831.
———. "Nobody's Lovin' Me." King Matrix K-5956. 14 September 1950. 4432.
———. "Not the Chump I Used to Be." OKeh Matrix W404968. 21 August 1931. OKeh 8916.
———. "Not Until You Came My Way." King Matrix K 5722. 8 April 1949. On *Lonnie Johnson Sings 24 Twelve Bar Blues*. King 958. 1966.
———. "Nothin' Clicken' Chicken." King Matrix K-5958. 14 September 1950. King 4411.
———. "Nothing but a Rat." Victor Matrix BS-044047. 2 November 1939. Bluebird B-8322.
———. "Nothing but Trouble." King Matrix K-5959-2. 20 September 1950. King 4432.
———. "Oh! Doctor the Blues." OKeh Matrix 74273-A. 13 August 1926. OKeh 8391.
———. "Old Fashioned Love." King Matrix K-5960. 20 September 1950. King unissued. On *Me and My Crazy Self*. Charly 266. 1991.
———. "Once or Twice." OKeh Matrix 403596-C. 8 January 1930. OKeh 8812.
———. "Playing Around." King Matrix K-5577. 5 January 1947. King 4293.
———. "Playing with the Strings." OKeh Matrix W400277-B. 21 February 1928. OKeh 8558.
———. "Pleasing You (As Long as I Live)." King Matrix K-5547-1. 13 August 1947. King 4245. 1948.
———. *Portraits in Blues Vol. 6: Lonnie Johnson*. 16 October 1963. Storyville 162. 1964.

———. "Racketeers Blues." Columbia Matrix W152260-2. 12 August 1932. OKeh 8946.
———. "Rambler's Blues." Bluebird Matrix 074068-1. 13 February 1942. Bluebird 34-0708. 1943.
———. "Roaming Rambler Blues." OKeh Matrix W81220-A. 12 August 1927. OKeh 8497.
———. "Rocks in My Bed." Disc Matrix D 492. 15 July 1946. Disc 6063. 1947.
———. "Romance in the Stars." King Matrix K-5725. 9 May 1949. Unissued.
———. "Sam, You Can't Do That to Me." OKeh Matrix W404438. 11 September 1930. OKeh 8831.
———. "Sam, You're Just a Rat." OKeh Matrix W405141-A. 9 February 1932. OKeh 8937.
———. "Seven Long Days." King Matrix K-9095. 26 October 1951. King 4503.
———. "She Ain't Right." Bluebird Matrix 059209-1. 7 February 1941. Bluebird B-8684.
———. "She Don't Know Who She Wants." OKeh Matrix W403672-B. 23 January 1930. OKeh 8775.
———. "She Just Won't Don't." OKeh Matrix W401669-B. 27 February 1929. Unissued.
——— ["Jimmy Jordan"]. "She's Dangerous with That Thing." Columbia Matrix 152062-1. 12 January 1932. Columbia 14647-D.
———. "She's Making Whoopee in Hell Tonight." OKeh Matrix W403594-B. 7 January 1930. OKeh 8768.
———. "She's My Mary." Victor Matrix BS-044046-1. 2 November 1939. Bluebird B-8322.
———. "She's Only a Woman." Victor Matrix BS-044046-1. 2 November 1939. Bluebird B-8363.
———. "She's So Sweet." King Matrix K-5724. 9 May 1949. King 4317.
———. "Sleepy Water Blues." OKeh Matrix W405098-A. 3 December 1931. OKeh 8926.
———. "So Tired." King Matrix K-5580. 19 November 1948. King 4263.

Discography / 185

——. "Solid Blues." Disc Matrix D 486. 15 July 1946. Disc 5063. 1947.
——. "Some Day Baby." RCA Victor Matrix D4AB-328. 14 December 1944. 34-0732. 1945.
——. "Somebody's Got to Go." Bluebird Matrix 059207-1. 7 February 1941. Bluebird B-8684.
——. "Something Fishy (Don't Lie to Me)." Decca Matrix 91345-A. 8 November 1937. Decca 7388.
——. "South Bound Water." OKeh Matrix W80742-B. 25 April 1927. OKeh 8466.
——. "Southbound Backwater." Decca Matrix 63524-A. 31 March 1938. Decca 7461.
——. "Southland Is Alright with Me." OKeh Matrix W404846-A. 11 February 1931. OKeh 8909
——. "Speedway Blues." OKeh Matrix W82088. 16 December 1927. Unknown.
——. "St. Louis Cyclone Blues." OKeh MatrixW81503-B. 3 October 1927. OKeh 8512.
——. "Stay Out of Walnut Street Alley." OKeh Matrix W81221-A. 12 August 1927. OKeh 8618.
——. "Steppin' on the Blues." OKeh Matrix W80748-B. 25 April 1927. Unissued.
——. "Stick with It Baby." Rama Matrix RR-30. Rama 14. 1953.
——. "Stompin' 'Em Along Slow." OKeh Matrix W400278-B. 21 February 1928. OKeh 8558.
——. "String Along with Lonnie." OKeh Matrix W81800-A. 9 November 1927. Unissued.
——. "Sun to Sun Blues." OKeh Matrix 73937-B. 19 January 1926. OKeh 8291.
——. "The Sun Will Shine in My Door Someday." OKeh Matrix W80747-B. 25 April 1927. Unissued.
——. "Sundown Blues." OKeh Matrix W402438-A. 11 June 1929. OKeh 8754.
——. "Sweet Potato Blues." OKeh Matrix W82053-A. 13 December 1927. OKeh 8586.
——. "Sweet Woman, See for Yourself." OKeh Matrix 74274-A. 13 August 1926. OKeh 8435.
——. "Sweet Woman, You Can't Go Wrong." OKeh Matrix W8119-B. 5 August 1927. OKeh 8512.
——. "Swing Out Rhythm." Decca Matrix 91343-A. 8 November 1937. Decca 7427.
——. "Take Me I'm Yours." King Matrix K-9027. 26 February 1951. King 4459.
——. "Tell Me Baby." Paradise 123. 1948.
——. "Tell Me Little Woman." King Matrix K-5554. 13 August 1947. King 4263. 1948.
——. "Tell Me Why." Disc Matrix 491. 15 July 1946. Disc 5060.
——. "That's Love." Bluebird Matrix 059206-1. 7 February 1941. Bluebird B8804.
—— ["Jimmy Jordan"]. "There Is No Justice." Columbia Matrix W151143-D. 17 March 1932. Columbia 14655-D.
——. "There's No Use of Lovin'." OKeh Matrix 74270-A. 13 August 1926. OKeh 8376.
——. "This Love of Mine." Rama Matrix RR-41. Rama RR-20. 1954.
——. "Tin Can Alley Blues." OKeh Matrix W81588-B. 31 October 1927. OKeh 8524.
——. "To Do This, You Got to Know How." OKeh Matrix W80075-A. 14 August 1926. OKeh 40695.
——. "Tombstone Blues." OKeh Matrix W82054-B. 13 November 1927. Unissued.
——. "Tomorrow Night." King Matrix 5313-1. 10 December 1947. King 4201. 1948.
——. "Tomorrow Night." Paradise 110-A. 1948.
——. "Treat 'Em Right." OKeh Matrix W80743-B. 25 April 1927. OKeh 8484.
——. "Troubles Ain't Nothin' but the Blues." King Matrix K5803-2. 29 November 1949. King 4346. 1950

———. "Trust Your Husband." Victor Matrix BS-044049-1. 2 November 1939. Bluebird B-8387.

———. "Two Tone Stomp." OKeh Matrix W401338-B. 17 November 1928. OKeh 8637.

———. "Uncle Ned, Don't Use Your Head." OKeh Matrix W405099-A. 3 December 1931. OKeh 8926.

———. "Unselfish Love." Columbia Matrix W152261-1. 12 August 1932. Columbia 14674-D.

———. *The Unsung Blues Legend: The Living Room Sessions by Lonnie Johnson.* Blues Magnet. 2000.

———. "Vaya con Dios." Rama Matrix RR-40. 1953. Rama 19. 1954.

———. "Very Lonesome Blues." OKeh Matrix 73935-B. 19 January 1926. OKeh 8282.

———. "The Victim of Love." RCA Victor Matrix D4AB-330. 14 December 1944. Bluebird 34-0742.

———. "Watch Shorty." RCA Victor Matrix D4AB-331. 14 December 1944. Bluebird 34-0732. 1945.

———. "Way Down that Lonesome Road." OKeh Matrix W400490-A. 13 March 1928. OKeh 8574.

———. "What a Real Woman." 14 December 1947. Federal. 12376.

———. "What a Woman." King Matrix K-5311-1. 10 December 1947. King 4201. 1948.

———. "What Do You Want That I've Got Pretty Baby." King Matrix K-5962. 20 September 1950. King unissued. On *Me and My Crazy Self.* Charly 266. 1991.

———. "When I Was Lovin' Changed My Mind Blues." OKeh Matrix 73936-B. 19 January 1926. OKeh 8309B.

———. "When I'm Gone (Will It Still Be Me)." King Matrix K-5961-1. 20 September 1950. King 4432.

———. "When You Fall for Some One That's Not Your Own." OKeh Matrix W401336-B. 16 November 1928. OKeh 8635.

———. "When You Feel Low Down." Bluebird Matrix 074075-1. 13 February 1942. Bluebird B-9006.

———. "Why a Man Does Wrong." 2 June 1947. Aladdin unissued.

———. "Why I Love You." Disc Matrix D 490. 15 July 1947. Disc 5062.

———. "Why Should I Cry." King Matrix K-9024. 26 February 1951. King 4459.

———. "Why Women Go Wrong." Victor Matrix BS-044045. 2 November 1939. Bluebird B-8363.

———. "Will You Remember (the Answer to Tomorrow Night)." Rama Matrix RR-29. 1953.

———. ["Jimmy Jordan"]. "Winnie the Wailer." Columbia Matrix W152142-1. 17 March 1932. Columbia 14655-D.

———. "Woke Up with the Blues in My Fingers." OKeh Matrix W80816-B. 2 May 1927. Unissued.

———. "Woman Changed My Life." OKeh Matrix 9634-A. 13 May 1926. OKeh 8358.

———. "Working Man's Blues." King Matrix K-5445-1. 11 December 1947. King 4212. 1948.

———. "Wrong Woman Blues." OKeh Matrix W400492. 13 March 1928. OKeh 8601.

———. "You Can't Buy Love." King Matrix K-9146. 3 June 1952. King 4572.

———. "You Can't Give a Woman Everything She Needs." OKeh Matrix W402437-A. 11 June 1929. OKeh 8722.

———. "You Don't Move Me." Prestige Bluesville 45-806. Unknown.

———. "You Don't See into the Blues Like Me." OKeh Matrix 74269-A. 13 August 1926. OKeh 8451.

———. "You Drove a Good Man Away." OKeh Matrix 74267-A. 13 August 1926. OKeh 8451.

———. "You Know I Do." Aladdin Matrix 4010A-1. 2 June 1947. Aladdin 3047.

———. "You Only Want Me When You're Lonely." King Matrix K-9026-1. 26 February 1951. King 4473.

———. "You Take Romance." King Matrix K-5723. 9 May 1949. King 4297.

———. "Your Last Time Out." Aladdin Matrix 4009-1. 2 June 1947. Aladdin 3047.
———. "You're Mine You." King Matrix K-551-1. 13 August 1947. King 4278. 1949.
Johnson, Lonnie, and Blind Willie Dunn [Eddie Lang]. "Have to Change Keys to Play These Blues." OKeh Matrix W401339-B. 17 November 1928. OKeh 8637.
———. "Midnight Call (Blues)." OKeh Matrix 403042-A. 9 October 1929. OKeh 8818.
———. "Two Tone Stomp." OKeh Matrix W401338. 17 November 1928. OKeh 8637.
Johnson, Lonnie, and Jimmy Foster. "I Want a Little Some O' That What You Got." OKeh Matrix W401670. 27 February 1929. OKeh 8691.
Johnson, Lonnie ["Tommy Jordan"], and Clara Smith. "What Makes You Act Like That." Columbia Matrix W150928-2. 31 October 1930. Columbia14568-D.
———. "You Done Lost Your Good Thing Now! Parts 1 and 2." OKeh Matrix 402491-B, 402492-B. 3 July 1929. OKeh 8733.
———. "You're Getting Old on Your Job." Columbia Matrix W150927-3. 31 October 1930. Columbia 14568-D.
Johnson, Lonnie, Victoria Spivey, and Clarence Williams. "Furniture Man Blues," Parts 1 and 2. OKeh Matrix 401244-A, 401245-B. 18 October 1928. OKeh 8652.
———. "Toothache Blues Parts 1 and 2." OKeh Matrices W401243-B, W401247-A. 17–18 October 1928. OKeh 8744. Parlophone 8744.
Johnson, Lonnie, and Clarence Williams. "The Dirty Dozen." OKeh Matrix W403749-C. 7 February 1930. OKeh 8775.
Johnson, Lonnie, and Spencer Williams. "Death Is on Your Track." OKeh Matrix 401730-A. 19 March 1929. OKeh 8691.
———. "It Feels So Good." OKeh Matrices W401622, W401623. 18 February 1929. OKeh 8664.

———. "It Feels So Good." OKeh Matrices W401981, W401982. 24 May 1929. OKeh 8697.
———. "Keep It to Yourself." OKeh Matrix W403750. 7 February 1930. OKeh 8812.
———. "Monkey and the Baboon." OKeh Matrix W403597. 8 January 1930. OKeh 8762.
———. "Monkey and the Baboon." OKeh Matrix W404042. 24 May 1930. OKeh 8802.
———. "Wipe It Off." OKeh Matrix W403598-B. 8 January 1930. OKeh 8762.
Johnson, Lonnie, with Elmer Snowden. *Blues and Ballads.* [Vol. 1]. Liner notes by Chris Albertson. Prestige Bluesville. 1990.
———. *Blues, Ballads, and Jumpin' Jazz.* Vol. 2. Liner notes by Lee Hildebrand. Prestige Bluesville. 1994.
Johnson, Lonnie, with Victoria Spivey. *Idle Hours.* Prestige Bluesville. 1992.
Lonnie Johnson's Harlem Footwarmers. [Duke Ellington Orchestra]. "Harlem Twist." OKeh Matrix W400032. 19 January 1928. OKeh 8638.
———. "Move Over." OKeh Matrix W401176. 1 October 1928. OKeh 8638.

JOHNSON, ALONZO ("LONNIE"): ORIGINAL RECORDINGS, SECONDARY ROLE

Alexander, Alger "Texas." "Bantam Rooster Blues." OKeh Matrix 400444. 9 March 1928. OKeh 8591.
———. "Bell Cow Blues." OKeh Matrix 400449-B. 9 March 1928. OKeh 8563.
———. "Blue Devil Blues." OKeh Matrix W402335-A. 16 November 1928. OKeh 8640.
———. "Boe Hog Blues. OKeh Matrix 400456-B. 10 March 1928. OKeh 8563.
———. "Corn-Bread Blues." OKeh Matrix 81223-A. 12 August 1927. OKeh 8511.
———. "Death Bed Blues." OKeh Matrix W400441-B. 9 March 1928. OKeh 8578.

———. "The Deep Blue Sea Blues." OKeh Matrix W400445-B. 12 August 1927. OKeh 8591.
———. "Don't You Wish Your Baby Was Built Up Like Mine?" OKeh Matrix 400448-A. 9 March 1928. OKeh 8603.
———. "Levee Camp Moan Blues." OKeh Matrix 81225-B. 12 August 1927. OKeh 8498.
———. "Long Lonesome Day Blues." OKeh Matrix 81213-A. 11 August 1927. OKeh 8511.OKeh
———. "Mama's Bad Luck Child." OKeh Matrix 400455-B. 10 March 1928. OKeh 8578.
———. "No More Women Blues." OKeh Matrix 400446-A. 9 March 1928. OKeh 8624.
———. "Penitentiary Moan Blues. OKeh Matrix W402334-B. 16 November 1928. OKeh 8640.
———. "Range In My Kitchen Blues." OKeh Matrix 81212-B. 27 November 1927. OKeh 8526.
———. "The Risin' Sun." Matrix W402331-A. 15 November 1928. OKeh 8673.
———. "Section Gang Blues." OKeh Matrix 81224-B. 12 August 1927. OKeh 8498.
———. "Sitting On A Log." OKeh Matrix 400454-B. 10 March 1928. OKeh 8624.
———. "West Texas Blues." OKeh Matrix 400443-A. 9 March 1928. OKeh 8603.
———. "Work Ox Blues." OKeh Matrix W402330-A. 15 November 1928. OKeh 8658.
———. "Yellow Girl Blues." OKeh Matrix 400442-B. 9 March 1928. OKeh 8801.
Alexander, Alger "Texas," and Lonnie Johnson. "When You Get to Thinking." *Blues Fell This Morning.* Philips BBL 7369, UK 1960.
Armstrong, Louis, and His Hot Five. "Hotter Than That." OKeh Matrix W82055. 13 December 1927. OKeh 8535.
———. "I'm Not Rough." OKeh Matrix W82040. 10 December 1927. OKeh 8551.
———. "Savoy Blues." OKeh Matrix W82056. 13 December 1927. OKeh 8535.

Armstrong, Louis, and His Savoy Ballroom Five. "I Can't Give You Anything but Love." OKeh Matrix W401691. 5 March 1929. OKeh 8669.
———. "Mahogany Hall Stomp." OKeh Matrix W401691. 5 March 1929. OKeh 8680.
Baby Cox with the Palmer Brothers Trio. "Since You Went Away." OKeh Matrix W401174. 1 October 1928. Unknown.
Blue Boys. "Memphis Stomp." OKeh Matrix W400238-A. 15 February 1928. OKeh 45314.
Blythe, Jimmy ["Duke Owens"], Willie Woods, Bud Wilson [Lonnie Johnson], and George Jefferson. "Bearcat Blues." Gennett Matrix 13300. 14 December 1927. Gennett 6378.
———. "It's Hot Let It Alone." Gennett Matrix 13289. 14 December 1927. Gennett 6423.
———. "Searchin' for Flats." Gennett Matrix 13288. 13 December 1927. Unissued.
———. "The St. Louis Train Kept Passing By." Gennett Matrix 13289. 13 December 1927. Gennett 6366.
———. "When a Man Is Treated Like a Dog." Gennett Matrix 13290. 13 December 1927. Gennett 6366.
———. "Why Should I Grieve After You're Gone." Gennett Matrix 13302. 14 December 1927. Gennett 6423.
Boyd, Raymond. "Bell Avenue Blues." OKeh Matrix 80811-A. 1 May 1927. Unknown.
———. "Blackbird Blues." OKeh Matrix 80812-A. 1 May 1927. OKeh 8528.
———. "Hard Water Blues." OKeh Matrix 80814-A. 1 May 1927. Unissued.
———. "Unkind Mama." OKeh Matrix 80813. 1 May 1927. OKeh 8528.
Brown, Joe. "Cotton Patch Blues." OKeh Matrix 80809-A. 1 May 1927. OKeh 8491.
———. "Joe Brown's Own Texas Blues." OKeh Matrix 80810-A. 1 May 1927. Unissued.
———. "Superstitious Blues." OKeh Matrix 80808-A. 1 May 1927. OKeh 8491.
———. "Yeller Freight House Blues." OKeh Matrix 80807-B. 1 May 1927. Unissued.

Charles Creath's Jazz-O-Maniacs. "Grandpa's Spell." OKeh Matrix 9429. November 1925. OKeh 8257.
———. "Market Street Stomp." OKeh Matrix 9426. November 1925. OKeh 8280.
———. "Way Down in Lover's Lane." OKeh Matrix 9428. November 1925. OKeh 8257.
———. "Won't, Don't Blues." OKeh Matrix 9427-A. November 1925. OKeh 8280.
Chocolate Dandies ["McKinney's Cotton Pickers"]. "Birmingham Breakdown." OKeh Matrix W401220. 13 October 1928. OKeh 8668.
———. "Four of Five Times." OKeh Matrix W401221. 13 October 1928. OKeh 8627.
———. "Paducah." OKeh Matrix W401218. 13 October 1928. OKeh 8627.
———. "Star Dust." OKeh Matrix W401219. 13 October 1928. OKeh 8668.
Cooper, Dolly. "Alley Cat." Savoy Matrix SDC-4369. 15 May 1953. Savoy 898.
Crawley, Wilton. "Crawley Clarinet Moan." OKeh Matrix W82079. 16 December 1927. OKeh 8539.
———. "Diamonds in the Rough." OKeh Matrix W82091. 17 December 1927. Unknown.
———. "Jewels of My Heart." OKeh Matrix W82090. 17 December 1927. Unknown.
———. "Let's Pretend to Be Sweethearts." OKeh Matrix 82081. 16 December 1927. OKeh 8555.
———. "Love Will Drive Me Crazy." OKeh Matrix W82080. 16 December 1927. OKeh 8539.
———. "She's Nothing But Nice." OKeh Matrix W82078. 16 December 1927. OKeh 8555.
Duke Ellington Orchestra. "Harlem Twist." OKeh Matrix W400032. 19 January 1928. OKeh 8638.
———. "Hot and Bothered." OKeh Matrix W401177. 1 October 1928. OKeh 8623.
———. "Misty Mornin'." OKeh Matrix W401352. 20 November 1928. OKeh 8662.
———. "The Mooche." OKeh Matrix W401175. 1 October 1928. OKeh 8623.
Dunn, Blind Willie [Eddie Lang], and His Gin Bottle Four. "Blue Blood Blues." OKeh Matrix W401843. 1 May 1929. OKeh 8689.
———. "Blue Guitars." OKeh Matrix W401870-A. 8 May 1929. OKeh 8711.
———. 'Guitar Blues." OKeh Matrix W401865-A. 7 May 1929. OKeh 8711
———. "Jet Black Blues." OKeh Matrix W401842. 1 May 1929. OKeh 8689.
Dunn, Blind Willie [Eddie Lang], and Lonnie Johnson. "Blue Room (Blues)." OKeh Matrix W403044-B. 9 October 1929. OKeh 8818.
———. "Bullfrog Moan." OKeh Matrix W401866-D. 16 May 1929. OKeh 8695.
———. "Deep Minor Rhythm Stomp." OKeh Matrix W403039-A. 9 October 1929. OKeh 8743.
———. "Guitar Blues." OKeh Matrix W401865. 7 May 1929. OKeh 8711.
———. "A Handful of Riffs." OKeh Matrix W401869-A. 8 May 1929. OKeh 8695.
———. "Hot Fingers." OKeh Matrix W403043-A. 9 October 1929. OKeh 8743.
———. "Midnight Call Blues." OKeh Matrix W403042. 9 October 1929. OKeh 8818.
Gilmore, Gene. "Brown Skin Woman." Decca Matrix 91824. 29 September 1939. Decca 7671.
———. "Charity Blues." Decca Matrix 91825. 29 September 1939. Decca 7671.
Gordon, Jimmie. "Bleed Heart Blues (Bleeding Heart Blues)." Decca Matrix 91531-A. 18 October 1938. Decca 7536.
———. "Number Runner's Blues." Decca Matrix 91532-A. 18 October 1938. Decca 7536.
Green, Violet [Clara Smith], and Lonnie Johnson. "Don't Wear It Out." OKeh Matrix W404524-A. 31 October 1930. OKeh 8839.

———. "You Had Too Much." OKeh Matrix W404523-B. 31 October 1930. Okeh 8839.
Hannah, George. "Hurry Home Blues." Brunswick Matrix SL42/3. 27 July 1926. Vocalion 1047.
———. "Setting Sun Blues." Brunswick Matrix SL44/5. 27 July 1926. Vocalion 1047.
Hayes, Nap, and Matthew Prater. "I'm Drifting Back to Dreamland." OKeh Matrix W400240-B. 15 February 1928. Unissued.
Hill, Bertha "Chippie." "Hard Time Blues." OKeh Matrix W82085-B. 16 December 1927. Unknown.
———. "Speedway Blues." OKeh Matrix W82088-B. 16 December 1927. Unissued.
———. "Tell My Why." OKeh Matrix W82087-B. 16 December 1927. Unissued.
———. "Weary Money Blues." OKeh Matrix W82086-B. 16 December 1927. Unissued.
Hot Lips Page Orchestra. "Dirty Deal Blues." King Matrix K 5377. December 1947. Unissued. On *Hot Lips Page: Shoutin' the Blues*. Blue Boar 1010. 1998.
———. "Don't Try To Fool Me." King Matrix K 5376. December 1947. King 4271.
———. "Sad and Disappointed Jill." King Matrix K 5375-3. December 1947. King 4207.
———. "Too Tight Mama." King Matrix K-5322. December 1947. King 4227.
Humes, Helen. "Black Cat Blues." OKeh Matrix W80803-B. 30 April 1927. OKeh 8467.
———. "Jam Up Too Tight." OKeh Matrix W80804-B. 30 April 1927. Unissued.
———. "Stomping Weaver's Blues." OKeh Matric W80806-B. 30 April 1927. Unissued.
———. "A Worried Woman's Blues." OKeh Matrix W80805-A. 30 April 1927. OKeh 8467.
Hunter, Ivory Joe. "It's a Sin." MGM Matrix 50-S-272A. 22 August 1950. MGM 10818.

———. "Sorta Need You." MGM Matrix 50-S-271A. 22 August 1950. MGM 10861.
Jim McHarg's Metro Stompers, with Lonnie Johnson. *Stompin' at the Penny*. Columbia CK 57829. 1965.
Jimmie Noone Orchestra. "Keystone Blues." Decca Matrix 93030. 5 June 1940. Decca 18095. Decca 25104.
———. "New Orleans Hop Scop Blues." Decca Matrix 93031. 5 June 1940. Decca 18095. Decca 25104
Johnny Dodds' Orchestra. "Gravier Street Blues." Decca Matrix 93033. 5 June 1940. Decca 18094. Decca 25103
———. "Red Onion Blues." Decca Matrix 93032. 5 June 1940. Decca 18094. Decca 25103.
Johnson, James. "Steady Roll." "Newport Blues." OKeh Matrix 73941-A. 20 January 1926. OKeh 8287.
———. "No Good Blues." OKeh Matrix 73940-A. 20 January 1926. OKeh 8287.
Johnson, James P., and Lonnie Johnson. "Johnson's Trio Stomp." OKeh Matrix 73946. 20 January 1926. OKeh 8417.
Johnson, Merline ["The Yas Yas Girl"]. "He May Be Your Man." Vocalion Matrix C-20600-1. 15 December 1937. Vocalion 04013.
———. "Love Shows Weakness." Vocalion Matrix C-2061-2. 15 December 1937. Unissued.
———. "Please Come Back Home." Vocalion Matrix C-2058-2. 15 December 1937. Unissued.
Johnson Boys [Lonnie Johnson, Nap Hayes, and Matthew Prater]. "Let Me Call You Sweetheart." OKeh Matrix W400237. 15 February 1928. Unknown.
———. "Prater Blues." OKeh Matrix W400244. 15 February 1928. OKeh 8708.
———. "Violin Blues." OKeh Matrix W400239-A. 15 February. OKeh 8708.
Jones, Karl, with Bob Shaffner and His Harlem Hot Shots. "Careless Love." Circa 1945. Mercury 1008.
———. "Mitzy." Mercury Matrix 104. 1945. Mercury 2002A.

Discography / 191

———. "Trouble in Mind." Mercury Matrix 106. 1945. Mercury 2002.

Keghouse. "Keghouse Blues." OKeh Matrix W400263-B. 17 February 1928. OKeh 8583.

———. "Lonesome Bedtime Jailhouse Blues." OKeh Matrix W400262-B. 17 February 1928. Unissued.

———. "Please Come Back to Me Blues." OKeh Matrix W400267-B. 18 February 1928. Unissued.

———. "Scott Levee Blues." OKeh Matrix W400264. 17 February 1928. Unissued.

———. "Shiftin' My Gear Blues." OKeh Matrix W400268-B. 18 February 1928. OKeh 8583.

———. "Yellow Woman Blues." OKeh Matrix W400265-B. 17 February 1928. Unknown.

Ladson, Ruth, and the Three Shadows. "Kicking My Man Around." Columbia Matrix C-3890-1. 30 June 1941. Columbia 06667.

———. "What Do You Bet." Columbia Matrix 3890. 30 June 1941. Columbia 06667.

———. "Why Do You Jive Me Daddy?" Columbia Matrix C-3891-1. 30 June 1951. Columbia 06667.

———. "Windy City Blues." Columbia Matrix 3890-1. 30 June 1941. Columbia 06667.

McFadden, Charlie "Specks." "Don't Bite That Thing." OKeh Matrix W402461-B. 14 June 1929. OKeh 8894.

———. "Gambler's Blues." OKeh Matrix W402455-B. 14 June 1929. Unissued.

———. "Misunderstood Blues." OKeh Matrix W402456-A. 14 June 1929. OKeh 8894.

Miller, Luella. "Dago Hill Blues." Brunswick Matrix C-547. 27 July 1926. Vocalion 1044.

———. "Down the Alley." Vocalion Matrix unknown. 28 January 1927. Vocalion 1080.

———. "Dreaming of You Blues." Vocalion Matrix E-4445. 28 January 1928. Vocalion 1081.

———. "Jackson's Blues." Brunswick Matrices C841-C843. 28 January 1928. Vocalion unissued.

———. "Pretty Man Blues." Brunswick Matrix C548. 27 July 1926. Vocalion 1044.

———. "Rattle Snake Groan." Vocalion Matrix E-4443. 28 January 1927. Vocalion 108.

———. "Triflin' Man Blues." Brunswick Matrix C-840. 28 January 1927. Vocalion unissued.

———. "Twelve O'Clock Blues." Vocalion Matrix unknown. 28 January 1927. Vocalion 1080.

Moore, Alice. "Doggin' Man Blues." Decca Matrix 91143. 25 March 1937. 7380.

———. "Don't Deny Me Baby." Decca Matrix 91156. 25 March 1937. Decca 7369.

———. "Hand in Hand Woman." Decca Matrix 91142. 25 March 1937. Decca 7380.

———. "He's Mine, All Mine." Decca Matrix 91157. 25 March 1937. Unissued.

———. "Humming Bird Man." Decca Matrix 91148. 25 March 1937. Unissued.

———. "Just a Good Girl Treated Wrong." Decca Matrix 91145. 25 March 1937. Decca 7293.

———. "Midnight Creepers." Decca Matrix 91144. 25 March 1937. Decca 7327.

———. "New Blues Black and Evil Blues." Decca Matrix 91146. 25 March 1937. Decca 7293.

———. "Tired of Me Blues." Decca Matrix 91147. 25 March 1937. Decca 7327.

———. "Too Many Men." Decca Matrix 91149. 25 March 1937. Decca 7369.

Morris, Clara. "Cry On, Daddy." Bluebird Matrix 53985-1. 27 March 1941. Bluebird 8767.

———. "I Stagger in My Sleep." Bluebird Matrix 53986-1. 27 March 1941. Bluebird 8700.

———. "I'm Blue, Daddy." Bluebird Matrix 53987-1. 27 March 1941. Bluebird 8700.

———. "Poker Playing Daddy." Bluebird Matrix 53988-1. 27 March 1941. Bluebird 8767.

Perkins, Cora. "Today Blues." OKeh Matrix W9699-A. May 1926. OKeh 8348.

———. "When I Rise Blues." OKeh Matrix W9698-A. May 1926. OKeh 8348.
Pettigrew, Leola B. "Boop Poop a Doop." Columbia Matrix W151716-2. 10 August 1931. Columbia 14625-D.
———. "You Need a Woman Like Me." Columbia Matrix W151717-2. 10 August 1931. Columbia 14625-D.
Ray, Herman. "I'm a Little Piece of Leather." Decca Matrix 74938 A. 20 May 1949. Decca 48105.
———. "President's Blues." Decca Matrix W 74937-A. 20 May 1949. Decca 48107.
———. "Trouble Blues." Decca Matrix 74936-A. 20 May 1949. Decca 48105.
———. "Working Man (Doing the Best I Can)." Decca Matrix 74935-A. 20 May 1949. Decca 48107.
Richardson, Mooch. "Big Kate Adams Blues." OKeh Matrix W40036-A. 27 February 1928. OKeh 8576.
———. "Burying Ground Blues." OKeh Matrix W400375. 29 February 1928. OKeh 8576.
———. "Fare Thee Well Blues." OKeh Matrix W400362-B. 27 February 1928. Unissued.
———. "Helena Blues." OKeh Matrix W400361-B. 27 February 1928. OKeh 8611.
———. "Southern Railroad Blues." OKeh Matrix W400212-B. 13 February 1928. Unknown.
———. "T and T Blues." OKeh Matrix W400213. 13 February 1928. OKeh 8554.
———. Untitled. OKeh Matrix W400214. 13 February 1928.
———. Untitled. OKeh Matrix W400377. 29 February 1928.
Scruggs, Irene. "Lonesome Valley Blues." OKeh Matrix W80817-A. 2 May 1927. OKeh 8476.
———. "Outsider Blues." OKeh Matrix W80818-A. 2 May 1927. Unissued.
———. "Smokey Rattler." OKeh Matrix W80819-A. 2 May 1927. Unissued.
———. "Sorrow Valley Blues." OKeh Matrix W80820-A. 2 May 1927. OKeh 8476.

Shepard, Ollie. "No One to Call You Dear-1 (Ain't It Tough)." Decca Matrix 91349. 8 November 1937. Decca 7408.
———. "Sweetheart Land." Decca Matrix 91350. 8 November 1937. Decca 7400.
Shepard, Ollie, and His Kentucky Boys. "At Your Mercy." Decca Matrix 63516-A. 31 March 1938. Decca 7541.
———. "Biscuit Rolling Time." Decca Matrix 63513-A. 31 March 1938. Decca 7480.
———. "Brown Skin Woman." Decca Matrix 63508-A. 31 March 1938. Decca 7448.
———. "Drunk Again." Decca Matrix 63512-A. 31 March 1938. Decca 7435.
———. "Good Woman." Decca Matrix 63510-A. 31 March 1938. Decca 7463.
———. "Hope You Haven't Forgotten Me." Decca Matrix 63515-A. 31 March 1938. Decca 7480.
———. "One Woman Blues." Decca Matrix 63507-A. 31 March 1938. Decca 7435.
———. "Outdoors Blues." Decca Matrix 65424-A. 18 April 1939. Decca 7613.
———. "Pee Wee, Pee Wee." Decca Matrix 63511-A. 31 March 1938. Decca 7541.
———. "S-B-A Blues." Decca Matrix 63509-A. 31 March 1938. Decca 7448.
———. "Sweetheart Land." Decca Matrix 91350-A. 11 August 1937. Decca 7400.
———. "What's Your Guess." Decca Matrix 63514-A. 31 March 1938. Decca 7463.
Smith, Bessie Mae ["Blue Belle"]. "Boa Constrictor Blues." OKeh Matrix W82048-A. 12 December 1927. OKeh 8538.
———. "Creepin' Eel Blues." OKeh Matrix W82004-B. 12 December 1927. OKeh 8553.
———. "Cryin' for Daddy Blues." OKeh Matrix W80821-A. 2 May 1927. OKeh 8483.
———. "Dead Sea Blues." OKeh Matrix W82049-B. 12 December 1927. OKeh 8553.

———. "Ghost Creeping Blues." OKeh Matrix W82045-B. 12 December 1927. OKeh 8588.
———. "High Water Blues." OKeh Matrix W8022-A. 2 May 1927. OKeh 8483.
———. "Mean Bloodhound Blues." OKeh Matrix W82052-A. 12 December 1927. OKeh 8704.
———. "My Daddy's Coffin Blues." OKeh Matrix W82051-B. 12 December 1927. OKeh 8588.
———. "Sneakin' Lizard Blues." OKeh Matrix W82050-B. 12 December 1927. OKeh 8538.
Spivey, Victoria. "The Alligator Pond Went Dry." OKeh Matrix W80769-B. 27 April 1927. OKeh 8481.
———. "Arkansas Road Blues." OKeh Matrix W80768-B. 27 April 1927. OKeh 8481. 1927.
———. "Be Careful." 15 November 1963. On *Three Kings and the Queen Vol. 2*. Spivey 1014. 1970.
———. "Big Houston Blues." OKeh Matrix W74265-A. 13 August 1926. OKeh 8401.
———. "Blood Thirsty Blues." OKeh Matrix W81589-A. 31 October 1927. OKeh 8531.
———. "Christmas Mornin' Blues." OKeh Matrix W81584-A. 28 October 1927. OKeh 8517.
———. "Christmas Without Santa Claus." 21 September 1961. On *Woman Blues*. BVLP 1054. 1962.
———. "Dope Head Blues." OKeh Matrix W81585-A. 28 October 1927. OKeh 8531.
———. "Garter Snake Blues." OKeh Matrix W81583-C. 28 October 1927. OKeh 8517.
———. "A Good Man Is Hard to Find." OKeh Matrix W81599-A. 1 November 1929. OKeh 8565.
———. "Got the Blues So Bad." OKeh Matrix W74266-A. 13 August 1926. OKeh 8401. 1963.
———. "Grow Old Together." 21 September 1961. On *Woman Blues*. BVLP 1054. 1962.

———. "I Got Men All Over This Town." 21 September 1961. On *Woman Blues*. BVLP 1054.
———. "I'm a Red Hot Mama." 21 September 1961. On *Woman Blues*. BVLP 1054. 1962.
———. "Idle Hour Blues." OKeh Matrix W80767-B. 27 April 1927. OKeh 8464.
———. "Jelly, Look What You Done." OKeh Matrix W81597-B. 1 November 1929. OKeh 8550.
———. "Let's Ride Tonight (Together?)." 21 September 1961. On *Woman Blues*. BVLP 1054. 1962.
———. "Lonnie's Traveling Light." 15 November 1963. On *Spivey's Blues Parade*. 1970.
———. "Mr. Johnson's Guitar Talks." 15 November 1963. On *Three Kings and the Queen*. Spivey 1004. 1963.
———. "Murder in the First Degree." OKeh Matrix W81596-B. 1 November 1927. OKeh 8581.
———. "My Baby Isn't Here." 18 June 1965. On *Queen and Her Knights*. Spivey 1006.
———. "New Black Snake Blues, Part 1 and Part 2." OKeh Matrices W401222-A, W401223-A. 13 October 1928. OKeh 8626.
———. "Nightmare Blues." OKeh Matrix W81590-A. 31 October 1927. OKeh 8581.
———. "No. 12, Let Me Roam." OKeh Matrix W80770-B. 27 April 1927. OKeh 8494.
———. "No, Papa, No!" OKeh Matrix W401242-B. 17 October 1928. OKeh 8634.
———. "Red Lantern Blues." OKeh Matrix W81586-B. 28 October 1927. OKeh 8550.
———. "Steady Grind." OKeh Matrix W80766-B. 27 April 1927. OKeh 8464.
———. "Stick by Me Baby." 15 November 1963. On *Three Kings and the Queen*. Spivey 1004. 1963.
———. "Stop Talking." 15 November 1963. On *Three Kings and the Queen*. Spivey 1004. 1963.

———. "T-B Blues." OKeh Matrix W80771-B. 27 April 1927. OKeh 8494.

———. "Thursday Girl." 21 September 1961. On *Woman Blues*. BVLP 1054. 1962.

———. "Wake Up Daddy." 21 September 1961. On *Woman Blues*. BVLP 1054. 1962.

———. "Your Worries Ain't Like Mine." OKeh Matrix W81598-A. 1 November 1927. OKeh 8565.

———. "We Both Got to Die." 6 April 1965. On *Queen and Her Knights*. Spivey 1006.

———. "West Texas Blues." 6 April 1965. On *Queen and Her Knights*. Spivey 1006.

Spivey, Victoria, with Lonnie Johnson, Little Brother Montgomery, Memphis Slim, and Sonny Greer. "1965." 6 April 1965. On *Queen and Her Knights*. Spivey 1006.

———. "Dig Me." 6 April 1965. On *Queen And Her Knights*. Spivey 1006.

———. "Every Dog Has His Day." 6 April 1965. On *Queen And Her Knights*. Spivey 1006.

———. "How's He's Gone." 6 April 1965. On *Queen And Her Knights*. Spivey 1006.

———. "Just a Rank Stud." 6 April 1965. On *Queen And Her Knights*. Spivey 1006.

———. "New Black Snake Blues, Part 1 and Part 2." 6 April 1965. On *Queen And Her Knights*. Spivey 1006.

Stovepipe Johnson. "Devilish Blues." Brunswick Matrix C2148. 26 July 1928. Vocalion 1203.

———. "Don't Let Your Mouth Start Nothing Your Head Won't Stand." Brunswick Matrix C2151. 26 July 1928. Vocalion 1211.

———. "Green Grass." Brunswick Matrix C2149. 26 July 1928. Vocalion 1203.

———. "Squabble Blues." Brunswick Matrix C2150. 26 July 1928. Unknown.

Sunnyland Slim and His Sunny Boys. "The Devil Is a Busy Man." Hy-Tone Matrix UB 21612. June 1947. Hy-Tone 33.

———. "Jivin' Boogie." Hy-Tone Matrix UB 21608. June 1947. Hy-Tone 32.

———. "Keep Your Hands Out of My Money." Hy-Tone Matrix UB 21611. June 1947. Hy-Tone 33.

———. "Miss Bessie Mae." Hy-Tone Matrix UB 21612. June 1947. Hy-Tone 33.

———. "My Heavy Load." Hy-Tone Matrix UB 21610. June 1947. Hy-Tone 33.

Sykes, Roosevelt, Big Joe Williams, Lonnie Johnson, and Victoria Spivey. "Feelings from the Fingers." 15 November 1963. On *Three Kings and the Queen Vol. 2*. Spivey 1014.

———. "Four Shots of Gin." 15 November 1963. On *Three Kings and the Queen*. Spivey 1004.

Temple, Johnnie. "Cherry Ball." Decca Matrix 91761-A. 13 September 1939. Decca 7678.

———. "Down in Mississippi." Decca Matrix 91759-A. 13 September 1939. Decca 7643.

———. "Evil Bad Woman." Decca Matrix 91760-A. 13 September 1939. Decca 7660.

———. "Good Suzie (Rusty Knees)." Decca Matrix 91758-A. 13 September 1939. Decca 7643.

———. "Let's Get Together." Decca Matrix 91762-A. 13 September 1939. Decca 7678.

———. "Streamline Blues." Decca Matrix 91757-A. 13 September 1939. Decca 7660.

Wallace, Sippie, with Albert Ammons and His Rhythm Kings. "Bedroom Blues." Mercury Matrix 117-4. 25 September 1945. Mercury 2010.

———. "Buzz Me." Mercury Matrix 121-5. 25 September 1945. Mercury 2010.

———. "Careless Love." 28 November 1945. Mercury 2008.

———. "Deep Water Blues." Mercury Matrix 119. 25 September 1945. Mercury 2016.

———. "Foggy City." 28 September 1945. Mercury 2008.

———. "She's A Mighty Fine Woman." 28 September 1945. Mercury 2005.

———. "Shorty George." 28 September 1945. Mercury 2005.

———. "Suitcase Blues." Mercury Matrix 118. 25 September 1945. Mercury 2016.

Wheatstraw, Peetie. "304 Blues." Decca Matrix 63535-B. 1 April 1938. Decca 7453.
———. "Banana Man." Decca Matrix 63538-A. 1 April 1938. Decca 7465.
———. "Beer Tavern." Decca Matrix 91775. 14 September 1939. Decca 7657.
———. "Black Horse Blues." Decca Matrix 91528-A. 18 October 1938. Decca 7568.
———. "Cake Alley." Decca Matrix 63545-A. 1 April 1938. Decca 7441.
———. "Confidence Man." Decca Matrix 91780-A. 14 September 1939. Decca 7692.
———. "Good Little Thing." Decca Matrix 63544-A. 1 April 1938. Decca 7498.
———. "Hard Headed Black Gal." Decca Matrix 63537-B. 1 April 1938. Decca 7453.
———. "Hot Springs Blues (Skin and Bones)." Decca Matrix 91526-A. 18 October 1938. Decca 7544.
———. "I Want Some Sea Food." Decca Matrix 91777-A. 14 September 1939. Decca 7657.
———. "Love Bug Blues." Decca Matrix 9179-A. 14 September 1939. Decca 7676.
———. "A Man Ain't Nothin' But a Fool." Decca Matrix 91527-A. 18 October 1938. Decca 7568.
———. "Me No Lika You." Decca Matrix 91530-A. 18 October 1938. Decca 7544.
———. "Road Tramp Blues." Decca Matrix 63540-B. 1 April 1938. Decca 7589.
———. "Rolling Chair." Decca Matrix 91778-A. 14 September 1939. Decca 7676.
———. "Saturday Night Blues." Decca 63542-A. 1 April 1938. Decca 7498.
———. "Shack Bully Stomp." Decca Matrix 63539-A. 1 April 1938. Decca 7479.
———. "Sugar Mama." Decca Matrix 91529-A. 18 October 1938. Decca 7529.
———. "Sweet Lucile." Decca Matrix 63541-A. 1 April 1938. Decca 7441.
———. "Truckin' thru Traffic." Decca Matrix 91525-A. 18 October 1938. Decca 7529.
———. "What More Can a Man Do?" Decca Matrix 63546-A. 1 April 1938. 7479.
———. "The Wrong Woman." Decca Matrix 63536. 1 April 1938. Decca 7465.
———. "You Can't Stop Me From Drinking." Decca Matrix 91776-A. 14 September 1939. Decca 7692.
White, Georgia. "Alley Boogie." Decca Matrix 91354-A. 9 November 1937. Decca 7389.
———. "Almost Afraid of Love." Decca Matrix 63547-A. 1 April 1938. Decca 7450.
———. "The Blues Ain't Nothin But . . . ???" Decca Matrix 91545-A. 21 October 1938. Decca 7562.
———. "Careless Love." Decca Matrix 91351-A. 9 November 1937. Decca 7419.
———. "Crazy Blues." Decca Matrix 63549-A. 1 April 1938. Decca 7807.
———. "Dead Man's Blues." Decca Matrix 91546-A. 21 October 1938. Decca 7534.
———. "Holding My Own." Decca Matrix 63551-A. 1 April 1938. Decca 7521.
———. "I'm Blue and Lonesome (Nobody Cares for Me)." Decca Matrix 63543-A. 1 April 1938. Decca 7450.
———. "Love Sick Blues." Decca Matrix 91547-A. 21 October 1938. Decca 7534.
———. "My Worried Mind Blues." Decca Matrix 91548-1. 21 October 1938. Decca 7562.
———. "Red Cup Porter." Decca Matrix 91353-A. 9 November 1937. Decca 7389.
———. "Rock Me Daddy." Decca Matrices 91352-A, -C. 9 November 1937. Decca 7436.
———. "T'Ain't Nobody's Business If I Do." Decca Matrix 63550-A. 1 April 1938. Decca 7477.
———. "Too Much Trouble." Decca Matrix 63548-A. 1 April 1938. Decca 7477.
Williams, Clarence, and His Novelty Four. "In the Bottle Blues." OKeh Matrix W401390. 23 November 1928. OKeh 8645.
———. "What Ya Want Me to Do." OKeh Matrix 401391. OKeh 8645.

Williams, Spencer. "It Feels So Good Parts 1 and 2." OKeh Matrix W401622-A. 18 February 1929. OKeh 8664.
———. "It Feels So Good Parts 3 and 4." OKeh Matrix W401981-A. 24 May 1929. 401982-B OKeh 8697.
———. "Monkey and the Baboon." OKeh Matrix W403597-B. 8 January 1930. OKeh 8762.
———. "Monkey and the Baboon Part 2." OKeh Matrix W404042-B. 5 June 1930. Unissued.

NORTH AMERICAN COMPILATIONS AND REISSUES

Johnson, Lonnie. *The Best of Lonnie Johnson: Tomorrow Night*. Bluesforever. 2001.
———. *Blues Roots, Vol. 8 (Swingin' with Lonnie)*. Storyville, 1983.
———. *Complete Recorded Works in Chronological Order, 1925–1932*. 7 vols. Liner notes by Chris Smith. Document Records, 1991.
———. *Complete Recorded Works in Chronological Order, 1937–1947*. 3 vols. Liner notes by Chris Smith. Document Records, 1992, 2015.
———. *He's a Jelly Roll Baker*. Bluebird 07863-66064-2. 1992.
———. *Lonnie Johnson Sings 24 Twelve Bar Blues*. King 958. 1966.
———. *Me and My Crazy Self*. Charly. 1991.
———. *Mr. Johnson's Blues, 1926–1932*. Mamlish S 3807. Unknown.
———. *The Originator of Modern Guitar Blues*. Blues Boy. 1980.
———. *Playin' with the Strings*. JSP. 2004.
———. *Rediscovering Lonnie Johnson*. Range RR00008-2. 2007.
———. *Steppin' on the Blues*. Columbia/Legacy C 46221. 1990.
———. *Tears Don't Fall No More: Blues and Ballads*. Folkways FS3577. 1982.
———. *Tomorrow Night*. Gusto Records GD 5039X(2). 1978.
———. *The Very Best of Lonnie Johnson*. Liner notes by Jeff Pearlin. Collectables COL-CD-2897. 2005.
———. *Woke Up This Morning Blues in My Fingers*. Origin Jazz Library OJL-23. 1980.
Johnson, Lonnie, and Otis Spann. *The Blues Collection, Vol. 1*. Storyville. 2013. Alexander Street Database Popular Music.
Lang, Eddie, and Lonnie Johnson. *Blues Guitars, Volumes 1 and 2*. Beat Goes On Records. 1997.

CITED WORKS BY OTHER ARTISTS

Armstrong, Louis, and His Hot Five. "West End Blues." OKeh Matrix W400967. 28 June 1928. OKeh 8597.
Austin, Gene. "The Lonesome Road." Victor Matrix BE-39188. 16 September 1927. Victor 21098.
Blind Blake. "Blind Arthur's Breakdown." Paramount Matrix 21460-2. October 1929. Paramount 12892-A.
Chatmon, Armenter "Bo" [Bo Carter]. "Bo Carter's Advice." Bluebird Matrix 02616-1. 15 October 1936. Bluebird B7073.
Crowded House. *Together Alone*. Capitol. 11 October 1993.
Duke Ellington Orchestra. "It Don't Mean a Thing (If It Ain't Got That Swing)." Brunswick Matrix 11204-A. 2 February 1932. Brunswick 6265.
Hicks, Robert "Barbecue Bob." "Motherless Chile Blues." Columbia Matrix 145134-1. 5 November 1927. Columbia 14299-D.
House, Eddie "Son," Fiddlin' Joe Martin, Willie Brown, and Leroy Williams. "Walking Blues." *The Land Where the Blues Began*. Liner notes by Alan Lomax. Rounder. 2002.
Jefferson, Blind Lemon. "Lemon's Worried Blues." Paramount Matrix 20375-3. February 1928. Paramount 12622.
King Oliver and His Dixie Syncopators. "West End Blues." Matrix E7389. 11 June 1928. Vocalion 1189.

Discography / 197

King Oliver's Creole Jazz Band. "High Society Rag." OKeh Matrix 8393. 22 June 1923. OKeh 4933.

La Vizzo, Thelma, and Richard Jones. "Trouble in Mind Blues." Paramount Matrix P1756. May 1924. Paramount 12206.

Johnson, Robert. "Hell Hound on My Trail." Vocalion Matrix DAL394. 20 June 1937. Vocalion 03623.

Memphis Slim and the House Rockers. "Mother Earth." 1950. Premium 50-221. 1951.

Morton, Jelly Roll. "Mr. Jelly Lord." Victor Matrix BE-38664. 15 May 1939. Victor 20164, Bluebird B-10258.

Patton, Charley. "34 Blues." Matrix 14739-1. 31 January 1934. Vocalion 02651.

———. "High Sheriff Blues." Matrix 14725-2. 30 January 1934. Vocalion 02680-A.

———. "High Water Everywhere," Parts 1 and 2. Matrices L0059, L0060. December 1929. Paramount 12909.

Rainey, Gertrude "Ma." "Ma Rainey's Lost Wandering Blues." Paramount Matrix P1698. March 1924. Paramount 12098.

Sonny Rollins Quarter. "Blue 7." Prestige Matrix 921. 22 June 1956. Prestige PRLP 7079, P-24050.

Smith, Bessie. "Back Water Blues." Columbia Matrix 143491-1. 17 February 1927. Columbia 14195D.

———. "In the House Blues." Columbia Matrix W151594-1. 11 June 1931. Columbia 14611-D.

———. "Muddy Water." Columbia Matrix W143569-2. 2 March 1927. Columbia 14197D.

———. "Need a Little Sugar in My Bowl." Columbia Matrix W151883-1. 20 November 1931. Columbia 14634-D, 1931.

Washingtonians. "Move Over." 19 October 1928. Cameo 9025, Romeo 829.

Bibliography

Abbott, Lynn, and Doug Seroff. *The Original Blues: The Emergence of the Blues in African American Vaudeville, 1899–1926.* Jackson: University Press of Mississippi, 2017.

———. *Ragged but Right: Black Traveling Shows, "Coon Songs," and the Dark Pathway to Blues and Jazz.* Jackson: University Press of Mississippi, 2007.

"About OKeh." Sony Music Entertainment. 2015. https://www.okeh-records.com/about/.

Albertson, Chris. *Bessie.* New York: Stein and Day, 1972.

———. "Lonnie Johnson: Chased by the Blues." In *Bluesland: Portraits of Twelve American Blues Masters,* edited by Pete Welding and Toby Byron, 38–49. New York: Dutton, 1991.

Alger, Dean. *The Original Guitar Hero and the Power of Music: The Legendary Lonnie Johnson Music and Civil Rights.* Denton: University of North Texas Press, 2014.

Anderson, Benedict. *Imagined Communities: Reflections on the Origin and Spread of Nationalism.* New York: Verso, 2016.

Anderson, Gene H. *The Original Hot Five Recordings of Louis Armstrong.* Hillsdale, NY: Pendragon Press, 2007.

Armstrong, Lillian Hardin. "Interview." Recorded 1 July 1959. Music Rising at Tulane: The Musical Cultures of the Gulf South, William Ransom Hogan Archive of New Orleans Jazz. https://musicrising.tulane.edu/listen/interviews/lillian-hardin-armstrong-1959-07-01/.

Armstrong, Louis. *Satchmo: My Life in New Orleans.* New York: Prentice Hall, 1954.

Auslander, Philip. *Performing Glam Rock: Gender and Theatricality in Popular Music.* Ann Arbor: University of Michigan Press, 2006.

Baker, Houston A., Jr. *Blues, Ideology, and Afro-American Literature: A Vernacular Theory.* Chicago: University of Chicago Press, 1984.

Baker, Vaughan B. "'Cherchez les Femmes': Some Glimpses of Women in Early Eighteenth-Century Louisiana." *Louisiana History: The Journal of the Louisiana Historical Association* 31, no. 1 (Winter 1990): 21–37.

Barker, Danny. *Buddy Bolden and the Last Days of Storyville.* Edited by Alyn Shipton. London: Cassell, 1998.

———. *A Life in Jazz.* Edited by Alyn Shipton. London: Macmillan, 1986.

Barrie, John, and Roynon Cillings. "True Blues." *Jazz Journal* 17, no. 2 (February 1964): 27.

Barry, John M. *Rising Tide: The Great Mississippi Flood of 1927 and How It Changed America.* New York: Simon and Schuster, 1997.

Barthes, Roland. "The Grain of the Voice." In *The Sound Studies Reader,* edited by Jonathan Sterne, 504–10. New York: Routledge, 2012.

Belford, Kevin. *Devil at the Confluence: The Pre-War Blues Music of St. Louis Missouri.* St. Louis: Virginia Publishing, 2009.

Berish, Andrew S. *Lonesome Roads and Streets of Dreams: Place, Mobility, and Race in Jazz of the 1930s and '40s.* Chicago: University of Chicago Press, 2012.

Bernhard, Blythe. "St. Louis Saw the Deadly 1918 Spanish Flu Epidemic Coming. Shutting Down the City Saved Countless Lives." *St. Louis Post-Dispatch*, 20 March 2020. https://www.stltoday.com/news/local/metro/st-louis-saw-the-deadly-spanish-flu-epidemic-coming-shutting/article_52e5e46d-1f30-5f31-a706-786785692bb5.html.

Bernstein, Barton J. "Plessy v. Ferguson: Conservative Sociological Jurisprudence." In *The Age of Jim Crow: Segregation from the End of Reconstruction to the Great Depression*, edited by Paul Finkelman, 2–11. New York: Garland, 1992.

Blesh, Rudi, and Harriet Janis. *They All Played Ragtime: The True Story of American Music*. 1950. Reprint, New York: Grove, 1959.

Brackett, David. *Interpreting Popular Music*. Berkeley: University of California Press, 2000.

Bridge, Donna, and Joel L. Voss. "Hippocampal Binding of Novel Information with Dominant Memory Traces Can Support Both Memory Stability and Change." *Journal of Neuroscience* 34, no. 6 (February 2014): 2203–13.

Brooks, Edward. *The Young Louis Armstrong on Records: A Critical Survey of the Early Recordings, 1923–1928*. Lanham, MD: Scarecrow Press; Rutgers: University of New Jersey Institute of Jazz Studies, 2002.

Broonzy, Big Bill. *Big Bill Blues: William Broonzy's Story as Told to Yannick Bruynoghe*. New York: Da Capo, 1992.

Brown, Ken, and Brian Rust. "Lonnie Johnson Discography." *Jazz Tempo* 19 (March 1944): 56–59.

Butler, Judith. *Gender Trouble: Feminism and the Subversion of Identity*. New York: Routledge, 1990.

Butterfield, Matthew. "When Swing Doesn't Swing: Competing Conceptions of an Early Twentieth-Century Rhythmic Quality." In *Music in Time: Phenomenology, Perception, Performance*, edited by Suzannah Clark and Alexander Rehding, 257–77. Cambridge, MA: Harvard University Press, 2016.

Carby, Hazel V. "It Jus Be's Dat Way Sometime: The Sexual Politics of Women's Blues." In *Jazz Cadence of American Culture*, edited by Robert G. O'Meally, 469–82. New York: Columbia University Press, 1998.

Carney, Court. "New Orleans and the Creation of Early Jazz." *Popular Music and Society* 29, no. 3 (July 2006): 299–315.

Casey-Leininger, Charles F. "Making the Second Ghetto in Cincinnati: Avondale, 1925–70." In *Race and the City: Work, Community, and Protest in Cincinnati, 1820–1970*, edited by Henry Louis Taylor, Jr., 232–57. Urbana: University of Illinois Press, 1993.

Catalog of Copyright Entries: Unpublished Music. 3rd ser., vol. 3, pt. 5B, no. 1, January–June. Washington, DC: US Government Printing Office, 1949.

Chafe, William H., Raymond Gavins, and Robert Korstad, eds. *Remembering Jim Crow: African Americans Tell About Life in the Segregated South*. New York: New Press, 2001.

Charters, Samuel B. *The Country Blues*. New York: Da Capo, 1975.

———. "Workin' on the Building: Roots and Influences." In Cohn, *Nothing but the Blues*, 13–31.

Chevan, David. "Riverboat Music from St. Louis and the Streckfus Steamboat Line." *Black Music Research Journal* 9, no. 2 (Autumn 1989): 153–80.

"Chicago Federation of Musicians: A History." Chicago Federation of Musicians. 2021. https://cfm10208.com/about/our-history.

Chilla, Mark. "The Mystery of Irene Higginbotham." *After Glow: Jazz and American Popular Song*, 8 June 2018. https://indianapublicmedia.org/afterglow/mystery-irene-higginbotham.php.

Cobb, James C. *The Most Southern Place on Earth: The Mississippi Delta and the Roots of Regional Identity*. New York: Oxford University Press, 1992.

Cohn, Lawrence, ed. *Nothing but the Blues: The Music and the Musicians*. New York: Abbeville Press, 1993.

Cole, Ross. "Mastery and Masquerade in the Transatlantic Blues Revival." *Journal of the Royal Musical Association* 143, no. 1 (2018): 173–210.

Collier, Geoffrey L., and James Lincoln Collier. "A Study of Timing in Two Louis Armstrong Solos." *Music Perception* 19, no. 3 (Spring 2002): 463–83.

Complete Vocal Technique Research Site. 2021. http://cvtresearch.com/.

Conforth, Bruce. "Ike Zimmerman: The X in Robert Johnson's Crossroads." *Living Blues* 194 (2008): 68–73.

Cressing, Peter. "Profile: Lonnie Johnson." *Jazz Journal* 4, no. 6 (June 1951): 15.

Cullen, Frank, with Florence Hackman and Donald McNeilly. *Vaudeville Old and New: An Encyclopedia of Variety Performances in America*. 2 vols. New York: Routledge, 2006.

Dahl, Bill. *The Art of the Blues: A Visual Treasury of Black Music's Golden Age*. Chicago: University of Chicago Press, 2016.

Dalton, James. "The Guitar Style of Lonnie Johnson." *Blues Revue Quarterly: An Acoustic and Traditional Blues Digest* 11 (1993): 48–49.

Daniel, Pete. *Deep'n as It Come: The 1927 Mississippi River Flood*. New York: Oxford University Press, 1977.

Darby, Cameron. "The Moldy Figs." *Toronto Telegram*, 22 July 1967, 12–13.

Davis, Angela Y. *Blues Legacies and Black Feminism: Gertrude "Ma" Rainey, Bessie Smith, and Billie Holiday*. New York: Pantheon, 1998.

Derrida, Jacques. *Writing and Difference*. Translated by Alan Bass. Chicago: University of Chicago Press, 1978.

Dicaire, David. *Blues Singers: Biographies of 50 Legendary Artists of the Early 20th Century*. Jefferson, NC: McFarland and Co., 1999.

Dietz, Howard, and Arthur Schwartz. *Alone Together*. Sheet music. New York: Harms Inc., 1932.

Dowden-White, Priscilla A. *Groping Toward Democracy: African American Social Welfare Reform in St. Louis, 1910–1949*. Columbia: University of Missouri Press, 2011.

Drake, St. Clair, and Horace R. Cayton. *Black Metropolis: A Study of Negro Life in a Northern City*. New York: Harcourt Brace, 1945.

Du Bois, W. E. B. *The Illustrated Souls of Black Folk*. Edited and annotated by Eugene F. Provenzo Jr. Boulder, CO: Paradigm, 2005.

Dunbar-Nelson, Alice Moore. "People of Color in Louisiana." In Klein, *Creole*.

Eidsheim, Nina Sun. *The Race of Sound: Listening, Timbre, and Vocality in African American Music*. Durham, NC: Duke University Press, 2019.

Evans, David. *Big Road Blues: Tradition and Creativity in the Folk Blues*. 1982. Reprint, New York: Da Capo, 1987.

———. "The Development of the Blues." In *The Cambridge Companion to Blues and Gospel Music*, edited by Allan Moore, 43–61. Cambridge: Cambridge University Press, 2002.

———. "Goin' Up the Country: Blues in Texas and the Deep South." In Cohn, *Nothing but the Blues*, 33–85.

———. "High Water Everywhere: Blues and Gospel Commentary on the 1927 Mississippi River Flood." In *Nobody Knows Where the Blues Comes From: Lyrics and History*, edited by Robert Springer, 3–75. Jackson: University Press of Mississippi, 2006.

———. *The NPR Curious Listener's Guide to the Blues*. New York: Perigee, 2005.

Everett, Donald E. "Free Persons of Color in Colonial Louisiana." *Louisiana History: The Journal of the Louisiana Historical Association* 7, no. 1 (Winter 1966): 21–50.

Eyerman, Ron, and Andrew Jamison. *Music and Social Movements: Mobilizing Traditions in the Twentieth Century*. Cambridge: Cambridge University Press, 1998.

Feldman, Martha. "Why Voice Now?" *Journal of the American Musicological Society* 68, no. 3 (Fall 2015): 653–85.

Ferris, William. *Blues from the Delta*. New York: Anchor, 1978.

Floyd, Samuel A., Jr. *The Power of Black Music: Interpreting Its History from*

Africa to the United States. New York: Oxford University Press, 1995.

———. "Ring Shout: Literary Studies, Historical Studies, and Black Music Inquiry." *Black Music Research Journal* 11, no. 2 (Autumn 1991): 265–87.

Floyd, Samuel A., Jr., and Ronald Radano. "Interpreting the African-American Musical Past: A Dialogue." *Black Music Research Journal* 29, no. 1 (Spring 2009): 1–10.

"Folkways Records." Smithsonian Folkways Records. 2021. https://folkways.si.edu/folkways-records/smithsonian.

Foner, Laura. "The Free People of Color in Louisiana and St. Domingue: A Comparative Portrait of Two Three-Caste Slave Societies." *Journal of Social History* 3, no. 4 (Summer 1970): 406–30.

Foster, Craig. "Tarnished Angels: Prostitution in Storyville, New Orleans, 1900–1910." *Louisiana History: The Journal of the Louisiana Historical Association* 31, no. 4 (Winter 1990): 387–97.

Foster, George "Pops." "Interview." Recorded 21 April 1957. Music Rising at Tulane: The Musical Cultures of the Gulf South, William Ransom Hogan Archive of New Orleans Jazz. https://musicrising.tulane.edu/listen/interviews/george-pops-foster-1957-04-21/.

———. "Interview." Recorded 24 August 1958. Music Rising at Tulane: The Musical Cultures of the Gulf South, William Ransom Hogan Archive of New Orleans Jazz. https://musicrising.tulane.edu/listen/interviews/george-pops-foster-1958-08-24/.

Foster, George "Pops," with Tom Stoddard. *Pops Foster: The Autobiography of a New Orleans Jazzman*. Berkeley: University of California Press, 1971.

Fox, Jon Hartley. *King of the Queen City: The Story of King Records*. Urbana: University of Illinois Press, 2009.

Frith, Simon. *Performing Rites: On the Value of Popular Music*. Cambridge, MA: Harvard University Press, 1996.

Garon, Paul. "Remembering Lonnie Johnson." *Living Blues* 1–2 (1970): 20.

———. "White Blues." Blues World. 2021. http://www.bubbaguitar.com/articles/whiteblues.html.

George-Graves, Nadine. *The Royalty of Negro Vaudeville: The Whitman Sisters and the Negotiation of Race, Gender and Class in African American Theater, 1900–1940*. New York: Palgrave Macmillan, 2003.

Giddens, Gary. *Visions of Jazz: The First Century*. New York: Oxford University Press, 1998.

Gill, Chris. "T-Bone Walker." In *Rollin' and Tumblin': The Postwar Blues Guitarists*, edited by Jas Obrecht, 17–24. San Francisco: Miller Freeman Books, 2000.

Gilroy, Paul. *The Black Atlantic: Modernity and Double Consciousness*. London: Verso, 2012.

Givan, Benjamin. "Gunther Schuller and the Challenge of Sonny Rollins: Stylistic Context, Intentionality, and Jazz Analysis." *Journal of the American Musicological Society* 67, no. 1 (Spring 2014): 167–237.

Goddard, John. "The Final Years of Lonnie Johnson." *Blues Access*, Winter 1998, 33–37.

Goffman, Erving. *The Presentation of Self in Everyday Life*. New York: Doubleday, 1959.

Grossman, Stefan, ed. *Early Masters of American Blues Guitar: Lonnie Johnson*. Van Nuys, CA: Alfred Publishing, 2007.

———. *Masters of Country Blues Guitar Featuring Lonnie Johnson*. Miami: CPP/Belwin, 1993.

Guralnick, Peter. *Searching for Robert Johnson*. New York: E. P. Dutton, 1989.

Gussow, Adam. *Beyond the Crossroads: The Devil and the Blues Tradition*. Chapel Hill: University of North Carolina Press, 2017.

———. *Seems Like Murder Here: Southern Violence and the Blues Tradition*.

Chicago: University of Chicago Press, 2002.
Hadlock, Richard. *Jazz Masters of the Twenties*. New York: Macmillan, 1965.
Hahn, Roger. "Lonnie Johnson." In *64 Parishes*, edited by David Johnson. New Orleans: Louisiana Endowment for the Humanities, 2010–. https://64parishes.org/entry/lonnie-johnson.
Hale, Grace Elizabeth. *Making Whiteness: The Culture of Segregation in the South, 1890–1940*. New York: Pantheon, 1998.
Halker, Clark. "A History of Local 208 and the Struggle for Racial Equality in the American Federation of Musicians." *Black Music Research Journal* 8, no. 2 (Autumn 1988): 207–22.
Hall, Stuart. *Essential Essays*. Vol. 2, *Identity and Diaspora*. Edited by David Morley. Durham, NC: Duke University Press, 2019.
Hamilton, Marybeth. *In Search of the Blues*. New York: Perseus, 2008.
Handy, W. C. *Father of the Blues: An Autobiography of W. C. Handy*. Edited by Arna Bontemps. London: Sidgwick and Jackson, 1957.
Hansberry v. Lee. 311 U.S. 32. 1940. https://supreme.justia.com/cases/federal/us/311/32/.
Harap, Louis, "The Case for Hot Jazz." *Musical Quarterly* 27, no. 1 (January 1941): 47–61.
Harker, Brian. *Louis Armstrong's Hot Five and Hot Seven Recordings*. New York: Oxford University Press, 2011.
Harrington, J. Winston. "Flood Refugee Shot to Death: 'Work or Die' Edict Again Perils Race." *Chicago Defender*, July 23, 1927.
———. "Refugees Herded Like Cattle to Stop Escape from Peonage: Plantation Owners in Fear of Raids by Labor Agents." *Chicago Defender*, May 6, 1927.
———. "Use Troops in Flood Area to Imprison Farm Hands: Refugees Herded Like Cattle." *Chicago Defender*, 7 May 1927.

———. "Work or Go Hungry Edict Perils Race: Flood Victims Driven by Labor Bosses." *Chicago Defender*, June 11, 1927.
Harris, Jay. "1945 Jazz Poll." *Jazz Session* 7 (May–June 1945): 3–15.
Harrison, Daphne Duval. *Black Pearls: Blues Queens of the 1920s*. New Brunswick, NJ: Rutgers University Press, 1988.
Hartman, Saidiya V. *Scenes of Subjection: Terror, Slavery, and Self-Making in Nineteenth-Century America*. New York: Oxford University Press, 1997.
Heidemann, Kate. "A System for Describing Vocal Timbre in Popular Song." *Music Theory Online* 22, no. 1 (March 2016): 1–17. https://mtosmt.org/issues/mto.16.22.1/mto.16.22.1.heidemann.php.
Hersch, Charles. *Subversive Sounds: Race and the Birth of Jazz in New Orleans*. Chicago: University of Chicago Press, 2007.
———. "Unfinalizable: Dialog and Self-Expression in Jazz." In *The Routledge Companion to Jazz Studies*, edited by Nicholas Gebhardt, Nichole Rustin-Paschal, and Tony Whyton, 367–76. New York: Routledge, 2019.
Hirsch, Arnold R., and Joseph Logsdon, eds. *Creole New Orleans: Race and Americanization*. Baton Rouge: Louisiana State University Press, 1992.
Hobson, Vic. "New Orleans Jazz and the Blues." *Jazz Perspectives* 5, no. 1 (2011): 3–27.
Howland, John. *Ellington Uptown: Duke Ellington, James P. Johnson, and the Birth of Concert Jazz*. Ann Arbor: University of Michigan Press, 2009.
Humphrey, Mark A. "Bright Lights, Big City: Urban Blues." In Cohn, *Nothing but the Blues*, 151–203.
Jackson, Joy J. *New Orleans in the Gilded Age: Politics and Urban Progress, 1880–1896*. Baton Rouge: Louisiana State University Press, 1969.
"Jheri Curl, Conk, Dreadlocks, and Afro: Black Hair History." Jazma Hair. 2021. http://www.jazma.com/black-hair-history.

Johansson, Mats. "Michael Jackson and the Expressive Power of Voice-Produced Sound." *Popular Music and Society*, 35, no. 2 (May 2012): 261–79.

Johnson, Jerah. "Colonial New Orleans: A Fragment of the Eighteenth-Century French Ethos." In Hirsch and Logsdon, *Creole New Orleans*, 12–57.

Jones, Max. "The Men Who Make the Blues." *Melody Maker*, 30 August 1969.

———. "You're in Love with the Blues." *Melody Maker*, 26 October 1963.

Jungr, Barb. "Vocal Expression in the Blues and Gospel." In *The Cambridge Companion to Blues and Gospel*, edited by Allan Moore, 140–54. Cambridge: Cambridge University Press, 2002.

Kant, Immanuel. *Critique of Practical Reason*. Translated by Lewis White Beck. New York: Macmillan, 1985.

Keil, Charles. "Motion and Feeling Through Music." In *Music Grooves: Essays and Dialogues*, edited by Charles Keil and Steven Feld, 53–76. Tucson, AZ: Fenestra Books, 2005.

———. *Urban Blues*. Chicago: University of Chicago Press, 1966.

Kenney, William Howland. *Jazz on the River*. Chicago: University of Chicago Press, 2005.

———. *Recorded Music in American Life: The Phonograph and Popular Memory, 1890–1945*. New York: Oxford University Press, 1999.

Kienzle, Richard. *Great Guitarists*. New York: Facts on File, 1985.

King, B. B., with David Ritz. *Blues All Around Me: The Autobiography of B. B. King*. New York: Avon, 1996.

Klein, Sybil, ed. *Creole: The History and Legacy of Louisiana's Free People of Color*. Baton Rouge: Louisiana State University Press, 2000.

———. "Introduction." In Klein, *Creole*, xiii–xxiv.

Lachance, Paul F. "The Foreign French." In Hirsch and Logsdon, *Creole New Orleans*, 101–30.

Lambert, Dan. "From Blues to Jazz Guitar." In *The Guitar in Jazz: An Anthology*, edited by James Sallis, 33–44. Lincoln: University of Nebraska Press, 1996.

Landau, Emily Epstein. *Spectacular Wickedness: Sex, Race, and Memory in Storyville, New Orleans*. Baton Rouge: Louisiana State University Press, 2013.

Le Menestrel, Sara. *Negotiating Difference in French Louisiana Music: Categories, Stereotypes, and Identifications*. Jackson: University Press of Mississippi, 2015.

"Moses Asch." Smithsonian Center for Folklife and Cultural Heritage. 2021. https://folklife.si.edu/legacy-honorees/moses-asch/smithsonian.

Lipsitz, George. *How Racism Takes Place*. Philadelphia: Temple University Press, 2011.

Logsdon, Joseph, and Caryn Cossé Bell. "The Americanization of Black New Orleans, 1850–1900." In Hirsch and Logsdon, *Creole New Orleans*, 201–61.

Lomax, Alan. *The Land Where the Blues Began*. New York: New Press, 1993.

———. *Mr. Jelly Roll: The Fortunes of Jelly Roll Morton, New Orleans Creole and "Inventor of Jazz."* 2nd ed. Berkeley: University of California Press, 1973.

Long, Alecia P. *The Great Southern Babylon: Sex, Race, and Respectability in New Orleans, 1865–1920*. Baton Rouge: Louisiana State University Press, 2004.

"Lonnie Johnson." *Coda* 9, no. 8 (July–August 1970): 31.

"Lonnie Johnson." In *AMG All Music Guide to the Blues*, edited by Michael Erlewine, Vladimir Bogdanov, Chris Woodstra, and Cub Koda, 227–28. 2nd ed. San Francisco: Miller Freeman Books, 1999.

"Lonnie Johnson Buried Quietly: N.O.-Born Jazzman Dies in Canada." Unknown source, 21 June 1970. Lonnie Johnson Vertical File, William Ransom Hogan Archive of New Orleans Jazz, Tulane University.

Malawey, Victoria. *A Blaze of Light in Every Word: Analyzing the Popular Singing*

Voice. New York: Oxford University Press, 2020.

Mazor, Barry. *Ralph Peer and the Making of Popular Roots Music.* Chicago: Chicago Review Press, 2015.

McCarthy, Albert J. "Lonnie Johnson." *Jazz Journal* 5, no. 6 (June 1952): 1–2.

McGinley, Paige A. *Staging the Blues: From Tent Shows to Tourism.* Durham, NC: Duke University Press, 2014.

Mertz, Paul E. *The New Deal Policy and Southern Rural Poverty.* Baton Rouge: Louisiana State University Press, 1978.

Meyer, Leonard B., *Style and Music: Theory, History, and Ideology.* Philadelphia: University of Pennsylvania Press, 1989.

Miller, Ernest "Punch." "Interview." Recorded 25 September 1959. Music Rising at Tulane: The Musical Cultures of the Gulf South, William Ransom Hogan Archive of New Orleans Jazz. https://musicrising.tulane.edu/listen/interviews/ernest-punch-miller-1959-09-25/.

Miller, Karl Hagstrom. *Segregating Sound: Inventing Folk and Pop Music in the Age of Jim Crow.* Durham, NC: Duke University Press, 2010.

Miller, Mark. *Way Down That Lonesome Road: Lonnie Johnson in Toronto, 1965–1970.* Toronto: Mercury Press and Teksteditions, 2011.

Morton, Jelly Roll, and Alan Lomax. "Library of Congress Narrative." Recorded 23 May 1938, in Washington, DC. Transcribed and annotated by Michael Hill, Roger Richard, and Mike Medding. Doctor Jazz. 2003. http://www.doctorjazz.co.uk/locspeech1.html.

Mosadomi, Fehintola. "The Origin of Louisiana Creole." In Klein, *Creole*, 223–43.

Muir, Peter S. *Long Lost Blues: Popular Blues in America, 1850–1920.* Urbana: University of Illinois Press, 2010.

Murray, Albert. *Stomping the Blues.* New York: Da Capo, 1976.

Nolen, Rose M. *Hoecakes, Hambone, and All That Jazz: African American Traditions in Missouri.* Columbia: University of Missouri Press, 2003.

Nystrom, Justin A. *New Orleans After the Civil War: Race, Politics, and the New Birth of Freedom.* Baltimore: John Hopkins University Press, 2010.

Obrecht, Jas. *Early Blues: The First Stars of Blues Guitar.* Minneapolis: University of Minnesota Press, 2015.

Odell, Jay Scott, and Robert B. Winans. "Banjo." *Grove Music Online*, 31 January 2014. https://doi.org/10.1093/gmo/9781561592630.article.A2256043.

Oliver, Paul. *Bessie Smith (Kings of Jazz).* 1959. Reprint, New York: A. S. Barnes, 1961.

———. *Blues Fell This Morning: Meaning in the Blues.* Cambridge: Cambridge University Press, 1960.

———. *Conversation with the Blues.* 2nd ed. Cambridge: Cambridge University Press, 1997.

———. *Screening the Blues: Aspects of the Blues Tradition.* New York: Da Capo, 1968.

Olwage, Grant. "The Class and Colour of Tone: An Essay on the Social History of Vocal Timbre." *Ethnomusicology Forum* 13, no. 2 (November 2004): 203–26.

O'Malley, Michael. "Dark Enough as It Is: Eddie Lang and the Minstrel Cycle." *Journal of Social History* 52, no. 2 (2018): 234–59.

Owsley, Dennis. *City of Gabriels: The History of Jazz in St. Louis, 1895–1973.* St. Louis: Reedy Press, 2006.

Packard, Jerrold M. *American Nightmare: The History of Jim Crow.* New York: St. Martin's, 2002.

Palmer, Vernon Valentine. "The Origins and Authors of the *Code Noir*." *Louisiana Law Review* 56, no. 2 (1996): 363–407.

Parrish, Susan Scott. *The Flood Year 1927: A Cultural History.* Princeton, NJ: Princeton University Press, 2017.

Pearson, Barry Lee. *"Sounds So Good to Me": The Bluesman's Story.* Philadelphia: University of Pennsylvania Press, 1984.

Peretti, Burton W. *The Creation of Jazz: Music, Race, and Culture in Urban*

America. Urbana: University of Illinois Press, 1992.

Peterson, Robert K. D. "Mean Old Bed Bug Blues." *American Entomologist* 60, no. 4 (Winter 2014): 241–43.

Pratt, Ray. *Rhythm and Resistance: Explorations in the Political Uses of Popular Music*. New York: Praeger, 1990.

"Preservation Plan for St. Louis, Part I: Historic Contexts." Cultural Resources Office, City of St. Louis. 1995. https://www.stlouis-mo.gov/government/departments/planning/cultural-resources/preservation-plan/Part-I-African-American-Experience.cfm.

Raeburn, Bruce Boyd. "Confessions of a New Orleans Jazz Archivist." In *Reflections on American Music*, edited by James R. Heintze and Michael Saffle, 300–312. Hillsdale, NY: Pendragon Press, 2000.

———. "Early New Orleans Jazz in Theaters." *Louisiana History: The Journal of the Louisiana Historical Association* 43, no. 1 (Winter 2002): 41–52.

———. *New Orleans Style and the Writing of American Jazz History*. Ann Arbor: University of Michigan Press, 2009.

Reich, Howard, and William Gaines. *Jelly's Blues: The Life, Music, and Redemption of Jelly Roll Morton*. Cambridge, MA: Da Capo, 2003.

Riesman, Bob. *I Feel So Good: The Life and Times of Big Bill Broonzy*. Chicago: University of Chicago Press, 2011.

Rogers, Charles Payne. "Lonnie Johnson's Instrumental Style." *Jazz Record* 57 (August 1947): 24–25. Lonnie Johnson Vertical File, William Ransom Hogan Archive of New Orleans Jazz, Tulane University.

Rose, Al. *Storyville, New Orleans: Being an Authentic, Illustrated Account of the Notorious Red-Light District*. Tuscaloosa: University of Alabama Press, 1974.

Rose, Tricia. *The Hip Hop Wars: What We Talk About When We Talk About Hip Hop—and Why It Matters*. New York: Basic Books, 2008.

Rosengarten, Theodore. *All God's Dangers: The Life of Nate Shaw*. New York: Alfred A. Knopf, 1974.

Rowe, Mike. Liner notes. In *The American Folk-Blues Festival, The British Tours, 1963–1966*. DVD. San Diego: Reelin' in the Years Productions, 2007.

Rusch, Bob. "Floyd Campbell: Interview." *Cadence*, March 1981, 5–9.

Rye, Howard. "The Southern Syncopated Orchestra." *Black Music Research Journal* 29, no. 2 (Fall 2009): 153–228.

Sallis, James. "Eddie Lang." In *The Guitar in Jazz: An Anthology*, edited by James Sallis, 20–32. Lincoln: University of Nebraska Press, 1996.

———. *The Guitar Players: One Instrument and Its Masters in American Music*. New York: William Morrow, 1982.

Schenck, John T. "Hot Club of Chicago's Second Concert." *Jazz Session* 11 (January 1946): 7–9.

Schuller, Gunther. *Early Jazz: Its Roots and Musical Development*. New York: Oxford University Press, 1968.

Scott, James C. *Domination and the Arts of Resistance: Hidden Transcripts*. New Haven, CT: Yale University Press, 1990.

Seligman, Amanda I. *Block by Block: Neighborhoods and Public Policy in Chicago's West Side*. Chicago: University of Chicago Press, 2005.

Shapiro, Nat, and Nat Hentoff. *Hear Me Talkin' to Ya: The Story of Jazz as Told by the Men Who Made It*. 1955. Reprint, New York: Dover, 1966.

Shaw, Arnold. *Honkers and Shouters: The Golden Years of Rhythm and Blues*. New York: Macmillan, 1978.

Sheridan, Chris. "Chapters in Jazz: Chapter 15: Strinin' the Blues." *Cadence* 7 (1981): 15–16.

Shute, Nancy. "Our Brains Rewrite Our Memories, Putting Present in Past." *NPR*, 5 February 2014. https://www.npr.org/sections/health-shots/2014/02/04/271527934/our-brains-rewrite

-our-memories-putting-present-in-the-past.

Simon, Julia. "Narrative Time in the Blues: Son House's 'Death Letter' (1965)." *American Music* 31, no. 1 (Spring 2013): 50–72.

———. *Time in the Blues*. New York: Oxford University Press, 2017.

Sitkoff, Harvard. *A New Deal for Blacks: The Emergence of Civil Rights as a National Issue. Vol. 1, The Depression Decade*. New York: Oxford University Press, 1978.

Sklaroff, Lauren Rebecca. *Black Culture and the New Deal: The Quest for Civil Rights in the Roosevelt Era*. Chapel Hill: University of North Carolina Press, 2009.

Slieff, Brennon, Kathy Bradshaw, Courtney Carver, and Charles Chamberlain. "The Tango Belt." New Orleans Historical. 2021. https://neworleanshistorical.org/items/show/1315.

Small, Christopher. *Music of the Common Tongue: Survival and Celebration in Afro-American Music*. Hanover, NH: Wesleyan University Press, 1987.

Smith, Jessie Carney, ed. *Notable Black Women: Book II*. New York: Gale, 1996.

Sotiropoulos, Karen. *Staging Race: Black Performers in Turn of the Century America*. Cambridge, MA: Harvard University Press, 2006.

Spalding, Philip, dir. *'Til the Butcher Cuts Him Down*. Delaplane, VA: Folkstreams, 1971. http://www.folkstreams.net/film-detail.php?id=306.

Spear, Jennifer M. "Colonial Intimacies: Legislating Sex in French Louisiana." *William and Mary Quarterly* 60, no. 1 (January 2003): 75–98.

Spivey, Victoria. "Blues Is May Business." *Record Research* 106 (July 1970): 9.

St. Cyr, Johnny. "Interview." Recorded 27 August 1958. Music Rising at Tulane: The Musical Cultures of the Gulf South. William Ransom Hogan Archive of New Orleans Jazz. https://musicrising.tulane.edu/listen/interviews/johnny-st-cyr-1958-08-27/.

Streckfus, Verne. "Interview." Recorded 22 September 1960. Music Rising at Tulane: The Musical Cultures of the Gulf South, William Ransom Hogan Archive of New Orleans Jazz. https://musicrising.tulane.edu/listen/interviews/verne-streckfus-1960-09-22/.

Suisman, David. *Selling Sounds: The Commercial Revolution in American Music*. Cambridge, MA: Harvard University Press, 2009.

Swenson, John. "Masters of Louisiana Music: Lonnie Johnson." *OffBeat*, June 2001, 20–21. https://www.offbeat.com/articles/masters-of-louisiana-music-lonnie-johnson/.

Taylor, Candacy. "The Roots of Route 66." *The Atlantic*, 3 November 2016. https://www.theatlantic.com/politics/archive/2016/11/the-roots-of-route-66/506255/.

Terrill, Tom E., and Jerrold Hirsch, eds. *Such as Us: Southern Voices of the Thirties*. Chapel Hill: University of North Carolina Press, 1978.

These Are Our Lives: As Told by the People and Written by Members of the Federal Writers' Project of the Works Progress Administration in North Carolina, Tennessee, and Georgia. Chapel Hill: University of North Carolina Press, 1939.

Thomas, Mark. "I'm a Roamin' Rambler: Lonnie Johnson." *Jazz Quarterly* 2, no. 4 (Summer 1945): 18–21.

Titon, Jeff Todd. *The Early Downhome Blues: A Musical and Cultural Analysis*. 2nd ed. Chapel Hill: University of North Carolina Press, 1994.

Townsend, Henry. *A Blues Life: Henry Townsend as Told to Bill Greensmith*. Urbana: University of Illinois Press, 1999.

Toynbee, Jason. *Making Popular Music: Musicians, Creativity and Institutions*. New York: Oxford University Press, 2000.

Tregle, Joseph C., Jr. "Creoles and Americans." In Hirsch and Logsdon, *Creole New Orleans*, 131–85.

Tsotsi, Tom. "Gennett-Champion Blues: Richmond, Indiana (1923–1934), Part 1." *78 Quarterly* 1, no. 3 (1988): 49–53.

Voce, Steve. "The Return of Lonnie Johnson." *Jazz Journal*, May 1963, 12–14.

Wald, Elijah. *Escaping the Delta: Robert Johnson and the Invention of the Blues*. New York: Amistad, 2004.

———. "Louis Armstrong Loves Guy Lombardo." In *Jazz / Not Jazz: The Music and Its Boundaries*, edited by David Ake, Charles Hiroshi Garrett, and Daniel Goldmark, 32–43. Berkeley: University of California Press, 2012.

Ward, Brian, and Patrick Huber. *A&R Pioneers: Architects of American Roots Music on Record*. Nashville: Vanderbilt University Press and Country Music Foundation Press, 2018.

Waterman, Richard A. "African Influence on the Music of the Americas." In *Acculturation in the Americas*, edited by Sol Tax, 207–18. Chicago: University of Chicago Press, 1952.

———. "'Hot' Rhythm in Negro Music." *A Journal of the American Musicological Society* 1, no. 1 (Spring 1948): 24–37.

Welding, Pete. "Lonnie Johnson." *Coda* 3, no. 4 (August 1960): 29–30.

Wells-Barnett, Ida B. "Flood Refugees Are Held as Slaves in Mississippi Camp: Men Who Escaped Death in Government Controlled Area Describe Viciousness of Southern Whites Ruling Workers." *Chicago Defender*, July 30, 1927.

White, Walter. "Walter White Reports that Peonage Conditions Prevail in Flood Area: Escape from Refugee Camps Barred by Soldiers—Tuskegee Graduate Tells of Brutal Methods Used." *New York Amsterdam News*, 8 June 1927.

Wilmer, Valerie. "Lonnie Johnson Talks to Valerie Wilmer." *Jazz Monthly*, December 1963, 5–7.

Woods, Clyde. *Development Arrested: The Blues and Plantation Power in the Mississippi Delta*. London: Verso, 1998.

Work, John W., III. "Untitled Manuscript." In Work, Jones, and Adams, *Lost Delta Found*, 53–126.

Work, John W., III, Lewis Wade Jones, and Samuel C. Adams Jr. *Lost Delta Found: Rediscovering the Fisk University– Library of Congress Coahoma County Study, 1941–1942*. Edited by Robert Gordon and Bruce Nemerov. Nashville: Vanderbilt University Press, 2005.

Wright, John A. *Discovering African American St. Louis: A Guide to the Historic Sites*. 2nd ed. St. Louis: Missouri Historical Society Press, 2002.

Wright, John J., Sr. *African Americans in Downtown St. Louis*. Charleston: Arcadia Publishing, 2003.

Wright, Richard. *Black Boy (American Hunger): A Record of Childhood and Youth*. New York: Perennial Classics, 1993.

Young, Nathan B. "Your St. Louis and Mine." In *"Ain't But A Place": An Anthology of African American Writings About St. Louis*, edited by Gerald Early, 337–46. St. Louis: Missouri Historical Society Press, distributed by University of Missouri Press, 1998.

Index

Note: page numbers in italics refer to figures. Those followed by n refer to notes, with note number.

Adams, Samuel C., Jr., 32
aesthetic works, and social change, 100
African American music, authentic, characteristics of, 18–19
African Americans performers, performance of Blackness
   adjustment to suit audience, 77–78
   blackface minstrelsy and, 52–53
   and hyperconsciousness about their perception by whites, 53
   and miscegenated style, 53–54, 71
   necessity of maintaining onstage and off, 76–77
   push against stereotypes in, 53
   similarity to offstage life, 53–54
   variation with audience, 53
Aladdin Records, Johnson's work for, 11, 12
Albertson, Chris, 14
Alexander, Texas, 8, 40, 59, 90, 124, 144
Alger, Dean, 38, 82, 172n22, 176n33
American Folk Blues Festival Tour of Europe, Johnson in, 15
Anderson, Benedict, 174n50
Anderson, Gene H., 139
Animal Hall, 17, 18
"Another Woman Booked Out and Bound to Go," 83
Armstrong, Lillian Hardin, 18, 96, 146
Armstrong, Louis
   admiration for Lombardo's "sweet" music, 158n117
   firing from Streckfus Steamers, 43, 89
   and "hot" to "sweet" scale of music, 20
   improvisation by, 19, 158n116
   and Jim Crow, 171n7
   Johnson's recordings with, 8, 47, 62, 90, 138–41
   Johnson's references to, 61–62
   musical influences on, 43
   work in Chicago, 8

Arnold, John, 50, 145
Asch, Moses, 4, 11, 14
Austin, Gene, 119
authentic African American music, characteristics of, 18–19
authenticity in jazz music, stock arrangements and, 44
authenticity of Johnson's blues
   as issue for critics, 1–2, 134
   issues of recording technology and, 12, 105, 109
   Johnson's failure to fit standard image of blues artist, 134, 142; due to background, 27; due to formal training in music, 145; due to range of instruments played, 145; due to versatility of styles, 25–26, 144–45, 149–50; due to work as successful professional musician, 144; due to work in groups, 144, 145; musical style and, 26, 159–60n129, 160n131, 160n134; singing style and, 12, 25, 26, 50, 59, 159n125, 160n131
   as product of social and existential issues addressed in his work, 150
   See also blues artists, authentic, standard image of
"Away Down the Alley Blues," 148

"Baby, Please Tell Me," 81–82
"Back Water Blues," Johnson's cover of
   critiques of, 26
   on homelessness caused by floods, 114
   Johnson's alternation between personal and general views in, 112, 113
   musical techniques in, 117, 118
ballads, prohibition on Black males' singing on white stages, 162n20
ballads by Johnson
   and charges of inauthenticity, 25–26
   critics' dislike of, 159n126
   recordings of, 13–14, 155n70
"Ball and Chain Blues," 84
Barbarin, Isidore, 17

Barker, Danny, 16–17, 39, 43, 78, 93
Barrett, Robert, 163n41
"Be Careful," 75
Berish, Andrew S., 18, 119, 157n107, 178n10
B. F. Keith circuit, Johnson's work on, 6, 47
Bigard, Barney, 138
blackface minstrelsy
   described, 52–53
   and performative aspect of race, 52–53
   and permeability of racial lines, 53
   post-Civil War Black performers in, 53
Blackness, African American performance of
   Johnson's awareness of, 52, 76
   permeable racial lines in New Orleans and, 52
   rituals of, 77
   similarity to on-stage persona, 53–54
   white expectations and, 53–54
   See also African Americans performers, performance of Blackness
Black popular culture, as contradictory space, 26
"Black Water Blues," 174n46
"Blue and All Alone," 107–10
   composer of, as unknown, 107
   Johnson's vocal performance on, 109
   on loneliness, 109
   music of, 109–10
   reuse of old Johnson lyrics in, 108
   weather as indication of emotional states in, 108–9
Bluebird Records. *See* RCA Victor-Bluebird, Johnson's recordings for
"Blue Ghost Blues," 126–27
"Blue Is Only a Ghost," 127–28
blues
   on death as great equalizer, 176n32
   and jazz, difficulty of separating genres, 21, 164n59
   major race record labels in early 1920s, 151n6
   as music of lower classes, 17–18
   origin of, in interplay of African and European musical traditions, 161n18
   prostitutes' interest in, 17–18, 157n100
   rediscovery in late 1950s, 14
blues artists, and song copyrights, loss of, 9
blues artists, authentic, standard image of
   audience, minimal acknowledgment of, 142, 143–44
   blues piano and, 179n21
   designated characteristics of, 30–31
   groups responsible for construction of, 134
   as inauthentic by virtue of being self-conscious, 149–50
   and only casual work with other artists, 144, 178–79n17
   radical independence as part of, 142, 143–44
   typical background and characteristics of, 27, 178n13
   women artists' failure to meet, 134, 143–44, 177n1
   See also authenticity of Johnson's blues; rural-urban distinction in blues scholarship
Blues Fell This Morning (Oliver), 161n9
"Blues in G," 148
blues scholarship
   early, shaping of, by record collectors, 21–25
   unexamined assumptions in, recent work on, 29–30
   See also rural-urban distinction in blues scholarship
Bluesville label, Johnson's recordings for, 14
Bolden, Buddy, 17–18, 40
Booker T. Washington Theater
   blues contest won by Johnson, 7, 153n38, 166n108; as OKeh records scouting event, 7; as start of his recording career, 46–47
   Creath's involvement with, 45
   Johnson's work as musician at, 46
   location and ownership of, 153n34
   ties to Theater Owners Booking Association, 46
   types of entertainment at, 7, 46
Bottley, Dude, 17–18
"Broken Levee Blues"
   critique of racialized economic exploitation in, 96–97, 112, 115, 143
   detailed, coherent narrative in, 143
   evocation of general racialized oppression in, 116
   as first-person account, 115
   musical techniques in, 118

playing of, at meeting of International Association of Jazz Record Collectors, 22
recording of, 174n46
Broonzy, Big Bill, 5, 146, 153n17, 174n48
Brown, Willie, 144
Brunswick Records, 46
"Bullfrog Moan," 154n48
Butterbeans and Susie, 134

Campbell, Floyd, 25, 162n20
"Can't Sleep Anymore," 75
career of Johnson
  ability to support himself without day job, 47
  adaptation to musical and social expectations, 27
  commercial constraints on, 25, 86
  as long and varied, 16, 25
  willingness to take direction, 86
Carey, Thomas "Papa Mutt," 19
Carr, Leroy, 179n21
"Cat You Been Messin' Aroun'"
  child in, as indeterminate sign in need of interpretation, 71–74
  guitar technique in, as reinforcement of ambiguity in theme, 73
Charters, Samuel, 14, 30, 31–32, 161n11
Chicago
  discrimination in, mid-20th century tensions over, 95–96
  as jazz center, 1920–25, 8
  Johnson's recording sessions in, 11, 12, 60
  Johnson's work as musician in, 11, 12–13, 13
"Chicago Blues"
  critique of colorism in, 98–99
  recording of, 98
Chicago Defender, 6
Chicago Federation of Musicians, 12, 155n63, 155n66
Cincinnati
  discrimination in, mid-20th century tensions over, 96
  Johnson's move to, 13
  Johnson's recordings in, 13–14
Clapton, Eric, 134, 177n1
classification of music
  by Johnson, difficulty due to large range of genres and styles, 20–21
  lack of clear criteria for, 26
Cleveland, Johnson's move to, 11
Cobb, James C., 111
Cole, Ross, 160n131
Columbia Records
  copyrighting of Johnson's songs, 10
  Johnson's recordings for, 3, 15, 71
Complete Recorded Works in Chronological Order, 1925–1932, 145
"Confused," 14
Cook, Will Marion
  Johnson's claim to have performed with, 58–59
  Johnson's work with in England, as disproved, 5
copyrights of Johnson's music
  Johnson's filing of, in 1928–29, 9, 10, 154n48
  as mostly owned by others, 8–10, 12, 14
copyrights on music, and exploitation of artists and composers, 8–10
corpus of Johnson's work
  avenues of fruitful inquiry in, 26–27
  embeddedness in social world, 27
  genre boundaries as distraction in analysis of, 15–16
  as intervention in immoral relations of society, 85
  songs about exploitative social relations in, 99
  as subject of this study, 15
The Country Blues (Charters), 14, 31–32
Courlander, Harold, 30
Cox, Gertrude "Baby," 3, 61–62, 138
Creath, Charlie
  as bandleader on Streckfus Steamers, 45, 56
  and cruises for African Americans out of St. Louis, 7, 45
  Floyd Campbell's work with, 25
  hiring of Johnson for Streckfus Steamers, 43
  involvement in St. Louis music venues, 45
  Jesse Johnson as promoter for, 7
  Johnson's work with, 7, 8, 45
  Pops Foster's work with, 8
Creole Jazz Band, 55

Index / 211

"Crowing Rooster," 94–95
  critique of class relationships in, 94, 95
  growing anger at discrimination as context of, 95–96
  instrumental performance in, 96
  working class call to action in, 95–96, 100, 102
"Crowing Rooster Blues"
  critique of class relationships in, 94–95
  instrumental performance in, 96

Dalton, James, 16
Dandridge, Louis "Putney," 11
Davis, Blind John, 122, 146, *147*
Davis, Joe, 86, 172n25
death, songs about, 128–30, 136–37
"Death Is on Your Track," 128–29
"Death Valley Is Just Half Way to My Home," 120–21
Decca Records, Johnson's recordings for, 11, 12, 59–60
"Deep Minor Rhythm Stomp," 10
"Deep Sea Blues," 123–24
De Luxe Music Shop (St. Louis), 7
Desdoumes, Mamie, 157n100
"The Devil's Woman," 69, 83
"dicty," as term, 17
Disc Records, Johnson's work for, 11
Dixieland, as term, 165n78
Document Records, Johnson collection by, 25
Dodds, Johnny, 11
Dodds, Warren "Baby," 12–13, 43
"Don't Be No Fool," 75, 81
"Don't Ever Love," 75
"Drifting Alone Blues," 122–23
drinking, songs about, narrator in, 64–66
Dunn, Blind Willie (Eddie Lang), 24
Dusen, Frankie, 17

Edwards, David "Honeyboy," 175n8
Ellington, Duke
  Johnson's recording work with, 3, 47, 138
  Johnson's references to, in lyrics, 61
  and "Move Over," 2, *3*
  multiple recordings of songs on different labels, 3
  and song copyrights, loss of, 9
embeddedness of individual in social world, Johnson's appreciation of, 27, 47–48, 59, 137–38

"End It All," 129–30
England
  Johnson in (1952), 14, 156n73
  Johnson's possible travel to (1917–19), 5, 41, 56
Erby, John, 117, 145
Evans, David, 31, 176n29, 177n1, 178n13
exploitative social relations
  Johnson as shrewd observer of, 99
  songs about, 93–99; critique of class relationships, 94–95, 96, 97–98, 99–100; critique of colorism, 98–99; critique of racialized economic exploitation, 94, 95–100, 175n8; evolution toward more forceful expressions of, 96; growing anger at discrimination as context of, 95–96; on Jim Crow laws, 97–98; and pimps as symbol of exploitative classes, 95; protection of Johnson's professional networks and, 99; as small percentage of total corpus, 99; working class call to action in, 95–96, 100
Eyerman, Ron, 91, 101

"Falling Rain Blues," 116
  as B side of "Mr. Johnson's Blues," 50
  copyright on, 8–9
  described, 50
  as display of Johnson's versatility, 40, 50
  Johnson's singing while playing violin, 40, 50
  lyrics of, 51
  lyrics, later reuse of, 108
  publication of, 154n52
  and sonic boundaries of blues, pushing of, 51
Federal Writers' Project, 110–11
"Fickle Mamma Blues," 83, 91, 105
Fisk University–Library of Congress Study, 32
Flanigan, Fan, 111
floods
  disproportionate impact on African Americans and poor, 110–12, 175n9
  shifting of costs onto to poor farmers, 112
floods, songs about
  critique of racialized economic exploitation in, 96–97, 112
  first-person accounts of, 115

and flood as individual and collective experience, 114
groups of, 110
on homelessness caused by floods, 114
Johnson's alternation between personal and general views in, 112–14
on lack of collective action in response to floods, 114–15
literal level of, 110–11
metaphorical meanings of, 115–16
musical techniques in, 117–18
"us vs. them" narrative created in, 115
See also Mississippi River Flood of 1927
"Flood Water Blues"
on homelessness caused by floods, 114
Johnson's alternation between personal and general views in, 113, 114
musical techniques in, 117–18
folklorist methodology in blues scholarship
binary oppositions in, as echo of musicology-ethnomusicology divide, 33, 161n12
and rural-urban distinction, 31–32
Foster, Abby "Chinee", 54–55
Foster, George "Pops"
on Clarence Williams, 9–10
on Dixieland, 165n78
on jazz centers in early 20th century, 8
on Johnson family band, 39, 139
musical influences on, 43
on Streckfus Steamers, work on, 7, 165n74
work with Creath, 8
"Four Walls and Me," 90, 124–25
Frankie Dusen's Eagle Band, 17
French colonial cities, different view of race in, 35, 42, 52

Gay-Shattuck Law of 1908, 163n38
Gennett Records, Johnson's recordings for, 3
genre boundaries
as distraction in analysis of Johnson's work, 15–16
permeability of, 47
stylistic differences marking, 18
genres and styles of music
constraints on musicians from, 89–90
Johnson's facility in large range of, 1, 8, 16; and ability to play in multiple

venues, 47; and adjustment of music to audiences' taste, 47–48; childhood in New Orleans and, 16, 38–42, 47, 134–35; and creative use of artistic restraint, 90–91; and dialectic between individual and community, 103; and difficult of classification, 20–21; early musical influences and, 47; "Falling Rain Blues" as display of, 40; as indication of blues inauthenticity for some, 25–26, 144–45, 149–50; and long, successful career, 47, 137, 145
socioeconomic factors affecting (race, class and gender), 16–19; classification of Johnson's music and, 20; and different meanings for different audiences, 18–19
See also musician, Johnson's versatility as
Georgia Music Co. of New York, 10
Glenn and Jenkins comedy team, 5, 6
Goffman, Erving, 76, 77, 160n134, 170n53
"A Good, Happy Home," 106–7
on loneliness, 106
music of, 106–7
Goodman, Bennie, 20
"Good Old Wagon," 69
"Got the Blues for the West End," 60
Grainger, Porter, 9, 145
Great Depression
collapse of race record companies in, 59
and fall in record sales, 11
as great equalizer, Johnson on, 102
and Johnson's hiatus in recording, 59–60
and traveling theater groups, 10
Great Migration, New Orleans and, 41
Grossman, Stefan, 24–25
groups, Johnson's playing in
and creative tension of varying partners, 145–46
discipline required for, 89, 90
in early years, 5, 40–41
in family band, 4, 38–39, 56, 139
in jazz bands, 15, 139–41
Johnson's ability to switch easily between rhythm and lead guitar, 146–48
Johnson's skill in, 146–48

Index / 213

groups, Johnson's playing in (*continued*)
    numerous examples of, 137
    as sign for some of Johnson's inauthenticity as blues musician, 144, 145
    skills required for, 137–38
    and social embeddedness of Johnson's identity, 27, 137, 148, 149
    and soloing within group dynamic, 139, 140–41
guitar, adoption by swing bands, 178n10
guitar, Johnson's playing of
    ability to switch easily between rhythm and lead guitar, 148
    characteristic style on, 50
    development as lead instrument, 41, 164n67
    electric guitar, transition to, 11
    as focus of first recording, 50
    and Johnson's roles in ensemble as similar to his social roles, 141
    in recordings of late 1930s, 60
    role in rhythm section of band, 41
    solo work, sense of dialogism in, 148–49
Guy, Buddy, 15

Hale, Grace Elizabeth, 35–36, 52, 53, 168n17
Hall, Stuart, 26
Harap, Louis, 158n114
"Hard Times Ain't Gone No Where," 102
Harker, Brian, 158n116
Harris, Andrew, 96, 122
hauntings, songs about, 125–28, 136–37
    death as theme in, 126
    as meditations on loneliness, 125–28
    threats of racial violence in, 126
"Headed for Southland," 101–2
"Hell Hound On My Trail" (Robert Johnson), 51
Hersch, Charles, 18, 37, 54–55
"He's a Jelly-Roll Baker," 80
Hicks, Mary, 169n29
Higginbotham, Irene, 86, 172n25
"High Sheriff Blues" (Patton), 178n16
"High Society Rag" (Creole Jazz Band), 55
"High Water Everywhere" (Patton), 143
Hildebrand, Lee, 107–8
Hill, Alex, 145
Hirsch, Arnold R., 35, 163n36

Hogan, Ernest, 53
hokum blues, 123, 176, 176n29, 177n1
"hot," as term, 18–19
"Hot and Bothered," 3
Hot Five, 8
"Hotter Than That," 18–19, 138–39
"hot" to "sweet" scale of music, 18–19, 138, 157n107, 158n115, 158n117
"hot" music characteristics, 18–19
    musician's location on, and public reception, 20
    racial overtones of, 18–19, 138, 157–58n109, 157n107
House, Son, 27, 33, 144
housing covenants, racially-restrictive, 95, 173n41
"How Could You?," 67
"How Could You Be So Mean?," 102
Howland, John, 58
human behavior, Johnson's knowledge of, 99
    and awareness of social systems' conditioning of immoral behavior, 82, 85, 91, 99, 100, 137
    as product of insights gained from observing human interactions as musician, 79–82, 88, 99, 102, 136
    and success in professional relations, 99
    See also social world depicted by Johnson

"I Ain't Gonna Be Your Fool," 69
"I Don't Hurt Anymore," 176n30
"I Found a Dream," 14
"I Got the Best Jelly Roll in Town," 80
"I Have No Sweet Woman Now," 84
"I'm Gonna Dodge the Blues, Just Wait and See," 101
"I'm Just Dumb," 81
immoral behavior, as conditioned by social systems, Johnson's awareness of, 82, 85, 91, 99, 100, 137
"I'm Not Rough," 21, 139–41
improvisation
    as characteristic of jazz, 44
    as present in all performance to some degree, 44; as characteristic of "hot" music, 19, 158n114; limits on, aboard Streckfus Steamers, 44
Indiana, Johnson's work as musician in, 13
instruments played by Johnson, 1, 40

and difficulty of categorizing his music, 21
in early years, 5, 38, 39, 55–56
and persona as sophisticated musician, 59
variety of, as evidence for inauthenticity of his blues, 145
and versatility as musician, 40, 50, 145
See also guitar, Johnson's playing of; violin, Johnson's playing of
intermediaries between Johnson and public, shaping of Johnson's work by, 1–2
International Association of Jazz Record Collectors (IAJRC), Johnson's late-life appearance at, 21–24
interviews with early-20th-century African American musicians
  inaccurate information, reasons for, 3, 152n10, 153n17
  and performance of public image, 3–4
isolation, for self-protection
  Johnson's advocacy for, 102, 103, 104, 136
  loneliness resulting from, 104, 136
isolation and loneliness
  as consequence of self deprived of community, 130
  of death, as inevitable, 130
  as preparation for death, 133
  songs about, 104; evocation of emptiness, 124, 128, 130; feelings of confinement from, 124; on isolation as prefiguration of death, 130; on loneliness as existential condition, 128, 137; on loneliness of traveling alone, 119–23, 136; from loss of home, 104; musical techniques in, 131–33; on nighttime as loneliest time, 124, 128; as paradoxical sharing of isolation, 131; and paradox of seeking comfort from those creating loneliness, 130; on psychological effects of loneliness, 125; and psychological isolation of blues, 104–5; repetition as technique in, 119; richness and complexity of, 133; on self alone in empty space, 118–25; sexual betrayal as cause of, 104, 105–10; and songs about death, 128–30, 136–37; and songs about hauntings, 125–28, 136–37; and songs about

suicide, 129–30; throughout his career, 130
"It Don't Mean a Thing (If It Ain't Got That Swing)" (Ellington), 61

Jackson, Michael, 177–78n3
Jamison, Andrew, 91, 101
jazz
  and blues, difficulty of separating genres, 21, 164n59
  improvisation as characteristic of, 44
  of New Orleans, eclectic styles of, 55
jazz bands
  preference for banjo over guitar, 178n10
  typical early composition of, 178n11
Jazz Journal, Johnson on cover of (June 1951), *24*
jazz music
  inauthenticity in, association with use of stock arrangements, 44
  spectrum from "hot" to "sweet," 18–19, 138
jazz musician, Johnson's work as, 13, 15
  and charges of inauthenticity of his blues, 26
  and creative tension of working with others, 145
  revolutionary guitar solos, 21, 139–41
  scholars on, 158n119
jazz musicians
  pressure to record blues music, 162n20
  and song copyrights, loss of, 9
Jazz-O-Maniacs, 7, 8
jazz scholarship, early, shaping by record collectors, 21–25
Jefferson, Blind Lemon, 8, 20, 27, 151n3
Jim Crow laws
  impossibility of escape from, 101–2
  learning of behavior required under, 171n7
  New Orleans and, 34, 41
  and restrictions on travel, 10, 165n73
  songs evoking, 97–98
Jim McHarg's Metro Stompers, 15
Johansson, Mats, 177–78n3
Johns, Lewis, 32
Johnson, Alonzo "Lonnie"
  in 1946, *147*
  as inconvenient for scholars, 1, 134
  vs. Lang, scholars' views on, 158n119

Johnson, Alonzo "Lonnie" (*continued*)
    multiple recordings of songs on different labels, 3
    publicity photograph (1920s), 56, *57*
    roles as musician, variety of, 1
    views on Lang, 158n119
    See also life of Johnson
Johnson, Bunk, 40, 157n100
Johnson, James (brother)
    move to St. Louis, 5, 42
    musician work with brother, 46, 81, 105, 106, 117, 145–46, 166n103
Johnson, James P., 145
Johnson, Jerah, 162n27
Johnson, Jesse
    and Black cruises out of St. Louis, 45, 46
    and copyright to Johnson's songs, 9
    multiple jobs in music industry, 7
    as scout for Black record labels, 46
    work for Booker T. Washington Theater, 46
Johnson, Kay Armstrong (second wife), copyrights of Johnson's songs owned by, 14
Johnson, Mary Smith (first wife), and lyrics in Johnson's songs, 82
Johnson, Robert
    influence of Johnson on, 51
    love of country music and polkas, 34
    public image of, 51
    and standard image of blues artists, 144
Jordan, Jimmy, as Johnson pseudonym, 71

Keghouse, 8, 144
Keil, Charles, 30–31, 174n50
Keith, B. F., 6
Kenney, William Howland, 18, 43
Keppard, Freddie, 8
Kienzle, Rich, 151n3
King, B.B., on Johnson, 151n3
King Records
    Johnson's recordings for, 13–14, 75
    ownership of copyrights on Johnson's songs, 14

Lambert, Dan, 179n23, 179n25
Landau, Emily Epstein, 37, 163n38
The Land Where the Blues Began (Lomax), 51–52

Lang, Eddie
    vs. Johnson, scholars' views on, 158n119
    Johnson on, 158n119
    Johnson's duets with, 8, 21, 90, 146, 179nn22–23
    as pseudonym, 154n44
    songs written with Lang, 10
    work as Blind Willie Dunn, 24
"Laplegged Drunk Again," narrator in
    as separate from but similar to Johnson, 65–66
    as simultaneously self-aware and self-deceived, 64–66
"The Last Call," 67–68
Ledbetter, Huddie, "Leadbelly," 174n48
Lee, Russell, 13, *13*
Lenoir, J. B., 174n48
"Let All Married Women Alone," 69
"Levee Camp Moan Blues," 90
Lewis, Walter E. "Furry," 86
life of Johnson
    early years, 4–11; birth, 4, 34; blues contest won by, 7, 46–47, 153n38, 166n108; death of family in 1918 influenza pandemic, 5, 41–42, 175n17; and embeddedness of individual in social world, appreciation of, 27, 47–48, 59, 137–38; influence on his idea of genre and style, 16, 38–42, 134–35; mixed-race audiences in, 5; move to New York, 8; move to St. Louis, 5; and musical family, 4; playing in family band, 4, 38–39, 56, 139; recordings, 7–8; wide range of gigs and music types, 38–39; work as musician, 4–5, 38–39, 56; work as musician on riverboats, 5, 7; work in clubs, 7; work in traveling theater troupes, 5–6, 10
    middle years, 11–14; gigs in nightclubs, 11, 12–13, *13*; jobs outside music industry, 11; move to Chicago, 11; move to Cincinnati, 13; move to Cleveland, 11; move to Philadelphia, 14; recordings, 11, 12, 13–14; work as backup musician, 11
    late years, 14–15; appearance at International Association of Jazz Record Collectors (IAJRC), 21–24; death,

216 \ Index

15; final show, 15; health problems after being hit by car, 15; move to Toronto, 15; recordings, 14, 15, 156n77; rediscovery of, 14; songs about sexual betrayal in, 75; touring with American Folk Blues Festival, 15; work outside music industry, 14
"Little Rockin' Chair," 14, 177n35
Logsdon, Joseph, 35, 163n36
Lois Publishing Co., ownership of copyrights on Johnson's songs, 14
Lomax, Alan, 30, 31, 32, 51–52, 161n9, 178–79n17
Lombardo, Guy, 20
loneliness. *See* isolation and loneliness
"Lonesome Ghost Blues," 126–27
"The Lonesome Road"
    as frequently covered, 175–76n19
    Johnson's versions of, 119; ballad version, 121–22; blues version, 120, 121, 175n17
"Long Black Train," 129
Long Head Bob's Social Orchestra, 17
Lonnie Johnson's Harlem Footwarmers, 2, *3*
Louis Armstrong and His Hot Five, 90
Louisiana, rural, Johnson's work as musician in, 4–5, 39
"The Loveless Blues," 11
lyrics
    about Jim Crow laws, 97–98
    about men's mistreatment of women, 84
    apparent misogyny of, 83–84; as critique of observed social world, 85; as depiction of world as observed by Johnson, 83–84; as trope of blues as genre, 84
    autobiographical interpretation of; critics' tendency to accept, 82, 172n22; flawed logic of, 83–84
    avoidance of traditional rhythm and rhyme structures, 51
    clear and correct pronunciation of, as characteristic of Johnson's style, 58
    as framework for interpreting role-playing in human interactions, 91
    greater social complexity of, *vs.* rural blues artists, 88
    indictment of social system in, 99
    influence of, 51
    moral advice in, as shield from censorship, 100
    narration of, as more coherent and complex, 142–43
    natural phenomena as reflections of psychological states in, 51, 60
    on pressure to play roles, 90
    on signs: lack of stable meaning underlying, 71–74; misuse for deception of others, 69–70
    songs of self-awareness and self-deception, 63–66
    See also exploitative social relations, songs about; floods, songs about; hauntings, songs about; isolation and loneliness, songs about; narrator; natural disasters, songs about; sexual betrayal and deception, songs about; social criticisms of racial and economic victimization; social world depicted by Johnson; suicide, song about; traveling alone, songs about loneliness of

Magnolia Band, 17
Malawey, Victoria, 155n60, 159n125
"Man Killing Broad," 83
Marable, Fate, 7, 43, 56
Marshall, Wendell, 107, 117
Martin, Chink, 54–55
Massaro, Salvatore (Eddie Lang), 154n44
McCormack, Mack, 30
McGinley, Paige A., 29, 56, 177n1
McHarg, Jim, 15
"Mean Old Bedbug Blues," 86–89
    artist's recording, 172n28
    basic conceit of, 86
    social critique in, 86–89
Melrose, Lester, 12, 155n62
Memphis
    Johnson's recordings in, 8
    as part of Jim Crow South, 93, 173n34
Memphis Slim and the House Rockers, 176n32
"Men, Get Wise to Yourself," 68, 75, 81
Mercury Records, Johnson's work for, 11
Midnight Steppers Tour (Smith), 10
Miller, Ernest "Punch," 4–5, 39, 41
Miller, Karl Hagstrom, 29
Miller, Luella, 45

Miller, Mark
  on ethnographic music records, 161n12
  on inaccuracy of Johnson's stories, 152n10
  on Johnson's appearance at International Association of Jazz Record Collectors (1967), 21–22
  on Johnson's travel to England, 41
  on Johnson's work with traveling theater groups, 6
  on race-based recording policies, 161–62n20
  on racial overtones of rural-urban distinction in blues scholarship, 33
  on record collectors' influence on early scholarship, 24
Mills, Irving, 3
miscegenated style, 53–54, 71
Mississippi River Delta, chronic flooding of, 111
Mississippi River Flood of 1927
  deaths of African Americans in, 175n9
  Johnson's songs about, 110, 174n46
  Johnson's songs about racialized economic exploitation in response to, 96–97
  living conditions for refugees of, 97, 174n47
  Patton's song on, vs. Johnson's, 143
Montgomery, Little Brother, 179n21
"The Mooche," 3, 61, 138
Moore, Alice, 11
Morton, Jelly Roll
  in Chicago, 8
  as Creole, 54
  name, and persona, 54
  watching of audience during performance, 78
"Mother Earth" (Memphis Slim and the House Rockers), 176n32
"Move Over," 2, 3
"Mr. Jelly Roll Baker," 26
"Mr. Johnson's Blues," 49–51
  B side of, 50
  copyright on, 8–9
  described, 49
  focus on guitar ability in, 50
  as Johnson's debut recording, 49
  and Johnson's persona, 51–52, 135, 141–42, 149

"Mr." title for African American, as controversial, 51–52
  referencing of, in "Mr. Johnson's Swing," 60, 63
  vocal elements, characteristics of, 49–50
  See also "Falling Rain Blues" (B side)
"Mr. Johnson's Blues No. 2," 169n45
"Mr. Johnson's Swing," 11, 60–63
  citations of other artists in, 61–62
  focus on quality of guitar playing in, 60–61, 63
  and Johnson's persona, conscious construction of, 62–63
  reflections on Johnson's career in, 60
  self-referentiality in, 60–62
  ties to Johnson's jazz work of 1920s in, 62, 63, 169n48
Murphy, Matt, 160n131
music, ability to read
  advantage of, for keeping up with popular tunes, 39
  gradations of, 44
  Johnson and, 39, 40, 55–56, 137
  Johnson's instruction from father in, 39
  Marable's insistence on, for his band members, 43
  as marker of inauthenticity, 19, 32
  racial overtones of, 19
  and violin vs. guitar players, 39, 40
musical education of Johnson
  as evidence of blues "inauthenticity," 145
  exposure to blues, 39
  exposure to wide range of music in New Orleans, 38
  father's instruction in reading music, 39
  and mix of rural and urban cultures in New Orleans, 40
  music jobs in rural areas of Louisiana and, 4–5, 39
  through family band, 4, 38–39
musical identity of Johnson
  complication of, by muddied musical identity, 20
  creation of in recordings, 50
  flexibility of, 71, 135
  record collectors' role in shaping of, 21–25
  See also reception of Johnson
musical notation, European system, limitations of, for transcribing blues and jazz, 44

musical performance, effect of market forces on, as inescapable, 32–33
musical style of Johnson
   and charges of inauthenticity of his blues, 26, 159–60n129, 160n134
   critics supporting authenticity of, 160n131
   discipline of: factors contributing to, 150; range of performance types and, 90; work on Streckfus Steamers and, 47, 86, 89; work on theater circuits and, 47, 86
musician, Johnson's versatility as, 55–56, 135, 146
   and ability to work in multiple formats and venues, 47, 135, 137, 144
   and flawless sense of time, 146–48, 179n25
   and jazz solo guitar, innovations in, 21, 139–41
   as key to long career, 47, 137, 145
   New Orleans' eclectic music and, 55, 137
   number of instruments played and, 40, 50, 145
   as obstacle to creation of legible musical identity, 20
   prowess as solo artist, 138
   and recognition of social embeddedness of his identity, 27, 47–48, 59, 103, 137–38
   success in semi-soloist roles, 138
   See also genres and styles of music, Johnson's facility in large range of
musicians
   ability to cross racial and social boundaries, 36, 37, 52, 76, 168n25
   constraints on: audience preferences as, 90; genres and, 89–90; practical constraints in ensemble play, 89–90; record companies and, 90; social constraints, 89
   work for scale, in 1930s–40s, 12, 155n66
music of Johnson
   categorization of, difficulty of, 1–2, 16, 20–21
   as "city blues," 58
   dramatic style change in 1940s–50s, 25

   influence of early life in New Orleans on, 5, 16, 39–42, 134–35
   key of D used in most early work, 24–25
   professional style, embrace of, 59
   See also copyrights of Johnson's music; corpus of Johnson's work; genres and styles of music, Johnson's facility in large range of; musician, Johnson's versatility as
"My Mother's Eyes," 25
"My My Baby," 14

narrator in Johnson's songs
   as first-person male, 82, 84
   as Johnson himself: critics' tendency to accept, 82, 84; flawed logic of, 83–84
   narration of, as coherent and complex, 142–43
   role in exposing power dynamic in human interactions, 70, 75
   as role performed by Johnson, 82
   in songs about drinking, as both self-aware and self-deceived, 64–66
   See also lyrics; persona of Johnson in recordings
Nathan, Syd, 14, 155–56n71
natural disasters
   human loss and suffering in, 112
   magnification of effects by racially discriminatory practices, 112
natural disasters, songs about, 110–18
   on emotional trauma, 116
   on isolation and loneliness, 112, 114, 115–16, 118, 136
   Johnson's narrative in, alternation between personal and general views in, 112–14
   metaphorical meanings of disaster, 115–16
   multiple layers of meaning in, 112
   storms as metaphor in, 116–17
   See also floods, songs about
natural phenomena as reflections of psychological states
   in "Blue and All Alone," 108–9
   as characteristic of Johnson's lyrics, 51, 60
   "The New Falling Rain Blues," 108, 116–17

Index / 219

New Negro ideology, emphasis on Black professionalism, 58–59
New Orleans
changes with start of World War I, 41
complex socioeconomic, legal, racial, and ethnocultural structures in, 35
"crazy quilt" demographic mix in, 38, 134, 162n27
creolization of music in, 135
and French colonial heritage, 35, 52
and Great Migration, 41
and Jim Crow laws, 34
as Johnson's birthplace, 4
Johnson's exposure to many genres and styles of music in, 16, 38–42, 47, 134–35
Johnson's return to, after World War I, 41–42
Johnson's work as musician in, 4; early years playing in family band, 4, 38–39, 56, 139; jobs outside family band, 40–41; venues played in, 5, 41
location of Johnson family home, 38
mix of rural and urban in area around, 40
personas adopted by Black musicians in, 54
porous boundaries between racialized spaces, 36–37, 168n26; and blurring of racial identities, 54–55; and eclectic music styles, 37, 55; and musicians' ability to cross racial boundaries, 36, 37, 52; and performative aspect of race, awareness of, 52; and racial mixing in music venues, 37
racial identities, influence on Johnson's persona, 51–55, 59
resistance to simple racial binary in, 34–37, 41, 52, 134, 162n24, 163n36, 163n38
See also Storyville district, New Orleans
"New Years Blues," 90
New York
as jazz center, after 1925, 8
Johnson's move to, 8
Johnson's recordings in, 8
"No Love for Sale," 102
Noone, Jimmie, 11
"Nothing but a Rat," 69, 92
"Nothing but Trouble," 176n33

OKeh records
exploitation of artists and composers, 9, 154n51
headquarters in New York, 154n43
Jesse Johnson as scout for, 46
Johnson's contract with, 7–8, 46, 144; and copyrighting of Johnson's songs, 10; as indication of his versatility and talent, 144; and recordings for other labels, 3
Johnson's recordings for, 22, 26, 110
Race Records catalog (1926 or 1927); ad for Johnson's records in, 23; cover of, 22
recruiting of Johnson, 46–47
scouting by, 7
traveling recording crews, 154n43
OKeh studios (New York), Johnson's recordings in, 2
Oliver, Joe "King," 8, 20, 31, 54, 55
Oliver, Paul, 1, 6, 30, 41, 161n9
Ollie Shepard and His Kentucky Boys, 11
O'Malley, Michael, on show business, racial transgression in, 168n25
one-drop rule, three-tierd racial structure in New Orleans as challenge to, 34–37, 52
Ory, Edward "Kid," 54, 169n29
Oster, Harry, 30

Paramount Records, Jesse Johnson as scout for, 46
Pathé Studio, Ellington's recordings in, 3
Patton, Charley
authenticity of, 20
characteristics as artist, 27
as folk blues artist, 8
"High Sheriff Blues," 178n16
"High Water Everywhere," 143
repertoire of, 33
and standard image of blues artists, 144
penal system, blues songs evoking, failure to indict larger society, 172n29
performance of race, ethnicity, and class roles
as characteristic of all humans in Johnson's songs, 82, 99
and development of race consciousness, 171n7
by Johnson, 76; and alienation, 149; both onstage and off, and blurring of

persona and person, 76; experience of racialized space and, 76; need to continually maintain, 76–77; and success in professional relations, 99, 135, 149 and misogyny in blues, 84, 85
See also signs

performers
appreciation of parallels between stage persona and masks worn by deceivers, 70, 76
privileged insight into construction of personas, 54, 70–71, 77, 79, 80–81, 136, 149, 170n53
privileged vantage point for observing human behavior, 78, 79–80
separation from audience: as never complete, 77; variation with physical distance, 78–79; variation with social distance, 79

persona of Johnson
blurring of onstage and offstage persona, 58
characteristics *vs.* other blues artists, 51
construction of community through, 142, 143
creation through his music, 49, 51, 135, 141–42
dependence on gaze of others, 141–42
and dialectic between individual and community, 103
in early New Orleans years, as largely unknown, 55–56
and enactment of respectability, 55–59
and fine clothes, preference for, 56–57, 57
and Harlem Renaissance, emphasis on musicians' professionalism, 58–59
identification with victims of sexual betrayal, 68–69
influence of Black women performers on, 56
influence of racial identities in New Orleans and St. Louis on, 51–55, 59
and inherent instability of identity, as creative opportunity, 71, 135
and inherent instability of identity, Johnson's awareness of, 71–74, 75
manipulation of signs in creation of, 71
"Mr. Johnson's Blues" and, 51–52, 135, 141–42, 149

and "Mr. Johnson's Swing," 62–63
muddying of, by large range of genres and styles, 21
multiple instruments played and, 59
and performative aspect of race, awareness of, 52
and professional style, embrace of, 59
rare labile quality of, 135–36
record collectors in shaping of, 21–25
and self-commodification, 149
self-conscious creation of, 51, 59, 78, 135, 149
and self/other dynamic, 141–42, 149–50
shaping by tour with TOBA, 56
shaping by work on Streckfus Steamers, 56
and social embeddedness of his identity, recognition of, 27, 47–48, 59, 137–38
and speech patterns, clear and correct, 58, 59

persona of Johnson in recordings, 59–63
advice given to listeners, 75–76
identification with victims of sexual betrayal, 68
multiple elements of, 74
on parallels between performers and masks worn by deceivers, 70
as revealer of hidden truths, 70
self-consciousness construction of, 63, 70, 74
as separate from but similar to Johnson himself, 63–64, 65
as simultaneously self-aware and self-deceived, 64–66
in songs about his musical career, 60–62
special insight into human capacity for deception, 70, 75, 135
strong sense of self-worth, 63
on world as place of deception, 66, 68, 69–70
See also narrator in Johnson's songs; social world depicted by Johnson

personas
of Black women artists: conscious contesting of minstrel imagery, 56; white fantasies and, 168n17

Index / 221

personas (continued)
  of musicians: adjustment to audience, 54; names adopted by Black New Orleans musicians and, 54; offstage continuation of, 54
  performers' privileged insight into construction of, 54, 70–71, 77, 79, 80–81, 136, 149, 170n53
  See also signs
Philadelphia
  Johnson's move to, 14
  Johnson's work outside music industry in, 14–15
Piron, Armand, 9
playing by ear, as characteristic of "hot" music, 19
"Playing with the Strings," 148
Pleasants, Cousin Joe, 160n131
"Pleasing You (As Long as I Live)," 13–14
Plessy, Homer, 34, 162nn22–23
Plessy v. Ferguson (1896), 34, 134
poor people
  disproportionate impact of floods on, 110–12
  ignorance of those with money about plight of, 111
Powell, Rudy (Musheed Karweem), 168n25
Pratt, Ray, 174n50
Prestige Records, Johnson's recordings for, 14
prostitutes
  in New Orleans' Storyville district, interest in blues, 17–18, 157n100
  and race categories, 169n29, 171–72n17
public records on lives of early-20th century African American musicians, as scarce and unreliable, 3

race
  categories of, prostitutes and, 169n29, 171–72n17
  different view of, in French colonial cities, 35, 42, 52
  and genres and styles of music, 16–19
  and rural-urban distinction in blues scholarship, 33–34, 161–62n20
  See also performance of race, ethnicity, and class roles; segregation
race, in New Orleans

  complex socioeconomic, legal, racial, and ethnocultural structures, 35
  porous boundaries between racialized spaces, 36–37, 168n26; and blurring of racial identities, 54–55; and eclectic music styles, 37, 55; and musicians' ability to cross racial boundaries, 36, 37, 52, 76; and performative aspect of race, awareness of, 52; and racial mixing in music venues, 37
  racial identities, influence on Johnson's persona, 51–55, 59
  resistance to simple racial binary, 34–37, 41, 52, 134, 162n24, 163n36, 163n38
race, in St. Louis
  porous boundaries between racialized spaces, 36–37, 76
  racial identities, influence on Johnson's persona, 51–55
  three-tiered racial structure in, 42, 52
race consciousness, episodes leading to, 95, 171n7
Raceland, Louisiana, Johnson's stay in, as working musician, 4–5, 39
racism, artists directly mentioning in blues songs, 174n48
"Racketeers Blues," 97–98
Radio-Keith-Orpheum circuit. *See* RKO [Radio-Keith-Orpheum] circuit
Raeburn, Bruce Boyd, 16, 37, 38
Rainey, Ma, 7, 9, 51
Rama Records, Johnson's recordings for, 156n73
"Rambler's Blues," 122, 124
"ratty," as term, 17
"ratty" music, venues for, in New Orleans, 40
RCA Victor-Bluebird
  and Black recording artists, 46
  Johnson's recordings for, 11, 12, 26, 59–60
reception of Johnson, 20–27
  complication of, by muddied musical identity, 20
  shaping of, by audience preconceptions, 31
  shaping of, by record collectors, 21–25
  See also musical identity of Johnson

222 \ Index

reception of musicians, and perceived location on "sweet-hot" scale, 20
record collectors, in shaping of Johnson's musical identity, 21–25
record companies
  constraints on musicians from, 90
  and explicit social criticism, rejection of, 86, 87–88
  exploitation of artists and composers, 9, 12, 86
  exploitation of Johnson, 12
  Johnson's contracts with, as constraint on content of his songs, 86
  shaping of perceptions of artists and styles, 3
recordings by Johnson
  in Chicago, 11, 12, 60
  final phase of, loneliness as theme in, 107–8
  geographical locations, and typical patterns for jazz vs. blues musicians, 8
  hiatus in, during Great Depression, 60
  jazz recordings, with Armstrong, 8
  large number of, 1, 151n2
  in late life, 14
  lyrical themes in, 60
  in New York, 10–11, 156n77
  for Okeh records, 10–11
  resumption in late 1930s, 60
  in St. Louis, 7–8
  start of recording career, 46–47
recording technology, and subtleties of Johnson's vocal style, 12, 105, 109
Rega, F. Wallace, 8–9
rhythms
  class and racial associations of, 18–19
  difficulty of notating, 19
rhythm section of band
  Johnson's ability to switch easily between rhythm and lead guitar, 146–48
  role of, 19, 41
  syncopation and, 19
  as traditional location of guitar, 21, 41
Richardson, Mooch, 8
RKO [Radio-Keith-Orpheum] circuit, Johnson's work on, 6, 47
Robichaux, John, 17, 164n59
Rogers, Jimmy, 148, 179n24
role-playing in human interactions
  and alienation, potential for, 149
  Johnson's awareness of, and self/other dynamic, 149, 150
  Johnson's lyrics as framework for interpreting, 91
  Johnson's mastery of, as opportunity, 99, 102–3
  and Johnson's narrator as role, 82
  Johnson's observation of, as musician, 80
  performers' privileged insight into, 54, 70–71, 77, 79, 80–81, 136, 149, 170n53
  as product of social structure, 82, 85, 91, 99, 100, 137
  as ubiquitous, 80, 137
  See also performance of race, ethnicity, and class roles; persona of Johnson; personas
Ross, Alexander, 21–22
rural blues artists, social criticism as unavailable to, 92–93
rural-urban distinction in blues scholarship
  and authentic blues artists, designated characteristics of, 30–31
  and disparagement of women artists, 33
  "folk" and "popular" spectrum created by, 29
  folklorist methodology and, 31–32, 33
  Johnson's awareness of, 31
  Johnson's urban origin and, 34
  vs. mix of rural and urban in greater New Orleans area, 40, 164n60
  and posited authenticity of rural blues, as result of artists' cultural isolation, 31, 32, 161n9
  and professionalism as kind of impurity, 32–33
  and race-based recording policies, 33–34, 161–62n20
  racial division underlying, 33, 34
  rural side as African American, 29, 33
  rural side as male, untutored, and authentic, 29, 31
  scholar's characterization of rural side as authentic, 30–31
  scholar's motivations for, 31–32
  unexamined assumptions created by, 29–30
  urban side as female and professional, 29
  urban side as segregated space, 29

St. Cyr, Johnny
    on guitar as foundation of orchestra, 138
    on "hot" to "sweet" music spectrum, 158n115
    and learning of blues, 164n59
    musical influences on, 43
    on syncopation and musical notation, 158n111
    work on Streckfus Steamers, 7, 165n74, 166n102
    work with Armstrong and Johnson, 139
St. Louis
    African American population growth in early 20th century, 42
    French colonial heritage of, 35, 42, 52
    Johnson's move to, 5, 42
    Johnson's recordings in, 7
    Johnson's work as musician in, 7, 8; and broad exposure to many types of music, 47; clubs played in, 45–46
    limited segregation in, 42, 165n76
    music community: importance of Johnson's ties to, 47; as small and tightly-knit, 45, 46
    as OKeh field location, 8
    porous boundaries between racialized spaces in, 36–37, 76
    racial identities, influence on Johnson's persona, 51–55
    similarities to New Orleans, 42
    three-tiered racial structure in, 42, 52
"St. Louis Blues," 26
St. Louis Publishing Co., 9
St. Louis ragtime
    influence on jazz in New Orleans, 42
    See also Streckfus Steamers
Sam, as generic name for untrustworthy person, 91
"Sam, You Can't Do That to Me," 91–92
"Sam, You're Just a Rat," 81
San Antonio, Johnson's recordings in, 8
Savoy Ballroom Five, 8
Schuller, Gunther, 158–59n119
Scott, James C., 53–54, 171n3
Searcy, De Loise, 81, 105, 145
segregation
    and Black crossing of racial lines as servants, 36
    as necessary feature in white supremacy, 35

and white crossing of racial lines to reassert white authority, 36
    See also Plessy v. Ferguson (1896); race, in New Orleans; race, in St. Louis
self/other dynamic
    in Johnson's creation of persona, 141–42; construction of community through, 142, 143; as different from stereotypical blues artist, 142, 143; and Johnson's self-commodification and alienation, 149–50
    in Johnson's dialogic guitar work, 149
    in work with other musicians, 148
sexual betrayal and deception, songs about, 66–69, 75–76, 81–82, 94, 96, 136
    on betrayal as expected, 68
    critique of social system underlying, 100
    with narrator as transgressor, 69
    narrator's identification with victims of sexual betrayal, 68
    narrator's role in exposing power dynamic in human interactions, 70, 75
    potential metaphorical meanings of, 137
    and resulting loneliness, 105–10
    on world as place of deception, 66, 68, 69, 75
Shepard, Ollie, 11
"She's Making Whoopee in Hell Tonight," 69, 83
"She's So Sweet," 14
Shilkret, Nathaniel, 119
Shines, Johnny, 34, 144, 178n17
Shipton, Alyn, 152n10
signifying, 44, 135, 165–66n92
signs
    of deceitful behavior, Johnson's songs about learning to read, 66, 82
    lack of stable meaning underlying: as fluidity of self-construction, 135; Johnson's awareness of, 71–74, 135
    manipulation of, in creation of Johnson's persona, 71, 85, 149
    misuse for deception of others, Johnson on, 69–70, 136
    in music: different meanings for different audiences, 18, 20, 90, 138; Johnson's expertise in manipulation of, 21, 28, 90, 135

See also performance of race, ethnicity, and class roles; persona
singing by Johnson
   characteristics of, 49–50
   clear and correct speech patterns characteristic of, 58, 59
   differences from classic blues style, 12, 25, 26, 50, 59, 159n125, 160n131
   recording technology and, 12, 105, 109
   while playing violin, 40
Singleton, Zutty, 43, 139
slavery, and interracial rape, 36
Smith, Bessie
   and copyright rights, 9
   public persona of, 51, 56
   recordings by, 86
   relationship with Johnson, 10, 154n53
   and standard image of blues artists, failure to meet, 134, 143–44
   and TOBA circuit, 7
   vocal style of, 106, 109
Smith, Chris, 84, 85, 86, 145
Smith, Clara, 6, 47, 56, 144
Smith, Mamie, 6, 56, 143–44
Smith, Mary, 153–54n39
Smithsonian Folkways series, Johnson in, 14
Snowden, Elmer, 14, 107, 110, 117, 156n77
social change
   aesthetic works and, 100
   Johnson's work as catalyst for: and difficulty distinguishing good from bad people, 100; and elusiveness of truth in world of deception, 101; as issue, 100; and Johnson's production of moral rather than political community, 100–101, 136, 174n50
social change, Johnson on
   difficulty of effecting: awareness of, 90, 91; in system forcing self-interested behavior, 100, 103
   focus on individual behavioral change, 101
   focus on self-protection, 102, 103, 104
   songs advocating avoidance and escape, 101–2
   songs invoking karma, 102
   songs with working class call to action, 95–96, 100, 102
   strategies for, 91
   veiled critiques of class- and race-based abuses in lyrics, 92–93
social criticisms of racial and economic victimization, 85–91
   implied parallels between abusive personal relationships and, 85–86, 88
   indirect representation of, reasons for, 86, 87–88
   in "Mean Old Bedbug Blues," 86–89
   as unavailable to rural blues artists, 92–93
social world depicted by Johnson
   and bad behavior as conditioned by social systems, 82, 85, 91, 99, 100, 137
   complexity of: and ability to call out racialized injustice, 136; as different from traditional blues songs, 136; *vs.* world of rural blues artists, 88
   as complex system in which all are enmeshed, 88–90, 91, 136; and difficulty of effecting change, 90, 91, 100, 103; ubiquity of role-playing in, 80, 90, 137
   and constraints on musicians, Johnson's willingness to work within, 89
   indictment of system underlying, 99
   and Johnson's experience with social and financial side of music business, 90
   misogyny in, 83–85
   as place of deception, lying, and betrayal, 66, 68, 69–70, 76, 79–81, 135, 136; as problematic for political organization for change, 101; and roles played by all, 80, 90, 137; self-protection as only option in, 102, 103, 104, 136
   as place of instrumental use of others, 82
   as product of insights gained from observing human interactions as musician, 79–82, 88, 99, 102, 136
   as product of professional experiences, 102–3
   and two types of people, good *vs.* bad, 91–92, 100; as cognitive practice, 91; difficulty distinguishing, in world of masks, 100; and Johnson's advice to "friends" on self-protection, 136; and potential community of good people, 104; as veiled critique of class- and race-based abuses, 92–93

social world depicted by Johnson
    (*continued*)
  zero-sum view of human relations in,
    80, 82
  See also exploitative social relations,
    songs about; performance of race,
    ethnicity, and class roles
socioeconomic factors affecting genres and
  styles of music, 16–19
  and classification of Johnson's music, 20
"So Tired," 14
Sotiropoulos, Karen, 53
South, rural, suppression of Black dissent
  in, 93
"South Bound Backwater," 113, 114, 117
"South Bound Water"
  on homelessness caused by floods, 114
  Johnson's alternation between personal
    and general views in, 112–13
  musical techniques in, 117
Southern Syncopated Orchestra
  Johnson's claim to have performed with,
    58–59
  Johnson's work with in England, as disproved, 5
"Southland Is Alright with Me," 101–2
Spivey, Victoria
  criticism of, 160n131
  Johnson's recordings with, 8, 14, 15, 47,
    76, 144
  performance style of, 159n126
  recruitment by OKeh Records, 46
  and standard image of blues artists, failure to meet, 134, 143–44
  vocal style of, 106
Spivey Records, 14
"Stay Out of Walnut Street Alley," 75–76,
  80, 172n19
Stompin' at the Penny (LP), 15
"Stompin' 'Em Along Slow," 148
Storyville district, New Orleans
  as area of racial mixing, 36
  closing of, 5, 41
  Johnson's work as musician in, 5, 41;
    effect on his view of life, 80; insights
    into human nature gained from,
    79–80
  and prostitutes' interest in blues music,
    17–18
  as red-light district, 5

Strassberg, Bernie, 58
Streckfus, Joseph, 18, 43
Streckfus Steamers (St. Louis)
  cruises offered by, 42–43
  firing of Armstrong, 43, 89
  Johnson as musician on, 7; boat
    assigned to, 43; comfort with requirements, 43, 44, 45; and discipline as
    performer, 47, 86, 89; and need to
    maintain persona, 76–77; opportunities opened by, 47; and shaping of his
    persona, 56; work with Creath, 45
  Marable as musical director aboard,
    43, 56
  Monday night cruises for African Americans, 45
  musicians aboard: from New Orleans,
    42–43; reading music as required
    skill for, 43; year-round work for, 45
  primarily white audiences on, 43
  steam calliope concerts every evening,
    43
  types of music played on, 43–44,
    165n89
  winter port stays in New Orleans, 43, 45
subordinate groups, hidden transcript created by, 171n3
Sumlin, Hubert, 148, 179n24
Sundown Towns, 10
"Sun to Sun Blues," 145–46
"sweet music"
  as term, 17
  See also "hot" to "sweet" scale of music
"Sweet Woman, See for Yourself," 101
swing era, range of jazz types in, 157n107
"Swing Out Rhythm," recording of, 60
Sykes, Roosevelt, 46, 60, 64, 117, 126,
  179n21
syncopation
  difficulty of notating, 19, 158n111
  as mark of authentic African American
    music, 18–19

Tampa Red, 134
Taylor, Myra, 12
tempo, class and race associations of, 18
Tharpe, Sister Rosetta, 160n131
Theater Owners Booking Association
  (TOBA)

Johnson's work for, 6, 10; and obstacles to travel in the South, 10; opportunities opened by, 10, 47; as opportunity opened by St. Louis connections, 47; and shaping of his persona, 56 ties to Booker T. Washington Theater, 46
"There's No Use of Lovin'," 76
"Tin Can Alley Blues," 9
titles of blues recordings of 1920s-30s, 167n1
TOBA. See Theater Owners Booking Association
Tom, Georgia, 134
"Tomorrow Night," 13, 75–76
Toronto, Johnson's move to, 15
Townsend, Henry, 45–46
travel by African Americans, restrictions on, in early twentieth century, 10, 165n73, 168n25
traveling alone, songs about loneliness of, 119–23
    atmosphere of threat in, 120–21, 136
    death as theme in, 119–20, 125
    evocation of transit racism in, 120
"Treat 'Em Right," 75, 84
"Truckin' thru Traffic," 11
"Trust Your Husband," 174n54

union. See Chicago Federation of Musicians

vaudeville, Johnson's work in, 169n29
venues for music, socioeconomic factors and, 17
"Very Lonesome Blues," 123–24
    on loneliness, 105–6
    music of, 105, 106, 107
    on self alone in empty space, 118–19
violin
    and blues, in Louisiana, 21
    early blues players using, 167n6
violin, Johnson's playing of
    in blues numbers, 21, *23*
    in early years, 39
    recordings of, 40, 50, 105, 106
    unusual bowing technique, 40
vocabulary of early twentieth century musicians, notable terms in, 16–17

Walker, George W., 53
Wallace, Sippie, 51

The Washingtonians, 3
Waterman, Richard A., 157–58n109
Waters, Ethel, 7
Waters, Muddy, 15, 146–48, 159n126
"Way Down That Lonesome Road," 119–20
Welding, Pete, 25–26, 30
"West End Blues" (Armstrong), 61–62
    Johnson's cover of, 170n47
Wheatstraw, Peetie, 11
    public image of, 51
"When I Was Lovin' Changed My Mind Blues," 81
"When You Fall for Some One That's Not Your Own," 69
white supremacy, segregation as necessary step in, 35
Whitman Sisters, 6, 56
Williams, Bert A., 53
Williams, Big Joe, 160n131
Williams, Clarence, 9–10, 47, 144, 145
Williams, Spencer, 8, 128
Williamson, Sonny Boy, 146
Wilmer, Valerie, 39, 58
"Wipe It Off," 145
"Woke Up with the Blues in My Fingers," 131–33
"Won't You Share My Love Nest," 12
Wood, Leo (aka Jack), 86, 172n25
Woods, Clyde, 177n1
Work, John W. III, 32
"Working Man's Blues"
    critique of class relationships in, 94, 95
    growing anger at discrimination as context of, 95–96
    instrumental performance in, 96
    working class call to action in, 95–96, 100, 102
World War I, and opportunities to play in Europe, 5
World War II, recording shutdown during, 155n58
Wright, John J., Sr., 46

"You Can't Buy Love," 14
"You Drove a Good Man Away," 83
"You Know I Do," 12
"Your Last Time Out," 66–67
"You Will Need Me," 81

Zimmerman, Ike, 179n18

CPSIA information can be obtained
at www.ICGtesting.com
Printed in the USA
BVHW091949250222
630059BV00001B/4